The Farming Game Now

The Farming Game Now

J. P. Makeham

Department of Agricultural Economics
and Business Management
University of New England, Armidale

L. R. Malcolm

Agricultural Economics Section
School of Agriculture and Forestry
University of Melbourne

CAMBRIDGE
UNIVERSITY PRESS

Published by the Press Syndicate of the University of Cambridge
The Pitt Building, Trumpington Street, Cambridge CB2 1RP, UK
40 West 20th Street, New York, NY 10011-4211, USA
10 Stamford Road, Oakleigh, Melbourne 3166, Australia

Printed in Hong Kong by Colorcraft

National Library of Australia cataloguing-in-publication data

Makeham, J. P. (John Patrick).
The farming game now.
Bibliography.
Includes index.
1. Farm management—Australia. I. Malcolm, L. R. II. Title.
638.68

Library of Congress cataloguing-in-publication data

Makeham, J. P.
The farming game now/J. P. Makeham, L. R. Malcolm.
Includes index.
1. Farm management—Australia. I. Malcolm, L. R. II. Title.
S562.A78M35 1992
630′.68—dc20   92-17527

A catalogue record for this book is available from the British Library.

ISBN 0 521 40452 5 Hardback
ISBN 0 521 42679 0 Paperback

Contents

List of Figures

Preface

The farming game is not just a way of life but a business. Or is the farming game not just a business but a way of life? This book is about the farming game now. This title has been chosen carefully, as 'game' can mean any of the following:

- any arrangement or contest intended to furnish sport, to test skill or strength, or simply to try chance;
- measures planned; schemes pursued; projects organized;
- having an undaunted spirit; unwilling to admit defeat; full of pluck;
- to be happy; to rejoice; to receive pleasure.

Much of farming practice, in essence, has never changed. Modern farmers would quickly find a lot of common ground with fellow farmers from any era in history.

It is ironic that one outstanding feature of farming is the unchanging nature of the task and that an equally prominent aspect of farming is the constant need for change which all farmers confront. Farmers can either willingly embrace and adopt change, or have change imposed on them; avoiding change is not an option. The way of farming life is unchanging in essence but the business is constantly changing.

Like other businesses, the motivation for and rewards from farming go beyond making money and material wealth. Nevertheless, the farmer doing a few sums about the hoped-for cash flow of the coming year who scrawled next to proposed family drawings 'a bit more than last year', typifies an important element of the farming game.

Most farm business people are keen to get a bit more out of doing what they love doing, and are keen to do a bit better. One reason is that they have to do so. For reasons mostly beyond their control farmers have to get a bit more out of the resources they manage in order to stay in the game of farming.

As authors, we need to answer the question: 'Who are we trying to help?' The answer is, many people: progressive farmers; students at agricultural colleges and of farm management-orientated courses at universities; private and public farm advisers; financiers, and people who service the rural sector; policy formulators for agriculture; prospective farmers, and people who wish to know what the farming game is all about.

Our emphasis in this textbook is on evaluating how a farm business is performing. The focus is on identifying and on evaluating changes which help the farm family to make the 'bit more' that they need, and to do the 'bit better' that they want.

We have written the book in a simple style, but not simplistically. Some jargon is inevitable, but we have kept this to a minimum. A glossary of terms follows the text.

In the book a balanced approach to farm management between modern farming technology, economics, finance, institutional matters, the risks, and the all-important human factor is presented.

This is not a 'recipe' book for farm management analysis and planning. It is our belief that it is much more important to understand the reasoning behind the techniques used in farm analysis and planning. This done, then practitioners can apply the techniques explained, adapting these to the particular circumstances of different cases. All farm situations are unique, and each has to be treated on a case-by-case basis.

In this textbook each chapter is aimed to be fairly self-contained, although each chapter has many ideas, concepts, and techniques linking to the other chapters and, just like a farm, the whole is more than the sum of the parts.

Use the whole book and refer to different chapters rather than try to master the material in any single chapter in isolation; it is best to do so in the context of analysing problems and of making decisions about real farm case studies.

In Chapter 1 we discuss the general question 'how do we see farm management? What is it?' Our answer is a 'state of the art' view; some elements of which progressive farmers have espoused for the last 7,000 years. The importance of 'economic ways of thinking' is stressed.

Our aim is to enlighten the reader about some commonly held but wrong-headed notions about analysing and solving problems in farm management. Finally, some general points about budgeting and key aspects of farming are made.

In Chapter 2 all of the important parts which make up the farmer's world are outlined. Thus each subsection deals with a topic we consider to be important, which needed to be stressed early in the book.

First, we cover factors to remember when analysing and planning any farm, anywhere. As a farm has to be analysed before it can be planned, it is necessary to look at: the present situation; its potential; and the things which may restrain or prevent the potential from being achieved. Then the farm is considered from the human; technical; and economic and financial perspectives.

The concepts of capital, returns, costs, profit, and budgets are explained in the section on economic aspects of the farm business. Many examples are given to help explain these concepts.

The basic concepts in the economics of production follow: diminishing returns; equal–extra returns; and opportunity costs.

These concepts are stressed many times in various chapters. The meaning of these economic terms and concepts is given. Often, in subsequent chapters, the concept of the time value of money and the techniques of discounting and compounding are put to practical use. So in the next subsection we explain these concepts. These are fundamental to many farm management decisions. Although the first time a farmer confronts the discounting techniques and their applications they are a little bewildering; in reality they are simple, commonsense ideas.

In keeping with the idea of presenting the whole picture of agriculture early in the book, next we stray beyond the farm gate, browsing in the field of how and where agriculture fits into the whole of a developed economy such as Australia.

Marketing is defined, then demand, supply, the equilibrium price, price elasticity of demand and supply, and marketing margins and efficiency are discussed. Attention is given to the specific features of agriculture as these affect marketing. Finally, we look at some of the 'rules' of the farming game. In particular, what are the implications which changes in the rest of the economy hold for agriculture as a sector and for farm families?

Then follows a major chapter (3) on a subject of increasing importance to farmers: finance. First, profit and loss, sources and uses of cash and balance sheet (or net worth) statements are described and their links explained. Assets, liabilities, equity, liquidity, solvency, gearing, growth, and costs of capital, are discussed.

We focus on various forms of credit; loan repayments; rates of interest; and short- and medium-term bank lending. Taxation is important and this is explained in the context of farming. Its relation to practical farm business management decisions is shown. The final part is about financial and physical records.

In Chapter 4 technical and economic aspects of animal production and breeding are covered. Ways of maintaining the numbers in a herd or flock of animals are explained, as well as economic analysis of any animal enterprise. The importance of the role which feed plays in animal systems is emphasized. How to assess animal feed demand and supply are also discussed. Finally, animal gross margins and livestock schedules are explained. We discuss practical aspects of genetic gain. The importance of improvement in the production environment as a determinant of the improved production performance of animals is stressed.

In Chapter 5 is broad-ranging coverage of various forms of crop production. The technical and economic features of broad-area crops, vegetables, pasture improvement, and tree and plantation crops are covered.

Personal, technical, financial, and economic aspects of cropping are covered. The economic analysis of crop rotations (sequences) is explained, and the use of crop gross margins. We discuss features of managing vegetable farms; such as gross margins; estimating future prices; and deciding whether to harvest a crop. In the section on pasture improvement we deal with general aspects of pasture improvement; analysis of pasture development decisions; costs, returns and net cash flows; and risk. The main biological and economic features of tree crops are discussed, including the role of discounting in planning and replacing tree crops and the comparison of tree crops with other activities on farms.

In Chapter 6 the focus is on economic and technical aspects of acquiring the services of machines. These services can be obtained in different ways, namely by purchase; leasing; from contractors; or by sharing with other farmers. Issues raised are the different effects of fixed and variable costs, depreciation; interest; tax; effects of numbers of hours or hectares worked per year; replacement; size; timeliness; and new versus second-hand machinery.

The greatest spending decision a farmer ever faces is whether to buy more land. We examine this issue in Chapter 7. Land value is a big question. How much should you, could you, would you pay for farmland? We discuss the amount of money involved in buying a farm, and land values in terms of real and nominal dollars. The importance of expected operating profits, and sometimes capital gains, in determining the value of land is stressed. Timing of land purchase is stressed as it is the key to safe farm expansion and continued success. Then we describe financing land purchase. Finally, leasing land and sharefarming are discussed.

Risk is dealt with in Chapter 8: the first half is essential theory; the latter is practical. In the theory part we cover such things as probabilities and the use of techniques such as break-even budgets; scenarios; sensitivity testing. In the practical section on risk the topics include drought, booms and busts, climatic and yield variability, measures to cope with variability, and alternatives to increasing activity productivity to increase profits.

In Chapter 9 is a mixture of topics about analysing and planning a change on the farm. We start by highlighting, in some detail, the main things a farmer should think about when trying to decide on a new activity or project. We distinguish two types of change: simple (changing from wheat to barley) and complex (putting in a new irrigation system, developing land, pasture improvement).

We develop a sound partial budget. This is the major tool to use when deciding whether or not to make a change on a farm. Then we talk about the different ways of judging a complex change using the discounted cash flow techniques: net present value (NPV), internal rate of return (IRR) and benefit–cost ratio (B:C). We give an example of a partial development cash flow budget using discounted cash flow techniques. As well the uses and limitations of using gross margins in planning a change are outlined, and the technique for planning changes on a mixed farm is explained.

In Chapter 10, 'Farm Management History', we look back. Read this chapter after the rest of the book has been worked through thoroughly. Chapter 10, like all history, is about helping readers learn from past efforts. In order to know where we are going it is a help to know where we have been and where we are now coming from. We are optimistically overlooking the dictum that 'people and governments never learn from history'.

The theme of change in farming relates to our previous book *The Farming Game* (1981) which we called 'a farm management text for the 1980s'. *The Farming Game Now* is a text for those people aiming to be involved in farming into the 21st century. It is a markedly different book because the world has changed and we have learnt a great deal. Different areas of farm management are given more emphasis, particularly financial management; new issues are dealt with; and the analytical techniques used are more reliable than they were in the past: as one should hope when trading up to a new model.

The adage which sums up best the position of farmers is: 'If you are standing still, you are going backwards.' This applies equally well to us and it is a primary reason we have written *The Farming Game Now*.

That is the book. We hope that this preface stimulates you to read those parts of this book which are of interest to you.

Acknowledgements

This book is about the many bits which make up the whole farm business. It has bits of many people's thoughts in it.

Our most special thanks is to Nanette Esparon who organized, presented, re-read and corrected the manuscript, as well as helping us in many, many other ways. Thanks, Nanny.

Robin Derricourt, Editorial Director at Cambridge University Press, Sydney, has bravely backed us and was most gracious in coping with us.

Many readers and reviewers of other farm management works by us, our students, and, most importantly, the numerous farmers with whom we have done case studies and courses, have taught us much about the intricacies of the farming game. We say thanks and, whatever part you are playing, may your cows be fat, your pastures green and your crops bountiful.

David Honybun and John Cary of the Agricultural Economics Section, School of Agriculture, University of Melbourne and Brian Hardaker, Jack Sinden, Vic Wright and Austin Adams of the Department of Agricultural Economics and Business Management, University of New England, have helped us to get various difficult topics 'right'. We appreciate their help very much.

The copy-editor, Robin Appleton, also helped.

To all the players involved in the farming game, this book is for you.

I

Hard Work and Worry, Worry, Worry:
Introduction

Farming mostly is the process where families use their management skills to combine the land, labour and capital they control to produce agricultural commodities. It is the main way that farm families try to achieve some of the many aims they have.

People, often well-off urban folk, often have unrealistic, romantic notions that farming is always the way to pastures of plenty. Farming is no easy way to make a living. Farmers need a very broad knowledge. Farming involves a lot of routine, repetitive menial tasks which can neither be avoided nor postponed; efforts with highly uncertain outcomes and rewards. There are hard times and there are good times. A reasonable living can be made by farmers who are smart and who can stick it out but it can be a hard row to hoe. Most farmers love it.

Farm management is partly about the processes of deciding what to do on a farm; processes which combine human, technical, economic, financial, risk and institutional elements. Understanding farm management has to be built on wide disciplinary knowledge. Acquiring this breadth of knowledge at sufficient depth, too, is hard work.

The fields of agricultural science and agricultural economics are fundamental to farm management. Knowledge from both these fields is necessary but will still not be enough for sound analysis of farm management problems, and knowledge of either, alone, will not be sufficient.

The importance which different people attach to each of the many fields of study involved in the management and operation of a farm business varies. It depends often on which of the particular fields the person concerned is most interested in and knows most about.

History

Before 1940 in Australia, farm management as a discipline was about mostly technical aspects of the business, with a little bit of rudimentary accounting as well. The focus was on the average technical efficiency of production; that is, the emphasis was on average output from the total inputs such as land, feed, labour, and fertilizer. This led to early research workers in farm management losing relevance to practical decision makers on farms. Economic, or marginal, thinking was needed. This came with the advent of production economic thinking in the 1950s.

Economic aspects of the business became the chief concern in farm management for those involved in investigations and instruction at the academic level. In days past when production economics was king, little emphasis was placed on the human, technical, financial and management aspects of farm production, or on the operation of individual businesses. This led to more workers in academic farm management losing relevance to practical farm management.

However, the enduring legacy of production economics is the economic way of thinking about problems. There is the definite widespread relevance of a couple of key, commonsense principles, about a bit more of this (input, output) and a bit less of that (input, output), in order to make a bit more in total from limited resources.

Financial management of the farm business is now the focus of much attention. Mostly, this is appropriate, particularly when the farmers' refrain worldwide is remembered: 'We worked through spring and summer, through winter and the fall; But the mortgage worked the longest and the hardest of us all.' Farmers know all too well the rest of the story about how the mortgage 'worked through drought and boom-time, through the night and through the day, it settled down among us and never went away!'

Still, there is always the danger of over-emphasizing any one aspect of farm management at the expense of focusing on other important aspects. As history shows, too much emphasis on any part of the farming picture always carries with it the associated risk of becoming irrelevant to practical farm management. To us, then, good farm management analysis and planning is all about applying the appropriate balance between all of the various disciplines involved, to the problem at hand.

Relevant fields

Economists are often viewed as being professionals whose role is to tell people that they cannot do things. This is not wholly correct. Well-trained farm economists attempt to explain, as well as possible, how the farmer's world works and point out the likely costs and gains from taking alternative actions.

The interdisciplinary nature of agricultural and farm management economics, and the quest for problem-solving relevance, should compel farm management economists not to assume too much of the real world 'out' of their analyses. Their disciplinary specialist, technical counterparts at times have a limited view of the farm management spectrum.

We believe that the technical aspects of agricultural production make up a very large part of the farm management story. But, it does not follow from this that understanding the technical aspects alone is sufficient for a farmer or adviser to be able to get the farm management 'right'.

The farming game can be such a tricky and difficult affair that long-term survival and prosperity needs more than just doing the very important technical side of things well. It is better to solve the problem moderately well than to just solve part of the problem very well. The 'whole farm' approach used by good agricultural consultants and other farm management specialists is the relevant approach to farm management problem solving because it is based on getting the disciplinary balance 'right'.

The theme of this work is the belief that applying economic ways of thinking about problems and making intelligent decisions is vital. Thoughtful analyses of the human, technical, economic, financial, risk and institutional ramifications of alternative actions makes for success in business. Using reasoned analysis, taking into perspective the farm family's objectives, some actions can be seen as predictably inappropriate. If a farmer avoids taking such 'predictably inappropriate' actions or decisions, it follows that the business will be more successful in fulfilling family goals and hopes.

To succeed in analysing farm management situations and in providing sound advice it is essential to identify problems correctly, in accord with the relevant time horizons. Often the solutions are relatively few, and obvious. It is a truism that, as the world becomes more complex, the depth of knowledge needed about any particular aspect of the farm business increases. It also gets harder to identify the problem correctly and precisely. Identifying the problem and appreciating all of its dimensions flows from having the right mix of knowledge and the right breadth and depth of knowledge.

The essence of the economic ways of thinking is the economist's standard, querulous retort to claims that some particular action is good or bad. The retort is 'Compared with what?' The outcomes of actions taken on farms have to be judged in terms of 'is this a good move compared with that move?' or, 'is this a better outcome in terms of the desired objectives than would be achieved by doing some realistic alternative?' Economic ways of thinking amount to going beyond 'apparent' or superficial conclusions; it permits people to see if a proposed action is wise, once the important, wider and deeper ramifications are weighed up.

The answer to the questions 'Is economic analysis of some possible action necessary?' and 'If so, what sort of economic analysis ought to be done?' is the same: 'It depends'. Generally, expected gains and losses (both measurable and unmeasurable) need to be assessed if the economist's 'Compared with what?' test is to be passed. That is, how well do the expected net gains (measurable and unmeasurable) compare with the expected net gains from a realistic alternative use of the same resources.

In this book, economic and financial knowledge is added to the existing body of agricultural scientific wisdom about farming. Much of the emphasis in the book comes from the fields of agricultural economics and financial management. We are not sure how much of the ability to gather insights and form good judgements about the human condition can be formally taught and learnt: the personality and experience of the adviser seem to be the keys here.

In some ways 'good management', like luck, remains a partly mysterious, intrinsic part of operating a farm business well. We recognize that both management and luck have important parts to play in effecting results in business. Not much can be done about bad luck. However, in the farming game, as in all other sports, it is possible to some degree to 'make' your own 'good luck' or, at least, to put yourself and your business in a position of being able to capitalize on good fortune, and to lessen the impact, to some degree, when the worst happens.

Fallacies

Rational ways of thinking often lead to debunking commonly held but wrong-headed notions. Common fallacious beliefs held by people who do not have a good understanding of economic reasoning include the following:

- technical ratios of amount of input to amount of product produced, or getting maximum physical output (physical productivity), are the same as economic efficiency (profitability), and that these are a good guide to farm management action. This is false;
- comparisons of average technical ratios such as kg of wool per ha or litres of milk per cow, or comparisons of average activity gross margins, or costs per dry sheep equivalent (dse), between farm businesses are valid and thus performance measures on one farm are useful guides to action for another farm. This is invalid;
- activity gross margins indicate profit. However, activity gross margin is not profit;
- the average gross margin achieved by an existing activity is the figure to apply to the gain to be derived from a change in an activity. It is unlikely to be correct to use this figure;
- net cash flow is profit. It is not;
- tax considerations can often be ignored in farm financial planning. They cannot;
- a change to the operation of part of a farm business can be adopted and implemented without affecting the operation, costs and returns of other parts of the operation of the whole farm. This is usually untrue. There are always numerous complementary and competitive results in the case of multi-enterprise farm businesses. Often, these effects are 'hidden';
- the last unit of potential stock-carrying capacity is worth attaining. It might not be the best investment, once all costs are considered, including the cost of extra risk, and opportunity costs;

- land is the only limiting factor. So the highest return to land should be the only test used. In fact, it might be capital which is limiting, e.g. less physically productive but less capital-using improvements might be more profitable than a more capital-using method. For example, irrigation or drainage which leads to higher physical productivity from the land can use a lot of money;
- net risk to the business remains the same, despite intensification. This is not so. Some risks will increase and some will decrease as a business intensifies, e.g. risks of suffering drought and its effects increase as stocking rate intensifies, but the risk of losing assets might be greater if a farm business does not intensify. Chances of long-run survival will be improved by increased farm profitability. Short-term chances of losses or financial ruin can be increased by increases in cash costs, borrowings and the debt–equity ratio as a result of intensification or a major development program;
- the present (real) value of the dollars, and real interest rates and real returns on capital, are the same as nominal (inflated dollars) market interest rates, and nominal returns on capital. This is not so. Real and nominal values are different, and hybrid real and nominal sums are misleading.

Reasons why the above types of beliefs are mistaken are made clear throughout the rest of this text.

Budgets

Making a few budgets of expected cash flows and profitability of the existing or a changed farm plan is more important nowadays than ever before, because making a living from farming is a more difficult and complex process than it has ever been. Budgeting involves getting information which the decision maker can use. The best farm managers have mastered the art of getting, analysing and using information. Simple farm management budgets, done properly, are very useful, if common mistakes are avoided.

The actual form and extent of the analyses used to judge any farm management decision depends on the nature of the proposed course of action. The detail of the question being asked governs the form and extent of the budgets needed.

Later we explain the many forms of farm management budgets which are useful. There are few rigid rules about what gets included and accounted for in particular farm management budgets, as each applies to the unique farm situation. However, there are important rules based on economic logic which should not be broken. People tend to 'make up their own rules' about budgeting, and their budget 'bottom line' gives a misleading message: a wrong turn, or undue optimism or pessimism, is indicated; or the prescription might be to flog a horse which has already passed on.

The essence of making good farm management budgets is good judgement as most of the numbers which are used are 'soft'. Good budgeting requires good judgements, plenty of information, and a calculator. A computer is not necessary, but for some farmers it is extremely helpful. Sound decision making also requires time to consider all the information made available by the process of budgeting.

An important aspect of judgement and budgeting is to decide what factors are most influential in the eventual outcome of a proposal. A common mistake is to regard all numbers in the budget as being equally important. Then, wrongly, the same attention is devoted to, say, the likely future drench needs and costs as to the likely movements in the price of wool, or interest rates, or debt levels or the overall effects of climatic or market disasters occurring early in the life of a project.

Information, judgement, and contemplation: these are the essence of the decision-making task.

Farming

These following points are what we believe are some enduring truths about farming which deserve wider and more thoughtful recognition than is often given.

- Farming is a human activity—with all the uniqueness, foibles and satisfactions which this implies. Start with the farmers;
- being a good farmer involves having continually to confront changes in climate, prices paid for inputs and prices received for outputs. Also there is the constant need to make the relevant changes to keep up with new technology;
- apart from reasonable luck the key factors which govern financial survival and success in farming are probably knowledge of, and ability with, agricultural technology. Also important is technical efficiency in applying the available resources to the production system. This varies among farmers. There is apparently lots of scope to survive for quite a long time even when things are done poorly. This can be seen where considerable technical and economic inefficiency is evident on some farms over quite long periods;
- the key to good farm management is to identify the problems, accurately and early. Once all the relevant information is gathered the feasible solutions are often relatively clear-cut, and few. When doubt remains more information is needed. Walk the paddocks and assess the overall situation. Remember, the relevant problem on which to focus depends on the time in question;
- what a farm family does is often not as important as how they do it. In many ways, particular mixes of activities are less important than ensuring that whatever activities are carried out, are done well;
- the relations between gearing and growth, and managing and controlling cash flows, are probably the crucial factors affecting financial performance;
- risk, yield, price and income variability, is the outstanding feature of Australian farming and this pervades all thinking and action. Risk is something which farmers live with, and they even exploit it. The potential consequences of risk are tackled step by step. Farmers take many different actions to counteract the effects of risk and be in an overall position which they believe will let them achieve, to a degree which satisfies them, the most important of their many goals;

- budgeting and planning to help make decisions is a start, but not an end. Implementing, controlling, learning, adapting, and revising plans, all play a big part in determining the extent to which farm families' goals are achieved.

Here we have shown how we view the farming game. The themes raised here recur throughout the book. In Chapter 2 we look at the component parts which are the essence of the whole farm business, as well as how to identify the current state of the business and to assess its potential.

2

Many Bits and Pieces Make Up The Big Picture:
The Farm Business

■

Here we introduce the nature of and scope for managing, analysing and planning a farm business. We present a sketch of the farm business, including each of the important bits which go to make it up and determine its success or failure.

A farm business is made up of human, technical, economic and financial parts. At the same time it is subject to seasonal, market and institutional influences, all of which involve risks and uncertainties. The human element is the starting point: what the farmer wants to do, whether the farmer can carry it out, and how much of the rewards to take in dollars.

Technology determines what is possible. Technical factors which underlie what is being achieved and what could be achieved are discussed.

Key economic and financial concepts are explained. Economic analysis indicates what is most profitable, and finance indicates what money is involved. Criteria are presented for judging how the farm business has performed, or might perform, in future, and for judging whether an idea is a good one, economically and financially. It is not just returns which matter, but riskiness as well.

The role of 'economic' thinking and the use of farm management budgets are discussed. Forces beyond the farm gate partially dictate the end result, so to complete the picture, the importance of market and political factors beyond farmers' control are outlined briefly. Despite farming being a risky business, most of Australia's agricultural production is world-class, passing the economists' test of efficiency by competing without government subsidy, on world markets.

Analysis and planning of a farm business involves evaluating current performance and potential changes. Every farm business is unique. The relevance of changes to the farming system have to be discerned on a case-by-case basis. In farm analyses it is vital to take full account of the business' unique combination of land, labour, capital, and the farm family's goals, interests, skills, and resources.

The aim is to help the farm manager to make more effective decisions, based on the steps of perceiving problems, collecting information, and analysing possible solutions. These are the questions that should be asked: What should I produce? What method of production should I use? How much should I produce? When should I buy and sell? How much capital do I need? Should I borrow? How much should I borrow? Giving good answers to each of these questions needs an understanding of human aspects; economic principles; of finance; risk; of factors at work in commodity and in financial markets; of management analytical techniques; and most important, of the technology. Decisions have to be made under conditions of limited information, unpredictable change, market and climatic uncertainty and risk. There are two major challenges facing today's farmer:

1 How to incorporate new technology profitably into the existing business organization.
2 How to be sufficiently flexible, mentally and financially, to adjust resource management to meet both changed economic circumstances and widely varying climatic conditions.

The business management principles and planning techniques we present can help farmers to meet these two challenges with some success. Remember though, that the outcome of efforts put into farming, as in all aspects of life, results in part from 'luck' and 'circumstance'. However, we are convinced that in the gamble known as 'farming', work put into understanding the 'game' thoroughly can help overall.

To survive and prosper, farmers have to keep up their rates of gain in productivity to maintain their profitability. Productivity increases have been greatest where up-to-date technological information has been combined with business management techniques, farming skills, and enough capital to devise and implement farm plans aimed at lifting income. Successful plans have to take account of the variability of prices, costs, yields, and seasons. The farmer, after investigation, should put figures on these things in the process of deciding what to do and how to act.

The 'management' or 'whole farm' approach to the problem of lifting productivity on farms has been shown to work. Such increases do not occur unless farmers are competent and progressive. Intensive management analysis and advice is of little use unless the farm operator has a good level of technical management and skill. Contrast per ha net farm income on those farms where farmers use sound information and knowledge, and apply that resource known as 'management skill', and use technological advances and capital, including prudent borrowings, with those farms on which the managers are unwilling or unable to do so. The contrasts become sharper each year. Mostly our message is to progressive farmers.

This book is mainly about using some of the useful techniques which apply 'economic' ways of thinking to farm management. Farming is mostly a biological activity; however the human aspect cannot be ignored. In general our approach is to pretend that the reader is to go out to a farm that he or she has never seen before, and to bring back a report on what the farm is like. Some of the questions to answer in the report are what:

- is the nature, quantity and quality of basic production resources?
- makes the farmer and the farmer's family work?
- does the farmer and that family need from the farm?
- do they want to do with, or to have, or to get from their lives?
- are the main problems of the farm?
- is the financial situation?
- are the limitations (weaknesses), and the potentials (strengths)?

As this subject is approached from an 'economic' view, one objective is to think about how you could advise the farmer to make more 'profit'. To give sound economic and financial advice you need to get the human, technical, and biological bits right.

Farm analysis and planning— components of a farm

A farm has to be analysed before it can be planned: the potential, and the restraints and risks have to be considered.

Not all the topics covered in Table 2.1 below, will apply to every situation being analysed. Also there will be some factors that do apply, which we have not mentioned. After studying Table 2.1, use it as a guide to compile your own list for the specific situation you are analysing.

Table 2.1: Key factors in analysis and planning of the whole farm business

Each part of this table has three components:
- factors to be considered when analysing (or knowing) the present situation on the farm;
- the potential for improving the existing situation through better technology and management and exploiting some possible options;
- factors which could prevent the perceived potential from being fully achieved, including risk.

Present	Potential	Some restraints on achieving potential
Human conditions		
goals of family	scope for change of goals	lack of knowledge of opportunities
		resource base limited
		content with present situation
skills of farm family and workers	prospect for improving skills	few informal or formal ways of acquiring more skills
• technical		• lack of confidence in ability
• economic thinking		• lack of ability
• mastery of information		• age and attitude

Present	Potential	Some restraints on achieving potential
farm family labour supply • numbers • age • sex	better use of labour through diversification into both rural and non-rural activities, or through some changes in who does what, when and how	small scope for extra enterprise diversification knowledge and skills for non-rural activities difficult to acquire traditional labour roles for different members of the family and employed workforce
farmer's attitude to risk		
farm management		

Technical conditions

feed supply for animals
soil types, nutrient status, and topography

from pasture and crops

proportion of non-edible vegetation	increased feed supply by better pasture, fertilizers and fodder crops	cost of fertilizer, pasture, seed and growing fodder crops, compared with value of production which would result from animals which consumed the extra feed
pasture species and crop residues		
pasture composition, species density	improving strategies to reduce losses in bad seasons and increased profit in good seasons	lack of capital to finance fodder crops and pasture improvement
fodder crops for animals		
expected seasonal (green and dry) feed production from pasture and crop	improve feed use water	pasture establishment limits
variability in seasonal pasture production		
availability and use of feed from agistment, leasing		
production strategies used to cope with climatic variability		

from grain and purchased feed from factories

if home-mixed feed, what are sources of grains, etc., used	improving quality of home-mixed rations by getting better advice on nutrition values of feeds and needs of livestock	lack of relevant information lack of suitable equipment for storage and feeding, or lack of funds for equipment
how is the best ration decided		
how is the feed mixed, stored, and fed to animals	reducing wastage in storage and feeding	
performance of animals on factory feed versus home-mixed feed	independent testing of feeds supplied by factory reducing cost of feed mix	

continued

Present	Potential	Some restraints on achieving potential

animal activities (converting feed)

type of animals

cattle, sheep, goats, chicken, pigs, horses, fish, other	introducing other species or strains	climate and environment
		disease risk
		costs and risks of change (including tax implications)

structure of herd, flock or group

numbers	increasing numbers and proportions of females	low reproduction rates
proportion of females to males		poor nutrition
age of various classes of stock	reducing average age of group	
source of semen (natural or artificial insemination)	specializing in a certain type of class of animal	
productive life of breeders	improve turn-off rate	
timing of lambing, calving, etc.	reduce mortality rate	
timing of key operations	reduce age of animals sold	
reproduction and weaning rates		

how system is replaced

self-replacing	increasing weaning rates	lack of knowledge on ways to increase weaning rates
bought-in replacements	acquiring better quality bought-in replacement stock	unavailability of suitable bought-in replacement stock
		preference for own bred stock

system of feeding

grazing, crop and crop residues, agistment, home-mixed or purchased concentrate feed, feed supplements in dry season	improving use of feed supplied	lack of knowledge
	increased use of feed supplements in dry season	inadequate facilities
		price and availability of suitable supplements

husbandry

labour for care of stock	reducing disease and parasites	lack of competent people to care for animals
housing, yards and veterinary chemicals and medicines	improving housing and yards to improve efficiency of handling and of disease control	cost of appropriate veterinary services and medicines
season of birth and young	change time of birth of young	

continued

Present	Potential	Some restraints on achieving potential
genetic quality		
methods used to maintain or improve quality	introduce improved strains	outdated ideas on selection methods
	use of artifical insemination	lack of suitable new strains adapted to environment
	crossbreeding for hybrid vigour	prejudice against crossbred animals
cropping		
soil types and fertility status		
type of crop		
short-term (3 to 4 months)	new crops	uncertainty of performance of new crops
medium-term (4 to 7 months)	change in mixture of crops	availability of land for development
year-long (12 to 14 months)	more land development	
perennial (2 to 50 years)	improved cultivation practices	cost and difficulty of development
cultivation practices for each type of crop		new crops might not fit in with the existing system
	new crop sequences made possible by new strains and chemical and cultural technologies	risk of changes
cropping system		
crop sequences	increased cropping intensity	rainfall inadequate
cropping intensity		labour needs
crop mix in any year and over time	alternative sequences which satisfy both return and risk criteria	relevant technology lacking
		risk from increasing cropping intensity
		soil degradation
		long-term objectives about soil quality
methods of maintaining soil fertility		
fallow	increasing legume crop percentages in the rotation	vigorous growing legume species are not available or successful
legume-based rotations		
non-legume rotations		
chemical and mechanical means	using longer or better fallows	
mixture of the above methods	more effective use of crop residues and stubbles to maintain structure	
	different chemical or machine services	
erosion control measures	reduce erosion through better techniques	cost of reducing erosion too great
		limited supply or organic matter to maintain fertility over the whole farm

continued

Present	Potential	Some restraints on achieving potential
inputs used		
planting materials, type and amount	improved or cheaper types available	no suitable alternative plant, materials or types
availability and cost		
machinery		
cropping labour needs		
main operations	developing cropping systems which reduce peak labour demand	no feasible alternative cropping system available
amounts		
skilled or unskilled		high wage rates for casual labour at peak times
how seasonal peak demands are met (share, hire, exchange)	improving arrangements for obtaining labour and machinery at peak times	
crop product use and marketing		
marketing channels	improving presentation or marketing arrangements for products	no facilities available to improve presentation, marketing channels
sales and domestic use		
on-farm processing		cost of improved storage too great
storage costs and storage loss	reducing storage losses	
irrigation		
system of irrigation	irrigation development	lack of capital
how limited water is used among competing activities	better use of water	lack of water
	improved drainage and recycling of water	poor water distribution systems
		topographic restraints
machinery services		
how machinery services acquired		
owned	acquiring machinery services which do a timely, better and cheaper job	capital cost of investing in own machinery
contract		
sharefarm		availability of reliable contract services
exchange	improving existing machines and equipment	
leased		
need for timeliness in operations		
age and value		
number of years before it has to be replaced	increasing life of machine through improved maintenance	operator's skills
expected cost of replacement		overcapitalizing
annual overhead and operating costs	using better designed machines	
adequacy for the job		
work rates		
adequacy of maintenance		

continued

Present	Potential	Some restraints on achieving potential

Economic and financial conditions

Present	Potential	Some restraints on achieving potential
total capital of farm, stock, plant	expected future returns to farm resources	poor management
activity gross margins	increasing gross margins of activities	no relevant new technologies to increase gross margin
reasons for level of gross margin	best mix of activities	credit very limited and not geared to realities of farm production or development cycle
levels of overheads, which includes essential household payments	introduce new activity(ies)	interest paid for loans
total gross margins minus overheads	expected rate of return on extra capital investment in new or expanded activities	no good advice available to help work out investment alternatives and cash management
debt level and terms of loans	avenues for extending terms of loans, getting new loans	
return on resources		
structure of 'business', e.g. family or group holding, partnership, small company, trust	possibility for changing structure	
debt compared to equity	prospects for increase in land value	
farm cash surplus	exploiting money market better	
	use of futures markets	
liquidity (i.e., whether some resources are readily saleable, e.g. cattle)	change in farm activity mix	seasonal pattern of cash flow
hedges agains inflation	expansion and spreading overheads	debt:equity too high
expected operating profit	intensification	
expected cash flow	expected extra return from a change in farm plan	
expected activity gross margins		
time effects and the present value of money		
tax		
farm management budgets		

Beyond the farm (Factors mostly beyond the farmer's control)

- markets
- marketing
- demand
- supply
- marketing margins
- rules of the game
- inelastic demand

- technological change
- unstable and declining prices
- cost-price squeeze
- inflation, exchange rates, interest rates
- balance of payments
- protection to industries
- adjustment assistance

Table 2.1 covers the key human, technical, and economic and financial aspects. We expand these sections in this chapter, as well as discuss the marketing and policy aspects. For a full explanation of many points you need to read the relevant chapter(s). As in economics, unlike much of science, many of the terms used can mean different things to different people and we discuss (in later chapters) the ranges of meanings and interpretations commonly given to key terms and ideas used in economic analysis and planning.

The examination of Table 2.1 follows the topics, point by point.

The human conditions

There are many skills important in good management. Farm management analysis and decision making is about identifying correctly the real nature of the problem. The critical skill is to identify this and relate it to human, technical, economic and financial, conceptual and analytical skills. Pertinent information, processed by sound analytical and planning techniques, makes for good decision making, that is, evaluating and acting on information. During the 1990s more and more useful information will become more available, more quickly, to more farmers, than in previous decades. The outstanding feature of the best farm managers is their mastery of information about the whole spectrum of the process called 'farm management'. Of the skills necessary in farm management, how much can be taught and learnt? Technical skills, both applied and theoretical, can be learnt. 'Economic' ways of thinking, the ability to recognize the essence of a problem and to draw on general principles and budgeting techniques, can also be learnt. The human side of management, the personality, understanding, intuition, ability to see an issue through another's eyes, and other intrinsic human qualities, are probably difficult to learn or to radically change other than through experience. Management flair, business acumen, entrepreneurial skills, intelligence, shrewdness, judgement, mastery of information, ability to assess and cope with riskiness, all vital features of top managers, are mostly innate qualities. Individuals might or might not have them, and they probably are not gained from formal teaching and learning. But, many analytical skills can be demonstrated and applied in formal teaching and learning situations to help owners of farm businesses to avoid some of the naive basic errors that were made through the 1980s by so-called 'entrepreneurs' and 'managers' in Australia's non-farm businesses and financial institutions.

Farm family goals

When considering why members of farm families do or do not take certain actions, the starting point is with their needs, wants, and goals. The goals of members of farm families ultimately determine how properties are managed and how the farm families might exploit the potential of farms.

Knowing the goals of both the farmer and the family helps to explain why the farm is managed in the way it is. Goals also help indicate how (if at all) the farmer might be able to exploit the potential of the farm.

Common goals of farmers are for the business to survive and to grow, and to set and to overcome challenges. Other goals are numerous: to farm well and to be recognized for this; to improve the physical state and appearance of the farm; to acquire extra land or to control a larger business for the future and for heirs; to have a reasonable but not profligate standard of living which compares reasonably with others in farming and society at large; to earn enough profit to be able to improve and develop the farm so as not to have to work so hard as the farmers age; to achieve capital gain and increase wealth; to have good quality animals and crops in good condition; to reduce income tax; to have a satisfying rural way of life; to have children well educated (often, better educated than themselves so they have the option to not go farming); to have enough leisure, increasing over time; to be a respected member of the community; and to have enough money to pursue non-farm interests. Importantly, some of these goals are in conflict, thus trade-offs are involved between achieving various goals at various levels.

Most farmers are moderately profit-orientated, and take a medium-term view of using and husbanding their resources, all done to the extent that more immediate economic forces allow. A reasonable supposition is that most farmers are largely motivated to do a bit better and to make a bit more gain in the short and the long term, when most, but not all of that gain, is dollar profit. This applies as long as not too many of the other things they value highly, have to be sacrificed, such as health, family life, leisure and outside interests. 'Farm to make a living and you can get a good living, farm to make lots of money and it will often deny you a living' is an adage whose truth is widely recognized in farming communities.

A role of professional farm management advisers is as 'professional goal adjusters'. Farmers might state definite objectives but might not see that their physical and managerial resources do not match their wishes. It is essential to find out if the product markets and the resources of land, technology, capital, credit and skills are compatible with these goals. If they are not, then the goals might have to be modified or re-defined. Sometimes, farmers might not be aware of the possibilities for exploiting the full potential of the resources which they and their families operate.

They might have 'vistas unperceived' and might be persuaded to raise their expectations. Others might be content and not have high hopes, wants, and expectations. Advisers can have an inspirational role when the goals are limited compared to the potential of the resources under the farmers' control. Mostly some kind of adjustment about stated goals has to be made when the situation is assessed, taking full account of the agricultural, economic, financial, and human realities. Given this, however, the adviser cannot know more than the farmers do about what is 'good' for them.

Supply and skills of farm labour

The numbers, ages, and skills of farm families and workers have to be considered in an analysis of farms. Of particular interest are the methods used to meet peak work loads and the skills available to do such specialized tasks as basic maintenance, repairs and adjustments to machines, pumps and generators, or the care of animals and crops.

Identifying where the managers' strengths, weaknesses and preferences lie in performing the various physical and mental tasks helps to explain the way farm businesses are being operated and how well these are performing. Operators' skills are one of the main inputs to farm production and these mostly determine the potential profitability of the businesses. Importantly, if changes were being considered, it is vital that the farmers should have the necessary skills, knowledge and personal make-up to handle the new, maybe more intensive and technically complex situation.

The extent to which casual and contract services are used are important in determining the output per permanent labour unit. The way in which work loads and specialized tasks are met form part of any farm analysis. In the appraisal of the potential of the farm, see if the existing permanent labour force, as well as convenient and reliable contract services and casual labour have the skills to handle an intensified or more diversified operation. If not, ask what training is needed to equip them to cope with the new situation? Would additional skilled people have to be hired?

Possibly, the numbers and skills of the farm family labour force can be used more productively if the farm were more diversified, and if sideline activities were introduced. Perhaps, there is also the potential for engaging in some non-farming activities.

Farm management

Broadly, the main management functions of a farm operator are: (1) planning and deciding (2) organizing resources and putting decisions into practice (3) controlling the operation of the business and reappraising actions. Usually the action farmers take have elements of each of the three functions in it. Also, the emphasis on different aspects of management changes over time. A farm business, and the farm family, go through different stages from starting out, to consolidating, to expanding, to winding down and to transferring control. It is not worthwhile treating the categories of management functions rigidly.

Making decisions usually involves choices. The process has some generally recognized steps:

• recognizing problems and need for action;
• making observations, collecting facts, getting ideas;
• analysing observations, and testing alternative solutions to problems;
• making the decision;
• acting on the decision;
• implementing;
• controlling the implementation;
• taking responsibility for the decision;
• reviewing the outcomes and adapting the intended and expected to the actual;
• doing it better next time, i.e., learning from one's mistakes.

Management cannot be assessed solely by goals achieved. In part, management is about making the best decision with the available information at the time. Even so, the decision might not be the correct decision. Management decisions are made before the event. Whether it is the right or wrong decision is only known after the event. A 'good' decision could still turn out to be the wrong decision because of the way the many previous unknowns and uncertainties turn out. Once a decision is made and action taken, the operation of the farm differs from that which existed before the decision. After putting the decision into practice, management has a new set of circumstances to manage.

One feature of managing farms which distinguishes it from managing many non-farm businesses is the close relationship between the household (consumption unit) and the business (production unit). This means that non-production issues have a larger role in how the business is managed than is the case with many non-farm businesses.

Some characteristics of good farm managers are that they:

- are aware of all the relevant information about whatever particular task or projects are at hand;
- know the technology thoroughly and keep up with new technological developments;
- emphasize getting jobs done on time;
- think ahead (using a bit of paperwork helps here);
- discuss ideas, procedures and alternatives with others;
- make provision to cope with the unexpected;
- have a system for keeping up-to-date with daily work achieved, for regular consultation, and for making sure that the employees have regular, clear instructions;
- have vision;
- are adventurous but sound;
- have sufficient grasp of farm management to decide on well-analysed and economically sound plans of action;
- can carry out plans.

Management and communication

In most of this textbook emphasis is placed on analysis and planning, using relatively simple farm management budgets. However, the importance of the human condition in business success cannot be overstated. Ultimately, it is the personal qualities of individuals involved in conducting the business which determines the results. Often the vital aspect of management is the task of getting the most from each person according to each person's ability. Communication is at the core of the management of labour. For instance, effective communication between the farmer and employee(s) is fundamental. Without good communication and mutual understanding the best of plans do not work. Within the family workforce it is also critical. But, the means of attaining good communications where it does not exist is usually difficult because of complex and close interpersonal relations. So much of the skill of getting things done by people (communication and leadership) depends on personality, fairness and respect-earning behaviour by management. Most of these traits are innate.

The technical conditions

Animals: feed conversion activities—present

In analysis of feed conversion activities see what system the manager uses to convert feed into money. On most farms this is done through animals, but there are some enterprises which convert it directly into such saleable products as hay or pellets. The potential for these activities seems to be increasing, as animal industries become more intensive. The scope for these forms of conversion are worth looking at.

Consider the chief features of animals as feed conversion mechanisms:

- type of animal activities;
- structure of the flock or herd, by age, sex, and numbers;
- system used to replace the herd or flock.

There are two systems of replacement:

1 Breed own replacements.
2 Buy-in replacements.

System of feeding

There are three possibilities:

- grazing (set stocking, rotational or both);
- hay, silage, fodder crop, grain, agistment;
- totally or partially fed on purchased concentrate feed.

Husbandry

Husbandry covers the use of medications and chemicals; veterinary services; the method of harvesting the product (milk, wool, eggs); the supervision and management at mating and birth; and the time and interval (frequency) of parturition (calving, lambing, and farrowing).

Use of genetics

The use of genetics includes artificial insemination (AI), embryo transfer, selection based on performance recording, use of progeny-tested sires, cross-breeding, and purchase of special hybrid animals, as in the case of the intensive industries.

Animals: feed conversion activities—potential

In the analysis of the animal-based feed conversion system consider the potential and the scope for improvement under the headings used in the previous section. The opportunity to improve performance by exploiting new or different systems of feeding is worth investigating, because it is in this area that these are some of the greatest gains in profitability. Under animal activities, it is necessary to consider whether there is a role for new activities, and expansion or modification of any of the existing activities. With herd or flock structure, there might be potential for increasing the ratio of female breeding stock to males, for selling animals at a younger age, and for mating animals at a younger age. The replacement system might be improved by changing partly from a self-replacing system to buying hybrid animals of superior performance, or by mating cull females to sires of another breed.

Husbandry practices on many farms can often be improved by using the latest developments in the rapidly changing technology of control of internal and external parasites; in shearing, milking, poultry shed, and piggery design and operation; and in the development of minimum care animal husbandry practices. Medicines, chemicals, and veterinary advice are also integral to insect and parasite control. These are often cheap when the improvement in animal performance and 'profits' are considered. The first need is for animals to be properly fed, as poor nutrition makes them more susceptible to disease and parasites. Capitalizing on the various techniques for improving the genetic worth of animals is not very expensive. A little time and effort spent on investigating techniques for achieving genetic gain often gives good returns.

Using feed supply efficiently is the key factor affecting the profitability of animal enterprises in both grazing and 'factory farm' production. There are numerous possibilities for ensuring efficient use of feed, e.g. timing of lambing or calving, more controlled grazing; segregation of age groups; using feeding facilities which reduce wastage; mixing different species of grazing animals (cattle, sheep, and goats). Strategic feed supplementation is also very useful, e.g. last stage of pregnancy; early lactation; weaning.

Animals: feed conversion activities—restraints

Some important restraints on the exploitation of the potential for improving animal enterprises include climate, environment, and risk of disease.

Though replacement through bought-in replacement stock rather than through a self-replacing system might appear better, it is not always possible to get 'superior' quality replacement stock of the type that farmers want. This method can also carry increased risk of introducing disease.

Barriers to using feed more efficiently include not knowing the best way of doing it, a shortage of labour or proper facilities (sheds, yards, equipment), or the risk and other changes associated with changing the timing of lambing or calving and operations. Often, better husbandry practices are not possible because of lack of competent people to care for the animals.

The main restraints on exploiting genetics to the full are that the animals are already being adapted to maximum performance in that environment; ignorance of the practical implications of genetic research; prejudice against crossbred animals; and the absence of AI skills and facilities within easy reach. There is also the problem, where introducing new strains (not species) is wanted, of finding those strains which are as well adapted to the local environment as the strains that have been traditionally used.

Feed supply—present

The two main sources of feed supply are pasture and the concentrate feeds used in intensive industries. In an analysis of a farm's pasture supply look at the topography (whether steep, undulating or flat); the soils and nutrient status; presence of rocks and non-edible vegetation such as trees, thorny shrubs and unpalatable bushes; also, the incidence of plants toxic to animals. Next to be assessed are the pasture species present; their palatability and digestibility; their density; their nutritional value; and what crop residues are available, and when; also, whether special crops are grown for animal fodder.

Topography

The feed supply varies with the slope and aspect of the land. An almost vertical slope facing south does not have the pasture production of a river flat. Even so, a balanced combination of flats and hills can often provide more flexibility if grazing pastures in different seasons.

Soil types

Soils vary greatly in structure, in nutrient status, and in fertility. Soils can be classified into major and minor groups according to their ability to produce pastures and crops. A breakdown of the area and range of soil types on a farm is essential for physical analysis: it is the basis of both present and potential land use.

Present soil nutrient status and fertilizer history

The commonest deficiencies in Australian soils are phosphorus and nitrogen. Soil tests indicate the pH (degree of acidity or alkalinity), the levels of the major elements phosphorus, potassium and sulphur, and are fairly reliable for use in a fertilizer program. Tissue tests of green growing plants are more useful tests for the significant trace (or minor) elements such as molybdenum, copper and zinc. The fertilizer history is useful mainly to help detect deficiencies other than phosphorus. If a farm has had a history of 2.5 tonnes per ha of superphosphate over the previous 15 years, and the pastures are not vigorous, it is likely that some element other than phosphorus is lacking and so that is limiting production. In practice, a combination of soil tests every few years, records of past fertilizer use, some simple, moderately sized trial plots and the farmers' observations of how the paddocks have been responding to recent applications of fertilizer, is an effective way of determining present fertilizer needs.

Pastures

The following aspects of the pastures have to be defined:

- composition: native, introduced legumes, grasses, weeds;
- balance between legumes and grasses;

- density of plant population;
- vigour, persistence of species, expected life;
- suitability for various classes of livestock, e.g. non-breeders, young growing animals, breeders, sheep or cattle;
- weed control: when, how;
- use of sprays and grazing;
- pasture improvement, establishment methods.

Expected seasonal pasture production

Based on rainfall records and farmers' experiences, there is for each region an average expected pattern of seasonal pasture production, as a result of the rainfall pattern. Thus, in southern Australia, rain-fed pastures usually begin active growth in late autumn, slow down in winter, reach a peak in spring, and do not grow in summer and early autumn. The further north the region is, the greater the tendency for pasture production to be summer-dominant and winter-dormant. Generally the lower the annual rainfall the greater the degree, and impact, of unreliability or variability of pasture. The expected average seasonal pasture production has to be defined because this determines the system of animal production which is best suited to use the pastures most profitably. For example, in Victoria it is more likely (but not necessarily more profitable) for ewes to lamb and cattle to calve in autumn than it is in northern New South Wales where winter-pasture production is low.

Another often important aspect of feed supply is whether some of the feed comes from agistment or leasing; the reliability and tenure of this source of feed needs to be determined.

Strategies to cope with variations above and below the expected pasture supply

Rarely does the average season occur. For example, in southern Australia, the opening rains, on average, fall during April. Yet these can begin as early as February, or as late as June. Winters in that region can be very wet, with the paddocks becoming waterlogged, and this impedes pasture growth and use; or winters can be very dry and warm, and good winter pasture supply results. There are similar variations about the average season in other areas, often with wider fluctuations.

The strategies and the particular tactics which the manager of an individual farm adopts to meet these variations about the average, vary greatly as do their degrees of profitability (or loss saving). The general aim is to reduce the harmful effects of adverse situations, and to exploit favourable circumstances. Thus it is essential, when analysing a farm, to discover what measures the operator adopts to handle variability of feed supply, e.g. supplementary feeding, stock trading, fodder conservation, reduction in body condition of stock. Skill at managing the fluctuations about the normal pasture supply is one of the main requirements for the successful running of pasture-based animal production enterprises.

Concentrate feed

The chief issues on concentrate feed are whether it is best for the operator to mix the rations or to buy pre-mixed feed from a miller, how much labour is saved from using pre-mixed feed, and the relative quality of the two sources of feed. The trend is now to use pre-mixed feeds, and to use the labour saved to do other things such as run more stock. The person studying the situation on the farm needs to find out if the grain is home-grown or bought; how the best mixtures of grains and additives are determined; and the methods of mixing, storing, and feeding. Where feed is bought from a company which mixes feed, the reliability of the feed supply, the quality and the consistency of quality, are important. Ascertain the relative performance of animals on home-mixed feed and factory-supplied feed, and the relative costs.

Feed supply: potential

Increasing feed quantity and quality by better species and fertilizer use

This always remains the single most important action available to farmers who manage pasture-based animal production systems. Technical information exists to help farmers implement the physical part of a development program if they decide that it is economic to do so.

Fodder cropping

Winter and summer fodder crops are often valuable as a means of increasing the supply of high quality feed when seasonal pasture is low. The scope for exploiting the potential contribution of fodder crops has to be examined in any farm analysis. Critical here is assessing the quantity of feed which a crop may provide.

Developing irrigation

On pasture-based farms there is increasing interest in using supplementary irrigation from water harvested from run-off which would normally be wasted. As well, a number of engineering developments have led to supplementary irrigation schemes that can be run more cheaply than by using traditional methods. Generally, because of its cost, feed grown using supplementary irrigation schemes needs to be fed to animals which can convert it into a high value product such as milk, stud stock, lamb or veal. It can also be used as hay or pellets as part of the ration of intensive animal systems such as pigs and poultry.

Feed supply: restraints

The main restraints on getting the full potential feed supply are the costs of seed, fertilizer, and growing fodder crops, relative to the amount of extra feed that grows as a result of using such techniques, and the use to which the extra feed is put. If lots of extra feed grows, and it is used efficiently by animals whose product (e.g. milk, carcase) is bringing a high price in the market, then it could be worth doing. Otherwise it could be a waste of money. Also, it might not be possible to match feed requirements to feed availability efficiently. Another restraint can be lack of knowledge about livestock and feed prices, particularly in situations where the farmer wishes to exploit the good years and cut losses if the season is bad.

There are two ways of supplying grain-based feed to animals: mix the grains on the farm, or buy the feed ready-mixed from a processor. There may be potential for improving the quality of farm-mixed rations (and hence animal performance) by getting advice from the extension service on nutritional values of various grains and on the specific feed needs of the different classes of animals being fed. In some situations, a feed-analysis service provided by the extension service or commercial laboratories can help ensure that the right blend of grain and additives is being used. Wastage during storage (through, e.g. insects, rats, or weather damage) and when feeding out, could be important causes of loss which could be prevented or reduced by better structures and equipment.

The main barriers to achieving the potential for improvement in grain-based feeding systems are lack of specific knowledge by extension workers and farmers about particular animal production methods and requirements; no readily available feed-testing services; and inadequate attention given to animal health. Animal health is usually a bigger issue in intensive feeding systems.

Cropping activities: present

Types of crops grown

These are the main points which need to be examined when analysing the cropping enterprise on a farm:

- the soil types and nutrient status;
- the types of crops grown: whether they are (1) short-term (three to four months) crops such as tomatoes (2) annual crops such as wheat or sorghum (3) longer term (18-month) crops such as sugar cane (4) crops which take three to four years to reach maturity, or (5) tree crops which grow for many years (e.g. apples);
- what cropping system is being followed, what sequences of crops are grown;
- the methods of preparing, planting, husbandry and marketing used for each crop;
- on orchards and in forestry the age of the trees, and the expected life of each stand or block, have to be defined;
- in cropping areas, the crops which are grown need also to be classified into winter and summer crops.

Maintaining soil fertility

Most progressive farm managers aim to have a cropping system which yields consistently well while not reducing the long-term fertility and erosion status of the soil. However, there are many farms where the arable soil has been plundered. It is essential, when examining the cropping activities, to find out what (if any) measures are being taken to maintain soil fertility. Fertility is defined in terms of structure, freedom from weeds, nutrient status, absence of harmful micro-organisms, and erosion. The question of how best to maintain fertility is critical on intensive vegetable farms as it is to orchard farmers and growers of plantation crops and broad-area grain crops. The commonest method of maintaining fertility on broad-area farms is to have legume–crop sequences.

In some areas where crops are more profitable than stock there is a trend to have non-legume or reduced-legume systems of maintaining soil fertility. Among the techniques used are stubble retention to maintain structure and reduce erosion, applying nitrogen fertilizer or herbicides to control weeds, and chemicals to control harmful micro-organisms. Minimum cultivation techniques using herbicides are increasing in favour. Assessment of the scope for expansion of one or other of these two basic systems to maintain fertility in the future is a vital step in any farm appraisal. On intensive vegetable farms where there is little crop residue to work back into the soil, gypsum and poultry manure might have to be used to help maintain structure.

Irrigation system
The chief aspects of the present irrigation system which need to be looked at are the amount of water available, water quality, salinity problems, labour requirements, the system of delivering water to the growing crop, and drainage. Of particular interest is the reliability of the water supply and water quality. Salinity and some idea of the content of toxic materials in the water must be known.

Cropping activities: potential
When evaluating the potential for the crop enterprise, a number of things need to be examined, including: the scope for new crops; changing the mixture of crops; having better sequences of crops and intensifying cultivation (say, through shorter rotations and sequences and land improvement).

Change in mixture of crops
It might be biologically better to change the mixture of crops. Increasing the proportion of summer to winter crops might lead to better weed and disease control. Alternatively, increasing the area sown to, say, stone fruits relative to apples and pears, might lead to a reduction in labour demand for a whole orchard operation.

Factors restraining (or preventing) the farm from achieving its full potential could be uncertainty about how well a new crop grows; market for the crop; the labour needs; the new mixture of crops not satisfying the full needs of a rotation; no suitable land for development; or the cost as well as the difficulty of development being so great that it would not be worthwhile to plant the crop. The latter situation is common at present in areas where there is considerable pressure on any land suitable for cropping.

The main limitations on more intensive land-use through mixed, double and inter-row cropping are soil structure and fertility; shortage of rainfall at critical times; labour; lack of relevant information, and lack of local experience.

Having looked at what is being done on the farm about soil fertility—whether it is being 'plundered', maintained or improved—it is then necessary to see what potential there is for improving the situation. Ask these questions:

- can more, or better legume crops be grown?
- can more crop residues and stubbles be returned to the soil, either directly or through grazing animals?
- what happens if more cash crops and fewer legume crops are put into the rotation?
- how can 'fertility' be improved by using more chemical fertilizers and sprays in a better way?
- could more grazing animals be introduced into the land-use system?
- what role is there for strip cropping and/or reduced tillage?

As water is usually a scarce resource the way in which it is distributed between the various alternative uses for it—annual crops, tree crops, animals, households—has to be analysed to find the most effective use for it. Some aspects of exploiting the potential of the limited water supply include: reducing waste; distributing water better; giving priority to activities which respond best to irrigation at times of annual water shortage; improving drainage so that no salting and waterlogging occurs; and being able to recycle some of the drainage water. Pumps, piping, spray jets, drips, and land levelling and contouring improvements all justify the costs. Timely (early) application of water, i.e., before plants are stressed, is invaluable.

On many farms more efficient use of water; reduction in labour; higher yields and greater areas cropped can result from applying new developments in engineering and irrigation technology for cropping. The payoff can be quite high.

Cropping restraints

Evaluate circumstances which might act against (restrain) the achievement of cropping potential.

Fertilizer restraints

Some farmers lack knowledge of the finer (but crucial) points on how to use and when to apply chemical sprays, especially for weeds, for best results, and to avoid killing half of the crop (or the succeeding crop) with them. Long-term effects of some chemical sprays are unknown and with the help of the extension service and chemical companies over four to five years many problems could be overcome. The main restraints on organic fertilizers to improve soil fertility is the small supply available compared with the large amount demanded by 'fertility-draining' cropping systems.

Labour in cropping

Sometimes, in cropping, there are peaks of demand for workers but there are not enough available hands to do the job on time. There are many possible arrangements for getting the job done. For example, farmers sometimes agree to share the labour cost among themselves, i.e., exchange. Farmers can also hire workers at the current rate of pay. In between these extremes there are sharefarming, renting, and bonus deals, payment of which relies on crop yield and price. The potential for improving either the timing of the job or the standard (quality) of operation is worth investigation.

Extending length of cropping phase in the rotation or sequence
Since cropping is usually more profitable per ha than the grazing component it might be technically possible, through the use of additional fertilizer and herbicides, to extend the length of the cropping phase in a legume–pasture–crop rotation or sequence and to still maintain fertility.

Irrigation development
Some restraints on developing irrigation are geological and hydrological. Other restraints include lack of capital either to develop more irrigation land or to buy the equipment to distribute the water properly; unreliable distribution systems from the main source of supply; and lack of knowledge about new developments in irrigation technology.

Machinery services

When analysing how the farmer uses machinery, the question is not 'what machinery equipment do you own', but 'from what sources do you get your machinery services?' These services come from many places: from equipment which the farmer owns (solely or jointly); from contractors; from sharefarmers; through one of the many arrangements with other farmers; hiring or leasing; and possibly from other sources. These are the main points to be covered in analysing the present machinery services of a farm:

• how are the machine services provided?
• are the machinery services available to do each operation properly and on time?
• age, current value and the anticipated timing and cost of replacement;
• overhead and operating costs of machines;
• whether the implements match the tractors;
• work rates;
• how well machinery is being maintained;
• what equipment and facilities for maintaining it are needed (and available).

• availability of spare parts and repair services needs to be defined:
• whether the machine is the right size and design for the range and the size of the jobs it has to do.

Machinery potential
When considering the future needs of machinery on the farm, it is necessary to know such things as:

• can the overhead costs be reduced by, say, providing some contract services;
• whether a change in the form of acquiring machinery services would be profitable;
• what measures could be taken to improve either the standard or timeliness of operations;

- if it would be profitable to replace labour with more or larger machines;
- given that inflation in machinery costs is likely to continue, how will the money be found to replace machinery when the time comes;
- if the power source and the implements can be better matched.

The areas which offer greatest potential for improving 'owned' machinery services are matching of capability and requirements; better maintenance to prolong the life of machines; and correct adjustment of equipment to enable the machine to do its job properly. The ingenuity of some agricultural engineers and the many farmer–inventors results in many simple modifications to existing machines, and better designed machines.

Economic and financial aspects of a farm business: introduction

Once farming was called a 'way of life'. Then, it became a business. It is both. We emphasize assessing the profit in farming but we recognize that most people do not really understand the term 'profit' in its pure sense. Most people relate to, and understand better, 'cash'. People want to earn enough cash to meet their aims, one of which will be the aim of continuing farming, to cover the cash costs to pay their labour and management what it is worth; and reward the capital in the business something akin to what the capital could earn elsewhere. (Remember though that there may be some non-cash gains to help cover this.) People also wish to replace aged equipment and to make improvements when these are needed. A business which makes enough cash to do all this is probably making a profit.

Costs and returns need to be assessed. The gross margin, i.e., gross income less variable costs, per unit of land, or labour, or head of livestock, or for each activity, and farm total gross margin, is estimated. The reasons why the gross margins of each activity are at the level which they are at present, should be investigated.

Overhead costs which must be met each year, whatever activities occur, have a big influence on profitability. Total gross margins need to total more than overhead costs for profit to be made. Total unavoidable cash requirements (both farm and household) also must be identified.

In an economic and financial analysis of the present situation of the farm family it is important to consider the market value of the resources the farmer uses or controls. Resources are usually classified as the value of the land and buildings, livestock, equipment, tools and machinery, and cash savings. A useful measure of the efficiency of the farm as a business is to express the annual profit it earns as a percentage of the total resources of the farm. This is known as the 'return on capital'.

As well as knowing the total value of the resources, it is useful to find out how much capital is tied up in each activity, e.g. the value of cattle, sheep, and machinery. This information plus information about activity net return, is then used in planning which activities to expand, and which activities to reduce.

Other essential information is about the amount and type of debts, types of creditors, and terms of the loans, e.g. short, medium or long term. The amount of expected annual cash surplus available to service existing debts is critical. The amount of debt compared with equity, and if the farm family could borrow more money if they wanted to invest in developing their farm is useful information.

For commercial farms the ownership structure, e.g. partnership, company or trust has to be determined. The business structure of the farm firm influences the amount of tax to be paid and how the farm assets are passed from one generation to the next. It is worth paying the professional fees of experienced lawyers and accountants to create a structure tailor-made to the unique situation of each farm household-cum-business. The cost is small relative to the benefits which normally result from having the appropriate structure.

Economic and financial potential

The financial potential of the farm under scrutiny can be evaluated after a number of issues have been examined. It may be possible to increase the gross margins of the existing activities by better 'management'; a change in the mixture of activities can produce more income, e.g. more crops, fewer animals; and there may be prospects for introducing new activities. If so, the expected profitability, the amount of extra capital needed, the estimated gain and the riskiness has to be calculated and assessed. It might be feasible to re-arrange loans so that they are converted from short- to medium- or long-term loans. This usually means lower annual repayments, but higher total interest.

Estimate whether it is likely there will be an increase in land value each year, after allowing for the effects of inflation and deducting any capital spent on development. If so, this results in an increase in the farmer's wealth (even though he or she may not choose to sell the farm), and thus in his or her capacity to borrow funds to increase production. From estimates of the anticipated total gross margins and overheads, and of the future total value of the farmer's assets, the expected return to farm resources can be calculated and compared with the present figures. Finally, there may be scope for changes in structure or arrangements for ownership, control and distribution of profits which may lead to more harmonious and efficient working of the business.

Economic and financial restraints

The main barriers to developing the financial potential of the farm include lack of knowledge and lack of management skills and the absence of any new technologies or activities which would enable total gross margin to be increased. These are real barriers, but often can be partly overcome.

It might be hard to get loans on more favourable terms, given the shortage of capital for lending for risky uses and the keen competition for it from the non-rural sectors of the economy. Also staff in many lending institutions do not fully understand the risky and cyclical nature of annual farm costs and receipts, or the time taken for many farm development programs to become fully operational; often six to eight years.

Sometimes it is difficult to change family arrangements or the business structure of the farm. Further, the scarcity of competent advisers, trained in farm financial planning and in appraising farm development proposals, leads to difficulty in getting sound and useful advice on the financial aspects of development. This prevents the farmer from getting the most from the farm.

Budgets for economic and financial analysis

Farmers and their advisers need to make well-informed, soundly based decisions on activity mix, farm investments and financial management, so that the best use can be made of the limited resources available. Together they can make effective use of simple budgets when analysing and making decisions about the farm business. Budgets are models of what can happen if a certain course of action is taken. Budgeting is a technique to simulate probable and possible real-world scenarios. With this knowledge the decision maker is equipped to exert more control over developments later on.

A farmer or an adviser ought to do a few sums when thinking about taking any action which (1) involves a change in direction from what he or she presently does and knows; and (2) it involves spending a significant amount of money by the farmer. Budgets are useful in such cases as follow:

- weighing up the expected benefits and the costs when thinking about buying another block of land;
- developing a pasture to increase the carrying capacity or changing from one activity to another, such as changing from fat lambs to vealer production or setting up an intensive sideline;
- putting in some irrigation;
- investing on-farm versus off-farm;
- growing a new crop;
- using a new chemical;
- buying better breeding stock;
- buying machinery;
- comparing different sources of machinery services;
- comparing different types of loans;
- changing selling methods;
- changing the strain of animal;
- clearing or draining some land;
- taking soil conservation measures;
- redesigning farm layout;
- changing the time of key operations such as lambing, calving, cropping and harvesting;
- comparing selling or conserving or buying fodder;
- introducing a new activity;
- taking action to reduce the effect of a drought.

Economic and financial analysis: detailed explanation

To be able to analyse a farm business and to construct and to use budgets for farm management, a number of key concepts are introduced, and briefly described and explained in this chapter, and dealt with further in later chapters. These concepts must be understood.

Capital

The total capital value of a farm business is the market value which would be received if all the land and improvements, stock, machinery and equipment, and stocks of inputs and product were sold. The cash sum available from the sale, after paying any debts owed by the business, is the owner's own capital. This is called 'equity' or 'net worth'.

Example
Calculation of farmer's capital (net worth or equity)

Assets	$	Liabilities	$
land and improvements	1,800,000	overdraft	30,000
plant and machinery	250,000	3-year loan	150,000
livestock	600,000	10-year loan	300,000
fixed deposit	100,000		
cash in bank at call	10,000		
total assets (A)	2,760,000	total liabilities (B)	480,000
		equity (A − B)	2,280,000

The farmer's equity can be expressed as a percentage of the total resources of the farm. The equity percentage of the farm described above is 83%:

$$\text{equity (\%)} = \frac{\text{equity}}{\text{total assets}} \times \frac{100}{1}$$

$$= \frac{\$2,280,000}{\$2,760,000}$$

$$= 83\%$$

The real net return, i.e., return adjusted for inflation and after tax, on capital owned is a useful indicator of profitability of the farming business. The profit made from the total capital invested in a farm, expressed as percentage return to capital, is a measure of the economic efficiency of the use of this capital.

The percentage return to capital used in one way can be compared with possible and expected returns to capital put to other uses in the economy.

It is necessary to know about costs and returns before profit can be identified. There are several different types of returns and costs in a farm business. It is essential to understand the different types as they are important when planning future farm activities.

Returns

Farmers' returns might come from a number of sources, as follows:

1 Income made from the annual farming operations. There are five broad sources or categories of such farm income:
 • sales of crops and animals produced as part of the annual farming operation;
 • non-cash income from extra stocks on hand at the end of the trading year, called 'inventory change', from the annual farming operation. This could be change in livestock numbers and value from retained potential sales, change in the value of livestock on hand as a result of their ageing by one year, or change in stocks of produce on hand;
 • dividends from co-operatives or farm-related companies of which the farmers are members;
 • saleable farm products used by the households;
 • payments for farm work off the farm (such as sharefarming or sale of contracting services).
2 Personal income not derived from farming such as income from off-farm investment or non-farm work. Such income is not part of farm-operating income and operating profit, although it will be part of the cash available to service debts.
3 Cash received from sales of capital assets such as sales of machinery, land or other capital items, which are not products of the annual business operations and so such sales are not part of the annual farm income. They are irrelevant to estimates of the annual profit produced by the farm business, but are a source of cash.
4 Cash can become available when investments with financial institutions reach the end of their term.

Inventories

Inventories are stocks of produce on hand. That is, they have been produced but not sold and converted to cash. When attempting to measure the amount of farm profit earned in a given period (usually one year) it is necessary to define precisely all the income made by the farming activities for that period. Changes in inventory over this period have to be counted. Assume that two farms of comparable size and efficiency each produced 15,000 kg of grain worth 20 cents a kilogram. They used the crop as follows:

Example

	farm A		farm B	
	quantity kg	value $	quantity kg	value $
sold	15,000	3,000	10,000	2,000
kept	0	0	5,000	1,000
total	15,000	3,000	15,000	3,000

Although the cash income from farm A is $3,000 and from farm B is $2,000, the true yearly income of the farms is the same. The grain that is kept is valued at the market price. In measuring the true income of a farm, both cash sales and the value of the change in inventory are included as income items. Sometimes there is a decrease in value of inventory over the year. In such cases the decrease in value is deducted from the sales to give the true income, as follows:

	$
A value of grain inventory at start of year	5,000
B value of grain inventory at end of year	2,000
C change in value of inventory over year (A − B)	−3,000
D cash sales of grain during year (from both inventory and current production)	+15,000
E true income from current year crop (D − C)	12,000

The value of saleable crop and animal products which are produced and consumed on the farm by the farm family and staff is also counted as part of the farm income. This is 'income in kind', not in cash. It is usual to count only those items which have a market value. For instance, if the produce which was home-consumed was unsaleable because it had suffered some damage or because there was no market for it, then it would not be counted as part of farm income.

When a farmer is a member of a co-operative society annual dividends and rebates on purchases are often received. These are accounted for under annual farm income.

Treatment of items of returns in analysis depends on the purpose of the analysis. Money earned from different types of off-farm work may or may not be regarded as part of the income produced by the farm. When a capital item such as land or machinery is sold, the money received is not part of the annual farm-operating income, although it is treated as part of the total cash receipts. Similarly, interest earned is part of taxable income, but mostly not part of annual farm operating profit. Interest earned on positive working capital balances is sometimes counted as 'non-operating' farm income. Money received from non-farm sources such as gifts from relatives, personal insurance, lotteries or non-farm share investments is not part of farm-operating income, and is classed as personal receipts. A loan brings money to the farm business but it is not annual income produced by the farm.

Thus these are the main sources of farm operating income:

- sales of farm produce;
- changes in inventory;
- saleable produce grown but consumed on the farm, and dividends and rebates from farm co-operatives or merchants.

Costs

Farm business costs fall into two broad categories:

1 Variable costs (sometimes called 'direct costs').
2 Overhead or fixed costs.

1 Variable costs

Variable costs are costs which vary directly as the output of an activity varies. If the area under wheat increases by 50% then most of the major costs such as sprays, fertilizer, seed, fuel, cropping labour, and machinery running costs will increase also by about 50%. Similarly, if cattle numbers are doubled variable costs such as feed, husbandry, and marketing costs will just about double.

Here are typical examples of variable costs:

- chemicals;
- insurance on animals, crops;
- irrigation running costs;
- casual labour costs;
- marketing costs;
- veterinary expenses;
- fertilizer;
- seed;
- fuel;
- shearing costs;
- bought feed;
- repairs to machinery.

Many variable inputs determine the yield or level of output of the activity. Thus with crops, for a given level of rainfall, the amount and kind of fertilizer, seeds, sprays, and cultivations largely control the crop yield. Similarly, with animal activities, the level and type of feed, and the amounts and types of drenches and of vaccines used have a major effect on production. Other types of variable costs do not determine yield or production, but the product could not be harvested or sold unless the cost was incurred. Examples of this type of variable cost are transport costs, marketing costs, milking costs, and to a large extent, harvesting costs.

Little output would occur on farms unless money was spent on variable cost items. Conversely, although a large amount of money was spent on meeting overhead costs, most of this has little effect on the level of crop yield or animal production because overhead costs are not related to a specific activity. A reason for identifying the variable costs of an activity is to show the size of the change in costs which would occur if a farmer were to expand or to contract one or more activities.

If a farmer decides to decrease the area of barley and increase the area of wheat, the variable costs change, but the overhead costs remain about the same. Knowing the likely gross margin of an activity such as barley or wheat, that is the gross income minus the variable costs, the farm operator is in a position to assess the merit of changes in the mix of activities on the farm. Where more significant changes are made involving extra capital investment such as pasture improvement and increases in livestock carried, then overhead costs, and the interest, tax and loan repayments are likely to change. In such cases account has to be taken of more than just the variable costs and activity gross incomes.

2 Overhead (or fixed) costs

Overhead or fixed costs do not change as small changes in the level of an activity are made. Thus an increase of 20% in the area of a crop or in the number of animals is unlikely to lead to a rise in overheads, but an increase of 100% would. Some typical overhead costs are listed:

- permanent workers' wages and employee on-costs;
- annual repairs to water supply, roads, buildings and structures;
- insurance on employees, fixed structures, and plant;
- telephone and business expenses (stationery, travelling, accountant);
- power costs (unless related to a specific activity, such as irrigation pumping);
- shire rates and land taxes;
- annual fixed water rates;
- depreciation of plant and improvements;
- consultants' fees;
- operator's allowance for labour and management;
- running cost of a vehicle used for all activities and in all manner of ways (the farm utility);
- interest on short-term working capital borrowed for all activities (but not interest for fixed capital borrowings) is sometimes treated as a fixed cost (though interest on capital borrowed is more accurately a return to investors than a cost of production).

Depreciation costs

One class of overhead costs is called 'depreciation costs'. Depreciation costs occur with assets which have a life of more than one production period, or, for convenience, a year, such as machinery, equipment, buildings, fences, stockyards, irrigation equipment and water supply. Most capital items depreciate over time, and an allowance for this cost should be deducted from gross income each year so that all the costs of producing output in that year are set against all the revenues produced in that year.

Although depreciation cost is deducted from gross income, it is not a cash cost. There is no cheque made out to 'depreciation', but it is a real cost to the business. The depreciation charge represents the cost to the business of acquiring the services of the asset in that year using the current market value of the asset. Depreciation can also relate to the need to continue to acquire the services of such an asset in the future using the expected replacement cost of a new asset. When estimating depreciation of assets, assets are valued at either current market value or expected replacement value.

Historical (original) values are not relevant to management decisions so the current market value of a similarly used machine or the current replacement cost of a new machine, and the expected salvage value at the end of the expected useful life in current year dollars is used to estimate depreciation. In this way some allowance is made for the future replacement cost of the equipment possibly differing from historical values. The simplest but not the most precise way of calculating depreciation is to use the straight-line method which assumes that an item depreciates by the same amount each year. Depreciation then is calculated as shown below.

Example

method (1)	method (2)
current market value = $40,000 (1992 $ value) expected remaining life = 5 years expected salvage value after 5 years = $10,000 (1992 $ value) annual depreciation = $$\frac{\text{market value} - \text{salvage value}}{\text{no. of years}}$$ $$= \frac{\$40,000 - \$10,000}{5}$$ depreciation = $6,000	replacement cost of new asset = $60,000 (1992 $ value) expected remaining life = 5 years expected salvage value after 5 years = $10,000 (1992 $ value) annual depreciation = $$\frac{\text{replacement cost of new asset} - \text{salvage value}}{\text{no. of years}}$$ $$= \frac{\$60,000 - \$10,000}{5}$$ depreciation = $10,000

In this case the depreciation cost of the machine in this year (1992) is expected to be $6,000, or $10,000, depending on which method is used. The replacement cost method allows for the fact that the asset has to be replaced eventually. The market value method represents the cost to the business of acquiring the services of the asset in that particular year.

In situations where more realistic calculations of depreciation play an important role in assisting management decisions the diminishing balance method can be used. With this method a percentage of the machine's current market value is depreciated each year. Here, depreciation is greater earlier in the life of the machine than later, which is what tends to happen in practice. Thus if a machine is expected to depreciate in value at 10% per year, and its expected replacement cost is $2,000, the machine is depreciated by $200 in the first year. In the second year the same depreciation rate, 10%, is applied to the balance of the value, viz., $1,800, so the depreciation in the second year is $180.

As the annual depreciation cost is deducted from gross income, this amount is not available for distribution as profit. Thus funds are retained in the business and these are available for other uses. In theory, deducting depreciation is a way of ensuring funds are available to replace worn-out assets when the time is due. In practice, retained funds are used in many ways, hopefully to make enough profits and reserves to enable worn-out assets to be replaced when the time is right. If depreciation funds are used in the business, enough liquidity has to be maintained to let worn-out capital assets be replaced when the time comes.

Costs do not always fall into distinct categories. Some farm costs are partly overheads and partly variable costs. Machinery depreciation has both a time component (the machine loses value as it ages, regardless of use) and a use component (the more the machine is used, the greater the loss in value). Variable repair and maintenance costs allocated to an activity cover some of the use-depreciation cost, and the rest of the use-depreciation and time-depreciation cost is allocated as an overhead cost when the expected end value is deducted from current market or replacement value.

Further, depreciation estimates are different for tax purposes from those used for management purposes. When estimating taxable income there are standardized depreciation costs allowed. The Commissioner of Taxation estimates some standard effective life of assets and a set percentage of the item's original cost is used. For tax purposes some assets are able to be depreciated at accelerated rates as a special concession and incentive to upgrade plant. The rates for eligible assets are given in current tax manuals.

Operator's allowance

An allowance for the operator's labour and management is another difficult cost to estimate. Although the operator might not actually draw a regular full wage, the operator's labour and management are an input to make profit and so these must be costed and deducted if a true estimate of profit and the return to the capital in the business is needed. For calculations of the cash position of the business though, the actual amount drawn by the operator is the figure of interest.

An indication of the value of an operator's labour and management can be gained from what leading hands or overseers and professional farm managers are paid. These are a guide, but they can be misleading. The cost or worth of some farmers might vary. If a charge is not made for operator's labour and management then the estimated operating profit represents a return to total capital and to operator's labour and management as well.

Profit

Opinions differ greatly about what is profit and what is not profit. When different people try to define or estimate profit they often use different methods, count different items, and use different values for some of the costs and the income. There are a number of equally valid, alternative ways of estimating the size of a number of the items in the calculation.

As well, there are elements of personal judgement in estimates of the values of some items which make up profit. This is mainly because of difficulties with the notion of cost. Accountants and economists come up with different estimates of the profitability of an enterprise, as they do the sums for different purposes. An economist considers the opportunity cost of some of the resources used whereas the accountant focuses only on the actual costs incurred. Broadly speaking most people have some notion of the returns left over from all income as profit, after all the costs which were involved in earning the income have been deducted.

One of the commoner definitions of profit used is as follows:

(total receipts − variable costs = total gross margin) − overheads = operating profit

The range of opinions about profit comes about from the purpose of the analysis. An accountant may work out the profitability of a business's operations at the end of some period to assess how well the business has done, or to minimise a client's tax liability. A management economist is probably trying to decide which of a number of alternatives is best to use the business's limited funds in the future, or to foresee when the next cash crisis will come.

Again the range of opinions about profit come from different views of income and costs which are not cash figures but have to be estimated. An example already shown is depreciation. Another example is the cost of the owner-operator's labour and management. Similarly, the value of non-cash income is a matter of opinion about possible market price of stocks of product not yet sold.

In any year operating profit will show changes from previous years. Estimation of operating profit highlights the importance of overheads and size of operation in the ultimate profitability of the business. The absolute size of operating profit is not very informative until it is related to the amount of capital used to produce that profit. Operating profit as a percentage return to total capital indicates the efficiency of the use of resources invested in the farm business. Expected operating profit is important as it indicates how efficiently the resources in the business might be used, especially after a change in farm plan. Operating profit is important as it represents the reward to all the owners of the capital tied up in the business.

The reward to the farmer's own capital is called net farm income, as shown below:

operating profit − interest to creditors (return to lender's capital)
= net farm income (return to owner's capital).

Note. It is usual to count interest on overdraft or short-term working capital borrowed as an operating expense. The interest deducted in the calculation of net farm income shown above is the return to lenders of fixed capital. In economic analysis interest is a return, not a cost. In analysis of the financial state of a business interest payments are a cash cost.

Net farm income is available to the owner of the business to pay taxes or to provide living expenses, called 'consumption' (or for some other use such as repaying debt). If the operator's allowance has not been deducted from operating profit then net farm income represents return to the farmer's capital, labour and management. Anything left over from net farm income after consumption and tax represents an increase in the owner's equity or net worth. This might be used to reduce a debt, or to have a cash reserve in the bank, or to buy an asset, which all amount to an increase in equity.

operating profit − interest (return to creditors) = net farm income − income tax − personal consumption (above operator's allowance if it has already been deducted from operating profit) = change in equity.

Net farm income can be a misleading statistic when it is used to describe the relative economic position of the farming community. Net farm income, in an accounting sense, with depreciation deducted, bears little relation to the cash situation of a farm business. There is the description of farmers 'living off their depreciation'. This is the situation where they are using the notional depreciation allowance included in estimates of net farm income for more immediate practical purposes such as family living expenses and servicing the farm debt. For instance a crop farm business might have an annual depreciation charge of $25,000 on $250,000 worth of machinery and plant. Net farm income might be low in any one year. However, in that year there will be $25,000 in cash above net farm income available to the farm family.

The usefulness of estimates of profit depends on what is included in the calculations, and on how good the guesses are about the non-cash costs and income. The calculation of profit comes from both fact and opinion, and sometimes fiction, too.

Cash

Profit is an economic criterion and it is the true measure of economic performance. But, profit is not the same as net cash flow as profit includes non-cash items. Cash flow, a financial criterion, is more important in practice. It determines if all business cash costs and family cash needs can be met. Farmers tend to be more interested in the cash side of their business than in strict measures of profit.

Some costs are obvious and are easy to measure, such as cash expenses, others are hidden and can only be guessed, like the annual ownership costs of capital items. The same applies for income. There are obvious cash receipts, but as well there are changes in inventory values such as changes in the value of stock, and farm production consumed on the farm. To add to the complexity of this accounting, there are usually cash receipts which are not part of income made from the farm activities. Money from off-farm earnings, from loans, and cash from sales of capital items are all cash coming in but these have nothing to do with the profit made from the resources used on the farm in the year. Similarly, non-cash income is not much use for paying current cash costs.

There are uses of cash for personal living expenses, interest and principal repayments of loans, and income tax. These are not costs of production to be deducted in working out operating profit from the year's operation. They are payments that have to be met from the profit that is made and represent the way in which the profit is used. A useful practical idea for farm management is the expected annual cash surplus. Expected annual cash surplus estimated in a whole farm cash budget is useful for management as an estimate of the cash that might be available to put to various 'new' uses.

Example

Expected gross cash receipts (excludes non-cash income) less cash variable and cash overhead costs (excludes non-cash costs. This might include a cash allowance set aside to replace equipment) less other cash uses (such as interest, principal repayments, tax, consumption) = expected annual cash surplus (available for 'new' uses).

Expected annual cash surplus shows the amount likely to be left over for certain uses after all other commitments have been met. This surplus has more to do with the bank balance than operating profits. The amount of annual cash surplus after interest and loan repayments, personal expenses, necessary replacement of assets, taxes, and new investment from current income shows how much new debt could be serviced.

Cash flows are the fundamental practical measures used to assess the likely current state of affairs and prospects for change. One of the first things an adviser does is to estimate the likely gross cash income minus cash variable costs from activities. This gives total cash gross margin. Then the unavoidable cash requirements for overhead costs, living expenses, interest, principal repayments, income tax and in some cases for replacement of assets is estimated and deducted from total cash gross margin. The net cash position is then the critical bit of information in a farm analysis.

Operating profit as a return on total capital

The market value of the total resources on a farm is widely known as the total capital value, or the walk-in-walk-out value (WIWO) of the farm. It is calculated by adding, at some time, the market value of the land, improvements, machinery, equipment, animals and stocks of produce and inputs on hand. This is called the 'stock of capital' at a particular time.

The rate of return on total capital is calculated by expressing the annual operating profit as a percentage of the total capital. However, operating profit is made over a period (thus it is called a 'flow item'). The question arises 'what then is the value of the capital used to make that operating profit?' The value of this stock of capital varies over the period involved. The only realistic way to deal with this problem is to use the average value of capital invested in production over the period. This is given by the opening value plus closing value of the capital, all divided by two. If inflation occurs and capital values change as a result of inflation, this effect has to be recognized. One way is to use opening and closing value of capital before the effect of inflation, then to acknowledge a nominal capital gain if, say, land values have kept up with inflation.

$$\% \text{ return on total capital } = \frac{\text{operating profit} \times 100}{\text{average value of total capital (WIWO)}}$$

average value of total capital is $\dfrac{\text{opening + closing value of capital}}{2}$

In calculating the annual rate of return earned by these resources no account is taken of what debts are owed, as the focus is on the earning rate of the total bundle of resources used in the business. In practice farmers have to manipulate the total resources under their control, not just the proportions which are debt-free. Rate of return on total capital is the reward to all capital regardless of who has supplied the capital. That is, lenders to the business get interest payments out of this overall return to capital as their reward, and the remainder or balance, called 'net farm income', is the return to the farmers' own capital or equity.

Operating profit after tax is a useful measure of return to capital. Whether operating profit or operating profit after tax is calculated depends on the purpose for which the sums are being done. When the tax implications of alternative investments with which the farm return may be compared are different, then the after-tax return is the appropriate figure to use. Ensure that equivalent measures of return are used in comparisons of returns to capital from alternative investments.

For each farmer, the return to total capital measures:

- effectiveness as a combiner of annual inputs such as labour, irrigation, fertilizer, seed and machinery services, to produce annual income from the total resources currently employed in agriculture;
- the rate of earning of the total capital relative to the rate of earning of that capital if it were employed in some other income-producing field, such as housing or government bonds.

The real interest rate on bonds or the yield of safe investments gives some idea of the minimum relative fruitfulness with which capital can be used in the economy. The rate of return on the WIWO capital of a farm business is the equivalent of the dividend yield of a share listed on the stock exchange. The farm-operating profit is the equivalent of the annual dividend paid on the share; the counterpart of the WIWO value of the farm is the market price of the share. The dividend yield of shares quoted in the financial section of the press is based on the current value of the share.

Investment in a farm resembles share investments a little. Each normally provides both an annual income and some capital gain or loss. Agricultural investments do not have the spectacular capital gains and losses which a few share investments have. There is usually greater opportunity for spreading the risk through diversified investments in the share and financial markets than on an individual farm.

The main purpose of calculating the return on total capital is to show the economic efficiency of investment in a farm business. If the figure were only 1%, and other managers with similar land, climate, and capital were obtaining 4%, the following questions should be asked:

- could the rate of return on capital be increased by using better methods, by borrowing extra money to improve production, or by changing the mixture of activities on the farm?
- should the capital be transferred from this locality to a farm in a different locality where the return on capital is likely to be higher?

- does it really matter if the return is low? The annual rate of increase in the real value of the capital (for reasons unrelated to profits) could be so rapid that the farmer is better off with relatively low profits for several years and obtain a regular and large real annual increase in capital;
- should increased borrowing power be used to obtain money to put into profitable agricultural or to off-farm projects or investments?
- should some or all of the capital be transferred out of farming, and put into some other form of investment, such as real estate, shares or a shop?

The commonest course chosen by farm managers whose real return on capital is low because operating profit is low (and not because capital gains are high) is first to try to improve by using modern management and more up-to-date methods. If, after adopting this strategy, the returns are still low, then alternative uses for some or all of the farm capital and labour need to be investigated.

A relevant question is 'how useful a measure is the return on total capital?' Return on total capital is of more interest when there is a possibility that all of the capital might be shifted into another use. Where a farmer adopts a change to the farm plan, and then works out the new return to total capital it is not very useful. Rate of return on total capital is an average rate of return made up of the average profitability of all of the bits of capital which make up the total capital of the farm business. Averages sometimes conceal more than they reveal. Suppose the return on total capital before a change to farm plan is 3% real, i.e., after deducting the effects of inflation. A proposed change is expected to return 6% real on the extra capital involved. The project yielding 6% real will raise the average return on all capital a little. The return on extra capital is a more informative guide, unless shifting all capital out of farming is a possibility under consideration.

Return on farmer's capital: net farm income

Farm annual operating profit after paying interest and tax, expressed as a percentage of farmer's equity capital, gives the percentage return on farmer's own capital. This gives the farmer one guide to the effectiveness of the investment. It allows comparison with the performance of own capital, invested as it is in the farm, with possible alternative uses for it. Again, this is only one measure of performance. It tells the farmer nothing about whether the value of capital has changed over the year.

The percentage return after tax on farmer's own capital (equity) is calculated as follows:

$$\% \text{ return on equity} = \frac{\text{annual operating profit after paying tax and interest}}{\text{farmer's capital (average value)}} \times 100$$

The farmer's capital (or equity, or net worth) is calculated by adding the market value of all the resources in the farm business and subtracting from that figure the total of all the money it owes. As in return to total capital, the average value of the farmer's capital over the period is the figure to use.

Net return on extra capital

Net return on extra capital is a useful indicator of economic efficiency used in evaluating new investment on the farm. The addition of capital investment to the existing farm resources has to be justified by a large enough expected increase in after-tax profits. If extra capital were spent on improving pastures or irrigation or drainage on an existing property, and the project was fully operational in a short time, one way of judging the investment is to express the extra net profit in the steady state obtained as a percentage of the extra capital invested. Thus:

$$\% \text{ net return on extra capital} = \frac{\text{extra net profit after extra interest and tax}}{\text{extra capital invested}} \times 100$$

In many cases this figure can be 10% to 20% in real terms. The investor would want it to be so too. If perfectly safe investments in the economy promise 3% to 4% real return after tax, then the farmer would want to have a good chance of getting much more than this for additional and risky investment on the farm.

First, note that the capital is being added to existing capital invested in the farm. All the estimated extra return then is the result of the contribution of all capital involved in production, but when this is expressed as return to extra capital, the return is attributed only to the extra capital invested. This is why return to extra capital often seems high. But, as a decision criterion, it is valid as long as the investor would not consider removing all of the existing capital already invested in the farm and putting it elsewhere. That is, the farmer is only interested in the best thing to do with extra 'new' investment capital. Then the gain from the use of the extra capital in one way, say, adding it to existing capital in the farm, can validly be compared with an alternative use of the such capital, either on the farm or off it (see Chapter 9).

Uncertainty associated with the weather, prices, costs and natural hazards often leads to extra capital needing to be borrowed so as to carry out a project. The extra profit has to be enough to be attractive once the risk of less-than-expected results is considered; as well the profit has to be enough to pay interest on the money borrowed; and enough to pay tax on the extra income earned; and high enough to pay instalments on the loan.

The measure return to extra capital has limitations. It does not take into account the timings of cash flows of a project; or the differences in the size of the capital investment. It does not give a useful guide to the differences in lengths of time which different uses of extra capital involve. It is usually measured for an arbitrary period. Thus a change in the period can affect the average rate of return greatly. And as it is based on operating profit it is not equivalent to actual cash flows, that is, it does not 'reconcile'.

When change has been implemented and is fully operational this is a 'steady state'. Return on extra capital is only one test which a proposed change must pass. If the expected real return on extra capital involved in a change in farm plan, in the steady state, is better than the real return expected from alternative, similarly risky uses of that capital, then in some cases more study is warranted.

If a number of years are involved before 'steady state' then as well net present value and internal rate of return, cash flow and break-even budgets are required to assess fully the economic and financial feasibility.

Rates of return

Rates of return are misinterpreted at times and sometimes it is not clear whether they are real, i.e., adjusted to exclude the effects of inflation; or nominal, which includes the effects of inflation, and what has been deducted in calculating them. The decision maker needs to know whether the return is after the effects of inflation and of tax and sometimes, interest, have been deducted. Rates of return do not mean much otherwise.

Capital gain

Capital gain in real terms is measured as follows:

real value at end of period − real capital investment made during period − value at start of period = real capital gain.

Operating profit and capital gain are the two important things to consider about farm capital; viz., the profit from the annual farming operation and whether there has been a real change in the farmer's capital. Thus also consider different prospects for capital gains in comparisons between alternative uses of capital. Operating profit as a percentage return to total capital can appear low in all sorts of farming, compared with returns available in other businesses. If the value of a farmer's land increases at say a real 1% to 2% per year, then that is a benefit as well. The point is that if the total worth of capital is increasing it can be difficult to maintain a high percentage return on total capital. This is so, even though operating profit might be satisfactory and might even be increasing in absolute, if not percentage, terms. Usually, land makes up over 60% of total farm capital. The value of land reflects the capitalized values of expected annual operating profits plus the expected future net capital gains. It also has a value for any other functions it might fulfil in the owner's terms, such as the 'worth' of the farm-style of living. If operating profits per ha rise and are expected to continue, then buyers will bid more for the right to earn those operating profits in future. Thus the price of land goes up and the total capital value of the business increases. But, the annual operating profit expressed as a rate of return on total capital could remain low.

These are the three most important factors determining capital gain in agriculture:

- level of prices of the commodities which can be produced;
- the scope for applying new technology which will allow either increased productivity or new enterprises;
- the influence of non-rural factors, such as demand for housing sites, industrial land or recreational use.

Productivity increases of about 2% to 3% per year have historically been achieved in agriculture. If these continued and just offset the profit-squeezing effects of the cost–price squeeze in agriculture, then the real average profitability of farming would remain relatively constant, although it does fluctuate a lot from year to year. If profitability levels were to remain relatively constant, then the value of resources used in agricultural production would also remain constant (if other influences were absent). In that case there would be no capital gains or losses. However, individual farmers can reap capital gains by judicious or fortunate timing of purchases and sale of particular parcels of farmland. The reverse to this is also a well-established phenomenon in farming. Remember, capital gain in land value needs to have deducted from it the cost of any capital spent on improvements and capital gains can result from non-agricultural reasons such as encroaching urbanization and demand for farmland for housing development or for part-time farmlets.

Although farmers sometimes claim that capital gains are useless unless the farm is sold, and most farmers who own land are more interested in continuing farming than selling the farm, increase in real net capital value is still a return, albeit of a different type to operating profit. This is because increases in net worth mean that the relative share of debt in the business is lower and there is more security against which to borrow money for use to increase farm income or off-farm income from investments. It ought to be noted that, equally, a fall in real capital values represents a loss to the business. Capital gain and operating returns are not the same thing, and cannot be simply added. Each has different implications for liquidity, taxation, and growth of net worth. Still, both must be taken into account as different forms of addition to wealth.

Expected annual real capital gain is hard to estimate. Real capital gain can be large or small, depending on timing and price of land and other asset purchases and sales. As well, actual benefits from capital gains also depend on how the increased net worth is used, such as borrowing against it and gearing-up further.

Ways of thinking about the economics of production

A starting point in economic analysis is that there is not much sense in doing something if in the end you are worse off in some important way than you were before you started. Something is usually worth doing if you strongly believe that you will end up better off in some way(s) which you value.

In the economic approach to farm analysis, emphasis is on making the most of whatever is wanted from the limited resources available. A key idea is that the farmer uses resources so as to have a 'bit more' of something, to be better off in some way. The 'something' focused on is often money (income) because it is easily measurable. But the principles can apply equally to quantities of production, or peace of mind for the farmer because risk is less; or even farmer 'satisfaction', which could encompass all of these measures and more. Satisfaction cannot be measured adequately for use in analyses.

Economic principles can be used to help to decide how to choose between alternatives: how to split limited resources between competing uses; what to produce and how. Once choice is involved, economic analysis is relevant. If you choose to use resources in a certain way, then you have given up the chance to use these in another way. Making choices means opportunities are given up; these are called 'opportunity costs'. The concept of opportunity cost is helpful in deciding 'which is the best thing to do?' 'If I do this what am I giving up the chance to do?' 'Which choice makes me better off?'

In economic analysis, the economic 'best' amounts of inputs to use depends on the extra cost of using an extra unit of an input relative to the extra return from using it this way. We are interested in the return from using that extra unit of input in one way and not another. The focus is on the effects on some total outcome of doing a bit more of something, and doing a bit less of something else.

The analysis needed to judge whether the use of resources in one way is better than another way is based on budgets. Budgets are sketches of the expected costs and returns of a business or part of it. Behind farm budgets is the body of economic theory called 'production economics'.

When thinking about changing some part of the way the farm business is run there are a few key ideas and 'truths' to include in the analytical and planning processes:

1 There is the technical notion of diminishing extra returns to increases in some inputs to production while other inputs are unchanged. The general principle is that if there is a fixed level of a resource, say, land, then higher levels of output can be obtained only by adding more inputs to the fixed resource. If increasing amounts of one input are added to production, while the use of other factors is held constant, the amount of output for each extra unit of the input will eventually decrease.

2 There is the idea of extra cost and extra return. Is the extra return greater than the extra cost? If so, it might be worth doing, if it is large enough.

3 Then there is the idea of equal-extra return. Is the extra return minus the extra cost from doing this greater than the extra return minus the extra cost of doing something else? The rule is that you do whatever will make you best off. Pursue that line until the extra return minus extra cost of more input in one activity (say, activity A), is not as great as what you could get from putting more into another activity (say, activity B). With the ability to buy only a certain amount of inputs, and with the extra returns from these inputs declining as more and more are used, then using all inputs to get output A or all for output B would be a wrong strategy. Getting equal-extra net return from both A and B is the best strategy. Thus you need to know the amount of inputs available and have a good idea of the expected physical and dollar response from applying inputs to different activities.

4 If you do something with the inputs you have these inputs cannot be used another way. Therefore this is an opportunity given up, and this has a cost. If whatever you do has a better net return than the opportunity given up would have, then you have done the best thing.

5 When making decisions about what to do in a farm business, you cannot be sure about what is going to happen when you do it; how much product you will have to sell and usually you do not know what price it will bring.

Thus you have to think carefully about what will happen to the business if what you do turns out to be worse than you expected (and gambled on). You should also think about what you can do if the result is better than you expected. Part of any thinking about change has to involve: (a) will it make me better off in some way, and will it help my business grow, and (b) if it does not perform to expectation what will be the effect? Will I be able to meet all my needs and be able to pay my debts?

The economics of production is about the relative proportions of different inputs used in production. Just as the combination of inputs in one type of production is subject to the law of diminishing extra returns, the same effect can be seen with the allocation of 'bundles' of inputs to the alternative enterprises which can be carried out. One of the skills needed in business is to be able to manipulate the mixes of inputs, and of outputs, to get a good dollar profit.

Often, different products or inputs affect the contribution of each other to total profit of a farm. A good clover crop might fatten steers and contribute to some build-up of nitrogen in the soil and act as a break in the cycle of build-up of diseases, such as cereal cyst nematodes. This will benefit a following wheat crop.

Effects between products can be of a complementary or a competitive nature. A complementary relationship is where one activity such as a legume-based pasture helps another activity such as a following grain crop. A competitive relationship is where more of one activity on the farm is only possible if there is less of another activity. For example, at a high stocking rate, more cattle can be carried only if some sheep are removed. Sheep and cattle are competing for pasture.

There is also the possibility that supplementary relationships between activities might exist, at least over some limited range. In this case more of one does not add to or diminish the contributions of other activities at all, e.g. a sideline activity using surplus labour or spare time. Hence the cost will be leisure forfeited.

The best combinations of activities for total profit will be combinations which exploit fully any advantages of supplementary or complementary relations. Beyond this an activity could be expanded only by reducing some other activity. That is, there would be competition between activities for inputs.

If a minor livestock activity complements the major crop activities of a farm then the most profitable farm plan would have livestock, at least up to the level where the farm could run more livestock only if the crops were reduced.

In essence farm management is about shuffling the proportions of all inputs to all forms of production to achieve the objectives of the operators-cum-managers of the resources. An important goal is to make money. An understanding of the technical dimension of the law of diminishing returns and increased inputs, and the complementary, competitive and supplementary relationships between inputs are basic to the economic analysis and planning of farm activities.

Inputs, outputs and equal-extra returns

It is useful to discuss the above-mentioned principles about economic use of inputs to produce output within the following framework of gross income (GI), variable costs (VC), overhead costs (OH), total gross margin (TGM), and operating profit (OP).

$$(GI - VC = TGM) - OH = OP$$

A farmer wants to increase profit. What are the options? Firstly the farmer could increase gross income with costs remaining virtually the same by producing more output. But how can output be increased without greatly increased costs? This could happen if varieties of plants or breeds and types of animals were used which have higher yields but require virtually the same inputs (except, say, harvesting costs).

Again, the farmer could spend money on variable inputs such as fertilizer, crop chemicals, seed, casual labour, drenches, which add more to gross income than the cost of the extra variable inputs. For instance, $8 per ha spent on fertilizer which adds 100 kg per ha of grain which is worth $20 after harvesting, and if no other costs change, would add $12 to operating profit. It is worth spending on variable inputs as long as the expected extra return is more than the extra costs.

The amount of extra return expected to be produced by extra input is relevant. Note that the extra output and return from extra inputs can vary; at first extra output and return might increase as more variable input is added, then extra return might be fairly constant. Eventually, if only one input were being varied, if more and more of the one variable input such as phosphorus (P) were added, the extra output and return from the extra P would start to decline. This is because of the operation of diminishing returns. When extra variable costs are incurred, the expected extra returns have to be considered and compared with the extra costs. In theory, if it could be afforded, most profit would be made when extra return from the last extra variable input just exceeds the extra cost of that input.

This extra return–extra cost is an important idea. Here the farmer increases profits without spending more or buying more variable inputs by swapping some variable inputs out of one use into another. Suppose the last 10 kg of nitrogen per ha (N per ha) to a wheat crop cost $4 and the added wheat is expected to be worth $10, but the same 10 kg N per ha, if added to the pastures, might add 100 kg of pasture dry matter worth $20 net return from grazing. The farmer might not want to spend more on variable costs because of lack of funds; then operating profit could still be increased by transferring the last 10 kg N per ha ($4 of VC) from the wheat crop (extra return $10) and applying it to the pasture (extra return $20). The farmer gives up $10 per ha and gains $20 per ha, a net gain of $10 per ha over the initial situation. The addition to profit is $16.

The key idea is that when you have limited dollars to spend, most profits are made when the extra return from a dollar of variable input in one use, is about the same as the extra return from a dollar spent in an alternative use. We call this the equal–extra returns principle. When this is not the case, then gains can be made by swapping inputs out of a low extra return activity to a higher extra return activity.

The same equal–extra idea applies when adding a number of variable inputs to a single activity. Pretend that the variable inputs to a crop are three: seed, fertilizer, and chemicals. Each one costs $10 per ha. Imagine that the extra output and return obtained from extra units of seed, fertilizer and chemicals, are expected to be as shown in Table 2.2.

Table 2.2: Extra return from extra inputs and how much of each to use

| | cost per unit $ | Extra returns | | | total no. of units applied if plenty of $ available | total variable cost $ |
		1 unit $	2 units $	3 units $		
seed	10	22 (2nd)	13 (5th)	5 (no)	2	20
fertilizer	10	25 (1st)	15 (4th)	12 (6th)	3	30
chemicals	10	20 (3rd)	5 (no)	2 (no)	1	10
total		67	28	12	6	60

The extra variable costs are allocated according to their expected extra returns. The input which yields the highest extra return is chosen first. In this case the first $10 spent goes to one unit of fertilizer (1st, in parentheses), which gives an extra return of $25. The next $10 goes to extra seed (2nd, in parentheses) giving $22, and so on until the available money is all used. With plenty of money to spend, $60 is spent on variable inputs to reap a return of $107 ($67 + $28 + $12). With only $40 to spend on four variable inputs, return is $82 ($67 + $15).

We are looking at the extra return per dollar spent in one use compared with the extra return per dollar spent in another use. The decision rule is: to gain the most profit with limited funds to spread among a number of profit-able forms of production, producers need to allocate the inputs they have in such a way as to get roughly equal extra profits from extra money spent in each activity.

This equal–extra idea is one of the most useful and enduring ideas in production economics. If one activity brings in a higher profit than an alternative activity, increase the most profitable activity. Most total profit is made when the extra profits from more of any of the activities are about the same. Increased profit occurs when more resources or inputs are available, but this needs extra capital.

This equal–extra profit approach is relevant to decisions about the combination of inputs to any production process, and to the combination of products in making the total gross margin of the farm business. Farmers might not think about their actions in precisely those terms, but, all the time, they are adjusting input mixes and activity combinations. If labour costs go up, farmers substitute capital. If crop prices go down, farmers substitute livestock. Farmers definitely play the equal–extra profit game.

Increasing profit

By increasing total gross margin without increasing overhead costs profit can increase. The total gross margin might increase by farmers spending money on variable costs in various activities in ways according to the criteria of: (1) extra cost versus expected extra return (2) equal–extra expected returns from applying a particular input to alternative activities, and (3) equal–extra expected return from applying different inputs to particular activities.

   This way of solving the problem of how to increase profit has the effect of increasing TGM for the given level of OH costs, that is, the OH costs are spread over a greater output and higher TGM, thus increasing profit per unit of output, and increasing total profit.

Example

	$	$
GI	100–	200–
VC	50	120
TGM	50–	80–
OH	30	30
operating profit	20	50

   Another way to increase profits is to reduce the overhead costs per unit of output, not by increasing output for a given level of overheads, but by reducing the overhead costs for a given output. Remember that in practice both output increasing and cost reducing steps are taken.

   By substituting a lower cost fixed input for a higher cost fixed input total overhead costs can be reduced. Suppose a farm has 1,000 ha of crop worked by two permanent workers whose wages are costing $18,000 each (a total of $36,000 per year), using small plant (two tractors, two ploughs, two cultivators, one spray unit, two combines, one header, truck, etc.) worth $300,000 with annual depreciation, insurance, registration and shedding costs of $30,000. Total labour and machinery overhead costs are thus $66,000. A change might be made to a one-person, larger plant cropping operation of a single larger tractor and implements. Labour costs might now be $20,000 as a single operator of larger plant is paid more per labour unit, and total investment in plant and overhead plant costs might be the same. A saving of $16,000 per year on overhead costs is achieved by rationalising the workforce. Further savings come from reduced variable costs such as fuel, repairs, and maintenance of the single plant, and some increased variable costs might be incurred such as some casual labour for truck-driving. Overall, reduced overhead costs and similar output and TGM increase operating profit.

Example

	before change $	after change $
GI	200,000–	200,000–
VC	80,000	80,000
TGM	120,000	120,000
OH	100,000	84,000
	(incl. 66,000 labour and plant costs)	(now incl. only 50,000 labour and plant costs)
operating profit	20,000	36,000

Operating profit (OP) has nearly doubled with the savings in annual permanent labour cost.

Another example of reducing overhead costs per unit of output is where a 1,000 ha crop farm brings in $120,000 TGM worked by labour and plant costing $60,000 per year, and an extra 200 ha of land is added, which gives another $40,000 GI and $24,000 TGM. Extra overheads are $5,000. The extra 200 ha of land can be worked by the existing labour and at about the same plant investment because of technological improvements of plant increasing work capacity. Now:

	before change $	after change $
GI	200,000–	240,000–
VC	80,000	96,000
TGM	120,000	144,000
OH	84,000	89,000
operating profit	36,000	55,000

Operating profit has been increased by working 1,200 ha with nearly the same overhead costs required for working 1,000 ha. Total overhead costs have been spread over more production.

In practice, changes on farms usually affect both variable and overhead costs, with intensification (increased VC; output and TGM increase) and extensification (reduced overheads per dollar output) being applied to increase operating profit.

Opportunity cost

Another key economic principle is called 'opportunity cost'. This is a variation on the idea of equal–extra profit. If a bit more of this is to be done what opportunities for doing other things have to be given up? Is the opportunity given up more rewarding than the action being considered? If so, then it is better not to take that action but to do whatever brings in the greater reward.

The key to opportunity cost is the notion that if you do one thing then you forfeit doing some other thing. To be sure that a farmer is doing the best possible, it is necessary to take account of the rewards from alternative uses of the resources. One proviso here is that the opportunity foregone has to be realistic. The opportunity cost has to refer to a genuine possibility of an alternative action. In some situations as there is not much choice there is little opportunity cost which can be counted in a decision. Suppose that a farmer assesses the expected return on extra capital and other inputs such as labour in a particular use, and estimates an expected 10% return per annum after inflation and tax. This figure of 10% cannot be judged as being good, bad, satisfactory, poor or anything else until it is compared with what the capital and other inputs could earn in another use seriously contemplated. Returns from resources in one use only have meaning related to returns foregone by not using the resources in other uses, i.e., opportunity cost. Economists insist that investments must earn more than the opportunity cost to be worthwhile. In the example above if the most realistic and likely opportunity cost of the use of the resources were expected to be 4% which could be earned after inflation and tax, then this is charged against the investment. The true return then is 10% − 4% = 6%. The return after opportunity cost is positive and thus greater than alternative uses. So if the choices were equally risky the investment earning 10% is the best use of the resources.

Economic thinking: in summary

The principles of diminishing returns, complementary, supplementary and competitive effects, and marginal effects in production outlined so far, are the core of economic analysis. For economic analysis it is necessary to relate technical knowledge of production to the costs and returns associated with production. 'Economic' ways of thinking, or 'economic' ways of looking at and seeing what is happening are useful in analysing problems and making decisions on the basis of causes and expected effects.

Ask the following: if I apply extra fertilizer which costs a certain amount and it increases total production, is it worth doing; or if I use the land to grow crop A instead of crop B, in what ways will I be better off or worse off?

These are economic ways of looking at farm production choices and deciding what to do. Of particular interest are changes to inputs and outputs 'at the margin'; the idea of a little bit more, a little bit less. Farm management decision making is, in part, the skill of applying production economics' principles to the use of physical, human, and financial resources in producing agricultural goods. It is about approaching the problems of 'the resources are scarce, our needs are many and varied and we have to make the best use we can of our resources', as it applies to farming decisions and farmers' objectives.

For many practical reasons the theoretical 'best' levels of operation can never be reached as we can never know enough about the world or the future. As well, the technical basis of a decision is incompletely known, and economic aspects such as costs and prices can vary greatly from the levels which may have been expected at the time decisions about product were made. The major point is to implement the economic, rational way of thinking about a problem. The idea is 'if I do a little bit more of this, and a little bit less of that, then will it make more profit?' Production economic thinking gives a framework for rational decision making. The reasoning points roughly which direction to go.

The key connection to make is that economic and technical principles underlie many things which happen in farm activities and they also underlie the budgeting and planning tools used in decision making (described in later chapters).

The effects of time on the value of money

A further important concept is that money value differs over time. This is not from the effects of inflation but that money (in the hand) today is worth more than a similar sum in the future. Today's dollar invested can grow to be worth more than a dollar in the future. Most people are aware of the effects of inflation on the value of money such as how a dollar today is worth about 20 cents related to what money was worth in 1967. Here, however, we are referring to the opportunity cost idea, and the fact that money can be used in different ways to earn an annual rate of return, and it has a different value over time regardless of inflation.

A sum of money today could grow by 5% or 10% over a year. Thus, a dollar you have in a year's time is equal in value to a smaller sum today. Adding a year's interest to today's sum of less than a dollar, will give you a dollar in total one year hence. Thus a dollar received sooner is worth more than a dollar received later. The sooner a dollar is received, the sooner it can be put to work to earn and to grow in value.

Many decisions must be based on what value is placed on money which is to be received and spent in the future. Different projects have different patterns of cash flow over different periods. Such projects need to be compared to see which project will contribute the most to the net worth of a business. A technique called 'discounting' is used. This technique is a way of allowing that when money is invested in one use, the chance of spending that money now in another use is gone. Discounting means deducting from a project's expected earnings the amount which the investment funds could earn in its most profitable alternative use. This is how opportunity cost is allowed for. This is called the 'discount rate'. Discounting the value of money to be received or spent in the future is a way of adjusting the future net rewards from the investment back to what they would be worth in the hand today. This 'worth in the hand today' is called present value (PV). It is calculated as follows:

$PV = A/(1 + r)^n$

Where PV is the present value of the future amount

A is the future amount

r is the interest rate expressed as a decimal

n is the number of years it will take to receive the money

There are discount tables where the calculations of discount factors are done for particular combinations of years and interest rates. There are also calculators and spreadsheets which do it all at the push of a button.

To find the future value to which current dollars will grow is simple. The discounting formula is rearranged to get:

$A = PV(1 + r)^n$

This is the well-known formula for compound growth of money.

Rate of return on capital in an average year is the commonest method of appraisal of a proposed change on a farm but it is a rough approximation only. This might not matter as long as the method ranks correctly the choices under consideration. However, the theoretically correct method of determining the profitability of an investment is discounted cash flow (DCF) analysis. This involves budgeting all the expected flows of cash out and cash in, and adjusting these flows back to equivalent present value. The DCF approach is explained below.

Example

Suppose an investment has the following expected flows of cash in current (real) dollars.

years	1	2	3	4
A cash in	0	10,000	10,000	6,000
B cash out	10,000	5,200	5,000	4,000
C net cash flow (A − B)	−10,000	4,800	5,000	2,000
D net present value factor at 5%	0.9524	0.9070	0.8638	0.8227
E present values (C × D)	−9,524	4,353	4,319	1,645
F net present value (sum of E)	794			

This means that this four-year project has a net present value of $794 when a discount rate of 5% is used. The project is earning more than 5% return. The discount rate which makes the NPV equal to zero is 10%. This is called the 'internal rate of return', and it is the earning rate of the investment.

Net present value (NPV) is the measure of the discounted value of a number of future receipts minus the discounted value of a number of future expenditures.

From a range of alternative uses of funds involving different patterns of cash flow, the use which gives the highest NPV is the one which promises to add most to the investor's total worth. To estimate NPV it is necessary to allow for what these funds could earn in a realistic alternative use. If the NPV of the project after discounting is positive then this investment is better than the alternative earnings (opportunity cost). Examine its physical and financial feasibility. Ideally the investments in farm activities should return rewards greater than they would earn in alternative investments of comparable safety and, equally important, comparable growth prospects.

Note. The higher the discount rate used (which implies a fairly profitable alternative is available), the lower is the NPV. High discount rates tend to rule out investments whose returns are far into the future, simply because money in the hand earlier could earn the high alternative returns implied by the high discount rate (opportunity cost). Low discount rates imply that not much is forfeited by not receiving the returns until later. Hence projects with distant future returns stand a better chance of being acceptable if low discount rates apply.

Discounting procedures and tables

In analysing the merit of farm management options there can be discounting, compounding, sinking funds and annuities to consider. These are further explained in Chisholm and Dillon (1971). The derivation and use of discount tables is fully explained in their work. The diagram in Figure 2.1 captures the essentials of the derivation and use of discounting, compounding, and annuities.

Discount tables (see the Appendix) are based on the sum invested being one dollar. Figures in the tables show the proportion or multiple of a dollar which results for a given combination of number of years and for a particular interest rate.

Compounding

For example, what will $10,000 grow to if it were invested for 20 years at 5% compound interest? From Table A in Appendix, 'Growth at compound interest', that is

$10,000 × 2.6533 = $26,533

Discounting

What will $26,533, received in 20 years' time, be equivalent to in 1992, at a discount rate of 5% interest? From Table B in Appendix, 'Present value of a future lump sum', that is

$26,533 × 0.3769 = $10,000

Annuities

An annuity is an equal sum of money received or spent over a period. If you were to get a dollar each year for 20 years, and the relevant interest rate were 5%, then the value (in 1992) of this flow of one dollar is $12.46. This comes

Figure 2.1: The values of lump sums of money now and in the future, and the present and future equivalent values of sums received or paid in equal annual instalments

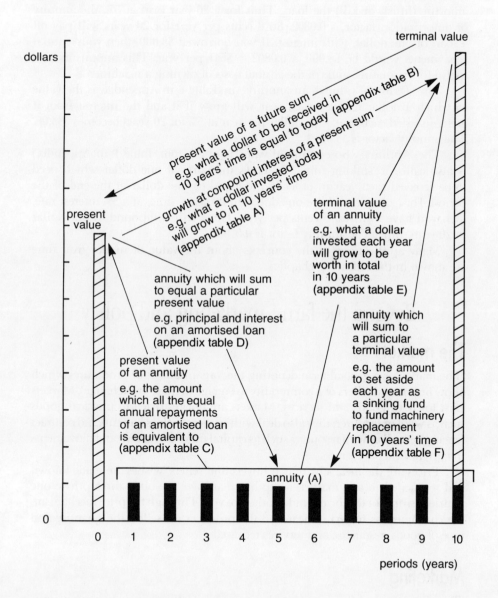

from Table C in Appendix, 'Present value of an annuity', and equals $1 × 12.4622. Thus you are equally well-off financially having $12.46 now, or a dollar a year for the next 20 years.

Table D in Appendix shows the 'Annuity whose present value is one'. This is most useful, especially when considering loans. It allows you to work out how much annual interest and principal you have to pay, in equal terms, to amortize (finish or kill) the loan. Thus for a 20-year loan at 5%, the annuity or amortization factor is 0.0802. So 8 cents per year for 20 years will pay off a loan of one dollar, with interest. If you borrowed $8,000, then your annual repayments would be $8,000 × 0.0802 = $641 per year. This annuity is also useful for estimating some of the annual costs of owning a machine.

The 'Terminal value of an annuity', in Table E in Appendix, is the value to which a dollar received each year will grow if it and the interest from it are re-invested each year. One dollar per year at 5% for 20 years becomes $33.06. The annuity factor is 33.06.

The 'Annuity whose terminal value is one' (from Table F in Appendix) is also called a 'sinking fund'. It shows the parts of one dollar which need to be received each year in order to grow and be one dollar at the end of the period. For example, to have one dollar in 20 years' time, at a 5% interest rate, then you have to invest 3 cents per year. These will compound to one dollar in 20 years' time. The annuity factor is 0.0302.

Many applications of the concepts about the value of money over time are shown in the following chapters.

Beyond the farm: marketing and policy

The market

'The market' is a general term denoting the 'organizations or procedures which allow buyers and sellers of a commodity to engage in trade or exchange'. Markets exist for both goods and services. Markets are not restricted to physical goods such as wool or fertilizer; they also deal with services such as haircuts and contract fencing, as well as with resources such as capital (rates of interest) and movements in currency exchange rates.

Prices are the means by which buyers and sellers' wishes are made known and reconciled in any market, accepting that there are often three prices: one for friends, one for the locals, and another for you. Through the price mechanism, the consumer (as buyer) indicates to the producer (as seller) the quantity and type of goods, resources, and services required.

Marketing

There is no single definition of 'marketing'. Many definitions and interpretations of marketing exist. Marketing can be seen as all those activities involved in getting farmers' products from the point of production to the point of consumption.

Other definitions define marketing in more specific terms:

- it involves co-ordinating supply and demand forces in forming market prices and quantities;
- it is a number of functional and institutional activities;
- it is essentially gathering and communicating information.

Marketing systems have a two-fold function, viz:

- to convert farm materials into consumer products;
- to direct production into the most profitable channels, so meeting consumer wants.

Functions of the marketing system

The functions of marketing are commonly divided into three broad groups, viz: (1) the physical functions (2) the exchange functions, and (3) the facilitating functions.

1 Physical functions

Transport is fundamental in a marketing system. Without cheap and efficient transport, the complex marketing systems and regional specialization in production, typical of advanced countries, would not exist. One of the serious obstacles to increased production of such perishable products as milk and vegetables in poorer countries is lack of reliable transport. Storage and processing are further physical functions of marketing.

2 Exchange functions

The exchange functions are buying and selling. In essence, buying and selling are two sides of the same transaction. The marketing system assembles products, i.e., it gathers them at central points and it helps disperse products. One of the major functions of wholesale centres is to break down rail wagon and truck-loads of product into lots of a size retailers can use. Further breakdown of bulk lots is done at the retail level. Dispersion of products at these levels increasingly involves packaging. At the retail level packaging is a means of protecting the product and catching the consumer's attention and giving information.

3 Facilitating functions

These functions make the physical and exchange functions operate more smoothly. They comprise:

- providing information;
- financing;
- risk-bearing.

The collection, interpretation and dissemination of market information is a vital function. We can distinguish between short-term and long-term information. The short term relates to decisions on the best time and places to dispose of products already produced. The long term is mainly relevant to decisions on what is to be produced and how it is to be produced.

Financing is required to bridge the gap between sale by the farmer and payment by the final consumer (often well after the final consumer's purchases).

An extreme example is wool, where distance, marketing methods and processing combine to produce a long period between production and final sale. This cost, together with the cost of other functions, must be borne by those in the market.

Risk-bearing is also an aspect of the information side of marketing, as it involves considering market information to take a view of the future. Actions which aim to make a profit from forecasting the future are called 'speculation'. Speculators aim to buy products cheap and sell dear. Speculators are often regarded by society as anti-social. In fact, however, they normally fulfil a valuable social role, shifting risks from those wishing to avoid or reduce risk and its associated costs to those willing to bear risk and reap appropriate rewards for doing so. Further, production has to be distributed through time. Ideally, the difference in price between any two periods will equal storage costs (including interest and profit to reward risk-bearing). Speculators bid up prices when prices appear to be less than expected future price minus storage costs. As well, by selling stocks they force current prices down when they are greater than expected future price less storage costs.

Demand and supply

Demand

We will consider demand first because the fundamental purpose of production is to satisfy the wants and needs of consumers. The demand for a commodity describes the effect of price on its consumption; it shows the amounts of the commodity which people are prepared to buy at various prices, with other things equal.

The demand for a commodity can be shown graphically, as in Figure 2.2. At price P_1, an amount Q_1 will be demanded; if the price drops to P_2, quantity Q_2 is demanded.

One fundamental reason why more of a commodity is consumed as price drops is that most commodities have substitutes. As the price of a commodity falls consumers use more of it, and proportionally less of competing commodities whose prices have not changed.

The response of quantity demanded to price changes varies between commodities, according to both the number of substitutes and how closely those substitutes resemble the commodity in question. This responsiveness is called 'elasticity of demand'. Margarine is the major substitute for butter as a spread; it resembles butter closely. Hence the demand for butter is sensitive to both the price of butter and the price of its substitute, margarine.

Elasticity of demand

The degree to which quantity demanded is sensitive to price change can be measured. This is called 'responsiveness' or 'elasticity'. The unit of measurement used is the percentage change in consumption which results from a 1% change

Figure 2.2: Demand for a commodity

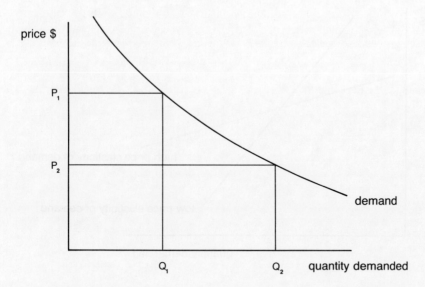

in price, and measures the price elasticity of demand. The price elasticity of demand for vegetable oils and butter is large, compared with the elasticity of demand for milk, or salt, neither of which have close substitutes.

The quantity demanded of a product with low price elasticity of demand changes little as the price of that product is changed, whereas quantity demanded of products with high price elastic demand is much more responsive to price (see Figure 2.3).

As the price for a commodity with a highly elastic demand decreases relatively large extra amounts of it are consumed. In the case of the commodity for which demand is price inelastic (low elasticity of demand), little more is consumed when its price falls.

The derivation of price elasticity of demand is shown in Figure 2.4.

Looking at Figure 2.4, with a rise in price of $10, 1,000 kg less is demanded. A $10 rise is a 5% increase. The 1,000 kg fall is a 10% fall. The price elasticity of demand for the product concerned over this range is:

$$\frac{\%\ \text{changes in quantity demanded}}{\%\ \text{change in price}} = \frac{-10\%}{+5\%} = -2.0$$

(−2.0 is a measure of how quantity demanded responds to a price change, and is known as the elasticity coefficient.)

The significance of the price elasticity of demand is in its implication for total revenue received. Take the following cases:

1 elasticity $\dfrac{\Delta Q/Q}{\Delta P/P}$ is equal to 1. This is called constant elasticity.

Figure 2.3: Elasticity of demand

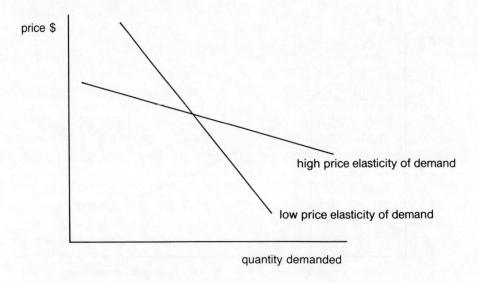

Figure 2.4: Elasticity of demand estimate

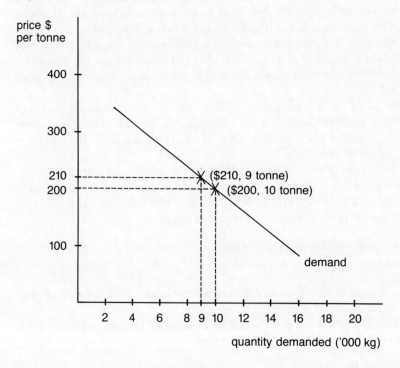

A 10% decrease in price results in a 10% increase in quantity demanded, or vice versa. In this case the total revenue (P × Q) received stays the same as before the price and quantity change.

2 elasticity $\dfrac{\Delta Q/Q}{\Delta P/P}$ is more than 1. This is called an elastic response.

In this case a 10% increase in price leads to say a 20% decrease in quantity demanded. The reduction in quantity outweighs the increase in price per unit, and so the rise in price causes a fall in total revenue (P × Q) received.

Alternatively a 10% fall in price might cause, say, a 20% increase in quantity demanded. The increase in quantity demanded outweighs the fall in price per unit and so the total revenue received increases.

3 elasticity $\dfrac{\Delta Q/Q}{\Delta P/P}$ is less than 1. This is called an inelastic response.

In this case an increase in price of 10% is accompanied by a fall in quantity of less than 10%, say, 5%. The increase in price outweighs the fall in quantity demanded and so total revenue (P × Q) increases, or, a fall in price of 10% is accompanied by an increase in quantity demanded of only 5%. The fall in price outweighs the increase in quantity and total revenue (P × Q) declines.

The price elasticities of demand of commodities thus has implications for farmers. If the response of buyers is inelastic, then price declines as a result of, say, increases in supply will lower the total revenue received as there will not be a corresponding sufficiently large increase in the amount sold. What this also means is that to get rid of an oversupply of a commodity which has a price–inelastic demand, the price will have to fall very low indeed. Most farmers would recognize this phenomenon when it comes to foodstuffs on domestic markets which generally have a price–inelastic demand.

Most farmers also recognize the other side of this price–inelasticity. If demand is inelastic to price changes then a certain increase in price is associated with a smaller decrease in quantity demanded, and so total revenue can be increased. This is the logic behind attempts by groups of farmers to control the supply of their production to force prices to rise and thereby increase the total revenue going to the farmers for the produce they sell.

This is only the case on domestic markets. When Australian farmers sell their production on world markets, they are one seller among many sellers and many buyers. They can sell a lot or a little and the price will not change. They face an elastic demand response for their products, and so they cannot affect the price by reducing their supply on the world market.

Factors affecting demand

The demand for a commodity varies over time, and depends on the influence of factors known as 'demand shifters'. The major demand shifters are population (i.e., number of consumers), income per head, prices of substitute products, and consumer tastes and preferences.

Population growth increases demand for all commodities by about 1%

year in Australia. Income per head is a less predictable shifter, as income grows
irregularly depending on business cycles.

Prices of substitutes are, for some commodities, the most important demand
shifters, e.g. synthetics consistently affect the demand for wool, natural rubber,
cotton, and jute.

Tastes and preferences account for shifts in demand not owing to the other
three influences. They may be either short or long term. Short-term shifts in
demand because of tastes and preferences are also associated with the time of
the year (turkeys at Christmas), the weather (salads on hot days), or promotional
campaigns. Longer term shifts in demand can result from taste and fashion
changes (demand for wines in post-war Australia, health concerns, a swing to
pure wool garments).

It is unlikely that the growth in demand for food in developed countries
will, in future, much exceed population growth. The effect of income
growth on demand for food is weak compared with the demand for, say,
microwave ovens, holiday travel, and tertiary education. The reason is that
most people in the developed countries have attained what they believe to be
a near-adequate diet.

As well, people tend to spend more of their increased income on marketing
services rather than the farm product. With increasing affluence and changing
lifestyles people tend to buy foods with more built-in convenience. Thus, they
substitute preparation, cooking and cleaning services provided by restaurants
and manufacturers for those previously supplied by the household. 'Trading-up'
in food-buying also takes the form of an increased demand for out-of-season
foods. Satisfying these demands involves considerable storage, processing,
packaging, and transportation services.

There is still an effect on demand from increased incomes for food, but
it is not strong. In countries such as the USA or Australia a 1% increase in real
income per head leads to an increase in demand for food at the farm level of
about 0.20%. In the economists' jargon, the income elasticity of demand for
food is only about 0.2%, i.e., if incomes increase by 1%, food demand increases
by only 0.2%. If incomes increase by $10, expenditures on food increases by
only $2 in more developed countries. A $10 increase in income can be associated
with an extra $4 to $6 spent on food in a less-developed country.

For agriculture as a whole the important point is that income is a relatively
weak shifter of demand. This means that as a country gets richer over time,
agriculture will play a smaller role in the economy. However, the poorer the
country the higher is likely to be its income elasticity of demand for food. But
even in poorer developing countries, population is the dominant demand shifter
because growth in income per head is generally slow.

Supply

The relationship of supply and price is shown on a supply curve as in Figure 2.5.

As the price of a commodity rises from P_1 to P_2, supply is increased from
Q_1 to Q_2.

Figure 2.5: Price and quantity supplied

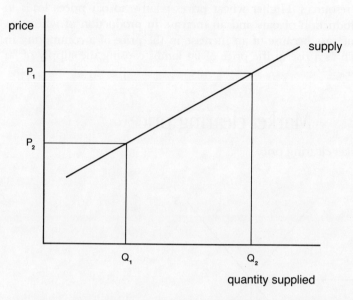

The explanation of why production rises when prices are high and falls when prices are low is found in the marginal (or extra) costs of the producer. Under higher prices the producer can expand output at higher costs until the cost of producing the last unit of product is just less than the revenue received for it, i.e., until extra costs and extra returns are approximately equal. The higher the product price, the greater is the cost the producer can incur from additional output and still make a profit on that additional output. Thus as wheat prices rise high marginal cost of production land is used for wheat production. Note that extra output is higher cost because of the effects of diminishing returns or diseconomies which may arise as activities are expanded.

Factors affecting supply

The major supply shifters in agriculture are the weather, technological advance, changes in the price of inputs, and alternative outputs.

The weather has a marked effect on seasonal price changes, especially with commodities for which demand is price inelastic. Technological advance means that more of a product is produced with the same amount of inputs involving a reduction in unit costs.

Changes in the price of inputs from season to season can also change supply. Changes in the price of feed grains have a marked effect on the extra cost of production of pigmeat, eggs, feedlot beef and, in certain cases, milk. Increased supply results from lowered input costs, other things being equal.

Increased supply of a commodity often results from reduced prices of inputs for that commodity, or from reduced prices of products competitive with that commodity for resources. Higher wheat prices relative to oat prices leads to a decrease in production of oats and an increase in production of wheat; or, supply might increase because of an increase in the price of a commodity in joint supply such as a rise in the price of fat lambs causing the supply of fat lambs to increase.

Market clearing price

Figure 2.6: Market clearing price

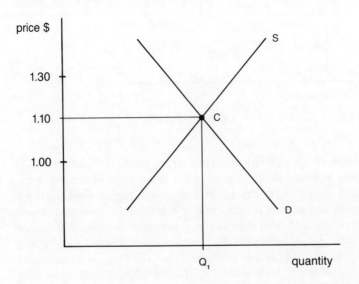

Point C is the market clearing or equilibrium price for the commodity in question in a free market. Forces exist in a free market which ensure that the market clearing price is formed, i.e., where the supply and demand curves meet. At $1.30, the amount supplied is in excess of the amount demanded. At $1.00 the quantity supplied is below what is demanded.

Prices are bid between buyers and sellers until the market clearance price C is reached; at C, the quantity supplied at $1.15 is enough to meet the demand of the buyers (or consumers) and the expectation of sellers (or producers), i.e. a mutually acceptable price. At any lower price the amount demanded would be greater than the amount supplied and vice versa.

Though this model of the market clearing price is an oversimplification of reality, it shows the fundamental relationship between supply and demand in a market, and the effects of a change in price, with no other changes occurring such as change in income, tastes, prices of other products and so on, i.e., movements along the demand and supply curves are shown (not shifts in these curves).

Another illustration of the clearing price is seen in the effects of technological change (better food conversion ratios) in poultry meats (Figure 2.7). Here changes other than price are involved. In such cases we refer to shifts in the supply or demand curves.

Figure 2.7: Shift in supply over time

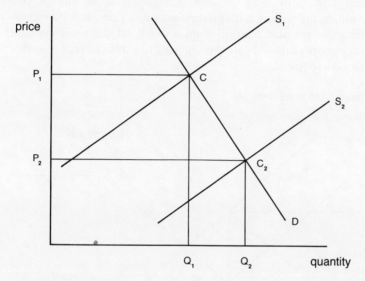

With technological developments the supply curve shifts to the right, i.e., supply increases from S_1 to S_2. Thus over time, if there is no shift in demand, the market clearing price changes from C_1 to C_2, a price decrease from P_1 to P_2.

As noted earlier the simple representation of the relations of supply, demand and market clearing price does not accurately describe what happens in practice; often governments or a few buyers or sellers acting together determine price and supply.

The free market mechanism is an efficient way of making known the wishes of consumers to suppliers, i.e., the consumers 'vote' for what they want by indicating the prices they are prepared to pay for the goods and services offered. However, this free market is idealized. In reality imperfections in the market distort market signals and prices. An example of this is found in the common agricultural policy (CAP) of the European Community (EC) where producers are paid far more than competitive world prices for their agricultural production. In Australia higher than competitive prices have prevailed to some extent in dairy and egg production, although this situation is now changing slowly.

The marketing margin and derived demand

The existence of a tiered or stratified marketing system means that the farmer sells to agents rather than to the consumer; the farmer receives 'farm gate' price rather than retail price; and faces so-called 'derived demand' rather than retail demand. The differences between the farm gate price and retail prices is known as the 'marketing margin'.

The derivation of farm level demand is represented as follows (see Figure 2.8). Consumers are willing to pay a certain unit of price, P_r, for a certain quantity of product as we may read off from a point on the retail demand curve; a certain amount per unit—the marketing margin—must be paid to attract the marketing services required.

Figure 2.8: Derived farm level demand

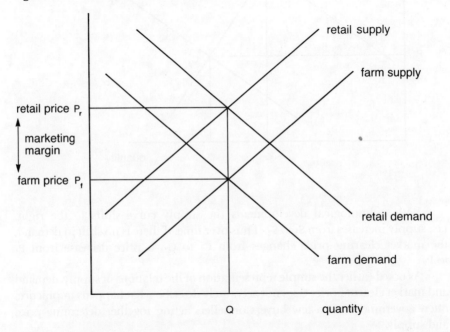

The willingness of consumers to pay that price at retail is therefore translated into a willingness to pay that price minus the marketing margin for the given quantity at the farm level.

Farmers and their organizations frequently argue, as part of a 'we'll all be ruined' syndrome, that marketing margins are 'too high'. The commonest explanation that they offer for these 'high' margins is that the marketing industry, or marketing system, is inefficient.

Marketing margins are the difference between the price the consumer pays for the product and the price the producer receives. This includes all the costs of transport, processing, and distribution through the marketing chain. The marketing system adds services to the farm product so that the product meets consumer needs. The marketing margin represents the value, or costs, of services added to the commodity through marketing. The size of the marketing margin for different products reflects the different amounts of services to be added to the product. The size of marketing margins, sometimes measured as farmers' share of the consumers' dollar, is not an indication of efficiency or inefficiency in marketing. The best indicator of efficiency or inefficiency or exploitation in the marketing chain is the degree of competition, or contestability, in providing marketing services and whether normal profits or greater than normal profits are being made.

In developed countries the demand for food increases little with an increase in income levels, but the demand for market services constantly increases. One result is that relative to farm prices marketing margins tend to rise. Thus the farmer's share of the consumer's food dollar tends to decline. However, this does not necessarily mean that farmers are suffering from falling incomes.

In fact, incomes might be rising because of an increasing consumer spending. As well, rises in margins are sometimes associated with improvement in farm level demand. Thus, potato producers would be worse off now (or there would be less of such producers) if new and appealing methods of processing had not been developed.

So, marketing margins might be increasing because of increasing demand for market services, virtually constant demand for food, and increasing costs of marketing. Different products require different amounts to be spent on them, thus different marketing margins and shares of consumer dollar indicate nothing about farm profitability or marketing efficiency.

Characteristics of agricultural production affecting marketing

The specific character of the farm marketing system is explained by the peculiarities of agricultural production. Agriculture is land-based and therefore dispersed, and subject to limited economies of farm size, and it is an industry of small firms. Hence, to a greater degree than in secondary industry, there is a need for some way of concentrating and assembling products. Further, agricultural production has greater variability in quality than secondary products, thus it needs more standardization during the marketing process.

Agriculture's dependence on the environment means that farm units engaged in production of particular commodities are not dispersed uniformly over the country, but are found in specialized producing areas. Another characteristic of farm products is that they are mainly produced in batches rather than continuously. To convert production at intervals into a continuous stream, storage is needed. Holding stocks involves the risk that prices will fall in the interim, so specialized risk-takers, and speculators, play a particularly important role in marketing farm products. Finally, the complexity of agricultural marketing services is increased because many farm products are bulky and perishable.

As agriculture is an industry of small firms, usually no individual farmer has an output great enough, in relation to the total market, for actions by the farmer to have any influence on the price received. Farmers are usually price-takers, not price-makers. They operate under conditions of competition among numerous relatively small farm firms. In most manufacturing industries, a few firms account for a large part of total output. By varying their output (or their promotion or product policies) these few firms can sometimes, to a degree, have some control over the prices they receive. The individual farmer generally can sell a lot or a little, without affecting price. This characteristic differentiates agricultural industries from manufacturing concerns. However, if many producers simultaneously expand or restrict production then price will be affected. This often happens in agriculture because each producer bases plans on broadly similar information. When optimistic expectations cause many producers to expand output the result might be not merely a fall in price, but even a fall in total revenue to the whole industry.

Farm producers face price uncertainty. Although demand forecasts can sometimes be roughly accurate, an individual producer can never expect to accurately predict supply. Accurate price forecasting is not possible because, if a price forecast is believed to be accurate, farmers and buyers would respond on the basis of this belief. Then forces would be put in motion which cause the eventual price to differ from the price which was originally forecast to happen.

Also agricultural production is in batches rather than a continuous flow; most producers cannot know future prices with certainty. So, misallocation of resources, often leading to over-production and under-production alternating in a cycle, is common in agriculture. Prices can similarly move up and down in a regular fashion. This can be seen in potato and pigmeat prices sometimes.

The structure of agriculture means that certain forms of competition, which are open to firms with larger market shares, are not open to the farmer. Manufacturers commonly employ advertising, packaging, product diversification, and research and development to keep up with their competitors. Farmers rarely control enough resources to make such expenditure worthwhile at the individual level. Further, the homogeneity of many farm products restricts the scope for individual farmers marketing their own product as something special or different. What might seem to be a good idea for some farmers, such as promotion of their own products, is no longer a good idea if all farmers do it.

A feature of farm life which is all too familiar to most producers is price and income instability. Income fluctuations can be a result of production or price variations, or both. Obviously, price fluctuations are because of the conditions of farm product supply and demand. Australian farmers sell a large proportion of total production of any commodities on overseas markets. The conditions of demand and supply in the rest of the world have a large effect on the prices farmers receive for their products. Demand for most Australian farm products might be affected by changes in such demand shifters as income per head overseas, and by changes in supply shifters such as weather in both importing and competitive exporting countries.

Demand in export markets is very elastic for most products (less for wool since Australia supplies a significant share of world production). And, the amount of farm produce that Australian farmers supply to world markets fluctuates considerably, i.e., the supply function shifts about a great deal. This is because the supply of farm products cannot be increased or decreased quickly (supply is inelastic in the short term), and weather conditions cause great fluctuations in the quantities produced.

As a result the prices that farmers receive on export markets often fluctuates considerably, as well as the exchange rate. Export markets are relatively small and are residual markets. Only a small change in total agricultural production can cause relatively large falls in prices received. Of the 600 m. tonnes of wheat produced throughout the world each year, only about 100 m. tonnes is sold on international markets. If 20% of total wheat production entered world markets, then a 10% increase in total production represents close to 50% change in the supply on world market. Given the nature of the demand, this causes a large drop in prices received for wheat on the world markets.

The dependence of Australian agriculture on exports also means it is vulnerable to the effects of overseas' political developments in the field of import regulations, and commodity agreements. Most countries protect their agriculture in some way from overseas competition to lessen the pressures on their own farming community for adjustment. Increasingly the 'going price' on overseas markets depends considerably upon the access which sellers are granted to those markets (through the plethora of bilateral and multilateral trade agreements) and on the extent to which competing sellers are disposing of subsidized production.

Farming in the economy and policy matters

Farm contribution to the economy

Agricultural activities contribute initially to the process of growth of an economy and the well-being of the people in five major ways:

1 Increasing production of food and fibre to provide for increasing population and income per capita.
2 Releasing of a surplus of labour for other activities, which helps improve living standards.
3 Earning net income to provide capital for investment in, and further development of, primary, secondary, and tertiary industries.
4 Providing a market for the output of other activities.
5 Earning export revenues.

The importance of these contributions varies from country to country. In Australia earning of income from exports has been a vital role of agriculture from the beginning of European settlement. Export earnings are primarily to enable the purchase of imports, not only of those consumer goods which Australia cannot produce efficiently, but also of raw materials and of capital goods (i.e., 'investment' goods used to produce consumer goods, such as machinery and equipment). Farm activities have valuable links to the rest of the economy through the suppliers of inputs and services, and through the many business activities which are needed between the farm gate and consumer.

Key aspects of the importance of agriculture in an economy are the share of national income from agriculture, the proportion of total exports, and the proportion of the labour force employed in agriculture. In each of these measures agriculture in Australia has declined in relative importance. Agriculture's contribution to Australia's national income declined from around 40% in 1840 to 20% in 1900, 14% in 1960, and about 4 to 5% in 1991. Agricultural production contributed 85% of total exports in 1950, and about 25% in 1991. However, as well, a significant proportion of Australia's 30% of exports which are manufactured goods are processed agricultural commodities.

In absolute terms, however, the agricultural sector is larger than ever and still very important, so percentages are a bit misleading. The state of Australian agriculture depends greatly on many factors over which farmers and governments have little control. The main factors are the nature of the season, and the state of world demand for, and supply of, agricultural commodities. The success or failure of agricultural activity in Australia depends on both the physical environment and economic circumstances for the production and marketing of the commodities.

A number of features of the economy beyond the farm gate dictate (1) that the agricultural sector's share of the gross national income will decline, and (2) that incomes per farmer must decline relative to everyone else in the economy unless some farmers leave farming. Fewer farmers or poorer farmers is the rule. These two features are so well-grounded in theoretical analysis and practical observation that they can be regarded as 'rules' of the game. As economic growth occurs and people become wealthier, they spend less of their increased income on the products of farming businesses, which are mainly food and fibre. There is a limit as to how much of these commodities people can use, no matter how wealthy they become. People's needs for food and fibre tend to increase at about the rate of population growth which also slows with increasing development.

As economic activities and income shares in the non-farm sector of the economy expand relative to the agricultural sector, the cost of farmers getting command of resources rises. This is inevitable as farmers compete in markets with non-farm businesses for inputs such as capital and labour. In recent times the major rise in costs has been the cost of capital (i.e., interest), which has affected most those who owe most.

These effects, along with rapid increase in production capacity mean that the prices farmers receive for their products decline over time in real terms. Declining prices mean that farmers have to improve their productivity continually so as to maintain their income. Most farmers do so. To maintain their income, they become more productive largely by adopting further supply-increasing technology, and expanding the size of their operations.

The least efficient producers, those with the relatively higher cost structures (often the small producers with consequently high overhead costs per unit of output), are subject to competitive pressure by the cost-price squeeze. They either adjust their operation, or become reconciled to receiving low incomes, or extract assistance through the political process, or move out of the industry. Adjustment (some get bigger, some diversify, some get out) plus large gains in productivity have, until recently, largely averted the persistent, widespread low income problems which have beset the farming sectors of other developed economies. While small pockets of low income farmers can always be found in any industry at any time, their existence in the past has had more to do with temporary market slumps, bad investment and management decisions and personal preferences, than with long-term structural problems. Such businesses are in financial troubles because the resources they command, or their command of resources, is not enough, and they do not make enough cash surplus to service their debts and meet family living needs.

The financial circumstances of farmers engaged in roughly similar types of production vary enormously. This is why it is always possible for some individual wool or wheat producers to be in financial trouble, and also why, at any time, not all of the farmers in a particular industry will be in serious trouble. Whether a type of farming is profitable or not depends a lot on how much was paid to get into the game. If the land, stock and plant are purchased at the right price, production will be profitable. If too much is paid for the assets, farming then can never be profitable. This is true of any business, e.g. television stations.

A fall in income is a potential problem if in the recent past a farmer has incurred a commitment to spend more money in the future, such as servicing new borrowings. In past downturns, virtually all farmers have managed to hold on until recovery happens. Then, here and there, a small number of farmers who were in financial difficulties, sold up. Generally when this has happened there were no shortage of buyers. Farmers who have been dealt a bad hand in one way or another almost always got out with something in their kick, with which to make a fresh start. Equally common, none of the neighbours, who are the ones to buy them out, are ever honestly surprised at the farmer having to get out. Many times the only surprise is how they managed to survive so long. So what is called a 'crisis in the bush' is never the case for all, or even the majority, of farmers. More realistically, these periodic downturns represent the much-needed opportunities for the most efficient farmers to expand.

Australian governments have had an active role in encouraging adjustment to change in agriculture since the 1970s. The rural adjustment schemes have been predicated on preventing the threat of major collapses in land prices, on identifying farmers without a future in farming and on assisting them to move out, and at the same time identifying those who, with a bit of help, will be able to continue farming, and giving them concessional credit. Welfare assistance, too, has been provided through the rural adjustment scheme to those farm families who have not enough cash to service their debts and buy their rations. All of these measures are mostly provided regardless of the relative asset ownership of the recipients. The point needs to be made that welfare problems cannot be treated on an industry-wide basis; they are treated case by case. Any approach which provides money to assist entire industries merely has the effect

that those who do not need help get more than they deserve, and those that
do need help then get less than they need.

Changes in the use of resources and people in agriculture has to happen,
as it does in the rest of the economy when crises occur. The crux of the problem
is, as always, the question of who is to bear the brunt of the costs? These costs
are the inevitable and unavoidable consequence of the adjustment which has
to occur in the current allocation of resources to agriculture. Up till now the
worldwide pressures for such adjustment, namely low farm incomes, have been
'exported' from the most highly developed and highly protected economies
to the export-dependent countries with less agricultural protection, such as
Australia. This has happened through the reduction in access to markets, and
through the inevitable low prices as supply increases faster than demand. The
problems caused by lower prices have since been worsened by the subsidized
sales wars to which the European community (EC) and the USA have resorted.

International and domestic policy

Mostly Australian farmers have to accept whatever price they are offered on
world markets, regardless of the reasons for the price being what it is. All they
can do is what they have done and continue to adopt and adapt to remain
among the most efficient farmers in the world. It would not be smart for
Australian taxpayers and consumers to attempt to help local farmers by
subsidizing production because they suffer as a consequence of what the
Americans and the Europeans, or the Japanese and South Koreans, do to help
their own farmers. To follow these examples would damage the well-being of
Australians in a number of ways. Australia cannot afford to compete with much
bigger, richer nations in subsidizing farmers.

Even if this were possible, it still would not be smart. Short-term benefits
achieved are eroded by increasing farm land values and the exchange rate. Farmers
receiving subsidies initially benefit, particularly if they sell out and reap the
higher land values which follow, but eventually highly protected industries lose
the dynamism engendered by the need for change and lose their worldly
competitiveness. No one would win. Taxpayers, consumers, other farmers, and
non-agricultural business people would be all made worse-off. Australia's
credibility in the world debates for freer trade in agricultural commodities and
greater access to international markets would suffer immeasurably. The ultimate
beneficiaries of Australia's participation in the push for doing away with
international farm subsidies and greater international market access are the large
number of exporting farmers.

Since 1970 the capacity of the world's famers to produce commodities
has increased considerably. This is in part as a result of increasing price and
income support given to farmers in the developed economies with highly
protected agriculture, notably the EC, USA, and Japan. As well, improvements
in agricultural technology and changes in pricing arrangements, along with
input subsidies, and protection from competition have caused increases in output
of grains in developing and newly industrializing economies such as China,

India, Indonesia, and South Korea. A lesson to come out of the 1980s of attempts to stabilise domestic agricultural prices is that doing so inevitably transfers the price instability to the world markets. Similarly, attempts to raise farm incomes by protecting farmers in agricultural importing countries lead to reductions in the incomes of farmers relying on export markets.

Despite the massive protection and assistance, it is obvious that using price and income supports to achieve the ultimate aim of maintaining the number of farmers and their incomes does not work. Increasing numbers of farmers in the EC and the USA are getting into more financial strife than their relatively lowly assisted, more efficient Australian counterparts. It is also becoming clearer that price and income subsidies cannot keep the incomes of inefficient farmers at some relatively high level for long without taxpayers and consumers providing steadily rising subsidies to farmers. Agricultural protectionism cannot protect farm people from the changes required by the decline in growth of demand, declining prices, and increasing productivity. Fewer farmers or poor farmers remain the options. In Australia though, those who remain are in one of the country's more efficient industries. They, thus, will earn a good living and have good prospects.

Deregulation of economic activities has been an idea that had received considerable currency during the 1980s. A major consequence of increasing deregulation of economies is more uncertainty. Furthermore, changes in the level of economic activity and in key economic variables like rates of foreign currency exchange, or interest and inflation, have more immediate impact on individual farmers' welfare than what happens where there is more regulation. The same also applies to the way international economic developments more directly affect individual economies. For instance, flows of capital are more readily 'internationalized' than in the past.

Nowadays, deregulated exchange rates reveal quite starkly the extent to which different sectors of the economy affect the profitability of each other. All sectors of the economy are linked through the exchange rate of the Australian dollar. Measures which protect domestic manufacturers from overseas competition, by reducing imports through tariffs or quotas, have the effect of raising the exchange value of the dollar above what would otherwise be the case. This might benefit domestic producers but it disadvantages exporters and it is, in effect, a tax on exports. Protection of the manufacturing sector of the economy through tariffs and quotas transfers potential wealth from export-orientated activities to industries producing for domestic markets.

A very important linkage in the economy is the exchange rate–interest rate–inflation nexus; what affects one of these factors affects all of them. This amounts to a further important rule affecting the farm economy. Farmer lobby groups tend to focus on one of these parameters, such as the level of the exchange rate. They then castigate governments for its magnitude. To do so overlooks the fact that when the domestic economy is growing rapidly a lower exchange rate will result in a tendency for a higher inflation rate, unless it is accompanied by higher interest rates. Alternatively, higher inflation rates in an economy will be reflected in lower exchange rates in the long term. It is not possible for government policies to attack one of these economic variables without a corresponding impact on the others.

Similarly the policy options facing any government, that is, monetary policy, fiscal policy, trade policy, wages policy, are all interconnected. 'Monetary policy' is actions by the Reserve Bank to affect the level of economic activity, the balance of payments, employment, and inflation. This is done by using interest rates and buying and selling bonds, etc., in the financial markets. 'Fiscal policy' is the government spending and collecting money to similarly affect the level of activity in the economy. The impact of both monetary and fiscal policy is different on producers in different types of industries and in different market structures. When monetary policy is tight, interest rates rise, and credit dries up for those businesses facing the bleakest prospects. The most vulnerable businesses in the economy are the hardest hit. Farmers who produce goods for export are among the types of business which are most vulnerable to the effects of monetary policy. This is because these, of all businesses in the economy, operate in highly competitive markets. Export farmers are not able to pass on increases in their costs to buyers of their products.

The decline in the relative importance of agriculture in the Australian economy as a whole has probably made farmers more vulnerable to changes which are occurring in the economy at large. Further, less regulation of key markets in the economy means that the welfare of farmers might be affected more readily by changes to fiscal, monetary, exchange rate, wage, tariff and general trade policies than traditionally was the case. Thus, now, maybe more than ever before, analyses of the situations of farmers need to be founded on a realistic, accurate picture of what is happening both on-farm and off-farm. It is only on this basis that sensible, appropriate, and equitable policy actions can be devised and implemented.

While there is little sentiment in business, there is a lot in farming. Whether it is because of bad luck or bad management, the hardships of some farm families when things go bad is as real as their feelings of helplessness at being unable to do anything about the markets and the climate and, ultimately, at being unable to keep the financier's 'wolf' from the door.

It is a competitive game, farming. If it is not the banker dropping in to discuss your situation, it is as likely to be the neighbours, dropping in to see how you are going and just to have a bit of a look around.

The following remains true. Most farm businesses are successful, have high equity, and are well placed to expand when the time is appropriate. Periodic cash crises in agriculture because of price falls and seasonal factors will continue to occur and will spell doom for those farmers with low equity. Herein lies the opportunity for the soundest farmers to expand their businesses in what is Australia's most important, world-class industry. This is our message:

the farming business is extremely complex, but often in practice the answers to a particular farm family's problems are fairly simple, if you are an experienced, competent farm management adviser. That is, if you can look at the whole picture, identify the important bits of it and the particular problem(s), and apply basic farm management tools of analysis correctly (i.e., resist the temptation to make up your own 'folk' economics).

2

Questions for discussion

1   There are many factors to think about when you start looking at the way a farm works. In problem solving, take a broad view and focus on those factors identified as being the 'key' elements. People tend to look closely at part of the farm, but not widely enough to have identified the true cause of a problem.
Discuss this statement.

2   Identify and discuss some cases where you might need to do some budgeting.

3   What do you understand by the following terms:
   • farm capital
   • equity
   • liabilities
   • returns
   • overhead costs
   • variable costs
   • inventories
   • depreciation
   • operating profit
   • return to capital
   • real capital gain

4   The principles of diminishing returns and equal–extra returns give guides as to how much of various inputs to use in production. How can these principles be used when thinking about farm production?

5   It is better to have a dollar now than a dollar in five years' time. We draw on this idea quite a lot in many later sections as we think that is important. Why is a dollar received now worth more than a dollar received sometime later?

6   In marketing there are also some basic economic concepts. There is the 'law' of demand and supply and the notions of market clearance price and elasticity.
Explain these concepts.

7   Overlooking the old edict on soothsayers and forecasters: 'May curiosity to foretell the future be silenced forever', and drawing on the material covered in this chapter about overhead cost, profit and returns to capital, weigh up whether a farm business you know well has a long and prosperous future.

2
Further reading

Barnard, C. S. and Nix, J. S., *Farm Planning and Control* (2nd edn), Cambridge University Press, Cambridge, 1986.

Barry, P. J., Hopkin, J. A. & Baker, C. B., *Financial Management in Agriculture*, The Interstate Printers and Publishers Inc., Illinois, 1988.

Boehlje, M. D. and Eidman, V. R., *Farm Management*, John Wiley & Sons, New York, 1983.

Castle, E. N., Becker, M. H. & Nelson, A. G., *Farm Business Management—The Decision Making Process*, Macmillan Publishing Company, New York, 1987.

Chisholm, A. H. and Dillon, J. L., *Professional Farm Management Guidebook No. 2*, ABRI, University of New England, Armidale, 1971.

Giles, T. and Stansfield, M., *The Farmer as Manager*, George Allen & Unwin, London, 1990.

Pollard, V. J. and Obst, W. J., *Practical Farm Business Management*, Inkata Press, Melbourne, 1988.

Williams, D. B. (ed.), *Agriculture in the Australian Economy* (3rd edn), Sydney University Press, Sydney, 1990.

3

Keeping The Wolf From The Door:
Financial Management

To know the many and diverse goals of farm family owners and operators is the starting point to any financial analysis of a farm business. These include making a living; maintaining and increasing the assets of the business; increasing net worth; and survival of the business in the long run. Also relevant are the stage of life of the business and those of the owner–operators; such as establishment; steady expansion; consolidation; then either more growth for offspring, or winding down and squatting on assets as a form of superannuation.

There are three basic financial statements about a farm business which are useful for analysis:

- the profit and loss statement;
- the sources and uses of cash statement;
- the balance sheet or net worth statement.

These statements deal with what has happened with the farm business in the past. All three contain data on the progress made in reaching some of the farmer's goals. They will differ markedly at the different stages in the life of the farmer and the business.

It is worth stressing here that many of the important numbers in these statements are 'soft', meaning that they can be defined and interpreted differently. Examples are depreciation of assets; valuation of assets on hand such as hay and grain for feeding; and imputation of the value of family labour.

Records and financial statements are about the past and the emphasis in business management is about the future. There is one basic tool for business management, the cash flow budget for the coming production year. This is used for planning and controlling the business' finances. Also, for the purpose of analysis and planning, estimates of expected profits and possible future changes in balance sheets are useful.

Profit and loss statement for farm management accounting

The profit and loss statement has the returns and costs of the business in the year just ended. The returns and costs in the profit and loss statement have both cash and non-cash items, such as depreciation and inventory changes.

Example
profit budget	$
gross income	320,000
less variable costs	100,000
total gross margin	220,000
less overhead costs	
cash overheads	20,000
depreciation	10,000
operator's allowance	30,000
operating profit	160,000

    The profit and loss statement is supposed to show the true 'profit' of the business. All income earned from farm operations and all operating costs incurred in that period are counted. Note that changes in the value of stock on hand is part of profit; income from the sale of an asset such as land might not be part of profit from annual farming activities, but it might still represent a capital gain if the sale price is greater than the book value used in the previous balance sheet. In accounting for most businesses, the proceeds from the sale of an asset is shown as a gain in the profit and loss statement, sometimes as an extraordinary item.

    The sale of land is a change in the form of an asset (land) which has a book value, into another asset (cash). This might then be changed into some other asset, such as a bank deposit or a reduced debt on existing assets.

    Capital expenditure incurred in a year is not all allocated as an expense in one year for the purposes of working out profit. This is because a capital expenditure such as buying a piece of equipment or improved pasture or new fencing, continues to provide services for many years. The cost each year of obtaining those services is equal to that year's share of the lifetime capital cost of the piece of equipment, improved pasture or new fencing.

    Net farm income (operating profit less the interest to creditors) is sometimes derived in the profit and loss statement. This is the return to the owner's capital. Sometimes operating profits and net farm income are calculated before a return is paid to the owner-operator for labour and management. In such cases care has to be taken when comparing farm business profits with profits of non-farm businesses. These will often have a different ownership–management structure and so treat labour and management costs differently. Other items such as interest on working capital might also be treated differently in different profit and loss statements. This is because there is no one way prescribed for treating some items in accounting.

Profit and loss statements are about what has happened in the past year. Farm management is about what might happen in the coming year(s). Information about the past is not necessarily relevant to the future. For management purposes, projections (budgets) of expected or possible profits and losses in the near future are needed. It is useful to look for major changes between the performance in the previous year or two and the expected performance in the coming year. The differences have to be explained. Some messages can be learnt from the profit and loss statements about the way the business has been run in the immediate past.

Sources and uses of cash and cash flow budget

Net cash flow is the difference between total cash payments and cash receipts in any given period. A source and use of cash statement shows cash at the start of the year, where cash came from and went to during the year, and how much was left at the end of the year.

This is then the cash balance for the start of the next year.

Example

	$
sources	
cash in	
sales	320,000
new borrowings	0
total	320,000
uses	
cash out	
variable costs	100,000
cash overheads	20,000
income tax	10,000
consumption	20,000
interest	45,000
principal	60,000
land improvement	50,000
total	305,000
net cash flow	15,000

A cash flow budget has the same information but it is about the future: where money might come from and might go to. The cash flow budget is designed to help the farmer to appraise the financial aspects of the proposed physical plan(s), either on a short-term (one-year) or medium-term (three-to-five-year) basis. Net cash flow is of vital interest to the farmer; it relates directly to the credit (plus) or debit (minus) balances of the business.

Cash flow budgets are used for two reasons: for budgeting and for checking or controlling the current year's finances. Cash flows can be done on a monthly or quarterly basis. They are used first to plan next year's activities, then to compare the year's actual results with the expected results which were put in the budget previously. When planning future activities or projects, after the physical plan has been decided, farmers need to know: How much money will the project produce? What will it cost? When will I receive the money? When will I have to pay money out? If the amount of money I expect to receive does not cover the amount needed to spend, how can the difference be made up. Is it to come from the bank, from savings, or from some other source?

The cash flow budget is used to provide continuous feedback or monitoring during the life of the plan. The actual cash income and costs can be compared with the estimates made when drawing up the budget. If the actual results differ greatly from the target results, then the farmer can try to modify the situation, before any serious harm results.

Balance sheet for farm management accounting

The third major financial statement, the balance sheet, should record the true worth of the business at a particular time. By contrast, cash flows and profit and loss statements refer to flows over time. The balance sheet gives a picture of the assets and debts of the business on a particular day of the year. Assets are things of value which the manager controls. Liabilities are debts or claims on the assets of the business. Equity is the value of the owners' share of the total capital invested in the business.

The balance sheet records all the claims on the assets of the business. Claims on assets come from whoever provided the means used to acquire these assets. The reason why equity appears on the same side of the balance sheet as the debt is that equity too represents a claim on the business assets. Equity in a business is what the business owes its owners. However, claims on debt are stronger than claims on equity. Debts have to be met before equity can be returned to the owners. The information in the balance sheet sums to total assets less total liabilities equals equity (or net worth).

Example

assets	$	liabilities	$
land	1,700,000	a 5-year, 15% term loan	300,000
stock	200,000	(in year 1)	
machinery	100,000		
(A) total assets	2,000,000	(B) total liabilities	300,000
		(C) equity (A − B)	1,700,000
			2,000,000

Assets in the balance sheet can usually be stated as current, intermediate, and fixed. Current assets are those expected to be converted to another form or used up within a year. They include cash, short-term bank deposits, and stocks of inventories such as grain, wool or trading livestock. Intermediate assets are those with a life of more than a year and up to seven to 10 years, such as most plant and equipment, breeding livestock, or medium-term financial investments. Fixed assets have a relatively long life, such as land and improvements, and buildings.

The category into which various assets fit depends partly on the nature of the operation. For instance, a livestock trader would regard the farm animals as 'work in process' and a current asset. To the operator of a commercial self-replacing animal activity, the breeding animals are an intermediate asset. A long-established elite stud might regard its animal bloodlines as being a relatively fixed asset. The farm land and most improvements are also fixed or long-run assets.

The same categories are applied to liabilities. Current liabilities are obligations to others which have to be met fairly soon (within the year) such as the bank overdraft, and accounts payable. Intermediate liabilities are loans up to seven to 10 years' duration. Fixed liabilities are the even longer term debts of the business, including such things as hire purchase commitments.

Assets and debts are put into categories because the length of life of an asset or a debt can have a major impact on, and implications for, future profitability, business survival, and growth.

Links between profits and loss sources and uses of cash and balance sheet

Changes in operating profit and in annual cash surplus from one year to the next end up as changes in the assets, liabilities and equity components of the balance sheet. The relation between the financial statements is shown in the following example.

Suppose at the start of a year the farm balance is as shown below:

Balance sheet 1

assets	$	liabilities	$
land	1,700,000	a 5-year, 15% term loan	
stock	200,000	(in year 1)	300,000
machinery	100,000		
(A) total assets	2,000,000	(B) total liabilities	300,000
		(C) equity (A − B)	1,700,000
			2,000,000

The profit and loss statement for the year reveals an operating profit of $160,000.

Profit and loss statement

	$
gross income (all from cash sales)	320,000
less variable costs	100,000
total gross margin	220,000
less overhead costs	
cash overheads	20,000
depreciation	10,000
operator's allowance	30,000
operating profit	160,000

Sources and uses of cash statement

	$
sources	
cash in	
sales	320,000
total	320,000
uses	
cash out	
variable costs	100,000
cash overheads	20,000
income tax	10,000
consumption	20,000
interest	45,000
principal	60,000
land improvement	50,000
total	305,000
net cash flow	+15,000

The sources and uses of cash statement has a cash surplus of $15,000. At the end of the year the balance sheet reads:

Balance sheet 2

assets	$	liabilities	$
land	1,750,000	term loan	240,000
stock	200,000		
machinery	90,000	(B) total liabilities	240,000
cash	15,000	(C) equity (A − B)	1,815,000
(A) total assets	2,055,000		2,055,000

What has happened?

The operating profit of $160,000 (from profit and loss) was equal to a cash sum of $200,000, once non-cash depreciation of $10,000 (from profit and loss), and non-cash operator's allowance of $30,000 (from profit and loss) is added back, i.e., $160,000 profit plus non-cash costs of $40,000 = $200,000 cash available. This $200,000 (from sources and use of cash) has been used as follows:

cash available (operating profit + non-cash costs)	$200,000
deductions	
less tax	$ 10,000
less consumption (drawings)	$ 20,000
less interest: 15% on $300,000 loan	$ 45,000
less principal on 5-year term loan:	
one-fifth repayment on $300,000	$ 60,000
less land improvement	$ 50,000
leaves annual cash surplus	$ 15,000

In balance sheet 2 at the end of the period:

* land value has increased by the $50,000 spent on improvement (from sources and uses of cash);
* machinery value has depreciated by $10,000 to $90,000 (from profit and loss);
* an extra $15,000 cash is in the bank (from sources and use of cash);
* debt has reduced by $60,000 principal repayment (from sources and uses of cash);
* equity has increased by $115,000 (from balance sheet 2) as a result of:

act	effect on equity
	$
improved land	50,000+
reduced machinery value	10,000–
increased cash	15,000+
reduced debt	60,000+
total change in equity	115,000

Interpreting a balance sheet

The contents of the balance sheet relate directly to three broad areas of concern to a farmer: liquidity, solvency, and growth. Less directly, the flexibility of the operator and his or her creditors to make changes to the operation of the business is determined by the structure of assets and debts. It is not just the relative levels of assets and debts which is of interest but the various forms of these debts and the marketability of the assets. For instance some debts may be able to be deferred longer than others, if times are tough. In particular, within-family debt is often like this, being more like equity than debt in many respects. (Although no doubt there are readers far and wide muttering 'you don't know my family').

Liquidity

Liquidity refers to the ability to meet all the cash commitments in the current period. A business is said to be 'liquid' if current assets exceed current liabilities. A test of liquidity is whether cash and liquid assets (current bank deposits, government bonds and securities, saleable stocks of grain, wool, trading livestock) can meet the debts which are due to be repaid. Liquidity is conventionally assessed as the ratio:

$$\text{current ratio} = \frac{\text{current assets}}{\text{current liabilities}}$$

or

$$\text{current ratio} = \frac{\text{cash and liquid assets}}{\text{current liabilities}}$$

However, this notion of liquidity is measured in terms of current ratios is usually more realistic for non-farm than for farm businesses. The ratio of current assets to current liabilities at any time is a more useful measure for businesses involved in producing batches of output such as piggery or broiler production than for businesses involved in longer term continuing production such as wool or cropping. The short-term credit system, such as the annual overdraft common to farming, or six-monthly bank bills, is geared closely to the production periods which may take six to 12 months and to the intermittent nature of cash flows associated with agricultural production.

At any time during the production period a farm could appear to have more current liabilities than current assets, and thus apparently low liquidity, but this need not be a major problem. For example, growing crops or sheep-growing wool are hard to value as current assets before they are harvested, but they are current assets and the clear promise of future cash flows to cover current liabilities is present. This is why projected cash flows for the year are a more useful indicator of liquidity over the coming production period than is the current ratio at any particular time.

The expected cash inflow compared with the more definitely known cash outlays reveals the way in which the liquidity of the business will change during the year. The financial system, through the bank overdraft and stock credit, takes account of the particular needs of farm businesses for liquidity. To the expected liquidity provided by expected cash inflows has to be added the liquidity available from other sources. These include cash in bank, tradable stocks and overdraft limits which might be granted because of the potential cash inflows. Only then can a good estimate of liquidity be gained. Not being liquid enough can be very costly to the business. For example a liquidity crisis can force a farmer to borrow from very expensive sources of short-term finance. There are also costs involved in holding too many assets in a liquid form, if their rate of earning is low. As always, a trade-off is involved between sufficient liquidity to be safe and the costs of being too liquid.

Another measure sometimes used is called the 'coverage ratio'. This is the ratio of a business' annual operating profit to the amount of interest to be paid annually. This ratio accounts for the relative claims of lenders to the business, and owners of the business, on the business' assets. However, debt servicing involves principal repayments as well as interest. Also, operating profit does not equate to cash flow. If the focus of an investigation into a business is on financial soundness, then 'cash flow coverage' is a better indicator than the coverage ratio. Cash flow coverage refers to cash receipts less the cash operating expenses, consumption and tax. The annual cash surplus is then expressed as a ratio of interest and principal repayments:

$$\text{cash flow coverage} = \frac{\text{annual cash surplus}}{\text{annual interest} + \text{principal}}$$

Solvency

Solvency and growth of the business are the other relevant aspects of the balance sheet. A business is solvent when total assets (TA) are more than total liabilities (TL) i.e.,

If $\dfrac{\text{TA}}{\text{TL}} > 1$

A business is said to be insolvent if the return from its sale does not meet all debts. Solvency is not profitability or liquidity. Assets have to exceed debt to be solvent, but assets also have to make enough profits to give a satisfactory return on all capital, and to be liquid enough to service the debt when it is due.

It is not just having more assets than liabilities which is of interest, but also the relative proportions of assets and liabilities. The value of debts is fixed, and is reduced by paying back principal. But, the value of many of a farm's assets depend on their profitability. Thus asset values can fall as profitability falls.

Example

start of year	$ m.
total assets	2.0
total liabilities	1.8
	solvent

After a fall in commodity prices and thus assets values

six months later	$ m.
total assets	1.5
total liabilities	1.8
	insolvent

If the farm had $1.8 m. debt and was solvent at the start of the year, it is vulnerable and could become insolvent with a relatively small fall in asset values.

Strengths and weaknesses in the asset and debt structure, the profit performance and the cash position, are obvious in a balance sheet. When interpreting the latest balance sheet information, look at changes in assets and liabilities over the past period(s). For management purposes, what is of interest is what might happen next year. A useful planning trick is to project expected profits, cash, asset, debt, and equity changes for the coming year's operations. This can show where problems might arise, such as the way a projected decline in operating profit and cash surplus might cause an increase in debt from carryover borrowings or an increased overdraft.

One important feature of the balance sheet is the matching (or balancing) of the earned potential assets with the need to pay interest and principal. Mismatched asset–debt structures, such as having too much in 'short' borrowings to be serviced by too many 'long' investments are revealed once a few profit and cash scenarios are explored. Most 'crashes' of businesses are because of serious mismatching between current asset earnings and the balance of long- and short-term debt.

There is also the phenomenon known as 'over-trading'. This is a problem of lack of cash. One index of over-trading can be an increase in assets and debt, without a corresponding increase in operating profit to service the increased debt. This is where a farmer borrows to develop the farm, say, by improving the pasture, and then there is not enough access to credit left to stock the improved pasture properly. The outcome is that, despite the investment, profit does not increase enough to service the increased debt load. Over-trading happens often. When considering the structure and type of assets and debts of a farm, having a reserve in borrowing capacity is of use. Another useful strategy is to have a reserve of potential liquidity to meet a cash crisis: for example, current assets in the farm of readily tradable livestock, or some short-term deposits with financial institutions.

The use of summary statistics like ratios of current assets to current liabilities, interest coverage, cash flow coverage, and solvency has limitations. These ratios are subject to similar limitations as other comparative statistics such as wool produced per head and crop yield per ha. That is, they are usually about the past, subject to a considerable range of possible valuations, and imply a cause and effect which might or might not be the case, or at least cannot be discerned without much more detailed analysis of the business (for more on comparative analysis see Chapter 10). It is the change in these ratios over time, and the forecast outcomes from now to the near future, which are of most interest.

Growth and gearing

A key aspect of credit use is the role which credit can play in the growth of a farmer's wealth over time. To do this, credit must be used to increase the earnings of the farmer's resources. The increase in earnings must exceed the full costs of borrowing, and allow the principal on the loan and interest to be repaid. The relation between debt and equity, and the rate of return on borrowings govern what the farmer will eventually be worth. First, net farm income (NFI) for a year is the return earned on assets (operating profit called 'rA') minus the interest paid on debts (called 'iD'). Income taxes (called 't') and spending on personal consumption (called the consumption rate 'c') from profits have to be deducted.

Tax is paid on taxable income, which is not the same as operating profit. Different values for some taxable income and costs are used. Calculations of taxable income includes different depreciation values, does not include operator's allowance, has interest as a deductable cost, and includes other tax deductable expenses different from the operating costs used in calculating operating profit. Consumption and all other off-farm spending is called the 'consumption rate'. This is subtracted from after-tax profit. Whatever is left is an increase in equity:

$NFI = (rA - iD)$ where
NFI = net farm income
 A = total assets
 r = rate of return (operating profit as a % of total assets)
 D = total debt
 i = interest

Growth in equity (GE) is defined as:
Return on assets (operating profit, rA) less interest on debt (iD) less tax (t) less consumption (c) equals growth in equity
i.e. $(rA - iD) - t - c = GE$

Note. Equity in the business can also grow from ownership capital introduced from an outside source, such as an equity partner.

When estimating rates of growth in equity, sometimes the 'r', 't' and 'c' proportions are confusing. The amount allocated to 'c' and 'r' depend on how the operator's allowance is treated. Strictly speaking, the return to assets should be after the operator's allowance is deducted. However, often a full allowance for the owner–operator's labour is not taken out by the owner–operator. Instead a certain amount of drawings, which we call 'consumption' is taken. The main thing is to depict accurately how much is withdrawn from the business as a reward for the operator's labour and as consumption. The rest is left in the business as retained earnings or growth in equity.

Example
full operator's allowance paid plus extra consumption

	$
operating profit before operator's allowance	50,000
less operator's allowance	25,000
operating profit after operator's allowance	25,000

continued

less interest	10,000
net farm income	15,000
less tax	5,000
	10,000
less consumption above operator's allowance	5,000
retained earnings or growth in equity	5,000

example of growth in equity

	$
assets (A)	500,000
debt (D)	50,000
equity (E)	450,000 (assets minus debt)
operating profit	25,000
interest (i)	10,000
tax (t) (0.33 of net farm income)	5,000 (from taxable income)
consumption (c) (0.5 of NFI − t)	5,000 (consumption above operator's allowance)
growth in equity equals	
operating profit	25,000
less interest	10,000
net farm income	15,000
less tax	5,000
	10,000
less consumption	5,000
growth	5,000
% rate of growth in equity	5,000
	450,000
	1.1%

It is important to ensure that the starting point asset values and debts are realistic estimates.

Alternatively:

Growth can be expressed differently. (Readers preferring the arithmetic explanation can move on.) A formula can be used.

First, tax 't' is the tax paid expressed as a proportion of net farm income (operating profit minus interest).

$$t = \frac{5,000}{15,000} = 0.33$$

Second consumption rate 'c' is the amount of consumption expressed as a proportion of the sum, 'operating profit minus interest minus tax', i.e.,

$$c = \frac{5,000}{10,000} = 0.5$$

Third, operating profit 'r' is expressed as a fraction of total assets, i.e.,

$$r = \frac{25,000}{500,000} = 0.05$$

Fourth, interest 'i' is expressed as a proportion of total debt, i.e.,

$$i = \frac{10,000}{50,000} = 0.2$$

A = 500,000
E = 450,000
D = 50,000

The formula for growth:

growth = $(r\,A/E - i\,D/E)\,(1 - t)\,(1 - c)$

$$\left[\frac{0.05\,(500,000)}{450,000} - \frac{0.2\,(50,000)}{450,000}\right](1 - 0.33)\,(1 - 0.5)$$

= $[(0.5)\,(1.11) - (0.2)\,(0.11)]\,(0.67)\,(0.5)$
= 0.011
= 1.1%

In summary, the message is that growth in equity in the farm business is directly affected by:

- rate of return on total resources (operating profit);
- interest on total debt;
- debt to equity ratio (called 'gearing' or 'leverage');
- rate of personal consumption of profits;
- rate of tax.

This focus on growth in equity puts attention squarely on the aspects of a business which count most for success and survival.

Gearing

The feature of most interest on the balance sheet is the ratio of debt to equity. This is called 'gearing' or 'leverage'.

$$\frac{\text{debt}}{\text{equity}} = \text{gearing}$$

The principle of increasing risk is about the way an increase in debt to equity ratio can increase the risk of going bankrupt. A chief concern is how borrowed money can be used to earn a rate of return greater than the cost of borrowing. The rate of return in farming can fluctuate a great deal, but interest charges have to be paid whether the rate of return is high or low. Gearing has this effect: when things go well and returns on assets exceed interest paid on debts, growth in equity occurs faster than it would have with the same return but no debts and no gearing. High gearing also means that when things go badly and returns do not exceed interest costs, equity is eroded at a far quicker rate than the rate at which it would have grown had returns been good.

Suppose you are assessing future prospects of the farm business. When budgeting a possible change in the operation of the farm, a good place to start is the debt-servicing ability and to apply the principle of increasing risk. The principle of increasing risk is about the lack of symmetry between the rate of growth in equity when things go well, and the rate of decline in equity when things go badly, for any given set of debt:equity, interest costs and rates of return. It is not all bad. Higher gearing might be riskier but it also has its own rewards when things go well. Then, equity grows at a much faster rate than would occur under a lower gearing ratio (see Table 3.1).

Table 3.1: Growth and gearing

Example (No taxes or consumption. So in this case,
growth in equity = operating profit – interest)

| | Proportion of total capital borrowed | | | | |
	0%	10%	25%	50%	75%
equity (A)	2,000,000	1,800,000	1,500,000	1,000,000	500,000
debt (B)	0	200,000	500,000	1,000,000	1,500,000
total assets (C)	2,000,000	2,000,000	2,000,000	2,000,000	2,000,000
10% return (D) (C × 0.1)	200,000	200,000	200,000	200,000	200,000
interest on debt at 8% (E)					
(B × 0.08)	0	16,000	40,000	80,000	120,000

Return to equity (return less interest) @ 10% return on assets
| (D − E) | 200,000 | 184,000 | 160,000 | 120,000 | 80,000 |

% change in equity (growth) at 10% return on assets
| $\dfrac{(D − E)}{A}$ | 10% | 10.22% | 10.66% | 12% | 16% |

Key principle. Higher gearing gives faster growth if return on assets exceeds interest costs.

return to equity @ 10% loss on assets (loss less interest)
| | −200,000 | −216,000 | −240,000 | −280,000 | −320,000 |

% change in equity at 10% loss on assets
| | −10% | −12% | −16% | −28% | −64% |

Key principle. Higher gearing gives faster decline in equity if loss is made

Gearing and the principle of increasing risk means that with an equal percentage profit and loss on total assets, the rate of growth of owner equity is less than the rate of loss of equity. Table 3.1 demonstrates that high gearing can mean going backwards rapidly.

Notice the effect of a change in the relationship between returns and interest at any given gearing ratio. Take the case in Table 3.1 of 10% debt at 8% interest rate, 90% equity, gearing ratio of 10:90. At 10% return on capital and 8% interest on debt, growth rate in equity is 10.22%. Suppose now that interest rates rise to 16%. Return to equity is then $168,000 ($200,000 less $32,000 interest), a growth rate of 9.3%. The change in interest from 8% to 16% reduces growth from 10.22% to 9.3%. This happens at a good return on assets (10%) and a high equity (90%).

If the return on total assets falls as it so easily can, say, to $20,000 or 1.0%, then with 10% debt and 90% equity at 8% interest, the growth rate is $20,000 minus $16,000 leaving $4,000 or 0.002% growth. Now, suppose interest rates rise as well to 16%. Return of 1% on assets and 10% debt at 16% interest is then $20,000 less $32,000, equity erodes by $12,000, a rate of decline of 0.007%. This is the case at the relatively high equity level of 90%. Imagine the consequences of increasing interest rates at slightly higher gearing ratios, particularly as reduced profitability is accompanied by a collapse in value of assets such as stock and land which automatically increases gearing.

In Australia the proportion of assets (A) to debts (D) is commonly expressed as equity (E) percentage, i.e.,

$$E = \frac{A - D}{A} \times 100$$

A high equity percentage means a relatively low proportion of debt (low gearing), and hence a greater margin of total assets over total liabilities, an indication that there is less vulnerability to insolvency because of a fall in asset values. In Australian farming for most farmers, equity percentage fluctuates between 85% to 95%. This implies a gearing ratio of around

$$\text{gearing ratio} = \frac{D}{E}$$
$$= \frac{5\%}{95\%} \text{ to } \frac{15\%}{85\%}$$
$$= 0.05 \text{ to } 0.18$$

In non-farm businesses gearing ratios around 50:50 = 1 are common. Farming is different from most business in a few key ways. A large proportion of total assets is land; incomes are highly variable year to year, and in a significant proportion of years there is not enough cash surplus to service significant debt. Thus it is not feasible to attempt to carry a large debt on the fixed asset component of the business. Non-farm businesses with greater investment in current and intermediate assets, and greater annual turnover of sales and current assets, are able to service more debt from current cash flows, which may also be less uncertain and less variable than farm cash flows. In farming it makes sense to borrow working capital on the basis of expected annual operating profits, but to expect current operating profits to be able to service significant debt on the fixed assets of the business is usually impractical. However, some debt has to be carried on fixed assets at various times in order to expand the business, and also for the business to get good rates of growth of equity during the good times.

Gearing and changes in asset values

As well as being affected by variable rates of return, growth is affected by unexpected changes in debts and assets. Low profitability in farming leads to equity being used to meet debts. The low profitability has the effect of reducing the value of the farm's assets. Asset values are affected by expected operating profits and interest rates. A decline in one, or a rise in the other, can affect the value of assets. Any decline in asset values resulting from, say, rising interest rates or declining profitability, further increases the ratio of the value of debt to value of equity. A change in asset values can be caused by changes in market conditions, or a run of above or below average seasons. If asset values fall, the gearing ratio increases automatically.

Example

	before (boom)	after (bust)
asset (A)	$600,000	$450,000
debts (D)	$200,000	$200,000
equity (E)	$400,000	$250,000
equity % $\left(\dfrac{E}{A}\right)$	66%	55%
gearing $\left(\dfrac{D}{E}\right)$	0.5	0.8

This change in gearing as a result of a fall in profitability could mean the difference between farm business survival and ruin. Higher gearing means that a given fall in price or asset values has a larger impact on equity than lower gearing.

Example

	farmer A		farmer B	
	$	%	$	%
assets	2,000,000		2,000,000	
debt	0		1,000,000	
equity	2,000,000		1,000,000	
Later: after a fall in asset values of $400,000				
assets	1,600,000		1,600,000	
equity	1,600,000		600,000	
change in equity	−400,000		−400,000	
change in equity		−20		−40

A reason why a high gearing ratio is risky is that the farmer's equity is at risk of eroding completely with major declines in asset values.

The availability of capital to a business reduces ('capital rationing') as gearing increases, for two reasons:

- at high gearing less capital can be borrowed by the business because risk is greater. Also, higher interest charges might apply. This is called 'external capital rationing';

- at higher gearing liquidity and 'reserves' of liquidity such as potential extra borrowings are reduced. This is called 'internal capital rationing'.

Probably the interest costs of extra debt will rise as gearing ratio increases and the rate of return on capital might decline as a reasonably large farm expands. This could be so if diminishing returns to inputs occurred, or costs increase because the business is too large and managerial inefficiencies happen. Alternatively problems might develop with the timeliness or quality of operations. Often business expansion involves adopting new technology. There could be a fall in expected return on assets in the short term. The above-mentioned reasons for declines in operating profit, rises in debt costs, and increasing risks, clarify why firms do not continually 'gear up' and expand. The financial risks to do with gearing and changes in liquidity as gearing changes help explain why farm businesses are relatively low geared. In sum, financial risk is a compound of:

- interactions between operating profit ('rA') and interest on debt ('iD');
- effects of 'rA' on asset and equity values;
- effects of gearing $\left(\dfrac{D}{E}\right)$ on debt-servicing ability and liquidity.

New equity

Historically, most new equity in farming comes from retained earnings kept in the business, and from capital gains which were not cashed. The 'residual (left-over) funds' hypothesis is one explanation of the source of capital invested in farming. That is, farmers re-invest most of surplus funds at the end of the year's operations. However, there is more to it than this. Specifically investment relates not just to a past or expected boom year or a run of good years, but it also relates to effects of income tax. Taxable income in a highly profitable year is potentially high. The marginal tax rate could be relatively high (even with income averaging for tax purposes). Thus the benefits from investment spending which is tax deductible, and which therefore reduce taxable income, is high. In a highly profitable year the after-tax cost of investing is less than at the time when a lower tax rate applied. The combined effects of good prospects, surplus funds and increasing tax rates make retaining funds in the business through investment on the farm an attractive option.

Cost of capital

The terms 'cost of capital' and 'returns to capital' are confusing. Whether something is seen as a cost or return depends on perspective. The return paid to the owner of some capital is a cost to the user or borrower (person or business) of that capital. Thus we can talk about the cost of equity capital to the business. This is the return to the owner of the equity capital in the business.

The cost of capital in a business has two components: the cost of debt capital which is the fee financiers are paid for lending the money, so the less

secure the debt, the more the lender wants in interest; the other is the cost of
equity capital which investors in the business (the owners) are paid (pay
themselves) for investing in the business, coincidentally also for risking losing
their capital if the business goes 'bust'. Equity is more vulnerable to being lost
than is debt, because debtors have first claim on the assets, thus a higher reward
is needed for equity than for debt capital. In theory, the 'cost' of equity capital
to the business is the return which the owners of the equity have to be paid
to keep their funds in the business. Further, for most businesses, the return which
equity capital has to be offered in order to attract it into, or keep it in the
business, has to be better than that capital could earn in alternative uses. With
farming it is slightly different as the owners get some non-money 'returns' as
well. Still, the true cost of capital to the business is the full costs of acquiring
the services of both debt and equity capital.

If the interest cost of debt were less than the return required for the equity
capital, then there would be the possibility of reducing the overall cost of capital
by gearing the business more highly by borrowing more. However the scope
for so doing is limited by financial risk.

As interest is an allowable tax deduction, the true cost of debt is the effective
interest charge after tax. If the average tax rate (t) is 20% and the interest rate (i) is
10%, then the after-tax cost of the interest is given by i $(1 - t)$, i.e., 10% $(1 - 0.2) = 8\%$.
Basing investment decisions on a realistic opportunity cost of capital means the
investor receives at least as great a return in 'this' use as in 'that' alternative use.

The source of equity, the ownership, the management, and much of the
labour force, are usually closely related in family farms. There are unmeasurable
returns to having equity invested in farming businesses and some unmeasurable
costs involved with using debt capital, e.g. sleeplessness. These unmeasurables,
(particularly the returns from the farming way of life, or fear and loathing of
debt; and thus benefits from being relatively debt-free), can significantly con-
found estimates of the true costs of debt and equity capital in a farm business.

Credit and interest

Influences on interest rates

Critical to analysis of investment on the farm is understanding of credit and
interest. In particular, borrowers need to understand how interest rates are formed
and what factors in the economy affect interest rates. With deregulated financial
and foreign exchange markets and a more open economy, farmers have to
compete vigorously with the 'players' in the rest of the economy for funds, mostly
paying current market rates of interest, and are vulnerable to the developments
in the rest of the local and international economy. In short, competition is fiercer
and variability greater; the farm financing game requires more sophistication
by both borrowers and lenders than in the past.

What are the forces in the economy which help determine the level of and
changes in interest rates? Interest rates are the price of borrowed funds; their

level depends on the willingness of borrowers to borrow at prevailing interest rates for projects with varying degrees of risk (demand), and the willingness of lenders to supply funds for various uses with varying risk, at various prices. Underlying the process are the expectations of borrowers and suppliers of funds about future trends in interest rates, that reflect expectations about the future trends in inflation, the balance of payments, economic activity, and the various and changing government monetary and fiscal policies.

There are two important forces at work on interest rates: the international scene where Australia's borrowers and lenders have to compete with borrowers and lenders worldwide. Thus Australia's interest rates partly depend on world market rates. There is then an adjustment for the different levels of performance in the Australian economy and other economies where funds can be placed.

Through the 1980s and 1990s Australia has had a serious deficit on the current account of the balance of payments. Australians, in business and the private sector, have been importing more goods and services than they have been exporting. The extra imports have been financed by borrowing from overseas lenders. Now, such a balance of payment deficit carries with it pressures for, and risks of, a fall in the value of the Australian dollar. This is one way the deficit corrects itself.

At the same time the federal government has certain economic objectives to achieve and uses monetary and fiscal policy as well as wages, tax, and trade policies. The government might be trying to run a tight monetary policy (high interest rates) to slow down domestic economic activity and to reduce the demand for imports which is causing a balance of payments problem, or to reduce pressures for inflation. An incidental effect of high interest rates is to keep the value of the dollar higher than it might otherwise be.

The Reserve Bank implements monetary policy, reducing the supply of money in the banking system by selling bonds and government securities, or by selling long-term rather than short-term securities. Again, the Reserve Bank can signal a change in interest rates by changing the rate of interest that it applies when buying back Treasury Notes sold at some earlier date to financial institutions.

A tight monetary policy might be accompanied by contractionary fiscal (budget) policies. Thus more money could be collected by the government than it spends, resulting in a budget surplus which has several effects. Tight fiscal policy can reduce the demand for funds by investors, reduce inflationary pressures, and indicate to overseas lenders the desire to solve the balance of payments problem by reducing imports. This does not rely on a large fall in the value of the Australian dollar. All these effects can ease pressure for interest rates to rise. However, interest rates will not decline much until monetary policy eases and allows interest rates to fall. So, insights into the level and movements in interest rates comes from knowing how the balance of payments on the current account is going, from government budgetary policy and from monetary policy implemented by the Reserve Bank.

Remember interest rates at any time are based on all the information and expectations currently available to borrowers and lenders. As soon as new information is available, or expectations of borrowers and lenders change, interest rates change. Levels of rates cannot be predicted, though the directions of change can sometimes be guessed on the basis of the above-mentioned types of factors. This is all subject to unpredictable influences, such as war or political disruption in the economies of major buyers of Australian exports, and so on.

Interest rates cannot be predicted accurately so it is prudent for a borrower to understand that when taking out a loan, he or she is immediately a part of a game subject to the complex interactions of many domestic and international forces which are uncertain and can be highly variable.

However, irrespective of the changes in the farm financial system, farmers increasingly depend on capital investment to maintain farm incomes. Rising costs and fluctuating prices for output keep farmers and their financiers under pressure to borrow and to lend wisely. Off-farm sources of finance for this investment are increasing in importance. A thorough knowledge of the intricacies of the many sources of farm finance will reap its own rewards.

Bank overdraft

The fluctuating overdraft system is the commonest form of lending to farmers. This provides funds up to an agreed maximum limit to meet normal seasonal working capital needs. It is well suited to meeting normal requirements for credit of primary producers because it is flexible. Interest is charged on the day-to-day debit balance. The borrower pays only for funds actually in use. The general practice of banks is to require periodic reductions with the aim of clearing the overdraft. Borrowings are re-negotiable periodically and the prime purpose is to meet short-term rather than long-term needs. Fully Drawn Advances are a similar credit form to the overdraft, but these are less flexible. They can run for a flexible term, and may extend up to six to eight years.

Bank bills

With bank bills the minimum amount involved is $50,000. The interest rate on the day of the transaction is set by the ruling interest rate in the bank bill market.

Example (minimum $50,000 for the bank bill)

A producer wishes to borrow $50,000 for 180 days with the intention of rolling over the bill at the end of this time for a further 180 days, giving the borrower finance for 12 months. At the end of this 360-day period it is the intention to repay the bill in full. A bill of $50,000 is sold by the farmer through the bank which endorses or guarantees it; using the farmer's security, usually land.

bill costs (based on 18% annual interest rate)
acceptance fee (banks discount share, varies 1% to 3%)

$$\text{using } 1\% = \$50,000 \times 1\% \times \frac{180}{365} = \$246$$

$$\text{interest } 18\% \times \$50,000 \times \frac{180}{365} = \$4,438$$

total costs = $4,684

The costs are met when the bill is negotiated and consequently the borrower receives $45,316. The borrower is required to repay $50,000 at the end of 180 days. The effective interest rate over 180 days, is $\dfrac{\$4,684}{\$45,316} \times \dfrac{365}{180} \times \dfrac{100}{1} = 21\%$.

Renegotiated bill (i.e., roll-over at end of 180 days)

To repay the $50,000, a new (renegotiated) bill for approximately $55,000 needs to be negotiated. The payments of interest 'up front' and bank charges mean the comparative rate of commercial bills to, say, overdraft accommodation is approximately 2% to 3% above the rate quoted for the bill.

Off-shore borrowing

In the mid-1980s many people made the mistake of borrowing off-shore at seemingly attractive low interest rates, overlooking the fact that borrowing overseas has the added risk of change in the Australian dollar exchange rate compared with the world currency which was borrowed. Borrowing in, say, Swiss francs when the Australian dollar declines in value against the Swiss francs means it will take more Australian dollars to repay the borrowed money. In practice there is seldom much difference between paying the current interest rates in the Australian financial markets and taking a properly hedged off-shore loan. This is because of the way different markets are linked and the role of informed operators in the markets.

Loan repayments

Loans require repayments of principal (the sum borrowed) as well as interest payments. Sometimes lenders allow a repayment holiday for the first one, two or sometimes three years of the loan. Interest, however, must still be paid. The two main types of loan repayments are term loans and amortized loans. The term loan is the commonest form of financing provided by the trading banks. Term loans are usually either for farm development or farm purchase. This type of loan is generally available for from five to 10 and possibly 15 years and principal is repaid in equal instalments (annual, half-yearly, quarterly, monthly). Interest is paid separately on the outstanding principal and thus this reduces as the principal is repaid. The ability of the newly purchased or developed property to meet all debt-servicing commitments as they occur is critical when a borrower considers the suitability of a particular loan. With a term loan the crucial period is during the first few years. It is then that repayments are greatest.

Pattern of annual repayments of a term loan

Figure 3.1: Pattern of annual repayments of a term loan

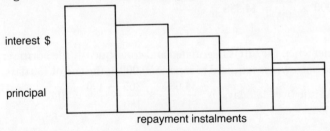

With amortized loans, repayments are made in equal instalments consisting of both principal and interest. As principal is repaid, the interest content of each payment is reduced, allowing more principal to be repaid. An amortized loan, by equalising the annual payments, is more easily serviced in the early years than a similar term loan.

Pattern of annual repayments for amortized loan

Figure 3.2: Pattern of annual repayments of an amortized loan

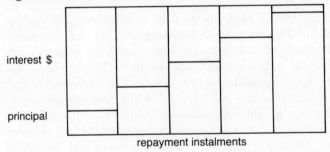

To calculate the annuity (equal annual payment) which repays an amortization loan, use the formula for an annuity whose present value is 1, viz:

$$\text{annuity} = P \, \frac{[i \, (1 + i)^n]}{(1 + i)^n - 1}$$

where P = the principal sum borrowed
 i = interest rate
 n = number of years

Alternatively, use discount tables (Table D in Appendix). For a $100,000 loan over 10 years at an interest rate of 10% (from Table 3.1), annuity whose PV is 1, the discount factor is $\dfrac{0.1 \, (1 + 0.1)^{10}}{(1 + 0.1)^{10} - 1} = 0.1627$.

Thus the annuity is $100,000 × 0.1627 = $16,270 annual repayment made up of both interest and principal.

In year 1 of the loan the interest component is $100,000 × 10% = $10,000 and the rest, $6,270 is principal. In year 2 the principal owing is $100,000 − $6,270 = 93,730. So interest in year 2 is $9,373 ($93,730 × 10%) and principal is $16,270 − $9,373 = $6,897, and so on.

Nowadays farmers contend with variable interest rates as a result of deregulation of the money markets (after 1983), as do all other borrowers.

Simple and flat interest

Simple interest is charged on the balance of the debt outstanding. Simple interest is the annual interest paid on the reducing amount of the loan outstanding. Flat interest is interest charged on the amount originally borrowed, for the full term of the loan, regardless of payments being made off part of the loan periodically. Total interest paid at flat rates is greater than total interest paid at simple rates. In some states now the true effective interest rate must be disclosed and flat rates can no longer be quoted legally.

Consider a 10% simple interest loan of $10,000 for two years with two equal annual repayments of $5,000 principal. The interest payment in year 1 is $10,000 × 0.1 = $1,000. The interest charge in year 2 is $5,000 × 0.1 = $500. The total interest is $1,500. If 10% flat interest were charged, the interest payment would be $1,000 in each year, or $2,000 in total. If confronted with a flat interest rate, convert it to its effective simple interest equivalent using this formula:

$$s = \frac{2\,ft}{t+1}$$

where

s = simple interest equivalent as a decimal
f = flat rate of interest
t = number of equal payments or instalments

For example a 15% flat interest for a loan with four annual interest payments is equivalent to:

$$s = \frac{2\,(0.15 \times 4)}{4+1}$$
$$= 0.24 \text{ or } 24\%$$

In the example above the flat rate interest of 15% is equivalent to 24% simple interest.

The simple interest rate equivalent to a flat rate is about two-thirds more than the quoted flat rate for three- to four-year loans, and nearer to double the flat rate for longer loans. When other compulsory charges sometimes associated with flat interest agreements are counted, the simple interest equivalent rate is often nearly twice the quoted flat rate.

Quoted interest rates must be converted to an effective annual basis for valid comparison. A quoted annual rate might not be all that it seems if there is some fine print about how frequently the interest is charged and if it is compounded as part of the debt. The way to know the true annual interest charge is to work out the total interest payments which will be required despite whatever is the quoted rate. The total annual payment is then expressed as a percentage of the sum borrowed. This is the effective annual interest charge.

There is also the 'sting': the various add-on charges which financiers charge: application fee, establishment fee, documentary fee, overdraft service fee, unused limit fee, composite bank charges, brokerage fee, and so on. These charges can be significant. A good way to compare the money costs of different loans and loan terms is to calculate the full repayment and up-front costs for the life of the loan and convert this to the equivalent annuity (the amortized average annual cost). This is the annual sum in present value terms needed to discharge the debt and interest obligations.

Duration of loan

What steps can be taken to reduce debt-servicing repayments to an acceptable level? This is a question most borrowers consider. There is scope for reducing the size of annual repayments by increasing the span of the loan or reducing the interest rate. In Table 3.2 below is shown the annual repayment on a $100,000 loan on which capital is repaid in equal annual instalments. On a $100,000 loan over 10 years an easing of interest rate from 18% to 12% reduces the peak annual repayment by $4,550. By extending the 18% loan from 10 to 15 years, the maximum annual repayment is reduced by $2,610.

Table 3.2: Annual repayments under different loan terms

$100,000 loan over years	interest rate	
	at 12% ($)	at 18% ($)
7	21,910	26,240
10	17,700	22,250
15	14,680	19,640
20	13,390	18,680

Increased length of loans has real advantages only up to a certain point. It is incorrect to think that very long-term loans are the answer to most financial problems. Lengthening the period of the loan does reduce the annual repayment required but often there is little reduction in annual repayment through extending the terms of loan repayment beyond 15 years at commercial interest rates. The situation for a $100,000 loan at 18% interest is shown in Table 3.3.

Table 3.3: Amortized annual loan repayment schedule for $100,000 loan at 18%

length of loan (years)	annual repayment ($)	annual difference ($)	total repayments ($)	total interest paid ($)
5	31,200		156,000	56,000
10	22,250	8,950	222,500	122,500
15	19,640	2,610	294,600	194,600
20	18,680	960	373,600	273,600
25	18,290	390	457,250	357,250
30	18,130	160	543,900	443,900

Thus as the loan term lengthens, the reduction in annual instalments becomes almost insignificant and the accumulated interest is very large.

Flexibility in loan terms is beneficial. An investment which promises a positive net present value at the desired rate of return might not be financially feasible because some of the returns are in the form of real and nominal capital gains, and are not cash available to service debt until the end of the planning period or at least well into it. Flexibility in repayments is needed in the early years of the loan to match repayments more closely with debt.

Inflation means the real burden of the debt is heaviest in the early years of a loan. This is at the time when the investment is usually least able to accrue all the cash which is needed. Amortization of long-term debt according to some graduated repayment scheme can be a help here.

Bank lending

Bank lending involves a series of step-by-step procedures undertaken by the loan applicant, bank manager, and head office staff. Banks judge loan applications according to such things as:

- what is the applicants' banking history; have they met previous repayments; who do they bank with; have they left credit funds in the bank when they have had them?
- what is the security available for the loan; is the bank well covered by mortgage over the land and fixed assets; does the bank rank highly among the business' creditors; what is the overall equity?
- what is their ability as farmers–technicians; what is the technical practicability and economic viability of the proposal?
- what is the expected net cash flow over the period of the loan?

Commercial lenders are generally not prepared to advance funds to projects which cannot be paid off in 10 to 15 years. Eight years is a common requirement, but it is usually too short a time for most agricultural investment projects to repay the capital borrowed.

Tax and interest must be deducted from any increased operating profit before the extra funds earned can be directed towards reducing the principal of the loan. The level of expected increase in the operating profit, less tax and extra interest, rather than the equity of the proprietor, determines the project's ability to service the loan.

Most lenders, quite sensibly, want farm borrowers to have more equity than debt, in order to secure the debt. Bankers tend to rely on the asset-backing of a proposal and often correspondingly rely less on the expected annual cash surplus of a proposal or a business.

In practice, it is the balance of annual cash surplus and equity, hence debt-servicing commitments, which determines the solvency and the security of a loan. Naturally, financiers do not want to see equity drop too low, as this means a rise in the interest payments and makes repayment difficult in the event of a drought, floods, an outbreak of disease, or a marked decline in product prices.

In many farm development projects there will be no positive cash flow (before borrowings) until the third year or later. The following two cases illustrate how cash operating surplus, less living costs, tax and interest, and principal repayments, rather than equity alone, determine the ability to service a loan. This is why the focus is on the debt-servicing ability of particular projects from entire farm plans.

Example

	higher equity farm proposed loan $100,000 10 years at 10%	lower equity farm proposed loan $100,000 10 years at 10%
	$	$
expected annual gross cash income	110,000	175,000
less		
cash variable and overhead costs	65,000	85,000
tax	5,000	7,000
living costs (minimum)	10,000	10,000
minimum asset replacement out of cash flow	4,000	7,000
current interest and principal repayments	10,000	25,000
balance cash surplus available to service new debt	16,000	41,000
less annual interest and principal repayments	16,270	16,270
balance margin for risk and variability	0	25,000

Neither business has much scope to defer nor to cut expenditures. The lower equity business has better scope for servicing the new debt after the possible variability of expected returns is considered.

As well other important aspects of borrowing to invest in a farm expansion or development include:

• capital needs;
• ownership and replacement costs of assets;
• changes in asset values;
• the terms and length of loans;
• the proportion of fixed, variable, and deferrable costs;
• expected and actual cash flows;
• timing of peak debt;

- the trade-off between having liquidity to meet known and unexpected calls on cash and using borrowings to achieve growth in equity.

A few rules of thumb common among those who finance farmers are: 'lend to the business having a 70% minimum overall equity', 'lend up to 50% of the value of the collateral put up', and 'lend an amount which can be serviced by only 70% of the amount expected to be available each year to service the debts'. Lenders sometimes apply the rule of thumb of lending up to about 70% of the current asset values. In this way the collateral can decline in value and the debt can still be redeemed, e.g. $1 m. invested in land, $700,000 borrowed with the land as collateral. If land values fall by 30%, the debt principal can still be covered if the land were sold.

Presenting a case for a loan

The way in which the case for farm finance is presented has a large bearing on the outcome. Knowing your way around the system, the sources of funds, and the lending criteria, are helpful, but not enough by themselves. A well-documented, well-planned case must be 'sold' to potential financiers; a definite proposal to which the farmer is firmly committed. Budgets of cash flow up to the steady state, and a budget of current and future steady state farm performance, are needed in applications for the funding of development projects. Written details of the proposal including firm quotes and prices and carefully costed capital requirements all help to establish the bona fides of a proposal. Written details of the financial position, debts, existing loans, and equity are essential for the lender to appraise the farmer and the farm proposal as a lending proposition. Also, sometimes borrowing for a project can mean arranging two or three loans from different sources.

Taxation

Here we are concerned with taxation matters as they affect the numbers to put in farm budgets and farm management decision making. There are three things to remember with taxation: there is always a tax angle; employ a good tax accountant; and emphasise actions to increase net income rather than tax-decreasing ploys. The marginal tax rate is not 100%.

In Australia it is compulsory to keep records for taxation purposes. Therefore, tax accounting of some sort has to be done, and it always has been done. The consequence of this has been that often the only measure of return available to farmers has been taxable income. However, taxable income is not a useful indicator of business profit or changes in owner's net worth, or business viability.

For the purpose of tax, a primary producer is defined as 'one who is engaged in the business of':

- cultivation of land;
- maintenance of animals or poultry for sale of these or their produce;

- fishing operations;
- forest operations.

Allowable deductions for taxation are operating expenses, some special 'approved' capital expenditures such as for land and water conservation, and depreciation. Farmers' wages and personal costs are taxable not deductable. Deductable depreciation costs include costs of plant, equipment and structures which gradually wear out. Depreciation is worked out on the basis of either the straight-line method or diminishing balance of the purchase price of the asset. Plant is written-off over its effective life in years as estimated by the Commissioner of Taxation (currently plus concessionary allowances such as an extra 10% to 20% of this value and accelerated rates for life of plant and equipment. Assets with a 5-years effective life have a write-off life equivalent to 3.75 years; 10 years, 6 years write-off; and 20 years, 7.5 years write-off). Structural improvements are depreciated at about 3% to 4% per year.

Capital expenditures which are deductable vary, but these often include investment in land and pasture improvements which are written-off at 10% per year over 10 years. At times special concessions such as 100% write-off for tax in the year of expenditure are available for things such as investments in water conservation and land preservation. Other concessions to farmers include rebate of diesel fuel, sales tax exemptions on specified classes of vehicles, and sales tax exemption of many inputs used in agriculture, such as fertilizers, etc.

Tax legislation in Australia also takes consideration of the variability of farming incomes, and the risky Australian climate. It has a number of helpful provisions for farmers, such as accelerated depreciation allowances; income equalization deposits; the treatment of fodder for stockfeed; and the spreading of proceeds of forced sales of stock over a period.

Ultimately, most changes in the operation of a farm affects the tax payable. An estimate of tax implications of changes is usually needed in assessing profitability. It is not good enough to compare expected profit before tax with alternative actions because different actions have different implications for tax. For instance, for a proposed investment, all capital expenditure might be tax deductions in the first year, which, at a high marginal tax rate of around 50 cents in the dollar effectively halves the cost of the initial investment. Another investment might have few tax-deductable expenditures and might be subject to capital gains tax.

The real return after tax is what counts with any action. Some people who think they are getting a good return on, say, fixed rate investment might be shocked to know what they are getting after inflation and tax. An investor receiving a nominal 15% a year return when inflation is 10% and the 40% marginal tax bracket applies gets a true return after tax of $15\% - (15\% \times 0.4) = 9\%$. Take away the effects of 10% inflation and the real return is -1%.

If paying 25 cents in the dollar tax, and inflation is 8%, then to receive a real return after tax of 4%, a nominal return of 4% real + 8% for inflation, giving 12% return after tax, is needed. To receive 12% return after 25% tax an investor needs a pre-tax return of 16%.

Income tax in Australia is a 'progressive' tax, so the more one earns the greater is the rate of tax paid. A set rate is charged for income in different brackets. As the income increases, the marginal rate of tax (i.e., the tax paid on the next unit of income) rises. If people start earning a higher income, they pay a higher rate of tax on the extra income they now earn. Companies are taxed at a flat rate of 39 cents in the dollar. With changes in both government policies and governments the rules affecting farmer taxpayers can vary considerably each financial year.

Tax accounting and farm management

For the purposes of farm management, tax accounting is misleading for a number of reasons. These are the main reasons:

- different costs are used to calculate taxable income and operating profit. For example, depreciation cost is derived from the Commissioner of Taxation's standard 'effective life' of a machine plus a concessionary extra percentage or a shorter life, and it is based on historic (original) cost. For management, operating profit uses depreciation based on expected life of machine and current value or replacement cost;
- different values of animal inventory income are used. For taxation accounting for 95% of businesses livestock are valued on the basis of average cost and concessional values for natural increase. Estimates of operating profit uses market values;
- for tax some capital expenditures are depreciated at accelerated rates;
- transfer items between activities such as feed supply from a crop activity to animal activity are important from management's view, but these do not come into tax accounting directly;
- livestock values for tax do not equal the actual amount of capital invested in livestock.

Taxable income and operating profit
Comparisons of operating profit and taxable income

operating profit	taxable income
income	income
1 sales of products from the annual farm operations	same
2 change in inventories shown at market values	livestock at average cost natural increase at concessional values
costs	costs
1 variable cost of production	same
2 overhead costs	excludes operator's allowance
3 interest is not treated as a cost	interest is a deductable expenditure
4 depreciation deduction should be based on expected replacement cost	deductions at concessional rates
5 capital investments not part of operating expenses	some capital expenditures might be deductable
6 no deductions for family dependants	dependants' deduction

Tax averaging

Farmers' incomes can be subject to tax averaging. Most farmers use it. 'Averaging' means the 'farmer's current income is taxed at the average rate of tax which applies to the farmer's average taxable income over the past five years'.

Example

year	taxable income	average taxable income
	$	$
1	12,000	14,000 (average year 1 and previous 4 years' incomes)
2	20,000	16,000 (average year 1, 2 and previous 3 years' income)
3	45,000	20,500 (average year 1, 2, 3 and previous 2 years' income)
4	15,000	17,400 (average years 1, 2, 3, 4 and previous 1 year's income)
5	26,000	23,600 (average of years 1, 2, 3, 4, and 5 years' income)

1990/1991 tax rates

taxable income	tax payable (at marginal rates)	average rate of tax
$1–$5,250	NIL	zero
$5,250–$17,649	NIL plus 20.5 cents for each $1 over $5,250	14.4
$17,650–$20,599	$2,542 plus 24.5 cents for each $1 over $17,650	15.8
$20,600–$20,699	$3,264 plus 29.5 cents for each $1 over $20,600	15.9
$20,700–$34,999	$3,294 plus 38.5 cents for each $1 over $20,700	25.1
$35,000–$35,999	$8,800 plus 42.5 cents for each $1 over $35,000	25.6
$36,000–$49,999	$9,225 plus 46.5 cents for each $1 over $36,000	31.5
$50,000 and over	$15,735 plus 47.0 cents for each $1 over $50,000	

In year 5 the tax payable on $23,600, using the tax scale above is $4,410.

The average rate of tax on the 5-year average taxable income is $\dfrac{\$4,410}{\$23,600} = 18.7\%$.

Remember tax averaging means that current income is taxed at the average current tax rate. Therefore in this year tax payable is the current taxable income multiplied by the average tax rate, viz., $\$26,000 \times 0.187 = \$4,862$.

Also, note that non-farm income above $5,250 is not eligible for tax at the average rate which applied to farm income, but it is taxed at the individual's marginal rate. As well though, the 5-year average used for averaging is based on both farm and non-farm income.

Provisional tax

Farmers also have to pay provisional tax which applies only to individuals. This is a type of pay-as-you-earn (PAYE) tax which enables the Treasury to obtain tax during the year in which income is earned. This is paid on 1 March in the year in which the income is earned, but it is assessed as the previous year's taxable income increased by a certain percentage to allow for growth. For 1993 tax, 1992 taxable income was increased by 8%.

Imagine that a farmer has just completed the first year of farming: tax is assessed at 30 June for income earned in the financial year of 1991/92 (farmer's first farming year). As well, a tax charge is estimated for the expected income for the next year, 1992/93 (based on the previous, 1991/92, year's income). Come 30 June 1993 tax is assessed for the actual income earned during the financial year 1992/93. Now some (or maybe more) of this tax bill will have already been paid as provisional tax which was charged at the start of the 1992/93 financial year, and probably was paid in March 1993. Having paid some tax in advance the taxpayer might receive a rebate or might have to pay more, according to whether the actual assessed taxable income was less or more than the expected income.

If a farmer's taxable income for the current year is higher than for the previous year and it is likely to remain high in future years, then the balancing extra tax in the current year and provisional tax in the ensuing year is also likely to be high. Unless some cash flow planning is done, the business could run into liquidity problems.

There is an option for self-assessment of provisional tax. This can be done if the farmer believes that the current year's income is going to be far lower than the previous year's income on which the provisional tax was assessed, not if income is expected to be higher. Note that there are penalties for being inaccurate in your estimate of income, though.

Livestock and tax

Livestock has a number of special provisions under the tax Act. To assess and to pay income tax it is necessary to identify what income has been earned, and it follows that it is necessary to know the value of livestock on hand at the end of the year. Two methods can be used to value the animals on hand at the end of the year: the average cost or market value.

Using the market value method requires that numbers of animals in various classes be known and their current market value is assessed. The average cost method of valuing livestock at the end of the year is based on the opening value plus purchases plus natural increase. A concession given by the Commissioner of Taxation is that the annual natural increase of livestock can go into the trading account at concessional values chosen by the operator.

In valuing closing stock and natural increase in the first year of operation an individual may value livestock at either average cost price or market selling price. If a stock owner makes no specific selection of method the Commissioner of Taxation uses the average cost price method. The farmer may not change the basis of valuation without the permission of the commissioner, and then only under special circumstances. The minimum concessional values per head for 1992 are:

stock	$	stock	$
sheep	4	pigs	12
cattle	20	goats	4
horses	20	deer	20

To determine average value of livestock it is necessary to know:
• opening number and value of livestock (last year's closing value);
• number and value of purchases for the year;
• number of natural increase.

At the end of a year a grazier had 1,000 head of cattle valued for tax purposes at $100,000. During the year 200 head were purchased at $300 per head. Natural increase was 400 head. The value used was the minimum value of $20 per head.

Average cost is calculated as below:

	number (head)	value ($)	
opening stock	1,000	100,000	
purchases	200	60,000	(200 × $300)
natural increase	400	8,000	(400 × $20)
	1,600	168,000	$\left(\dfrac{\$168,000}{1,600} = \dfrac{\$105}{\text{average value}} \right)$
sales	200	70,000	(200 × $350)
closing	1,400	147,000	(1,400 × $105 average value)
total	1,600	217,000	(closing value + sales)
trading profit		49,000	(closing values + sales) – (opening values + purchases + natural increase)

$$\text{average value per head} = \frac{\$168,000}{1,600} = \$105$$

At the end of the year there are 1,400 head of cattle on the property after sales of 200 (no deaths) at $350 per head. The closing value of the cattle is 1,400 × $105 = $147,000.

The concessional method of valuing natural increase causes the average value of the livestock for tax purposes to be pulled down over time. Average cost of the livestock will tend towards the value selected for natural increase. But, when animals are sold, their market value making up sales income is used for tax purposes.

There is little difference in the total amount of tax paid using either market values or average cost of stock on hand, although the timing of the tax payments differ, which can be a significant factor. With the market value method, taxable income in any year includes profit from changes in market values, which might or might not be realized by eventual sales of stock. Thus, with the market value method tax is paid on unearned profits, or tax is saved by 'paper' or market losses, although the animals have not been sold.

Using the average cost method tax is paid when the animals are sold. The difference between book value and sale price represents taxable profit in the year of sale. Thus the lower the value chosen for natural increase, the greater is the profit when animals are sold.

In the short term the choice rests between paying tax on unrealized profits year by year (market value method), or paying tax in years when profits are realized through livestock sales (average cost method). The average cost valuation means that tax on livestock profits is not payable until the livestock are sold. The advantage is that tax is deferred and tax due is paid from the sales to which the tax relates. Where the taxpayer is in a low tax bracket because of tax deductable development expenses, the advantage of using low stock values may be not significant. Also, the deferred tax might come due at a later date when, because of inflation, the taxpayer has moved into a higher tax bracket. Thus the advantage of being able to defer tax through using concessional book values for livestock can be reduced a bit if inflation puts the taxpayer into a higher bracket when the tax is eventually paid.

A major management implication of income tax on livestock income is the way in which the choice of method of valuation can affect the animal replacement system used. The calculation of average value of livestock at the end of the year means that purchases at market prices are added to the opening value of the stock. This adds more to the average value of the head/flock than does natural increase. Natural increase goes into the calculation of average value at less than market rates. Raising the average value per head by purchases means that the value of closing stock numbers is higher, and thus trading profit is higher, than when average value and closing stock value is lower (owing to low values for natural increase). Thus the tax-deferring effect of concessional values for natural increase (by keeping average value of head down) is greater than for purchased livestock. The tax system works in favour of having self-replacing flocks and herds over using a bought-in system of replacing animals.

Generally after-tax profits will be lower in early years under the average cost method than the market value method, but higher in subsequent years if sales are abnormally high. Sometimes the tax can be greater under the average cost method. This could happen if rising profits from other enterprises, or inflation, meant that the tax rate increased over the years. The higher profits will be earned from livestock in years with higher tax rates. However, some of this effect can be offset by various means of spreading the tax burden, such as using income equalization deposits.

Capital expenditures

The tax deductability of the annual costs of capital investments of the farm effectively reduces the real cost of such investment. For example, a farmer spends $50,000 on pasture development. This represents an annual tax deductable expense of $5,000 per year for 10 years. If the farmer's average marginal tax rate (that is, the marginal rate applying to the typical five-year average) is 35%, then the $5,000 deduction amounts to $1,750 savings in tax ($5,000 × 0.35). $1,750 per year for 10 years has a present value of $13,513 at a discount rate of 5% (1,750 × PV of annuity discount factor, 10 years, 7.7217). This reduces the real cost of the investment to $50,000 − $13,513 = $36,487. When we talk of $1,750 benefit per year this is the full saving only in the unlikely case where the alternative use of the $50,000 would have been in a use which did not produce any tax saving at all.

Machinery

Machinery can be depreciated at a range of rates, although rates of 10% to 20% per annum for the straight-line depreciation method and 15% to 23% per annum for the diminishing balance method are common for some pieces of farm machinery.

A 20% tax allowance for machinery depreciation works like this. Say the machine costs $10,000 to buy. The 20% tax deduction for depreciation from taxable income reduces taxable income by $2,000. The tax saving is not $2,000 but the saving in the tax which would have been paid on this amount had it remained as part of taxable income, instead of being deducted from it. The tax saving is the deduction from taxable income ($2,000) multiplied by the average tax rate, say 25 cents in the taxable one dollar. This comes to a tax saving of $500 for each year until the machine is written-off for tax purposes. These savings of $500 per year for five years would have a present value at 5% real interest of $2,165, leaving a real total cost of the $10,000 machine of $7,835.

Interest

Taxation affects the way in which resources are allocated to alternative uses. Treatment of costs such as interest as a tax deductable expense makes capital investment relatively more attractive than would be the case without tax deductability of interest. For an investor on a high tax rate, say near 50% in the dollar, with interest as a tax deductable cost, the true cost of borrowing at, say 16% interest rate is near 8% after tax. The tax deductability of interest makes for a higher rate of growth of equity for a profitable business than would be the case without tax deductability.

Note. The interest earned (above $5,000) is treated as non-farm income and is taxed at the individual's marginal rate.

Growth

Tax also has implications for growth of equity. Tax reduces the rate at which equity grows. Tax reduces the growth rate in a profitable year, particularly with a progressive tax system. But, it does not affect the size of a loss in a loss year. Therefore tax accentuates the effect of the principle of increasing risk, which has the effect that a loss reduces a highly geared farmer's equity more quickly than it would grow after a profitable year.

Capital gains tax

A tax is levied on inflation-corrected capital gain which has occurred since 1985. The tax is charged at the individual's marginal tax rate. Also in cases such as the purchase and sale of a property within 12 months, the real capital gain is added to the taxpayer's normal income.

Taxation and leasing

Usually lease payments for machinery and livestock are tax deductable, subject to some minimum residual values set by the Commissioner of Taxation. However, if the lease arrangement has the condition that the lessee will buy the leased asset at the end of the lease, the lease payments are not allowed as a deduction. Instead, for tax purposes, the transaction is regarded as a sale, and deductions for depreciation and for interest are allowed which are normally less than the lease payments although there should not be much difference.

Losses

Losses incurred by primary producers in one or more years can be carried forward unrestricted into the following years, i.e., no tax is levied until a cumulative profit is shown. This feature of taxation should not be confused with averaging where losses are treated as nil income.

Tax and budgets

The question of what tax rate to use in a budget is always difficult to answer. Suppose farmers paid income tax on each year's income, regardless of previous years' incomes. The relevant effect of any change in farm plan would be the addition to annual taxable income from the change. In this case the marginal tax rate would be the right rate to use in farm management budgets. However, averaging provisions are available to all primary producers, and most average their taxable income. For taxation purposes the relevant effect of a change in farm plans, costs and income, is the effect it has on the five-year moving average taxable income in any year. The question is then how much a change in farm plan will shift the five-year average taxable income. The effects of extra income will not be felt fully until it has been part of taxable income for every year of the averaging period.

There are many other matters affecting whether a farmer pays much tax or not. The deductable costs start in the first year and may extend for up to the next 10 years. For the above reasons it is hard to pinpoint all the effects of a change in farm net income on the farmer's average taxable income. The correct tax rate to use is the 'expected average marginal tax rate'. The true 'average marginal tax' rate to apply to the effect of the change is hard to define. So, a guess is needed about the average rate of income tax a farmer expected to be paying over the next few years. In most cases farm marginal tax rates are below 20%. Members of farm partnerships during the 1980s paid an average of $5,000 to $6,000 income tax per year each, an average tax rate of about 20%.

Income tax minimization

These are the main ways to reduce the income tax paid:

1 Splitting of incomes when additional taxpayers (usually family members) can be allowed to share in taxable income.
• partnerships;
• trusts–discretionary units;
• a company;
• payment of a salary to family members for services rendered;

2 Maximization of allowable deductions by means of:
• investment allowances;
• self-managed superannuation funds;
• income equalization deposits;
• income tax schemes which create 'artificial' losses.

Minimizing the tax bill is a specialist field. Farmers pay accountants to advise them on how to keep their tax bills down. Partnerships do not pay tax. The individual partners are taxed on their share of net income. The effectiveness of increasing the number of proprietors via a partnership is as follows:

	$	%
tax scale	5,250–17,649	20.5
	17,650–20,599	24.5

Tax payable on $20,000 = $3,118

Tax payable by a two-person partnership, each receiving income of $10,000 = $973 each, a total of $1,946: a saving of $1,172.

Income equalization deposits (IED)

An IED is an investment farmers can make in the IED scheme in high income years which is not subject to income taxation until the funds are withdrawn from the IED scheme. The deposits supplement the existing tax averaging scheme available to farmers.

The latest (1989) IED scheme has the following features: it is only available to primary producers; deposits can only be made by individuals, not partnerships, trusts, companies or company shareholders; the minimum deposit is $5,000 made for a minimum of 12 months before withdrawal; the interest payable on IEDs is the Commonwealth bond rate on the investment component which amounts to 61% of the total (the component which would remain after a tax rate of 39%). This rate is considerably higher than the actual marginal tax rate paid by the great majority of farmers. This is one reason why IEDs might not be used by farmers. Deposits are deductable from the assessment of tax on primary production income in the year of deposit. An upper limit of tax deductable deposits of $250,000 applies. When the deposit is withdrawn, a withholding tax is deducted at the rate of 29%. Tax is withheld to ensure that there is no excessive deferral of tax by the use of IED. The withheld amount of tax is treated as a tax credit when income tax is assessed for the year.

Summary
Income tax affects every decision on the farm which results in higher income or greater expenditure. Even so few general rules can be formulated about the part that tax plays in these matters because of the number of factors which have to be taken into account. However, it is important to consider the implications of tax because of the effect on an overall farm organization or development plan and not merely focus on expenditures as an instrument of tax minimization.

Business structure

Many family business structures eventually blow up or break down, and do so usually during tough financial times. The most favoured form of business structure in farming is the family partnership, with sole traders next, and a few farm businesses operating as companies and trusts.

Partnerships

The relative simplicity of the partnership, plus the advantages from tax spreading, makes partnerships more appealing than companies and trusts. In a partnership each partner has the same amount of control as held by the other members, unless a contrary arrangement has been made. Then the detail of the extent of partners' powers and areas of authority need to be defined and agreed. In a company the control is in the hands of the directors, subject to shareholders' power to appoint and to dismiss directors. The extent of the powers wielded by directors is set by company law and the company's memorandum and articles of association. Control of a trust is held by the trustee.

Taxation is often the main factor that determines the choice of structure, although concerns for succession are also important. The income-splitting aspect of partnerships makes these attractive for farm businesses. Partnerships are simple and flexible. However, care is needed at the outset to ensure that the 'rules' of the operation of the partnership are clearly defined; important issues to be decided include drawings; treatment of loan accounts; off-farm work commitments; administrative responsibilities; planning horizon for major decisions; land ownership; and arrangements for dissolving the partnership.

It must be remembered that each partner has an unlimited liability for the obligations of the business. As each partner has to accept the new partner transfer of interest can be difficult. Particular problems arise in evaluating the retiring partner's share.

Companies

A company is a separate legal entity with perpetual succession. Shareholders have a limited obligation to contribute capital to meet the company's liabilities. Company tax is payable at a rate of 39%. Losses cannot be offset against private income in any year (as in a parnership), but can be carried forward to future years.

Succession

Transfer of management, control and ownership of the farm is always an intricate, often troublesome, matter. The common transfer strategy is bringing the farming offspring into the partnership with their parents. This usually involves the transfer by purchase of some assets over time into the younger partners' names, e.g. some land, plant, stock. Transfer of the land can become complicated, often with the title staying in the parents' names until their deaths. Then the land is transferred by will. This protects the older people's retirement fund, and also pre-empts any potential splitting up of the land, or large payouts, resulting from divorces among the younger partners.

Farm viability

There are, and can be, no simple measures about the viability of a farm firm in the future. Viability is difficult to define. Still, notions of business viability should be included in any analysis of a business. Viability has elements of satisfactory rates of return and standards of living according to some wider community and local area 'norm'. But, many things determine an analyst's conclusions about the viability of a farm business. These include:

* the definer's image of what is an acceptable standard of living;
* the nature of the difficulties which have brought the farm's ability to survive into question;
* the extent of technical development of the farm;
* the state of financial affairs, and history, of the farm business;
* the period being dealt with. The question is: 'Will this farm business last until next Thursday, the end of the year, a couple of years hence or into the next decade?'

- the current and foreseeable state of commodity and financial markets;
- the farm financiers' view of the situation;
- abilities, aspirations, and capacity to work, of the farm family.

As with other aspects of the economic analysis of the farm business such as profit; capital value; ownership costs; returns to labour; management and capital; there are many opinions involved in assessments of the ability of a business to survive and in the viability of a business. Still, some key aspects of a 'farm with a future' or with ability to survive in the short and longer term, can be identified. The objective measures of potential liquidity and solvency detailed earlier are a good starting point in assessing the prospects of a business surviving and growing. A farm must have capacity to grow thus the flow of income must exceed that required to cover living expenses, current operating expenses, depreciation, and debt obligations.

In sum, a farmer with a future has to be able to:

- operate profitably in the current economic climate and grow in net worth over time;
- maintain and improve productivity, and to take advantage of new technologies;
- earn an income related to current cash and non-cash income which is roughly commensurate with others in the same community, and to accumulate sufficient wealth for a comfortable old age.

A farm business is solvent when total assets cover total liabilities if the business were to be sold. A business is liquid when assets which are reasonably readily convertible to cash, or soon will be, like a growing crop, covers liabilities such as overdraft, interest and debt repayments for the current period and the near future. A farm business is at risk of failing when debts cannot be serviced. Also, when the farm's current financial position and future prospects are so bleak as to make it possible that creditors will foreclose on the debts. This is often combined with the situation where the equity is so low as to stop renegotiations of debts or the arrangement of carry-on credit.

There are two parts to debt repayment capacity: the annual cash surplus after all the usual claims have been met; and there is the additional repayment capacity which could be available if needed.

A reserve of repayment capacity comes from current assets and from costs which can be temporarily deferred. The latter costs include some living expenses; some repairs and maintenance; replacement of capital items; family labour payments; maintenance of stocks of fodder and soil fertility. Also possibly deferrable is this notional item called 'returns to owners' labour, management, and capital'. In some cases the annual principal repayments will be deferred for a short time by creditors, but farmers cannot plan on this happening. Even interest payments owing are sometimes converted into a further loan, but this can be very dangerous.

Family debt can be slightly different to other debt, especially in tough times. When assessing the financial state of a business in financial difficulties it is necessary to identify debt-servicing commitments which must be met and debt commitments such as family debts, which may be deferred. A conundrum is that exercising any of these options depends on the business' prospects for survival, but the prospects for survival may depend on these options being exercised.

Even so, plans and actions ought to be based upon being able to service the debts of the business under 'normal' circumstances. There should be sufficient 'fat' and flexibility in the system to handle most variability without recourse to the more desperate of the options of cashing assets and of deferring expenditures. The financial and political system bends to avoid selling up farmers who are unable to meet their financial commitments, and to prevent dramatic collapses in land values. Forced sales of farms during a slump by long-established financial institutions happen only in the most extreme cases, despite the talk that might go on. On rare occasions private mortgagees force sales. Generally farmers' own resources and resourcefulness, and the political-economic system as a whole let them dictate the terms of their leaving the land. They might not get their initial price but usually farmers leave with a bankroll which, by community standards, is not too bad.

Income variability on farms causes total borrowings over time to be greater than would otherwise be the case. Although two farms might promise the same average income over several years, the farm with the more variable income has to borrow more and pay more interest so it needs more annual cash surplus and higher equity to survive.

Holding a large proportion of long-term debt in preference to higher interest but shorter term debt, to keep annual debt-servicing charges down, can be costly. Annual principal repayments are less the longer the loan but the increase in total interest payments sooner or later outweighs this effect; with high interest rates, this happens very much sooner.

The impact of different timing of the interest payment is also significant and has to be watched; a change from quarterly to monthly payments of interest changes short-term liquidity. Repayments should be matched to expected repayment capacity, which usually increases as a farm is developed. When a business is in trouble, the first thing to look at is the possibility of restructuring existing debt commitments to better fit expected improvements in annual cash surplus.

Changes in the rate of inflation can shift the real burden of a debt. With a fixed interest amortized loan, where equal annual repayments of interest and principal are made, high inflation transfers the real burden of the debt to the early years of the loan. This reduces the real cost of debt servicing in the later years. For most development projects, the reverse of this pattern is more appropriate. In practice there is usually some flexibility in some parts of the financial system to vary loan repayments. This means repaying a bit more in the good times, and a bit less in the bad times, without formal variable amortization schemes. In times of high interest some (affluent) farmers benefit by investing money so high interest is not all bad for all farmers.

A related point is the survival of farms in an industry. Some of the costs farmers face are determined by the profitability of the uses of the resources involved, and also by the profitability of the alternative uses of these resources. Some costs are determined by the prices farmers receive for their output. For example, land and livestock costs to individual farmers are determined by how profitable owning and using them is expected to be.

Declining returns in an industry will cause financial problems and test the survival capacity of some of the farms in that industry. But financial problems will not lead to the ruin of the entire industry. Survival of an industry, parts of which are in trouble, depends on whether there are more profitable alternative uses of the resources. If there are not, then the industry cost structure adjusts downwards, and the industry continues. The farmer who buys land or stock at sufficiently low prices after a fall in product prices gets returns which compare favourably with the returns on investment which prevailed in the industry before the fall in product prices. Those who go into the industry highly geared when product prices are at a peak, or when interest rates are unusually low, are at risk of having to adjust their financial arrangements when conditions change, or they may have to sell out and suffer capital losses.

Accounting

Management is about now and the future. Accounting is about what has happened, and, in some cases, what is the situation now. Some information about the past can be of some use to management, but in essence farm management is not really about farm accounting, given the present common methods of farm accounting. The major form of farm accounting is for taxation. This is different to the type of information which is needed for management. Management information is about how the business is going and might go, identifying problems and appropriate changes. It involves planning, decision making, and control.

There are now numerous accounting systems for use on computers. These vary in what they offer but all offer at least a cash flow budgeting facility. Information from the cheque butts and bank statements is transformed into statements of cumulative actual cash flows. This is compared with the expected cash flow budget prepared at the start of the planning year. Computer financial accounting systems also provide profit and loss and balance sheet facilities, as well as paddock and activity analyses of inputs, outputs and gross margins. For management accounting, computerized systems are available for livestock, crop and machinery schedules and for specialized animal recording and paddock recording needs.

Records of financial transactions and situation are useful for accounting and tax purposes as these:

* save the accountant's time (and probably yours, as well as your money);
* ensure that all tax deductions available are claimed;
* ensure you stay in control of finances and assets and can take advantage of opportunities as these arise.

Farmers were inundated with various types of accounting schemes, particularly in the 1980s, but none of these schemes are used by more than a few. A few simple records are of some use, generally, but detailed record-keeping is not the business of farm business management. Farmers tend to prefer to leave most of the book work to their accountant or a farm secretarial service. Farm secretarial services are slowly growing in their availability and in their management orientation. These services will play a larger role in the future of farm management, especially if consumption taxes are introduced as there will be a need for greater record-keeping by farmers. These services also have a role in teaching farmers the rudiments of simple uses of the computer spreadsheet in keeping and in analysing useful information, such as cash flows.

Although complex accounting schemes are unlikely to be widely used in Australian farming, there is an important place for an efficient system of keeping the key bits of information. First, the user has access to accurate facts and figures when needed. These are useful when borrowing funds. Also some records are necessary for tax purposes, particularly where a sizeable labour force is employed. Farm records can be used when the enterprise mix on the farm is evaluated. A farmer sees readily where he or she has done well or poorly in the past if those records are accurate. Records are interesting 'monuments to past folly' and to a small extent, this information can be used in planning future operations. Usually what happened probably will not bear much relation to what might happen in the future, but knowing the present situation is relevant to decisions about the future. An available course of action can be evaluated using present information.

The reason for the considerable emphasis usually placed on farm accounting, and the use of accounting packages, is that mastery of important information is the essence of good farm management. The key is to identify the important information and to spend time and money only on this information. Remember farm accounting information makes up only a small part of the range of information needed by good managers of farms. Of this, the expected versus actual cash flow budget for financial control is one of the most important and useful sources of information, with the monetary value of assets.

There are many books, pamphlets, and computer software 'packages' available from state government departments, extension agencies, and private consultants to help farmers decide what sort of records they should keep if they are to prepare accurate accounts under local conditions. We will not discuss these in detail here.

Records some farmers find useful

Information from the following records can be stored on personal computer, for the small number of users, or users of farm secretarial services.

Farm diary

The value of some sort of farm diary or notebook is often underrated. Farmers who do use a diary can permanently record important facts and figures otherwise easily lost or forgotten (although they can be hard to find quickly).

Paddock records

It is useful to record what happens to each paddock each year, e.g.:

* fertilizer application (season and amount);
* seeding;
* stocking rates;
* crops (grown and yields);
* gross margins per crop.

A very good, practical information system is one called 'Paddock Boss', which was developed by a farmer. It is simple, requiring only a bit of thought, a pencil, some arithmetic, and the user knowing what is happening in each paddock on the farm. It also allows an easy calculation of crop and livestock gross margins.

Livestock records

For management purposes, as well as for tax, it is important to keep track of production and numbers, e.g.:

* livestock feed and health records in intensive systems;
* livestock production (wool, milk, and animals sold);
* livestock numbers (split into breed, sex, and age groups);
* purchases;
* natural increase;
* dead and missing;
* rations.

There are many cheap booklets and stock diaries available for this.

Multi-column records

Books with multi-column sheets are useful in keeping farm financial records, especially the cash books. Give each column a heading which fits the specific situation on each farm. Use multi-column sheets for tasks such as recording receipts from the different farm activities or recording details of cost and income from each activity.

In many states agricultural extension and credit agencies have prepared books for financial and physical record-keeping. These are usually based on multi-column sheets, and make provision for the user to adapt some of the column headings to meet specific requirements. As well the computer spreadsheet is ideal for setting up multi-column records and for such things as cash flow budget.

Plant and improvement records

Here are examples of records that might be useful:

* costs and dates of purchase or installation. Annual depreciation (tax or market value depreciation);

- insurance;
- fuel use;
- hours of use;
- major repairs and maintenance.

Summary

Farm management accounting has a number of distinct features, viz:

- approximate realizable market value (not historical cost) is the basis of valuation of most resources analysed;
- inputs are related to outputs;
- direct costing or the gross margin is the basis of activity analysis;
- the production year, rather than the tax year, is the basic accounting period. Thus, depending on the industry, and the farm locality, the opening month of the accounts' year will differ. For example, it might start in March, April, or July;
- the full information needs to be readily available to the farmer within weeks of the end of the production year;
- physical records play an important part in preparing the accounts, e.g. tractor and casual labour usage, feed consumption by various classes of livestock, sex, and age composition of flocks and herds, crop yields;
- deferred payments for sales are accounted for by relating these to the year of production, and not the year of receipt;
- regular up-to-date reports of actual progress against budgeted projections are given.

The services of a first-class rural accountant is essential. Farm records and accounts can be useful for measuring performance and for improved farm planning. Adequate records make it easier to analyse farm performance. This is when physical and financial records come together. Both are needed for a critical appraisal of progress, and to change to annual farm plans. Keeping full records just for the exercise is a waste of time and energy. A little time spent keeping a few orderly records is useful.

One of the main skills needed by farmers is the ability to manage their finances. Farmers face trade-offs between equity, credit and gearing, and growth and risk. In particular, gearing for growth of equity has to be balanced with liquidity to meet cash demands and risk of income variability. Sources and uses of cash statements record when and where cash came in, and when and where it went out. Anticipated cash flows are very useful for planning. The comparison of expected with actual cash flows assist farm business control and it also enables problems to be pinpointed. A knowledge of the distinction between operating profit and taxable income is also imperative, as is the distinction between farm information for management purposes and for tax purposes.

3

Questions for discussion

1 How do you define 'profit'?

2 What is meant by 'costs are what you think they are'?

3 What is the difference between annual cash surplus or deficit and annual profit or loss?

4 Why must both annual operating profit and net annual capital gain or loss be considered when assessing the annual gain or loss in wealth of the owner of the farm business?

5 Define total capital (WIWO) value and marginal (extra) capital.

6 What is equity? What is the debt:equity ratio known as?

7 What are the main headings in the items called 'annual farm returns' and 'annual total farm costs'?

8 We say that cash flow budgets are among the most useful, practical planning tools which a farmer can use in financial planning. They are useful for both planning and control. How are they used for these two purposes?

9 Explain how the information in the:
(a) profit and loss statement;
(b) the sources and uses of cash; and
(c) the balance sheet;
can be fitted together to give a comprehensive picture of the finances of the farm business. Explain solvency and liquidity.

10 What do we mean by saying: 'There are as many definitions of profit as there are definers'?

11 What is meant if a business is said to be 'highly geared'? What do you understand by the 'principle of increasing risk'?

12 Items such as 'depreciation', 'operator's allowance', 'profit', 'valuation' of produce and livestock on hand, do not have one specific meaning in practice. They can be fiddled to suit the purpose for which they are used, yet they can still be within acceptable guidelines. What is (are) the best course(s) of action for farm business managers to take, so that their accounts are realistic and these can be used as an aid to decision making?

13 What use would a farmer make of the following:

(a) overdraft;   (f) hire purchase;
(b) term loans;   (g) solicitors trust funds;
(c) amortized loan;   (h) insurance company finance;
(d) bank bills;   (i) family loans;
(e) leasing;   (j) merchant credit?

14 'Ability to service a loan is the annual net cash flow after tax, but before principal and interest. Equity alone is a dubious basis for lending or borrowing.'
What do you think? What are the implications for
(a) a financier; and
(b) a borrower?

15 Explain how discount tables can be used to work out what is the annual debt servicing cost of an amortized loan.

16 Identify the major differences between farm accounts for taxation and for farm management purposes.

3
Further reading

Barry, P. J., Hopkin, J. A. & Baker, C. B., *Financial Management in Agriculture* (3rd edn), The Interstate Printers and Publishers Inc., Illinois, 1988.

Boehlje, M. D. and Eidman, V. R., *Farm Management*, John Wiley & Sons, New York, 1983.

Penson, J. B. and Lins, D. A., *Agricultural Finance: An Introduction to Micro and Macro Concepts*, Prentice Hall, New Jersey, 1980.

Pollard, V. J. and Obst, W. J., *Practical Farm Business Management* (2nd edn), Inkata Press, Melbourne, 1988.

4

Feeding and Breeding:
Animal Farm Management

▬

The aim of running an animal activity is to convert feed into saleable animals and animal products, and to do so profitably.

The key questions to look at when analyising the operation and performance of an animal production activity are as follows:

- how are animal numbers maintained? (This is called 'the replacement system'.)
- how is the health of the animal maintained or increased?
- what are the taxation implications of alternative animal replacement systems?
- how are the animals supplied with the amounts of feed, of the necessary quality and quantity, to meet the feed demands throughout the cycle of production and despite seasonable variability of feed supplies? (This is called 'the feeding system'.)
- how is the overall productive potential of the animals maintained and improved over time?
- how do different combinations of activities affect one another?
- what is the return to the various resources used in alternative animal activities?
- what net cash flows result from the animal activities?

These are the main components of animal production systems:

- the conversion mechanism and method of production;
- feed;
- costs and returns.

The animal is the mechanism by which feed is converted into saleable animal products. It is the overall economic efficiency of this conversion process which is the key to the success of animal enterprises. The main aspects of this process are discussed in this chapter.

Animal health

It is possible to control the major animal health problems by using vaccines, veterinary services, and by paying due attention to hygiene and husbandry, for both extensive and intensive animal production. Such expenditure is an essential precaution as the penalty costs of failure to take reasonable care of stock health are very high. In contrast, the cost of effective disease control is small. Intensive animal production, such as broilers, eggs, pigs, and livestock feedlots can be likened to sitting on top of a sometimes active volcano, such are the potential risks of disease outbreak if vigilance on animal health lapses.

Genotype

Usually some members of the one species are genetically superior to others in their ability to convert feed to animal products within the same environment. Demonstration of this biological fact is seen in the application of modern population genetics to production in the poultry and pig industries, where it has been possible to produce animals with efficient and predictable feed conversion ratios.

Stage of growth

Stage of growth has a big influence on the efficiency of feed conversion and the profitability of a feeding operation. The stage of growth of animals has a direct impact on the efficiency with which they convert feed into live weight. The older an animal is, the greater the amount of feed needed for each kilogram of weight gain. The higher the feed conversion ratio (fcr), the less efficient is the feed conversion process.

Suitability to environment

All animal species have their environmental limitations. Thus, it is extremely difficult to run sheep in the wet tropics. Also, within the genus, certain species are better adapted to particular environments. For example, *bos indicus* (Brahman-type) cattle are better suited to the wet tropics than *bos taurus* (British breeds). Over time the population of animals adapt, through breeding, to an environment (to the extent that environment is constant). Suitability to environment, or lack of it, and adaptability, is the result of complex but often subtle differences between animal genotypes, involving several trade-offs between performance characters. However, given the general suitability of animals to certain types of environment, the breeding industries produce animal genotypes which are finely tuned to intra-regional environment variation. The best example of this is in the wool industry where particular genotypes have developed to suit particular regions or environments extremely well. In the subsequent discussion on economic analysis it is presumed that the animals are suited to the environment. In the discussion on breeding the point is made that changes in the environment make possible genetic gains as environmental limits to production are met and then extended.

Exercise

Animal energy requirements above maintenance increase as the animal expends energy grazing the feed and then digesting it. In feedlots, the exercise factor is approximately 15% above maintenance; when grazing medium to good quality pastures the energy requirement for exercise increases to 35%. On poor sparse pastures it rises as high as 60% above maintenance. As well, as pasture quality deteriorates, energy requirements for digestion increase.

Disease, psychic and environmental stress

Inadequate diet is a precursor to disease. Also, many disease conditions increase energy requirements. Psychological stress which results from excessive concentration of numbers, rough handling, and frequent disturbance by people, dogs or pests also does this. Excessively high and low temperatures, and wet windy conditions raise energy needs. As animal production intensifies much greater attention needs to be given to the psychic aspects of production.

The method of production

Animal production methods are classed broadly as 'extensive' such as grazing enterprises, or 'intensive' such as piggeries, feedlots, eggs and poultry production. Dairying is an intensive grazing-based activity.

A major aspect of any production system is the method of replacing animals. Within these broad categories there are three major animal replacement methods:

- non-breeding;
- breeding with bought-in female replacements;
- self-replacing.

Non-breeding methods of production include wethers, store lamb fattening; growing out store heifers; finishing grower pigs, and egg and broiler production. Production with bought-in female replacements includes such activities as buying-in first cross ewes; Merino ewes; joined heifers; older joined cows with calves at foot; gilts; or sows and litters. Self-replacing systems of production involve breeding replacement animals on the farm and these are slightly more complex than the non-breeding and bought-in replacement systems. Examples of self-replacing systems include straight-breeding Merino × Merino, Hereford × Hereford, or a mixed straight and crossbreeding system such as having a self-replacing Merino ewe flock where most of the ewe progeny are mated to Merinos, and some to Border Leicester rams to produce first-cross ewes as well.

These are two important questions to be answered about any animal production:

- how are the animals in the activity replaced?
- what are the costs, other than feed and husbandry, associated with maintaining this method of animal replacement?

Non-breeding

The simplest example for answering these questions is a sheep for wool activity using wethers. Typically, the owner maintains the system by bringing in young replacements (in this case one-year-old [1 y.o.] wethers), keeping them for four years, and selling them as cast-for-age (cfa) sheep when they are about to turn 6 y.o. For every 100 young 1 y.o. sheep bought-in, only about 90 are available for sale when they are 6 y.o., because about 2% probably die every year.

The price paid for 1 y.o. wethers is greater than their sale price when they are nearly 6 y.o., because at 5 y.o. to 6 y.o. the wethers have not as much productive life, related to growing good quality wool, as they had when they were 1 y.o. Conversely, wethers might be bought at a young age, and grown out for sale at 2 y.o. to 4 y.o. to an overseas live-sheep market. In this case they usually gain in value from time of purchase to sale. If a farmer bought (at constant 1992 prices) 100 young wethers and kept them for four years, the costs of maintaining them would be as follows:

Buy 100 1 y.o. wethers @ $20 = $2,000
Sell (4 years later)
90 5 y.o. wethers @ $10 = $900
Depreciation and death (of the 100 wether asset over 4-year period)
$2,000 − $900 = $1,100
Flock average depreciation and death cost per 100 wethers over 4 years = $1,100
Flock average depreciation and death cost per 100 wethers per year

$$= \frac{\$1,100}{4} = \$275$$

Flock average depreciation and death cost per wether per year = $2.75

Therefore apart from the money needed for feed and husbandry (shearing, crutching, drenches, fly control, supplementary feed) it is expected to cost $2.75 per wether per year to maintain and to replace the animals in this activity.

Usually there is no depreciation in fattening activities such as steers, prime lambs, grower pigs, and broilers. There should be appreciation in the value of these animals. The cost of maintaining these systems is the purchases and losses because of deaths.

Breeding with bought-in female replacements

A depreciation and death cost also applies in the case of a first-cross breeding ewe enterprise. For example, suppose young 1.5 y.o. ewes cost $35 to $40, and sell at 6 y.o. for $10 to $15. Deaths may be 3% per year.

Example

	$
buy 100 1.5 y.o. ewes at $35	3,500
sell, after 4 years, 88 5.5 y.o. to 6 y.o. ewes @ $10 per ewe (expected)	880
flock average depreciation and death over 4 years	2,620
flock average depreciation and death per year	655
flock average depreciation and death per year per head (expected)	6.55

Another cost of maintaining this ewe system is the depreciation and death of rams. A ram might cost $200, serve 40 ewes per year in each of four years, and sell for $10 at the end of his usual working life. Further, some rams die, and some do not perform their stud duties. The ram cost per ewe, as a result of depreciation, deaths, and failure could be as follows:

	$
buy 10 rams at $200	2,000
1 ram dies in fourth year	
1 ram fails in first year and is replaced for $190 net	
(i.e., sold for $10, replaced for $200)	
total purchases	2,190
sell (after 4 years) 9 rams for $10 each	90
ram flock average depreciation (over 4 years) = $2,190 − $90	2,100
flock average depreciation per ram $= \dfrac{\$2,100}{11}$	191
flock depreciation per ram per year $= \dfrac{\$191}{4}$	48
ewes mated per year = 40	
average ram depreciation per ewe per year $= \dfrac{\$48}{40}$	1.20

In egg production young hens at point of lay might be bought at $6 and kept for 13 to 14 months, then sold as boilers for $2.00 each. The cost of maintaining this system is about $4 per head plus say 12% deaths, giving a total cost of $4.25 per bird for initial bird numbers.

It is a slightly different case when buying young beef or dairy females as heifers, or pigs as gilts, and then breeding from them for several years. The sale price of the cast-for-age (cfa) cows and sows coming from these systems usually exceeds the purchase price of the young female replacements. In these activities the costs then are deaths and the cost of acquiring semen, either through artificial insemination or by buying bulls and boars. Where bulls and boars are bought, there is an annual depreciation and death cost, just as there is for rams.

Self-replacing activities

These are the commonest replacement system in the sheep, beef, dairy, pig, and goat industries. In the poultry industry most replacements are purchased from specialist breeders. With thoroughbred horses semen is obtained by paying a service fee to stallion owners and the females typically are bought-in.

In a self-replacing animal system, some of the female progeny are retained and mated to replace the cfa females in the flock or herd. Suppose in a balanced breeding flock of 125 ewes equally divided into various age groupings, the ewes are first mated at 1.5 y.o. and kept in the breeding flock until after their fourth lamb at 5.5 y.o. If there were no deaths there would be 25 ewes in each age group. There would also be at least 25 immature (under 1 y.o.) females entering the breeding flock during the next year as replacements for ewes culled, either because of age or for reasons to do with reproduction performance. At least 25 female lambs born during the year would be retained as potential replacement breeding ewes in about 18 months' time. About 20 cfa ewes, depending on deaths in previous years, would be sold at five years of age after their fourth lamb.

The cost of maintaining this system are ram depreciation and death, and the loss of income from the area devoted to rearing the female replacements instead of running mature ewes. The following example will make the meaning of this cost clearer. Assume that there are five equal areas (paddocks), each capable of carrying one breeding ewe. In a self-replacing system, one area has to be devoted to growing out the young female replacement. The other four areas are grazed by breeding ewes. The situation is shown below.

1 y.o.	2 y.o.	3 y.o.	4 y.o.	5 y.o.
non-breeding	breeding	breeding	breeding	breeding

If there is 100% lambing (four lambs born, two male, two female) and there are no deaths, then the sale animals flowing from this system, approximately each year:

1 cfa 5.5 y.o. ewe after rearing her fourth lamb
2 wether lambs or hoggets
2 ewe lambs or hoggets (one of these ewe lambs or hoggets is retained for future replacement of cfa ewes)

One-fifth of the area produces just wool from a ewe hogget and no lambs, because it is used to grow out the 1 y.o. ewe to sufficient bodyweight for mating when 19 months. If the five areas were used to run bought-in ewes, then the system would produce five lambs for sale, but at a cost. The difference between the net income obtained from the area devoted to rearing the young ewe in the self-replacing system, and what could be obtained if the land were running a breeding ewe, is the annual cost of running the self-replacing system. Usually this difference is about equal to the annual death and depreciation of a bought-in ewe flock, plus the value of other unmeasurable benefits and costs associated with each system. So, the activity gross margins from the two systems, each using the five units of land, will be fairly similar, as long as sheep of a similar type are used.

Some people prefer to breed their own stock, sometimes because of legitimate fear of disease such as footrot. Others prefer the bought-in system which is easier to manage, or they are able to buy-in genetically superior stock from specialist breeders, or buying-in suits their pasture management and their other activities. Importantly the two systems, bought-in versus self-replacing, have different implications for taxation. All of these above-mentioned considerations are at least as important as the economic considerations. The reasoning used in this example can be applied to the economic analysis of self-replacing versus bought-in systems in any animal activity.

Another variant of the self-replacing system is to breed enough females of the straight-bred strain (say, Merinos) to maintain the Merino–ewe flock, and to mate the rest of the ewes to a ram of another breed, such as a Border Leicester (BL) or a Romney Marsh to produce first-cross fat lambs which might use more of the spring feed or a summer fodder crop. With 100% lambing, and no deaths (for simplicity), the situation in this case would be as follows:

(1) 50 M ewes × M rams produce
25 M ewe lambs
25 M wether lambs
(2) 50 M ewes × BL rams produce
25 MBL ewe lambs
25 MBL wether lambs

The annual livestock flowing from this system:

25 cfa 5 y.o. M ewes
25 MBL ewe weaners or 1.5 y.o.'s sold to become first-cross breeding ewes for fat lamb production
25 MBL and 25 M wether weaners sold
25 M ewe lambs retained as replacements

The same approach is often used with cattle breeding, where part of the straight-bred herd is joined to a European breed bull (such as a Charolais) for a terminal cross where all the progeny are sold. In practice, because of lower conception rates than we have assumed in this example, and deaths, and the need for some culling to maintain and improve standards, the percentage of females mated to sires of their own breed would usually need to be higher than 50%.

Flow charts

To carry out economic analyses of various animal production systems it is useful to make some form of flow chart for each enterprise that shows which animals go where within the system, in what numbers, and when it happens. Flow charts use rates of birth, culling, death and cast-for-age figures, to calculate the numbers of each class of animal within each activity which are on hand at various times, and which ones will be sold and retained. A flow chart is a sketch of what happens in the animal production system over the coming planning period. Thus in the sketch the changes occurring over time have to be described as it does not just represent the structure of an activity at any point in time but it must cover the changes occurring over the relevant planning period.

Example of flock flow chart

Figure 4.1: Flow chart—flock or herd dynamics—steady state, self-replacing Merinos

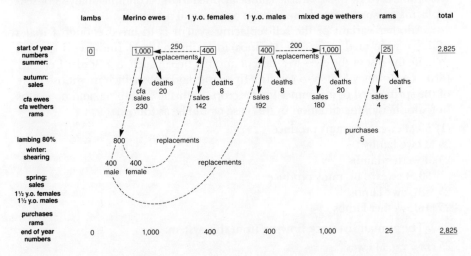

Modelling the flock or herd indicates the relationships between key parameters: the relation between productive life of ewes, lambing rate, survival rates, and the proportion of young ewes selected. These relationships determine the number of ewes which can be culled and the maximum possible rate of stock increase. This is important when pasture improvement occurs. If a self-replacing flock can produce more than needed for replacements, the surplus ewes can be used in some other way.

So far we have shown simple practical ways of working out the flock and herd dynamics and the cost of maintaining the system. A formal way is to use a livestock trading schedule (we explain this later in the chapter).

Replacement

The questions of herd or flock replacement is central to the analysis of an animal activity. Replacement policy involves a number of aspects of the farm business. These include animal health matters, selection pressure and animal improvement, the productive performance of various classes of animals, cash flow, and, importantly, taxation considerations.

In general the replacement problem in a breeding ewe block involves:

- to breed or to buy-in;
- if buy-in, at what age;
- at what age to cull ewes.

For any age class of stock the decision on whether to cull or to retain for further production depends on the likely price for the cull animal; the expected future production if the animal is not culled and the prices that can be expected for the products; the animal's expected variable costs over the future production period; and tax aspects. To the extent that the widespread practice is for animal activities to be self-replacing, then the key question concerns the most appropriate replacement age, keeping in mind that most measures of animal production performance tend to increase rather than decrease, over time.

An important point about self-replacing animal systems is that in practice rarely does the steady state, with a regular cyclical pattern of sales and retained replacements, or an enterprise with a constant size and composition happen. If this is the case it could be that the farm is not developing as it needs to over time to survive. Anytime an activity is analysed it is more likely to be changing in size or composition than to be routinely turning off and replacing stable numbers. This is because of ever-changing price ratios and fluctuating seasonal conditions farmers face, and farmers' opportunistic responses to these. Also flock size and composition alters when pasture improvement is carried out, when there are less culls of young animals. The aim then is to increase the size of the breeding stock or herd, and thus increased young replacements are required. The age structure of the flock or herd changes during a build-up phase. Another situation is where a grazier begins with a flock of the one age group. Replacements are low at first and then high later.

For valid comparisons between alternative activities based on expected animal gross margins it is generally necessary to compare activities as though they were operating with approximately stable numbers and composition. Flock and herd build-up phases have to be budgeted over a number of years for accurate comparisons between livestock activities. Once a relevant planning period for analysis is decided on, the flock or herd structure which will prevail in any year has to be worked through. Relevant parameters and prices have to be applied to the various animal types and classes comprising the flock or herd in any year. Genetic improvement over time can also be a factor to consider as it might affect reproductive performance or production per head.

Like planned crop rotations, in practice, planned 'stable' rotations of animals over time do not happen but are interrupted by uncertain real world phenomena such as market and seasonal fluctuations. A change in replacement policy has implications for the future age composition of the flock or herd and for the way the activity and other activities are conducted. In a breeding flock the number of animals in any particular age class that can be carried through the most limiting feed period is restricted by the number of stock in the immediately younger class coming forward; the number of these depends on the number of ewes in the breeding flock. There is thus interdependence between age classes. So a change in replacement policy has ramifications for the feed available for all the activities on the farm, and thus, for whole farm profitability.

Taxation is important in decisions about replacement. For tax purposes, natural increase of stock goes into the livestock trading accounts at concessional notional values decreed by the Commissioner of Taxation, or at some other value chosen by the farmer. Alternatively trading profit or loss is calculated on the basis of current market value of all numbers and classes of stock. For tax purposes trading profit or loss can be calculated on the basis of the change in average value of the animals from the start of the year to the end.

The use of concessional rates for natural increase understates the true animal income in any year, and defers the tax bill payable on some of the income produced by the activity until these concessionally valued animals are sold. Then, when sold, these are recorded as cash income and tax is paid on the difference between their book value and safe value.

With the alternative approach, using current market valuations for livestock, tax is paid on 'book' gains which may not be realized until animals are sold. In times of low inflation there is little difference in the amount of tax paid on animal activity income. Then the option to defer tax by using concessional values for livestock from self-replacing systems can be an attractive benefit. The option is less attractive if later, as a result of inflation, a higher rate of tax ends up being paid on the livestock income. The self-replacing system contrasts with a bought-in system which has greater cash sales and purchases in any year, and thus a higher current tax bill.

The economic concept underlying replacement decisions is that of maximizing average profit over time. In theory, it is possible to compare potential income streams from different replacement policies (akin to different crop rotations), and compare the net present values (NPVs) or annuities from each 'rotation' of animals. This is useful information to the extent that a stable rotation eventually occurs.

Costs and returns

In this section the main points about costs and returns are discussed.

To clearly demonstrate some economic principles which underlie all animal enterprises our discussion is confined to the 'simplest' animal system: steer-fattening lot-feeding. The two elements of a conversion mechanism, and feed, are involved.

Costs

The costs in a feeder situation, where cattle are bought-in, fattened and sold are overhead costs and variable costs. Variable costs include:

1 Feed costs, such as fertilizers, irrigation, supplementary feed, hay, and silage-making.
2 Running costs of plant, machinery, and casual labour used in feeding.
3 Husbandry and disease control: usually a constant charge per head for given

levels of stocking rate and animal throughput, increasing as both the stocking rate and throughput cost, and includes veterinary expenses, medicines, and vaccines.

4 Marketing changes (freight, commission, government levies, yard dues). For a given feed cost, husbandry and marketing charges tend to remain fairly constant per head. Their yearly total depends on the number of animals put through the feedlot, so they can be regarded as variable costs, i.e., costs which vary as throughput rises or falls.

Returns

To calculate the profit margin from feeding steers the initial purchase price of the stock is deducted from the gross income from sale of the fattened stock. The difference also covers loss through death.

For purposes of economic analysis it is convenient to subtract from this net gain the husbandry and marketing costs. We will call the figure so obtained 'the net value of animal product less husbandry and marketing charges' or 'net animal revenue'. The gross margin is calculated by subtracting feed costs from the 'net animal revenue' figure.

By using this modified expression of income or of gain from the feeding operation, we are able to broadly analyse any feeding operating as a one input–one output system. The overheads, since they remain constant, do not affect the point of maximum profitability, which is reached when extra costs are just slightly below extra returns. Modifying the income picture by deducting husbandry and marketing costs means that there are only three components for analysis, viz., overhead costs, feed costs, and 'net animal revenue'.

The output is controlled by the level of feed input. As the level of feed increases, the extra return per added unit of feed decreases. This is expected from the principle of diminishing returns (Figure 4.2).

Figure 4.2: Costs and returns in an animal activity

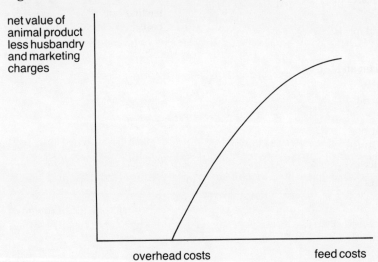

A stage is reached where the cost of an additional unit of feed is only slightly less than the value of the net animal product which resulted from it. This is the point of maximum profit, for a fixed level of overheads, i.e., where the $\dfrac{\text{extra return (ER)}}{\text{extra cost (EC)}}$ ratio is approximately equal to 1

Probably no livestock feeder in practice is in a position to organize the feed inputs such that $\dfrac{\text{ER}}{\text{EC}}$ is close to 1.

All livestock operations can be analysed in relation to the three components: overheads, feed, and 'net animal product less husbandry and marketing'. Once we leave the factory-type environment of the feedlot, the piggery, and the poultry farm, where the feed costs are readily identified, the problem of accurately defining the 'feed cost' figure for items such as pasture, silage, hay, and irrigation water arises. It is usually necessary to estimate the running costs of machinery involved in these operations, as well as the direct production costs. It is simplest where farmers use only maintenance dressings of fertilizer, (i.e., that level of fertilizer which maintains the pasture production at a constant level) and conserve their own fodder.

Direct feed costs are usually fairly easy to calculate. In most livestock enterprises these include the cost of buying supplementary feed and of growing and conserving pasture and fodder crops.

Table 4.1 contains the (1) feed and (2) husbandry and marketing costs for the main types of Australian animal production activities.

Table 4.1: Main cost items in animal systems

sheep	beef	dairy	poultry	pigs
feed				
fertilizer	(as for sheep)	(as for sheep)	bought feed	as for poultry
hay and silage			home-grown feed	
inventory decreases in stored feed			feeding-out costs	
grain, nuts and meals				
fodder crops				
allocatable plant and machinery costs				
licks and mineral additives				
agistment and grazing lease costs				
irrigation water				
feeding out cost				

continued

sheep	beef	dairy	poultry	pigs
husbandry and marketing				
shearing, crutching	bull replacement cost	running costs of milking sheds	medicines and disease control	as for poultry
dip, drench				
freight, levies, marketing	depreciation	veterinary and medicines	packing and preparation costs	
depreciation	freight, levies, marketing			
share of vehicle used in husbandry	share of vehicles used in husbandry	replacement rearing	marketing	
		bull or AI	freight, levies	
medicines and vet fees	medicine and vet fees	herd testing	flock replacement costs	
ram replacement costs		depreciation		
	anti-bloat measures	freight, levies, marketing		
		share of vehicle used in husbandry		

Note. deaths can be treated as either a cost or a loss of income

Fertilizer can present a problem in feed cost calculations. In the early years of pasture improvement much of the fertilizer cost could be regarded more as capital input than a maintenance cost. One convention treats the first three years' fertilizer as capital, the balance as maintenance. This convention is fairly useful in practice, although it takes no account of the different fertilizer needs of various soil types. Where the problem of allocation on a particular project or soil type is critical much more refinement is needed.

Agistment is readily identifiable as a feed cost; the cost of grazing leases is likewise easily isolated. In irrigation areas devoted to animal production, the cost of water, either bought direct from the irrigation authority or supplied from the farm's own pump, engine, etc., is part of the costs of producing feed for the animals and so this can be viewed as a feed cost.

With the exception of grossly under-stocked forage, the amount of feed supplied determines the level of output from a given animal-based system of feed conversion. The system of feed conversion using the same class of animal varies greatly. Thus, on similar pasture types, with comparable productivity, individual managers impose differing stocking rates and methods of supplementing seasonal pasture deficits.

However, once the conversion system begins to operate at reasonable levels of technical efficiency, feed input becomes the main determinant of output. By isolating the role of feed on output, farmers are in a position to use the principle of diminishing returns in determining the level to which funds should be spent on this item.

Gross margins of animal activities

The gross margin for an activity is the gross income made by that activity minus the variable costs incurred in earning the income from the activity. Gross margins are worked out per head for non-breeding activities. For breeding activities though, gross margins are worked out on a per breeding unit, or per herd unit basis. That is, the gross margin includes income from animal products and offspring, as well as costs associated with replacements and sires. The gross margin in this case is the difference between the total income derived from the breeding activity and the total variable costs associated with that breeding activity.

These are the main components of the variable costs of any animal activity:

1 Feed: maintenance costs of improved pastures, cost of forage, hay, straw, silage, purchased feed, home-grown grains, agistment, direct or casual labour costs.
2 Husbandry: medicines, cleaning materials for milking shed, contract plus casual labour, and services (veterinary, shearing).
3 Marketing: brokers' and agents' fees, transport, processing, and selling.

Expenditures on purchasing replacement stock (when not reared on the farm) are often included with variable costs in a gross margin calculation. This is done in order to capture the difference between sale value and purchase price, i.e., the depreciation cost, or appreciation. Depreciation is the relevant annual cost; the money spent to purchase replacements is a capital investment.

Animal income is made up of sales of animals, sales of animal products, sales of by-products, and inventory changes. In livestock activities, the change in value of the flock or herd because of a change in numbers or changes in animal class and age are an important part of the yearly profit. Increases in value of stock (appreciation) from changes in class through the year are also part of income produced by the animal activity. Alternatively, decreases in the value of animals (depreciation) from changes in class are a cost.

Example

The gross margin of any animal activity can be calculated as follows:

* sales of animals (animals produced for sale, not cast for age), and animal products;
* increase or decrease in value of stock on hand from change in stock numbers and classes from the start to the end of the year includes animals cast for age and replacement purchases. The values chosen here can have a major effect on income, e.g. if a current market value was unusually high or low. For this reason it is better to use the same value of similar stock at the start and at the end of the year;
* sales of animal by-products;
* the above points = gross income (A);
* cost of feed + cost of husbandry + cost of marketing (B);
* A − B = gross margin.

Cast for age and purchases, as well as inventory changes, are part of the calculation of gross margin. If the activity is not in a steady state then the profit components have to be separated from capital components of animal sales. All the receipts from cast-for-age breeding animals are not income produced by the farm. The receipts are mostly the conversion of an income-producing asset (the animal) into a different form of asset (cash). The reverse is true for cost of the purchased replacements. However the difference between purchase costs and selling price of animals is part of income earned (if animals have appreciated) or costs (if animals have depreciated), and this difference is thus part of operating profit. In the calculation of income from livestock, inventory values are adjusted for cast-for-age animals and for purchases of replacement, as well as for animals produced and retained on the farm. If there are more stock this year than last year, then the farmer has chosen to forego some of the potential cash income from the extra stock by retaining some which are normally sold.

Alternative methods of stock valuation can be used. A practical way is to use the same per head values of stock of the same class at the end of the year as at the beginning, i.e., ignore market influences. Then make a periodic revaluation of stock to account for market influence on stock values. The method of valuation chosen, be it market value or average cost or some other method, will all give quite different estimates of trading profit in any single year. Use of one method of valuation consistently means that assessed trading profit over time will be the same. Over a long time the effect of value chosen becomes less important. However, in a short time the effect of the valuation method, and the values used, can be so great that all the other numbers in the trading account become of little significance. If inventory values are to be included in a gross margin calculation, as necessary when herd or flock is expanding or declining, use the same values at start and end of year for particular classes of stock.

To estimate the activity gross margin from a steady state animal activity use cash sales which includes sales of cull animals, less variable costs less purchases for replacements. Short-term inventory changes are ignored, on the grounds that with a steady system, over time these changes cancel out. Mostly, in farm management planning, we are interested in both cash flows and longer term development planning. In either case, for a steady state gross margin and profit, annual inventory changes as a result of annual changes in animal age and class can be left out. Instead use net replacement cost (cast for age less replacement purchases) in the livestock gross margin calculation. Note that replacement of cast-for-age animals can involve a net cash cost or a net cash income, depending on whether the aged animals gain in value or depreciate as they age. Inventory changes within any year end up eventually as cash items when animals are sold and purchased.

With a self-replacing herd or flock, retained replacements are animals which could have been sold but are not. They are replacements for which no cash is spent, but cash is foregone from their potential sales. In this case, cash income from sales might appear to be overstated because part of total sales are the cast-for-age animals, which as mentioned above is equivalent to selling an asset, and is not produced income, and there is no apparent offsetting purchase of replacements. But sales resulting from cast-for-age animals being sold are not overstated. There is a hidden offset to the sales from cast-for-age animals. The total sales of animals has already been reduced by the value of the animals which were retained instead of being sold. Thus their 'purchase' cost has been incurred in the form of sales foregone.

So this is the gross margin of a steady state animal activity:

gross margin = gross income − variable costs − replacement purchases
where, gross income = sales of animal product + sales of animals produced during the year + sales of cast-for-age animals.

Gross margin: fat lamb activity

A flock of 100 Border Leicester × Merino ewes are mated to a prime lamb sire. Ewes lamb at two years' old, are kept for four lambings, and cfa at nearly 6 y.o. 100% lamb are weaned and sold. Ewe deaths are 2%. Replacement ewes are bought-in at about 1 y.o.

No account is taken of changes of inventory values of stock not sold during the year. Short-term changes can be transitory, and in a steady state flock changes in inventory values within a year balance out over time. Depreciation effects are captured by purchase price of replacements and cfa value four years later.

Fat lamb gross margin

wool:	$
gross income	
1,000 ewes at 4.5 kg greasy wool per head at $4.00 kg net of selling costs	18,000
cast for age:	
ewes: 1,000 − 2% deaths = 245 × $8	1,960
rams: 6 × $10 net of selling costs	60
1,000 lambs at $25 net of marketing costs	25,000
total gross income (A)	45,020
variable and replacement purchase costs	
shearing, crutching and shed costs at $4 per ewe	4,000
flock husbandry costs at $3.50 per ewe	3,500
ewe replacement: $\dfrac{1,000}{4}$ = 250 + 20 death replacements = 270 at $35	9,450
ram replacement: 6 at $250	1,500
total variable and replacement purchase costs (B)	18,450
activity gross margin (A − B)	26,570
GM per ewe	26.57

Gross margin: cattle activity

There are a total of 1,000 breeders (200 breeders aged 2 y.o., 200 breeders aged 3 y.o., 200 breeders aged 4 y.o., 200 breeders aged 5 y.o., and 200 breeders aged 6 y.o.) and 200 heifer replacements approaching 1 y.o. Therefore the herd consists of a total of 1,200 adult females. Ten cows in each of the 2 y.o. to 5 y.o. age groups (40 non-breeders) fail to get in calf and are culled. As well, two deaths occur in each of the 2–6 y.o. age groups (i.e., 10 deaths). Thus 50 mixed age replacements are purchased in calf or with calves at foot to keep herd numbers fairly constant and age composition in reasonable balance. For the 1,000 breeding cows a 98% weaning rate of calves is achieved, giving a total of 980 calves weaned. All 6 y.o. cows are culled, less two deaths (i.e., 198 cfa 6 y.o. cows are culled). Five bulls are culled and five bulls are purchased for the 25 bull herd. From the 980 calves weaned, 200 heifers are kept and the remaining 780 progeny (290 heifers and 490 steers) are sold as yearlings.

Cattle gross margin

	$
gross income	
sales: 780 heifers + steer yearlings at av. $280 per head net	218,400
198 cfa 6 y.o. cows at av. $350 per head net	69,300
40 cull cows at av. $350 per head net	14,000
5 cfa bulls at av. $350 per head	1,750
total gross income	303,450
variable and replacement purchase costs	
drench all females and 5 new bulls at $2 per head (1,200 + 980 + 50 + 5)	4,470
parasite control all animals at $1 per head × 2,235	2,235
veterinary at $3 per breeder ($3 × 1,000)	3,000
supplementary feed for breeders at $10 per head ($10 × 1,000)	10,000
purchases 50 mixed age breeders at av. $350 per head	17,500
purchases 5 bulls at av. $600 per head	3,000
total variable and replacement purchase costs	40,205
total gross margin	263,245
gross margin per breeder	263

Livestock trading schedule

A way of representing the dynamics and economics of animal flocks and herds is the livestock trading schedule. In a livestock trading schedule is recorded all the additions to and subtractions from the initial numbers and value of the animals in an activity for the period of interest (usually a year). A livestock trading schedule acts as a check on all of the movements into and out of an activity. It also acts as a record of changes in values of animals as they are born and age, bought, sold, through the year. The livestock trading schedule then forms the basis for calculating trading profit from the animals in the activity. When a herd or flock is in a build-up or reduction phase, the trading schedule identifies the income and cost components of the activity, as distinct from changes in the capital aspects of the flock or herd. This is done by subtracting from the total of sales, plus closing value on hand, the opening value plus purchases. Trading profit from animals plus animal product sold makes up total income from the activity.

A livestock trading schedule is shown below. In it is recorded:

• animal type and class;
• number and value at the start of the relevant period;
• births;
• purchase numbers and value;
• sales number and value;
• deaths and rations;
• transfers in and out of classes within an activity;
• transfers in and out of activities;
• numbers and value at end of period.

Example livestock trading schedule (wether flock)

| | A | | | B | |
	no.	value		no.	value
opening stock		$	sales		$
200 at 1, 2, 3, 4, 5 y.o.	1,000	20,000	cfa 6 y.o.	194	1,940
purchases			deaths	30	0
cfa replacements	194	5,820	rations	0	0
death replacements	30	900	transfers out	0	0
births	0	0			
transfers in	0	0			
no. unaccounted for	0	0			
			closing stock	1,000	20,000
totals	1,224	26,720 (A)		1,224	21,940 (B)

trading profit or loss (B − A)   (4,780)
(positive sum = profit, negative sum = loss)
(i.e. depreciation and death is
5820 + 900 − 1940 = 4780)

In this example there is a 1,000 head wether flock, of 200 head in each age group 1–5 y.o. At 6 y.o. wethers are culled for $10 per head. Replacements (1 y.o.) are bought for $30 per head. Some mixed age wethers are also bought to replace deaths and keep block numbers and age composition stable. The average value of the flock at start of year market prices is $20 per head. A loss on stock trading is incurred. This is because of animal depreciation and deaths. Culls sell for $10 per head and replacement costs $30 per head every five years then annual depreciation is $\dfrac{\$20}{5}$ = $4 per head.

This is the gross margin for the wether flock:

	$
gross income	
wool: 1,000 × 5 kg greasy × $6 net per kg	30,000
trading loss	4,780–
	25,220
variable costs	
husbandry $1 per head	1,000
shearing $3 per head	3,000
	4,000
activity GM	21,220
GM per head	21.22

For detailed analysis of changes to an animal production system, month-by-month livestock schedules can be set up on the computer spreadsheet. Livestock trading schedules on the spreadsheet can be adapted to capture the timing of events during the year, the timing of income and cost actions, activity gross margin per unit of feed, land and capital, the activity feed demands and cash flows through the year. In this way the dynamics and complementary effects of the operation of animal activities can be represented adequately. A model which uses the livestock schedule approach, and a computer spreadsheet, and puts together animal numbers, classes, changes, feed demand, gross margins, activity tasks, monthly cash flow, whole farm operating profit, net farm income, tax, and change in net worth, is shown later in this chapter in Table 4.6 (see p. 159). Such a model as shown in Table 4.6 is probably most needed for research purposes, but it can apply to analysis and understanding of any animal farm.

Feed supply and demand

Production of extra and better quality feed from pastures and fodder crops, especially at limiting periods of the feed year, is still the most important single technical measure available to most Australian livestock producers. For any age group of animals of similar breed, genotype, and stage of growth, which is receiving proper husbandry, and veterinary care and good grazing management, the major determinant of output will be the amount and quality of feed supplied in each season.

Knowledge of the energy requirements of livestock at the various stages of its productive cycle; of the economic outcome of failure to meet these requirements; and of the energy value of various classes of feed, reveals that a feed unit has a different economic value in each season of the year. The value is assigned according to its effect on the overall yearly economic performance of the animal which is being fed. Thus, an extra feed unit for a spring calving cow might have virtually zero value in late spring when feed is plentiful, but be worth a dollar in mid-winter when feed supply is limited. With a reasonable idea of the values of the feed at different times it is possible for farmers to calculate the upper limits they can afford to pay to supply feed at different times of the year to a herd or flock; whether from purchase, fodder conservation, fodder crops or fertilizer and pasture improvement. The value of extra feed depends on the amount which is produced and the contribution it makes to extra net activity profit. In turn this depends on the way in which the whole animal system operates, and the value of the extra production gained, or losses prevented, which is attributable to the extra feed. Further, the value of such gains depends on uncertain future prices.

In assessing the value of extra feed made available by a change in the operation of the animal, pasture and supplementary feed system, allowance also has to be made for the possibility of compensatory and substitution effects on animal performance. For instance, animals that lose weight in the minimum feed period might compensate by growing more rapidly in the feed surplus period than if they were fed better in the minimum feed period. Alternatively, an animal provided with extra feed, such as dairy cows fed in the bail, might respond by substitution of the supplementary feed for grazing pasture. This results in less use of pasture, and deterioration in pasture quality.

An aspect often overlooked of increasing stocking rate is the way that intensification of production can increase risk, and thus the associated costs of risk. All risk has a cost. Higher stocking rates mean that feed shortages and drought arrives sooner, or are more likely, than with less intensive stocking of pastures. Conversely, low stocking rates greatly increase the risk of pasture quality deteriorating and total feed supply declining. Probably more pastures are ruined by understocking than by overstocking.

Some people believe that the extra animals and the pre-existing animals consume the same proportion of available grass after the increase in numbers as they did before the herd or flock increase. In practice, as stocking rate increases so too will percentage of pasture use. The pasture composition changes as stocking rate increases. Thus the eventual change over time in animal performance per head over the whole flock or herd depends on the number of extra animals, the changes in pasture use by the animals, the change induced in the pasture itself, and the weather. The key point is that pasture helps determine animal production and animal production helps determine pasture production.

Substitution rates between types and classes of animals in relation to feed requirements is an idea which is often misused. For instance, it is common for farmers and advisers to rate one breeding cow grazing pasture as the equivalent of, or substitute for the equivalent of 12 to 18 dry sheep, depending on breed of cattle and the production system. The proviso is 'at a fully stocked stocking rate in which the animals are competing in earnest for feed'. It is only when substitution rates are expressed accounting for existing numbers and types of animals that there is any sense to substitution rates. For example, at some stocking rates of sheep, with no cattle, and at which pasture is relatively abundant, the initial substitution rate of cattle for sheep may be zero. An extra steer might be added without removing any sheep, because the extra steer might graze pasture of a species or stage of growth which the sheep would not use at this stocking rate; as well it might not compete for labour required for the sheep activity, and sufficient cattle might contribute to parasite control by enabling sheep-free areas on the farm for portions of the year. Extra investment in livestock capital would be required. At a higher stocking rate of sheep with no cattle, the substitution rate might be one steer for the equivalent of five dry sheep, as complementary grazing habits of sheep and cattle are further exploited. At an even higher stocking rate of sheep, and with a small proportion of cattle using all of the pasture available because of different grazing habits, and allowing for pasture changes because of higher stocking rates, then an extra head of cattle might require a reduction of the equivalent of 12 to 15 dry sheep. Under an even more intensive stocking rate, in which all the complementary advantages have been exploited, for the last cow to be added might require a reduction of 20 dry sheep.

Such complementary effects can apply to any resource. Labour supply at a certain time of the year might be the factor limiting the expansion of sheep numbers. Non-breeding cattle could be added if the labour requirements are at different times of the year than is the case with sheep. Another example of a complementary effect is where a small cattle activity complements a major sheep activity by enabling at least one paddock at any time to be devoted to non-sheep grazing; the cattle thereby playing a critical role in management for control of worm build-up.

Note that as stocking rates go up resources and considerations other than pasture production also assume increasing importance. Examples are labour requirements, disease control and risk. An important consideration is the extra risk costs which will arise as stocking rate goes up. These costs are for extra supplementary feed, or an increased cash 'drought reserve'. Heavier stocking rate changes the composition and life of a pasture, at times for better, at times for worse, depending on the initial season and subsequent seasons.

Animals, pasture, and economic thinking

The classic model of the animal–pasture complex, shown in Figure 4.3 emphasizes the role of time and timing of grazing inputs and outputs, and the consequent and dynamic interactions between animals and pasture. Also livestock decide how much of which feed they will eat. This characteristic is not trivial.

Figure 4.3: The animal–pasture complex

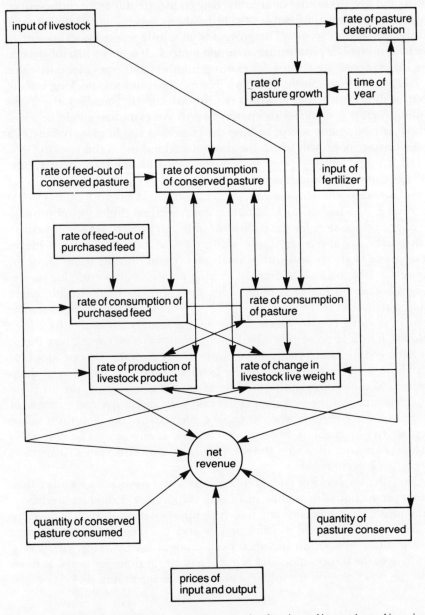

Source. J. L. Dillon and H. T. Burley, A note on the economics of grazing and its experimental investigation, *Australian Journal of Agricultural Economics*, 5(1), 1961.

There are two key points: there is an infinite assortment of possible sequences of timings of the many inputs to production and ultimately to net revenue, including numerous uncertain variables such as rainfall, sunshine, soil nutrients, and prices. Each sequence of events resulting in output and net revenue adds up to a distinct grazing system; the grazing complex involves interdependent phenomena. Livestock influences pasture composition and production and pasture consumed influences livestock production. Therefore realistic approaches to analysing grazing must allow for simultaneous determination of some variables. For example, matching feed supply and demand through the year has to take account that some of a surplus in feed supply in one period can be carried over into the next phase. Increased feed demand in a period affects the carryover into the next period, which eventually affects the carryover in the following year into the equivalent period in which the initial increase in stocking rate took place.

Gross margin and stocking rate

Production per animal is affected by the amount of feed available per head, which decreases as heavier stocking rates are reached. This is partly countered up to a point by improvements in the quality of feed because of the pasture responding to the heavier stocking rate. The response of increasing stocking rate can be linear over quite a range of stocking rates if pasture production growth responds sufficiently. Eventually a stage is reached where there are too many animals competing for feed and output and revenue per head and revenue per ha declines. Costs also increase. For example, supplementary feed costs per head will increase as stocking rate increases.

As stocking rate increases total gross margin per ha passes maximum and declines. Declining rates of extra production per ha as stocking rate increases, and extra costs and the costs of risk associated with higher stocking rates (greater health problems, more supplementary feed, earlier drought) will cause the rate of increase in total gross margin per ha to decline. (See the following figures.)

These figures illustrate the important point that maximum gross margin per head is unlikely to equate to maximum gross margin per ha. This is so for a number of reasons. Up to some stocking rate reductions in production per head are outweighed by increases in total production per ha. When hectares of feed is the limiting factor then output and profit from areas of land are of interest. If land were plentiful and labour to manage animals was the factor which limited production, then it would make sense to focus on gross margin per unit of labour.

The dry sheep equivalent (dse) or livestock unit (lsu)

To calculate animal feed demand it is necessary to break the animal production year into a number of sub-periods, such as non-pregnant, early and late pregnancy, lactating, growing, post-weaning, fattening. In practice these demands have to be matched with the feed supply. A common practice is to compare the total feed needs of various classes of animals in terms of the maintenance feed needs of a 45 kg (sometimes 48 kg) bodyweight grazing wether for a year. This unit is termed the 'dry sheep equivalent' (dse) or the livestock unit (lsu). Thus, a crossbred ewe rearing a lamb for sale at five months might be rated as having an annual feed requirement equal to that of 1.66 or 2 dse, a 320 kg steer growing slowly may be rated as equivalent to 8 dse and so on.

Figure 4.4a: Stocking rate and gross margin (GM) per ha

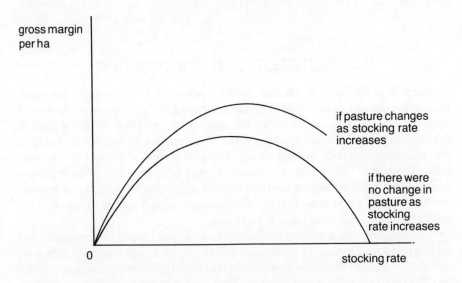

Figure 4.4b: Output per head and stocking rate

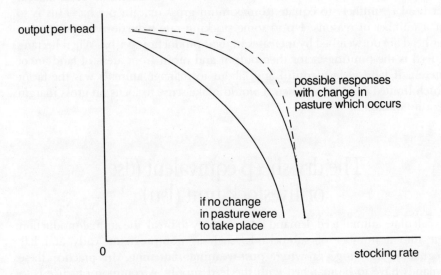

Stocking rate and supplementary feed costs

Figure 4.5a: Stocking rate and supplementary feeding

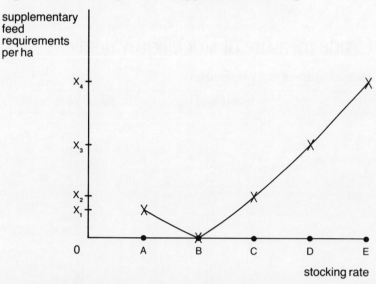

Note. At a very low stocking rate (SR) A; X_1 supplementary feed cost.
At (SR) B; no supplementary feed cost because the pasture has improved with increased stocking rate.
At (SR) C; X_2 supplementary feed cost.
At (SR) D; supplementary feed costs increase markedly to X_3.
Beyond (SR) D; supplementary feed makes up a lot of the total feed supplied.

Figure 4.5b: Gross margin (GM) per ha, stocking rate and supplementary feed

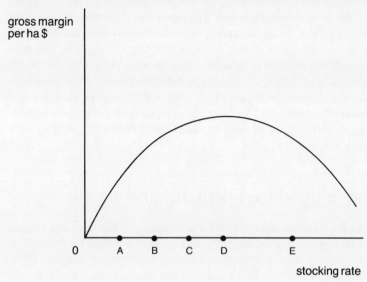

Some suggested dse ratings are given in Table 4.2. In predominantly dairy, beef cattle or fat lamb areas, the relevant measures might be the feed requirements of a milking cow unit, breeding beef cow, and ewe unit, respectively.

Crude measure of stock equivalents

Table 4.2: Crude measure of stock equivalents

	bodyweight (kg)	dse or lsu rating
sheep		
ewe	40	1.33
	47	1.50
	53	1.66
	63	1.83
wether	48	1.00
	53	1.16
weaner	27	0.90
ram	56	1.20
dairy		
Jersey cow	364	13.00
Friesian cow	545	15.00
beef		
beef breeder	455	11.00
weaner	204	5.80
steer yearling	318	6.65
two-year-old	386	7.50

Stock equivalent tables such as Table 4.2 have limited use. For example, it is common in farm management analysis to compare profits of various classes of livestock on a dse or lsu basis. However, this type of analysis does not account well for differences in the detail of animal reproduction systems and for feed demand by different types and classes of stock varying throughout the year, depending on stage of pregnancy, lactation, and growth. The 1.66 dse or lsu rating accorded to ewes in Table 4.2 is based on total feed demand for the whole year, rather than the demand at a particular time. Of interest to management is the feed demand of animals and feed supply at a particular stage of a season. Feed requirements and supply of feed to meet these requirements can vary markedly through the year.

More refined feed demand and supply

A refinement of annual stock equivalents for assessing feed demand and supply emphasises the energy needed by animals and energy supplied by feeds. It is important to remember that a complete animal ration must contain fibre, protein, minerals and vitamins. But energy is the major item. Details of the specific requirements of these nutrients for various animal functions are found in textbooks and pamphlets on animal nutrition.

Energy is required for the maintenance of normal body functions, as well as for exercise, growth, pregnancy, lactation, and environmental stress. Knowledge of the energy needs of animals for their various functions is well defined. One practical difficulty is that the energy used by animals varies depending on the quality of the feed they are consuming. Thus, energy requirements have to be specified in terms of particular feed qualities. Algebraic equations for animal energy requirements are readily available. The metabolizable energy (me) system is used in Australia to express the energy content of feeds. Metabolizable energy is the portion of total feed supply which can be used by the animal. It is the energy available for metabolic processes including maintenance, growth, and milk production after energy used in the production of urine, gas, and faeces has been counted. (Note that these are only approximations of requirements, often with some feed and metabolic interactions 'assumed away'.) The standard measure of energy is megajoules (MJ) of metabolizable energy (me) per unit of dry matter (dm).

Rickards and Passmore (1977) developed a system which allows livestock demand and feed supply to be measured on a common basis. It is known as the livestock month (lsm) system. An lsm is the amount of feed required to maintain one 48 kg dry sheep (called a 'livestock unit') for one month, grazing medium-quality pasture. (A similar term sometimes used is dry sheep month.) The bodyweight of any type of livestock largely determines their energy needs. To the basic maintenance requirements, expressed in lsm, has to be added allowances for gestation, lactation, exercise, quality of feed, and rate of weight gain. Part of the energy required by the livestock unit is used in walking and an exercise factor of from 20% to 40% is added to the basic maintenance energy requirements of a livestock unit in a stall or small pen. As well, digestion of one kg of dry matter of poor or medium-quality feed requires more energy expenditure by the animal consuming it than does one kg of dry matter of high quality feed such as young green pasture or concentrates or grain. So it is necessary to specify the feed type when defining the energy needed by an lsu to maintain itself for a month.

Exercise levels vary from 15% for lot-fed animals, to 35% under average grazing conditions, and 60% for sparse feed with harsh climatic conditions. To calculate the requirements for any given animal, there are tables in Rickards and Passmore (1977), which show the energy requirement in lsms for different exercise requirements and feed qualities, for:

- maintenance;
- pregnancy;
- lactation;
- weight gain (or loss).

One lsm represents the following amount of energy:

energy requirement for 48 kg wether fasting metabolism (me) × maintenance factor × exercise factor for medium quality pasture × 30 days

4,213 kJ $\times$ 1.47 $\times$ 1.35 $\times$ 30
= 250,821 kJ
= 251 MJ
= about 8 MJ of me per day

A dry 450 kg cow on medium-quality pasture, with a 35% exercise allowance, requires about 8 lsms of energy per month, or about 67 MJ of me per day (i.e., $8 \times \dfrac{251}{30}$).

The feed requirements for one month in lsms of a 450 kg bodyweight dairy cow, grazing medium quality feed, with an exercise factor of 35%, producing 13.5 L (3 gal.) of 4% milk, two months after calving (thus not pregnant) is calculated as follows:

	lsms
maintenance requirement	7.8
lactation requirement	7.9
pregnancy	0
total	15.7

Similarly, the lsm requirement of a 450 kg bodyweight beef cow, on good feed, with an exercise factor of 35%, one month before calving:

	lsms
maintenance requirement	7.3
pregnancy	3.6
total	10.9

lsm content of common feeds

Table 4.3: lsm content of common feeds

feed	description	approx. % of dry matter	approx. lsm of energy per 1,000 kg (normal range) fresh wt	dry wt	class of feed
roughages					
cereal straws	with no grain matter	90	26–30	28–33	poor
pasture hay	little leafy material	90	30–35	33–37	"
native pasture	no green pick	87	30–35	33–37	"
cereal stubbles	with green pick	87	28–35	33–37	"
pasture hay	fair quality	90	33–35	35–37	medium
native pasture	good condition	80	35–37	37–40	"

continued

feed	description	approx. % of dry matter	approx. lsm of energy per 1,000 kg (normal range)		class of feed
			fresh wt	dry wt	
sown pasture	poor–fair	80	35–37	37–40	medium
hay	good quality	90	35–37	37–40	"
succulents					
good pasture	short and leafy	25	9–12	37–47	good
maize,	actively growing	"	"	"	"
sorghum,	"	"	"	"	"
millets, oats,	"	"	"	"	"
wheat, barley,	"	"	"	"	"
rye, lucerne,	"	"	"	"	"
cowpeas	"	25	9–12	35–47	"
clover	"	20	7–9	35–47	"
cereal by-products					
wheat pollard		90	44	49	good
wheat bran		90	39	44	"
oat bran		90	39	44	"
grains					
wheat	suitably crushed	88	49	56	concentrate
barley	"	88	47	53	"
maize	"	88	51	58	"
oats	"	88	44	49	"
grain sorghum	"	88	47	53	"
protein rich meals					
meat		90	46	51	"
fish		90	46	51	"
meat and bone		90	40	44	"
peanut		90	46	51	"
cotton seed		90	42	46	"
linseed		90	46	51	"

Source. Rickards and Passmore (1977), 'Planning for Profit in Livestock Grazing Systems', *Professional Farm Management Guidebook No. 7.*

Similarly, an average seasonal feed supply in lsms for a good pasture in the Gippsland dairying area of Victoria is as follows:

	autumn (Mar. Apr. May)	winter (Jun. Jul. Aug.)	spring (Sep. Oct. Nov.)	summer (Dec. Jan. Feb.)
lsms per ha	66	19	110	57

The cow day (cd), another feed unit

In dairying, a convenient unit to measure stock requirements and feed supply is the cow day (cd). A cow day is the amount of feed required by a medium-sized Friesian cow to produce 1 kg of butterfat per day in early lactation. For green, succulent ryegrass and white clover pasture this amounts to 60 kg of pasture green matter, or 15 kg dry matter with 10.8 MJ of metabolizable energy per kg of dry matter. Here are some typical estimates of dairy feed requirements for dairy cattle:

feed requirements	no change body condition (cds)
cow in full milk producing 1 kg butterfat per day in early lactation	1
late in lactation	$2/3$
backward dry cow	$1/3$
springing Heifer	$1/2$
yearling	$1/4$
annual requirements	
42 weeks @ 1 cd	294
4 weeks @ $2/3$ cd	19
6 weeks @ $1/3$ cd	14
	327

Approximately 300 cds equal 4,500 kg good quality dm
330 cds equal 5,000 kg good quality dm.

These estimated cow day (cd) requirements assume that body condition is constant. Here are some estimates of feeding value, in cow days, of different feed sources:

feed	unit	cow day
good ryegrass and clover	15 kg	1
hay	25 kg bale	1
silage	1 t	10
oats	1 t	64
barley	1 t	68
wheat	1 t	62
N fertilizer (response 10 kg dm to 1 kg N)		
urea	1 t	330
nitram	1 t	240
S of A	1 t	140
fodder crop		
chou mollier	50 t per ha	550
rape	30 t per ha	450
forage oats	200 bale per ha	400

Estimating lsm feed from pasture and forage crops is often more difficult to determine than feed demand because of lack of data. In Table 4.3 is shown the lsm content of some common feeds. To use such a table as this the quantities of the various feeds produced on the farm have to be known. Specific data is not usually available. But the known grazing performance of the different farm areas and pastures on a farm can be converted into 'apparent' lsms supplied. Then judgements need to be made about how well the past pasture production and the known grazing performance (paddock days grazing by various classes of stock) can indicate the expected pasture production for the current planning period. In particular the magnitude of the surpluses and deficits, and the mechanisms and amounts of feed carryover between months and seasons need to be known.

Grazing and cutting trials are important sources of information, and increasingly devices are becoming available to assist in measuring and estimating feed quantity and quality. However, the experience of observant managers of individual properties is still the most important source of basic data for planning systems of livestock feeding and management of any particular farm.

Feed budgeting

In Table 4.4 is an example of a budget of feed transfer.

Autumn and winter are the most limiting periods of feed. Demand for feed is such that feed available in these periods is fully used as well as the feed carried over from the previous time. Now, what about attempting to lessen the effect of the feed limit in autumn? First, the current stock numbers in autumn are based on the current numbers in spring and summer leaving a surplus. Some of this surplus feed is already being transferred into the autumn and consumed by the existing stock. Any attempt to increase feed supply and stocking rate in autumn has to take into consideration that, unless these extra animals are removed before the winter, extra stock numbers in winter will also require extra feed.

Once this change in feed supply and increased stocking rate is established and with no consequent change in pasture production from the overall higher stocking rate, a feed shortage still occurs in autumn and, now, in summer as well. Other steps need to be taken, such as a fodder crop, agistment, or earlier turn off of stock, to reduce the feed deficiencies in autumn and summer.

This example shows how the feed supply through the year can be affected by actions at any time within the year. It is vital to account for this when planning a change in the animal production system. This type of feed budgeting as shown in Tables 4.4 and 4.5, though relatively crude, is informative.

Table 4.4: Example of a budget feed transfer—lsms of feed fully used

time	spring	summer	autumn	winter	spring
feed produced per ha	60	20	15	30	60
feed available per ha	60	28	17.4	30	60
feed demand per ha	40	22	17	30	40
feed surplus per ha	+20	+6	0	0	+20
feed carryover	8	2.4	0	0	8
(40% of surplus)					

Table 4.5: Feed and supply demand after a change: extra 10 lsms supply and demand in autumn and winter

time	spring	summer	autumn	winter	spring
feed produced per ha lsms before change	60	20	15	30	60 (from Table 4.4)
feed available per ha before change	60	28	17.4	30	60 (from Table 4.4)
feed produced per ha lsms after change	60	20	25	40	60
feed available per ha after change	60	24	25	40	60
feed demand	50	32	27	40	50
feed surplus per ha or deficit per ha	+10	−8	−2	0	+10
feed carryover per ha (40% of surplus)	4	0	0	0	4

One of the most important changes in an animal production system which warrants consideration is the timing of lambing and calving. A change from spring to autumn lambing transfers feed demand for lactation from the spring to the autumn, and changes peak feed requirements for pregnancy from winter to late summer and early autumn. The implications for resources on the farm other than feed may well prevent a change even though it is sound in terms of feed supply and demand. For instance the changed labour requirements might cause an excessive demand for labour because of, say, cropping requirements in the autumn. Additional feed and drought costs could be prohibitive. Always an expected change in weaning performance is a critical factor in evaluating the worth of such a change.

Variations and uncertainty about feed supply

Knowing the feed requirements of the various classes of stock and estimating the feed available on a particular property is the essence of feed budgeting. Comparisons of feed supply and feed demand indicate likely supplementary feed requirements, and hence alternative management strategies. As expected feed supply is based on average expected yields, and as the average year never occurs, it is essential that there be flexibility, in cash reserves, high equity (and thus access to credit), fodder reserves or readily saleable trading livestock, to cope satisfactorily with climatic variations.

There are many strategies for farmers confronting the problem of planning for uncertain seasonal feed supply. A flexible stocking policy allows the sale or purchase of a buffer group of animals (dry ewes, wethers, dry heifers, steers) according to seasonal feed supply. Fear of introducing disease and shortage of capital for short-term trading could act as restraints on this strategy, but there is considerable practical merit. The conventional wisdom of 'sell, prepare to repent, but sell early' indicates that this strategy has been adopted by many farmers with satisfactory results.

Fodder can be conserved in periods of feed surplus for feeding in periods of feed deficit, depending mainly on the length and frequency of bad seasons, and on the cost of conserving and storing feed, and the price to which feed rises during poor seasons.

Calving, lambing, lactation, buying and selling times can be arranged so that animal demand matches, as closely as possible, the expected feed supply. This will mean that the period of minimum expected feed demand matches the period of minimum expected feed supply. Feed deficits can be handled in the following ways:

* supplementary feed;
* reduce stock numbers (the success of this tactic depends mainly on keeping the animals in good, readily saleable condition);
* use the fat reserve of the animals as a partial reserve of energy during the period of the feed deficit.

When the feed supply in a given time exceeds the expected quantity required by the animals it can be used:

* to feed to existing stock to improve bodyweight;
* to feed to extra stock;
* or conserved;
* or carried over into the following period, with some loss of feed quality.

No tactic or combination of tactics can be applied generally for different areas and seasons. Each case differs. However, it is worth stressing the need for flexibility.

Use of purchased feedstuffs

Commercial and home-mixed feed compounds enable a range of high quality feeds to be directed to the specific nutritional requirements of each stage of livestock growth. Animals in the intensive industries are more efficient converters of feed than animals in extensive situations. Their rations also have a higher energy and lower fibre content than adult sheep and cattle rations, making these rations less costly to transport per unit of food. In the grazing industry purchased feedstuffs are used mainly to fill seasonal feed gaps. It is a characteristic of the more intensively stocked grassland properties that they become progessively more dependent on outside feed. As a general rule, in the better rainfall areas it is more profitable to stock to the point where most seasonal deficiencies are filled with purchased feed than it is to understock in order to rely on carryover or conserved feed to fill annual seasonal deficiencies.

One source of economic loss on livestock farms is from slow or retarded growth of young animals, especially females, caused by inadequate or unbalanced feed. This leads to a delayed breeding performance and often lower lifetime productivity. Expenditure on appropriate supplementary feed with the aim of producing good early growth rates can be very profitable when viewed from the lifetime performance of the animal. Expenditure on supplementary irrigation, for strategic use during critical times of the feed year, is another application of the same principle.

Irrigation

Here is a list of the main technical advances in irrigation:

- a reduction in the labour component involved in applying water to pasture and crops by replacing labour with capital investment;
- plant, structures and timing devices designed to automate the process and deliver water with greater precision;
- devices which indicate when pastures and crops require irrigation so that maximum benefit is received from the watering;
- more use of strategic applications of key fertilizers such as nitrogen on pastures and crops. This permits greater exploitation of favourable temperature and moisture conditions.

The development of supplementary irrigation on natural rainfall grazing or dairy properties is expensive. The opportunity cost of capital spent on such projects is often high when alternative uses for the funds are considered. Better pastures, higher stocking rates and better systems of using pastures are some of the options.

However, investment in supplementary irrigation projects can be profitable when quality feed production is low on the rest of the property, but the feed has to be used in activities which have a high extra return per hectare of irrigated pasture. Examples are finishing quality lambs or vealers, or producing for an out-of-season market, or growing replacement breeding stock to maturity rapidly, or finishing stud sires. The value of a unit of feed varies according to the season of the year because it can have a range of effects on animal performance and total gross margin and operating profit. Thus extra feed produced by irrigation can have a range of values.

Example of livestock schedule linking stock numbers, cash flows, gross margins, operating profit and feed supply and demand on a monthly basis

This model incorporates the livestock schedule, GMs, monthly cash flows, operating profit, and monthly feed supply and demand. It needs to be worked through step by step. Being a model used on the computer spreadsheet it is ideal for exploring how a change in one aspect of the livestock activity, such as lambing or calving, or time of turn off affects cash flows, feed supply and demands, activity GMs, and, ultimately, the key measure, operating profit after the change.

Table 4.6: Monthly analysis of animal activity (condensed example)

time: 1 April   enterprise: Merino ewes   comments: young ewes back from Horsham, drench weaners, crutch ewes

class	opening no.	value $	transfers in	transfers out	births	deaths	purchases no.	purchases $ per hd	purchases total $	sales no.	sales $ per hd	sales total $	closing no.	lsm per hd	total lsm	cash flow $	drench no.	drench $ per hd	drench total $	crutch no.	crutch $ per hd	crutch total $	suppl feed no.	suppl feed $ per hd	suppl feed total $
under 1 y.o. F	600	17				2			0			0	599	1.0	599		600	0.20	120						
1 y.o. ewes	0	0				0			0			0	0	1.0	0										
2 y.o. ewes	375	30				1			0			0	374	1.0	374					375	0.44	165			
3 y.o. ewes	375	30				1			0			0	374	1.0	374					375	0.44	165			
4 y.o. ewes	375	30				1			0			0	374	1.0	374					375	0.44	165			
5 y.o. ewes	375	15				0			0			0	374	1.0	374					375	0.44	165			
wet ewes						0			0			0	0		0										
lambs						0			0			0	0		0										
	2,100	49,575	0	0	0	6	0		0	0		0	3,095		2,095	−4,780	600		120	1,500		660	0		4,000

time: 7 October   enterprise: Merino ewes   comments: mark, drench & mules lambs, shear 1 y.o.s

class	opening no.	value $	transfers in	transfers out	births	deaths	purchases no.	purchases $ per hd	purchases total $	sales no.	sales $ per hd	sales total $	closing no.	lsm per hd	total lsm	cash flow $	mark, mules, vacc, eartag, ring no.	$ per hd	total $	drench no.	drench $ per hd	drench total $	shear no.	shear $ per hd	shear total $	income shear no.	kg per hd	total kg	$ per kg	total $
under 1 y.o. F	0	0				0			0			0	0		0															
1 y.o. ewes	591					1			0			0	590	1.0	590								591	2.00	1,182	591	3.00	1,773	6.00	10,639
2 y.o. ewes	73					0			0			0	73	1.0	73															
3 y.o. ewes	73					0			0			0	73	1.0	73															
4 y.o. ewes	73					0			0			0	73	1.0	73															
5 y.o. ewes	73					0			0			0	73	1.0	73															
wet ewes	1,185					3			0			0	1,182	1.6	1,891															
lambs	1,185					5			0			0	1,180		0		1,185	0.75	889	1,185	0.05	59								
	3,254	0	0	0	0	9	0		0	0		0	3,244		2,773	−2,130	1,185		889	1,185		59	591		1,182	591		1,773		10,639

continued

time: 12 March   enterprise: Merino ewes   comments: transfer young wethers to wether flock, transfer in young ewes from stud, sell young ewes, agist weaners, shear cull ewes

class	opening no.	value $	transfers in	transfers out	births	deaths	purchases no.	purchases $ per hd	purchases total $	sales no.	sales $ per hd	sales total $	closing no.	closing lsm per hd	total lsm	cash flow $	agistment no.	agistment $ per hd	agistment total $	shear no.	shear $ per hd	shear total $	income no.	income kg per hd	income kg	income $ per kg	income total $
under 1 y.o. mkf	1,164			582		3	0		0	544	20	10,874	579	0.0	0		1,164	1.30	1,514	544	2.00	1,087	544	1.50	816	6.00	4,893
1 y.o. ewes	584	17	367			1	0		0			0	0	1.0	0	406	350	1.30	455								
2 y.o. ewes	365	30				1	0		0			0	406	1.0	406	364											
3 y.o. ewes	365	30				1	0		0			0	364	1.0	364	364											
4 y.o. ewes	365	30				1	0		0			0	364	1.0	364	364											
5 y.o. ewes	1	15				0	0		0			0	364	1.0	364	364											
wet ewes	0					0	0		0			0	0		0	0											
lambs	0					0	0		0			0	0		0	0											
	0					0	0		0			0	0		0	0											
	0					0	0		0			0	0		0	0											
	0					0	0		0			0	0		0	0											
	0					0	0		0			0	0		0	0											
	2,843	49,318	367	582	0	7	0		0	544		10,874	2,077		1,498	12,711	1,514		1,969	544		1,087	544		816		4,893

feed demand—Merino ewes

month	lsm
1 April	2,095
2 May	2,090
3 June	2,233
4 July	2,376
5 August	2,518
6 September	2,780
7 October	2,773
8 November	2,766
9 December	2,857
10 January	1,332
11 February	1,328
12 March	1,498
total enterprise feed demand	26,645
total enterprise dses	2,220

gross margin—Merino ewes

		$
gross income	wool—shearing and crutching (total kg) 13,894	83,365
	trading profit	13,161
		96,527
variable costs	shearing	7,605
	crutching	660
	drenching and jetting	1,740
	mark, mules, eartag, ring	889
	vaccination	119
	supplementary feed	4,000
	agistment	5,910
		20,923
	gross margin	75,603
	GM per dse	34
	GM per $100 capital	153
	GM per breeding unit	48

annual trading schedule—Merino ewes

item	no.	value $	item	no.	value $
opening no.	2,100	49,575	sales	910	14,541
purchases	0	0	deaths	83	
between enterprise transfers in	367	11,021	between enterprise transfers out	582	9,898
births	1,185		killed		
trading profit		13,161	closing no.	2,077	49,318
				3,652	73,757

continued

whole farm feed demand

month	lsm
1 April	7,242
2 May	7,246
3 June	7,556
4 July	7,805
5 August	8,457
6 September	8,306
7 October	8,598
8 November	8,569
9 December	8,659
10 January	6,364
11 February	5,944
12 March	5,867
total farm feed demand	90,614
total farm dse's	7,551

depreciation schedule

item	opening value	rate %	amount	closing value
tractor	40,000	15.0	6,000	34,000
drill	20,000	12.0	2,400	17,600
sprayer	8,000	10.0	800	7,200
post driver	3,000	10.0	300	2,700
cost feeder	1,000	8.0	80	920
auger	1,000	8.0	80	920
land cruiser	20,000	15.0	3,000	17,000
wool press	3,000	5.0	150	2,850
tables	4,000	5.0	200	3,800
portable yards	3,000	5.0	150	2,850
	$103,000		$13,160	$89,840

(summary)

	11.3 dse per ha	4.5 dse per acre
total farm stocking rate		
total farm wool production	34,295 kg	
total farm gross margin	$266,846	
operating profit	$150,786	
total capital		
land and buildings	1,500,000	
plant	96,420	
livestock	308,699	
	$1,905,119	
return to total capital	7.9%	

unallocated variable costs

	annual	April	May	June	July	August	September	October	November	December	January	February	March
seed and fertilizer	12,000		12,000										
total	12,000	0	12,000	0	0	0	0	0	0	0	0	0	0

overhead costs

	annual	April	May	June	July	August	September	October	November	December	January	February	March
fuel	5,000	417	417	417	417	417	417	417	417	417	417	417	417
repairs and maintenance	15,000	1,250	1,250	1,250	1,250	1,250	1,250	1,250	1,250	1,250	1,250	1,250	1,250
rates	3,200												3,200
insurance	3,500							3,500					
registrations	500							500					
accountant	500											500	
power and phone	4,000			1,000			1,000			1,000			1,000
wages and casual labour	19,200	1,600	1,600	1,600	1,600	1,600	1,600	1,600	1,600	1,600	1,600	1,600	1,600
total		3,267	3,267	4,267	3,267	3,267	4,267	7,267	3,267	4,267	3,767	3,767	7,467

depreciation—plant	13,160
operator's allowance	40,000
total	104,000

monthly cumulative net cash flow*

April	-17,772
May	-57,519
June	-62,162
July	-3,432
August	-34,438
September	-40,902
October	1,392
November	54,508
December	47,239
January	51,173
February	50,230
March	100,280

* Cash flow includes interest, principal and tax.

Source. This livestock management model was constructed by David Honybun of the Agricultural Economics Section, School of Agriculture, University of Melbourne.

The detail contained in this model is relevant for research purposes such as where an agricultural scientist wishes to appraise the likely effects of a technical change to an annual production system, like the impact of change in timing of lambing or lambing percentage on feed demand and supply.

Animal breeding

In animal improvement the focus is on environmental constraints. In discussing genetics it is important to remember that much of the variation in production characters observed in farm animals is a result of environmental effects. People involved in animal breeding for genetic improvement sometimes confuse the gains coming from environmental improvement with genetic gains. Animal feeding and management have more influence than the manipulation of animal genes. The adage 'half the breeding goes down the throat', sums up much past experience with breeding programs.

Through selection animals become adapted to their environment, and perform up to the limits on reproductive performance which are set by the environment. Ultimately the scope for exploiting unused potential genetic gain depends on changes to the production environment which partly remove the environmental limits to performance, thereby increasing the scope for genetic gain. Because of the related effects between performance traits at any time and over time, lifetime reproduction performance is the critical indicator of reproduction. Orthodox genetic theory and analyses involve assumptions which reduce the relevance of quantitative genetics to practical animal breeding. This is the theory argued by Dr R. G. Beilharz of the School of Agriculture and Forestry, University of Melbourne.

As the genetic worth of the animals change through breeding, different environmental limiting factors come into play. These continually constrain performance. The production of genetically superior animals does not increase unhindered simply because of improvement in one part of the animal's potential capacity. Instead, as production increases occur, new environmental constraints are met. Thus key factors to consider in improvement of animal performance are the extent to which the environmental and management constraints are able to be eased.

In any given environment there are two ways of breeding livestock with superior production characteristics, viz:

• selecting within a given population or breed;
• crossbreeding.

The second method is the method chosen by farmers who have relatively small numbers of animals and by many owners of large flocks or herds who find that they can make a good deal more money by crossbreeding the poorer one-third of their females than by straight-breeding. It is this method that gives the quickest gains.

Some simple population genetics

Genes occur in all cells of an animal's body on chromosomes. The chromosomes are in pairs and one of each pair comes from the sire and one from the dam. Animal genes control the animal's biological processes. The characteristics of any animal depend to a large extent on the genes which it receives from its parents. In an animal of average growth the genes for increasing growth and the genes for decreasing growth balance out. The fast-growing animal has more genes for faster growth than genes for slower growth. In any unimproved animal herd or flock both fast- and slow-growing types exist. A selection program for growth aims to build up the number of cattle with a high proportion of faster growth genes and reduce the number of cattle with only an average number of faster growth genes. Since each animal has one of a pair of chromosomes from each parent, the key to selection is to choose sires and dams which have a high proportion of superior genes. The essence of selection of replacement sires and dams is choosing the animals with the highest proportion of superior genes. However, this is easier said than done because of the effects of environment on animal performance. In breeding the emphasis has shifted from the individual animal to the group or the population. Within any animal population there is a variation in individual performance expressed: in different milk production, growth rate, wool cut, carcase composition, lambing rate.

Figure 4.6: Production characteristics (e.g. wool cut, milk yield, growth rate) in a population

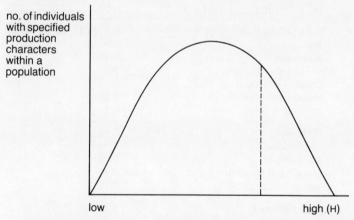

no. of individuals
with specified
production
characters
within a
population

low   high (H)

Animal breeders can use the variation in individual performance to gain genetic improvement by keeping, for future breeding, those animals which fall into the part of the graph denoted by H (high). However, only part of the better performance of the H group is because of a superior collection of genes; the rest of the variation is the result of environmental effects.

The characters commercially important in animals differ in the extent to which the expression of their gene qualities is affected by the environment. Heritability is the percentage of the superiority in any character which parents pass on to their offspring. The geneticist tries to isolate, in any breeding program, the relative contribution of genes and environment. Geneticists introduced the concept of heritability. A character is highly heritable when the environment effects on variation in a production character are small, relative to genetic effects, and vice versa.

Suppose replacement parents selected on pre-weaning growth have an average rate of weight gain of 0.8 kg per day, 0.3 kg above the herd average of 0.5 kg per day. The heritability of pre-weaning growth rate is about 33%. That is, only 33% of the superiority of 0.3 kg will be passed on to their offspring which will grow at the rate of 0.5 kg per day + 0.1 kg = 0.6 kg per day, environment and other traits permitting.

Heritabilities of some commercial characters

Table 4.7: Heritabilities of production characteristics of various classes of livestock

sheep	greasy wool weight	0.25–0.30
(Australian Merino,	% clean yield	0.40
Polworth, Corriedale)	wrinkle	0.3–0.40
	twinning	0.30
	weaning weight	0.50
	post-weaning gain	0.50 (high)
	milk yield	0.30
beef cattle	birth weight	0.40
	weaning weight	0.30
	post-weaning gain (on pasture)	0.50
dairy cattle	milk production	0.25 (0.41 1st lactation)
	fat	0.55
	body size	0.40
	snf (solids, non-fat)	0.55
	mastitis resistance	0.25
	ketosis resistance	0.25
	milking time	0.40
poultry	body weight	0.40
	egg weight	0.60
	shell colour	0.60
	blood spot incidence	0.75
	age at first egg	0.50
pigs	pigs farrowed	0.15
	pigs weaned	0.10
	economy of gain (feed conversion)	0.30
	6 month weight	0.30
	carcase length as % carcase weight	0.60
	ham	0.50
	shoulder	0.50
horse	racing ability	0.45
mouse	tail length	0.60

An example of the meaning of heritability can be seen when selecting cattle for weight gain at 400 days. This is a better selection criterion than weaning weight. In turn weaning weight is a more useful selection criteria than calving or ovulation rate as the output resulting from these measures is affected are both limited in turn by the lactation performance of the cow or ewe.

Let us assume a breed averages 300 kg at 400 days, with a range from 200 kg to 400 kg. If, after correcting for sex and minor age differences, the bulls of the 400 kg group are kept for breeding and are later mated with the group of females which averaged 300 kg, the average 400-day weight of the population of their progeny, if grown under comparable conditions, will be 320 kg.

This is explained as follows: The heritability of 400-day weight gain is about 40% or 0.4 kg. Thus, of the observed 100 kg superiority of the selected bulls, 40% or 40 kg is heritable. Since the females joined have no relative genetic superiority, they do not contribute to increasing the weight of their progeny.

males	×	female
+ 100 kg		+0.0 kg
× heritability 0.40%		0.40
contribution 40 kg		0.0 kg

progeny

total gain $\dfrac{40 + 0}{2} = 20$ kg

Average 400-day weight of progeny = 300 + 20 = 320 kg; not 350 kg as one at first might think.

If the animal breeder is trying to select simultaneously for two characters occurring independently of each other, e.g. high wool weight and high lambing percentage, the rate of genetic progress in each will be lowered. The more independent characters selected for at one time, the slower the progress that is made in each. Selection response reflects selection differential, but overall merit increases faster through index selection in the simple case than through any other method, even when the progress in each character is slower. If some characters have to be dropped from the program, they should be the ones of least economic importance. Usually characters affecting reproduction have low heritabilities but are of high economic importance. Carcase characters have both high heritability and economic merit. Beilharz's arguments on environmental limits to reproduction performance, and the importance of lifetime reproduction performance, are pertinent here.

Many of the characters of interest such as growth rate and carcase quality are of medium to high heritability, and the performance of an animal is a good guide to the genes carried for these characters. For characters with low heritability an animal's performance tells little about the genes for these characters carried and passed on to offspring. As an individual animal has some of its genes in common with its close relatives, more information can be gained about an animal's genetic value for low heritability characters by examining the performance of these relatives. This is the function of progeny and sibling testing. Reproductive characters are often difficult to improve by selective breeding because the heritabilities of reproductive characteristics is low and because existing adaptation via selection to the limits set by environments means environmental changes are needed to 'release' the potential for more gains (Beilharz 1984, 1986). On the other hand the higher heritability characters are fairly easy to improve by genetic means, particularly the growth characters, if the environmental limits on reproduction and survival allow. This is done through emphasis on selecting herd replacements on pre- and post-weaning growth measurements of young animals.

Some general requirements for getting good results from a breeding program warrants brief mention:

- choose foundation stock wisely;
- achieve a high selection differential, i.e., superiority of selected individuals over the average;
- test under uniform environmental conditions;
- turn generations over quickly;
- keep inbreeding rate low. Inbreeding percentage per generation is estimated as $\dfrac{100}{8 \times S}$ where S is the number of sires used, e.g. in a closed herd, six sires would achieve an inbreeding percentage per generation of about 2%.

Selection of superior animals

It is helpful for a farmer beginning a breeding program to understand some genetic terms:

Selection differential (SD)
The selection differential is the difference between the observed performance of selected animals and the average performance of the herd or flock to which they are being mated. If the flock averages a wool cut of 4.5 kg, and the cut of selected individuals averages (after age and sex correction) 6.0 kg, then the selection differential is 1.5 kg.

Heritability (H)
Heritability is the extent to which differences between animals are transmitted from one generation to the next, expressed as a decimal or a percentage. When using published heritability figures for budgetary calculations, it is important to ensure that the environment in which the heritability figures were derived resembles that in which the breeding program will be carried out.

Generation interval (GI)
The generation interval is the time between one generation and the next. The average age of the parents is a measure of the generation interval. The longer this period is, the slower the annual rate of genetic process.

The annual gain in any character under selection in a breeding program can be estimated as follows:

annual gain $= \dfrac{\text{selection differential} \times \text{heritability} - \text{inbreeding depression}}{\text{generation interval}} \times \$$

gain per generation $=$ (average SD of sires and dams) $\times$ H

gain per year $= \dfrac{\text{SD sires} + \text{SD dams}}{2} \times \dfrac{\text{H}}{\text{GI}}$

If the average SD of sires and dams were 1 kg, the H of wool weight 0.3, and the GI four years, the annual gain is thus:

$$\dfrac{1.0 \times 0.3}{4} = 0.075 \text{ kg}$$

These are the requirements for fast gains:

- maximize SD, H and dollar value
- minimize GI and I

Heritabilities for a number of important characteristics of animals have been calculated and these are shown in Table 4.7. The range in some of the figures for particular differences is a result of differences in environment. Remember that environmental–management effects are often mistaken, in practice, for genetic effects, even when comparing stock from two properties whose environments and management systems appear similar.

Relative genetic gains from sires and dams

So far, we have only considered the case of mating one or a selected group of males (with age and sex-corrected SD) to a population of females, i.e., the females have not been selected. If, instead of mating the selected males to the average female population, a superior group of females is selected to mate with the males, what will be the difference in the rate of genetic progress?

Since, for most species, one male can fertilize at least 40 females, it is difficult, in practice, to obtain a population of superior females with as large an SD, relative to the average female, as it is to select males, i.e., the selection pressure the breeder can exert is much higher for males than for females.

Therefore, the selection differential of a group of selected females will be less than that for a group of males.

A typical example is for wool weight within a given flock of sheep. Selection of ewes is likely to lead to an SD of only 0.2 kg of wool in most flocks, an SD for males of, say, 1.35 kg.

Let us compare the rate of genetic gain for the whole flock, for two situations, viz., where females are not selected and where females are selected. In both cases assume that they are mated to males which have the same SD, relative to the average female in the flock. This is the general formula for rate of genetic progress:

$$\dfrac{\text{SD ram} + \text{SD ewe}}{2} \times \dfrac{\text{H}}{\text{GI}}$$

case 1: no selection of ewes:
SD rams = 1.35 kg
SD ewes = 0.0 kg

$$\text{annual gain} = \frac{1.35 + 0}{2} \times \frac{H}{GI}$$

$$= \frac{0.67}{1} \times \frac{H}{GI}$$

case 2: selection of ewes
SD rams = 1.35 kg
SD ewes = 0.2 kg (say, after 25% culling)

$$\text{annual gain} = \frac{1.35 + 0.2}{2} \times \frac{H}{GI}$$

$$= \frac{0.77}{1} \times \frac{H}{GI}$$

Thus:
difference in SD of the two systems = 0.77 − 0.67 = 0.10 kg
difference in annual rate of genetic gain

$$= 0.10 \times \frac{0.3}{4} = 0.007 \text{ kg}$$

The advantage of culling the females (other than for serious defects) is very small. The old saying 'the sire is half the herd' conveys more vividly the same point, but now the criteria for selection of the sire are more rational than when this saying first appeared.

Note. It is tempting to calculate rate of gain for given SDs, Hs, GIs, but there is a severe limitation as to how far we can go in practice. The calculated gains would only be true if the 'numbers' were true, but these numbers are assumed to apply in an environment and to continue to apply as gains are made. The application of statistical analyses to genetic gain variables is advanced and elegant. But, at the start an assumption has to be made that these numbers will apply and will keep on applying in the particular environment. This can be dubious (see Beilharz).

While thinking about genetic gain in the above ways is beneficial, there is the danger of losing sight of the initial assumptions involved. Once change occurs in an animal system many related subsequent changes occur. It is dynamic. New environmental constraints to production gains come into play and limit the theoretical continuing gains until that constraint is overcome.

There is a parallel between the quantitative approach to genetic gain and farm reality, and production economics and farm management. In production economic theory the technology of production is assumed to be uniformly and efficiently applied. If this is so the rest follows logically and elegantly. In both quantitative genetics and production economics critical assumptions are made at the start of the analysis and onto this a logical and elegant superstructure is built. However, if the opening premise is incorrect, as we believe it often is, then the existing analyses are less relevant to practical farm management. But, given that, we strongly believe both the production economics and the quantitative genetic 'ways of thinking' remain fundamental to understanding these aspects of the farm business and to making good management decisions.

Economics and genetics

The genetic gains in particular production traits which appear theoretically possible, and the economic values attached to such gains, are strongly modified by each particular environment. Specific farm characteristics and management strategies determine the realistically achievable genetic gains and economic rewards.

With-without criteria

Assessing economic gains is more than identifying and valuing gains from breeding. The assessment of economic gains from animal-breeding efforts represents a good example of application of the economist's 'Compared with what?' criterion for almost any proposed action. The net gain from animal selection for improvement is the net value of extra output, but the true net gain is the extra net profit with the breeding program in place compared with the net profit from the animal production system without the breeding program. That is, the with-without criterion applies. The true gain is the net profit with the breeding program minus the net profit without the breeding program and with the next best alternative system of production and improvement. Production gains cannot usually be achieved without incurring the need for other changes to the previous system of animal production. To the extent that such changes occur, then by simply valuing extra production does not capture fully the gains from animal improvement. True net gain from a change is net gain from the new system minus net gain from the old system, or, minus net gain from the next best alternative system which would be implemented (if this were more profitable than the old system).

Valuing superior breeding stock

A couple of examples relating to the thinking about the economics of genetic gains follow. For example, how might we assess the maximum premium per head which could be paid for a group of animals of superior genetic merit such as rams, bulls or AI semen?

Assume a flock of 1,000 ewes and a source of sires is a stud producing rams run under like conditions to those on the farm on which they will be used, whose sale rams, after correcting for age and sex differences, could be expected to grow 1.5 kg more wool than produced by ewes (if no new constraints were encountered).

The question is, if these conditions were true, what is the most money premium which a buyer could afford to pay for these rams of proven quality compared with rams which had no real selection differential? Eight new rams per year would meet the needs of a 1,000 ewe flock. That is, the effective working life of rams is three years.

---

ram wool advantage	1.5 kg
generation interval	3 years
heritability of wool weight	0.3 kg

rate of gain per year if no new constraints are encountered

$$\frac{\text{SD sire} + \text{SD dams}}{2} \times \frac{\text{H}}{\text{GI}} = \frac{0.75 \times 0.3}{3} = 0.075 \text{ kg per year}$$

Note. We are only considering the genetic improvement of the flock affected by the rams and, since the sire is 'half the flock', the SD figure is 0.75, or one-half of 1.5 kg.

Suppose now that the environmental limitations on this and other traits allow these gains to be made. Then a diminishing returns effect occurs in a breeding program because the selection differential decreases each year with rising wool cut (or other character being selected for) of the ewe progeny in the program. Our example has the assumption that the rams have constant genetic worth. If rams of the same quality were always used in the breeding program the rams' contribution each year would be twofold:

- they will hold the gains already made above the base level;
- they will add to the existing gains another gain of slightly less magnitude than the gain made the year before.

In theory, if the program continues long enough, the wool cut of the whole population would gradually approach that of the (age and sex) corrected wool cut of the rams, provided that the environment of the stud and the flock under consideration were broadly similar.

A major practical point is that when applying genetic principles in the real world it is hard to make progress, but, conversely, it is hard to reverse completely.

Estimated breeding value

Animal breeders call the attributes of animals 'traits'. Of these 'traits', the ones which they wish to improve are called 'breeding objectives'. The key to success is to select objectives responsive to selection and which will contribute to greater profit. In order to select according to a trait breeders use estimates of an animal's breeding value from measurements for that trait in the animal and from measurements made on its relatives.

As there is often a correlation between traits, measurements on correlated traits can be used to improve the estimate of an animal's breeding value for an associated trait. Using statistical techniques best estimates are made of an animal's breeding value for each breeding objective. Breeding values achievable in given environments need to be converted into economic values in order to derive a selection index.

The estimated breeding value (EBV) for an animal's genetic merit can be estimated by detailed analysis of performance records. EBVs are expressed in physical units and as differences from a population average (flock, herd, breed).

The question is: how much could and should a producer pay for a sire (bull) with, say, an extra 40 kg of breeding value for yearling weights? If yearling weight is an important objective, bulls with high EBVs for yearling weight should command a premium. The price a producer should pay for this depends on how the producer is going to use the bull and the expected price of the product.

If the bull is going to be used purely as a terminal sire then the answer depends on the number of calves that the sire will produce and the time from the date of the purchase of the bull to the sale of the offspring. A bull with an EBV of +40 kg for yearling weight will result in progeny weighing an additional 20 kg.

Suppose the bull is put to work immediately after purchase; in about two years' time the first calves are ready for sale. If the bull is kept for four years then calves will be available for sale in the ensuing years 2, 3, 4, and 5. If the net price received for the 15-month-old yearlings is $1 per kg live weight, then the extra production per yearling attributable to the superior bull is $20. Assuming the extra 20 kg can be produced each year, then $20 earned in each of years 2, 3, 4, 5 would have an equivalent discounted present value. If the bull is mated to 35 cows per year, for four years, gets about 90% weaning per year and is sold for the equivalent of $400 (current) in year 4, then the present value of the benefits from the bull over a bull without the superior genes is $2,128. If the bull is salvaged after four years for $400, this has a total present value of $2,474.

Table 4.8: Worth of extra production

year	2	3	4	5	total PV
extra product @ $1 per kg	600	600	600	600	
(20 kg × 30 calves)					
5% discount factor	0.9524	0.9077	0.8638	0.8227	
present value of extra product	571	545	518	494	2,128
present value of bull salvage value			400		
5% discount factor			0.8638		
present value of bull salvage			345		345
total PV of bull purchase					2,474

If $2,474 more were paid for this bull now over a scrubber, and 20 kg per calf extra was then produced, and the bull was worth $400 (current) at the end of its working life, then the investment would earn 5% real return before tax. However, it is risky and there is doubt about the extra 20 kg of product being produced each year. Still, in a poor season the genetically superior animals might perform better than animals of less genetic merit. To allow for risk and uncertainty the producer might want the chance of getting 10%, 15% or 20% real return before tax on a risky investment. In this case the producer could pay an extra $2,002 at 10% and an extra $1,719 at 15% and $1,487 at 20% for the bull. The purpose of these sort of sums is simply to give a broad guide to how much extra could be paid, such as an extra $1,500 could be paid for the superior bull.

What happens if the producer intends to keep some heifers as replacement breeders? The value of the bull to the producer changes. There is a direct cost because less yearlings are sold, but replacement purchase costs will be saved. There is also an indirect gain. The progeny from each of these heifers are expected to be 10 kg heavier as yearlings, because their maternal grandsire had an EBV of plus 40 kg. It is two years later when the producer gains from these heifers, and this type of gain will be significant for a number of years into the future. Then these superior replacement heifers will produce superior replacement heifers, until eventually but slowly the superiority of the whole herd is upgraded and approaches the performance of the superior bulls.

The present value of these indirect effects depends on the replacement policy applied to the breeders, the expected calving percentage, the live weight price of beef and the discount rate.

One estimate can be made by simply putting dollar values on the immediate (next generation) gains. For example, say, the use of some superior rams will raise the average wool cut of the flock by about 0.25 kg over the next four years, without additional production costs. That is an average gain of about 0.05 kg per head per year. At $5.00 per kg a gain of 0.05 kg of wool is worth $0.25, or a total gain of $1 per head over the ram's life. This rough analysis gives a guide to the sort of maximum premium which could be paid for the superior sires in this case. With a ram to every 40 ewes, and a working life of four years, then the total increase in net revenue by the ram could be about $40 over four years.

However, the maximum premium which can be justified depends on genetic gains which are made, the benefits of which are hopefully maintained into the future. The direct economic 'gain' of about $40 over four years from using the superior ram is not the total gain, as the improvement contributed by the sire is maintained into the future. An estimation of the direct economic gain from the sire's lifetime gives a yardstick by which to assess the largest premium reasonable to pay for an above-average sire. The buyer needs to consider how much he or she is prepared to invest to get this uncertain extra $40 plus future benefits per ram (compared with lesser rams).

Performance testing

One practical application of the principles of genetic gain is animal selection based on measured performance. The benefits of herd improvement in dairying by selection based on production figures progeny testing and the widespread availability through AI and embryo transfer (ET) (and maybe cloning in future) of performance-tested superior sires, are well known. (As also are the dangers of widespread reliance on too few sources of genetic gain.) The use of production recording in beef production, often in conjunction with AI, and use of ET is growing slowly.

Identifying superior animals is the basis of all genetic improvement. Herd-testing has long been practised in dairying. Similarly there is the National Beef Recording Scheme (NBRS) which uses expected breeding values (EBVs) to estimate the genetic merit of animals. An application of this approach is Breedplan, which is a performance-recording system. Breedplan uses an animal's own performance plus the performance of all known relatives in the herd compared to the performance of all their contemporaries, to predict an animal's ability to produce superior progeny. Breedplan uses EBVs, expressed as differences from the herd base which is set at zero, to rank animals for different traits, such as birth weight; 200-day growth; 200-day maternal or milk ability; 400-day yearling weight; 600-day final weight; and the fertility traits scrotal circumference and days to calving. Selection is then based on animals with the highest EBVs for the traits important to particular production systems.

Participation in the performance-recording system involves collecting and recording data on animals. The conveniently sized laptop and personal computers can be invaluable aids in assembling and in storing this necessary information. Farmers involved in performance-recording schemes, such as the NBRS, are usually strong protagonists of the virtues and value of performance recording with a genuine fascination with and love for the animal breeding 'game'.

Remembering that it is not what you do so much as the way you do it, information from performance figures can be useful in the management and selection of good beef breeding stock. However, it is neither a panacea to mediocre management nor does it reduce the importance of the production environment on ultimate profitability.

One common practical difficulty is finding the so-called 'superior' animals we have been discussing. There are breeders who are working along progressive lines to produce superior animals and they can meet some of the demand. However, there can be a very good case, on non-stud properties where there are a sufficient number of breeding stock (e.g. 600 beef breeding cows) to initiate a selection program for 400-day weight based on the superior animals within the herd. The minimum number of breeders needed varies with the heritability of the character selected for. With wool weight probably close to 1,000 ewes are needed.

Where flock or herd numbers are small, use of AI and participation in group breeding schemes are likely to be worthwhile. The Western Australian-based Australian Merino Society is one of a number of breeding co-operatives which try to achieve flock genetic gain by using a central nucleus of objectively ranked superior breeding stock plus the use of AI. They apply the principle that if, in a normal distribution of levels of animal production, half the animals are below the 'average' and half are above the 'average', then by consistently culling the half below-average animals the production average consistently increases. Variations between animals within any population are great, and flock average figures are the major factor in such a program.

Crossbreeding

The benefits of crossbreeding are well established and widely exploited in the fat lamb, pig and poultry industries. Crossbreeding is not so widespread in the cattle industries. Still, crossbreeding between basically similar cattle breeds (Shorthorn, Hereford, Angus) can increase production compared with straight breeds. The hybrid vigour (heterosis) effect in the crossbred progeny, in the case of cattle, shows itself in higher:

- calving rate;
- calf survival;
- weaning percentage;
- weaning weight;
- post-weaning gain.

The advantage of the cross for each one of these production characters may be only 3% to 4% but their effect is additive: i.e., more calves are born, these calves survive better, more of them are weaned and at a greater weight, and after weaning they grow better. Thus the cumulative effect of these advantages can be significant. No great advantages in carcase quality have been observed from crossbreeding. Crossbreeding of British with Zebu (Brahman) types not only gives hybrid vigour but also allows other production characters to be introduced into the progeny, e.g. better heat tolerance and tick resistance.

A disadvantage with running crossbred animal systems can be the practical difficulties for management. If first-cross breeders are not bought-in, then two breeding systems have to be operated: one to supply the first-cross breeders and one to produce the terminal second-cross animals. Thus there are no 'free lunches' with crossbreeding, and farmers' preference for straight-bred herds is often well founded once all the management factors are considered. It depends.

Exploiting new breeds or species

One way for a few people to make money from the breeding game is to be one of the innovators or entrepreneurs in either introducing a new breed, or a new species. The rewards to those who introduced Landrace pigs, crossbred broiler chickens, Santa Gertrudis, and Charolais cattle, Tukidale sheep, and Quarter-horses to Australia were high. Those who adopted the innovation later did not profit nearly as much. In fact, as fashions changed, some lost money. Similarly, those who were among the first to develop and to promote such new and 'different' species as deer, mohair and cashmere goats, squab pigeons, pheasants, trout, donkeys, and mink have made quite good profits from their innovativeness.

It is folly to confuse the effects of the environment, especially feed, and management, with the effects of the genes.

4

Questions for discussion

1   Feed is the major determinant of output in any given animal feeding system. Discuss this assertion.

2   The economics of any animal system can be reduced to three major components. What are these?

3   What is meant by: In grazing systems, feed has different economic values, depending on the season of the year?

4   Explain the difference between a dry sheep equivalent (dse), a livestock unit (lsu), and a livestock month (lsm).

5   Animal demand at different seasons of the year can be fairly accurately predicted. The problem is *not* knowing what the future feed supply will be in each season. List five or six major strategies which different good managers adopt to handle this problem.

6   You are contemplating setting up an intensive 'factory farming'-type enterprise. What major lessons from present intensive animal production systems that you know of could you apply to your new venture? Is 'sitting on a volcano' an apt term?

7   What do the following statements on animal breeding mean:
'Half the breeding goes down the throat.'
'The sire is half the herd (or flock)?'

8   We claim:
'Probably no sector of agriculture has been more prone to the wiles of rapscallions than has the breeding game.'
Discuss this claim.

9   'In the section on breeding we try to separate scientifically based facts from the myths and mysticism hawked by those who stand to gain from the gullibility of some stud stock buyers.'
What facts are we talking about? What myths?

10 A selected sire has an age- and sex-corrected superiority of 100 kg over the average of the female population to which he is being mated. Therefore the average superiority of the progeny will be 50 kg more than if an average sire were used.
Why is this statement wrong?
What factor in the inheritance of observed superiority is missing?
What is the right answer to this statement?

11 Is performance recording really worth the trouble? State, if so, for whom?

4

Further reading

Barnard, C. S. and Nix, J. S., *Farm Planning and Control* (2nd edn), Cambridge University Press, Cambridge, 1986.

Beilharz, R. G., 'The Inheritance of Reproductive Performance' in *Reproduction in Sheet*, Australia Academy of Science, Canberra, pp. 240–242, 1984.

Beilharz, R. G. 'The Pivotal Role of Reproduction in Animal Improvement', Third World Congress of Genetic Applications to Livestock Production, Vol. XI, Lincoln, Nebraska, pp. 49–54, July 1986.

Beilharz, R. G. and Luxford, B. G., 'Inheritance of Reproduction Affects Gains Possible in Commercially Important Traits', *Proc. of Australian Applied Animal Breeding and Genetics*, 6, Perth, 1987.

Boehlje, M .D. and Eidman, V. R., *Farm Management*, John Wiley & Sons, New York, 1983.

Castle, E. N., Becker, M. H., & Nelson, A. G., *Farm Business Management—The Decision Making Process*, Macmillan Publishing Company, New York, 1987.

Dillon, J. L. and Burley, H. T., 'A note on the Economics of Grazing and its Experimental Investigation', *Australian Journal of Agricultural Economics*, 5(1), 1961.

Rickards, P. A. and Passmore, A. L., 'Planning for Profit in Livestock Grazing Systems', *Professional Farm Management Guidebook No. 7*, ABRI, University of New England, Armidale, 1977.

5

It's Not In The Bag Yet
Crop Farm Management

In this chapter economic and management aspects of crops, vegetables, pastures and trees are examined.

Part 1
Crops

In all cropping activities there are four main operations:
- preparing the seedbed;
- growing (planting, seeding, watering, weeding, fertilizing, spraying, protecting, pruning);
- harvesting;
- marketing (which can include processing, sorting, packing, and transport).

Generally, four types of cropping activities can be recognized. These occur when the crop:

- grows quickly (three to four months) from planting to harvest, e.g. many soft vegetables such as tomatoes or beans. Often two or more such crops can be grown on the same area of land within one year;
- takes four to seven months to grow; most of the commonly cultivated grain crops (such as wheat, sorghum, and maize) are in this group;
- has about a 15 to 18 months' growing season (sugar is an example);
- takes three to four years to produce the first harvest, maybe six to seven years after that to reach full production, and continues to produce for 20 to 30 years. Tree crops such as fruits, pines, vines, and nut trees belong here.

The special economic features of each will be discussed in this chapter.

The important factors affecting decisions about crops are of a personal, technical, financial and economic nature (Edwards 1989).

Personal factors, which refer to the human aspects, include the farmer's attitudes to risk, skills, needs, and desires to adapt change, attitudes to using chemicals, preferences for different crops, livestock and crop–livestock combinations, and desire to work and to be active in marketing.

Technical factors are the biological and physical aspects of crop production. These are important in determining what is possible in any paddock, and include crop type and cultivar; previous crop sequence; previous crop yield; previous and expected cultivations; herbicides and insecticides; weeds; disease and pests; and soil characteristics such as nutrient status; structure; and acidity or alkalinity (pH). Also important overall limits to cropping are environmental factors; machinery capacity; labour supply; grain storage and handling facilities; and farm lay-out.

Financial factors include prices and costs involved in cropping; expected gross margins; cash flows and timing of receipts and expenditure; possible fluctuations in outcomes; considerations of gearing and growth of the farm business; and taxation implications.

Economic factors refer to true measures of current and expected future profits from crop sequences such as net present value or annuity.

The term 'crop rotation' is commonly used when referring to a series of crops on a piece of land. However, the term 'rotation' has the connotation that crop selection is routine or habitual. The term 'crop sequence' is more apt. The choice of crop on any piece of land in any year is, in part, dictated by technical 'rules' of good agronomy for crop health and satisfactory yields. But within these technical constraints there are choices, and these are dictated by relative profitability of alternative crops. Further, the technical 'rules' are continuously being modified by technological developments. For example a run of cereal crops without a break crop such as grain legumes or canola, or a fallow period, in some areas, run into problems with cereal cyst nematode. With technological developments it is possible to crop cereals more intensively using nematicides and nematode-resistant cereal strains. Thus, at certain prices, it might be profitable to temporarily bend the agronomic rule which says that cereals without a break crop is not wise.

It is important in any analysis of annual crop decisions to allow for changes and differences in expected variable costs, yields, and prices. These decisions need to be made both year by year and paddock (area) by paddock, corresponding to the expected effects of the performance and type of the preceding crops. It is important to note the contribution to the net worth of a farm business by: (1) various crop and pasture sequences of varying lengths and (2) the different, unique combinations of technical inputs and outputs associated with various crop areas on the farm.

Personal factors

Farmers' decisions or actions have to be seen, and justified, according to all the relevant decision criteria, applicable to each situation. Each is unique. Each farmer's approach to crop decisions is aimed at achieving both short- and long-term objectives. Important aspects of a farmer's approach to decisions about the annual cropping plan include the following: attitude to risk; skills; age; stage of business development; need and desire to change; attitude to using chemicals; preferences for different crops and for livestock and crop-livestock combinations; desire to work at chosen degrees of intensity; desire to market crops where and when a farmer wishes.

Attitude to risk

Farmers' views of the risk in their jobs helps shape their responses to change. They do not consider some crops in a farm plan, because they are seen as being too risky. Farmers might be inexperienced with them, or might have had past crop failures. The trade-offs between return and risk have to be assessed with the financial state of a farm business in mind, and also those of the long- and short-term goals of the farm family. Risk means there is a chance that the outcome will reduce the net worth. As well, there is the danger of damaging prospects for achieving such objectives as increasing profits, living comfortably, or expanding the business. Farm families act in many ways to cope with all of the risk they face in conducting their business. However, the risk they face remains an ever-present factor. It demands action. It cannot simply be ignored.

Skills

Farmers have different amounts of the many skills needed to grow good crops. Adopting new technology such as alternative chemicals and tillage techniques occurs at different rates. Like everyone else, farmers do not instantly understand or implement new technology effectively. Hence the farmers' abilities to exploit current and new technology influence the cropping possibilities and choices made.

Wish to change

Commonly, some farmers are reluctant to alter current cropping strategies. There are many reasons for this: some are sound, some are not. New technologies or changes in farmers' approaches to cropping might be expected to increase profit more than by using current practices. But many farmers prefer to keep doing what they know well, in the short term at least. Local information and peer pressure influences the acceptance of major changes in farming practices.

Need to change

The need to make changes on farms comes from many factors. The financial state of the farm business is a key factor; each farmer reacts differently to changing financial states. The threat of possible bankruptcy stimulates some farmers to take more risks and to try new cropping strategies. Other farmers respond to a similar situation with increased caution.

Desire to work

Doing main jobs like sowing and harvesting quickly is a major factor in the choice of machine size, crop type, area sown, and crop mix. This objective can be because of technical factors and timeliness costs, but it also can result from peer group competition or a wish for more leisure. Further, some farmers place high value on being out on the tractor at certain (usually early) stages of their farming career; but it is common for cropping farmers to eventually grow to detest the drudgery of endless hours of tractor work. Decisions about crop types, crop areas, and the choice of technology to use are influenced by both 'desire to work' and leisure considerations.

Attitude to chemicals

Chemicals used for cropping influence costs and income from crop activities. Farmers' attitudes to using chemicals vary widely from a strong preference to not use chemicals through to a penchant for using as much chemical input as possible. The reasons for using or not using chemicals are numerous, and farmers' attitudes to chemicals and their use have a major impact, affecting the crop possibilities they consider, the techniques used and the returns.

Attitude to crops or livestock

Some cropping farmers dislike livestock. Others such as wheat–sheep farmers, gain immense satisfaction from knowing that their 'compulsive woolgrowers' will be at work. In some case, regardless of the short-term economic prospects of sheep and crops, farmers select a mix of livestock numbers and crop area for their farms and maintain this, through the ups and downs of crop and livestock returns. When this happens the maximum and minimum crop areas and sheep numbers on the farm limits the cropping choices. This can mean farmers' machinery, crop and livestock decisions are rigidly constrained.

Desire to be a 'marketer'

Different crops have different market outlets. Mostly the cropping farmer has little bargaining power. Some farmers select particular crops because they want to be actively involved in marketing. Others select certain crops because they do not want to worry about marketing.

Technical factors

Technical factors are unique to each crop area. The economic outcomes of crop decisions result, in large part, from the technical factors involved in the current year decision and effects these have on the future options. Technical considerations influence the type of crop selected, the inputs needed, and expectations about yield and quality of end product. They determine input costs both in the current year and future years. These are the important input costs affected by technical factors:

- seed, which includes the seed type, grading, cleaning, bagging, rate of sowing, testing, innoculation, and various chemical treatments;
- fertilizer, which includes the type, method, rate, number of applications and freight;
- machinery, fuel, repairs and maintenance, which include number and types of cultivation, harvesting, chemical application, and annual repairs and maintenance to plant. Any hired plant for special operations is also included;
- contractors and labour, which include hired casual labour and specialist operators and their machinery;
- chemicals which include all chemical treatments for weeds, disease and pests;
- marketing costs, which include post-harvest handling to point of sale. These can involve grading, cleaning, storing, transport, chemical treatments, and marketing changes.

Crop type

Choices must be made between broad types of crop such as cereals, legumes, and oilseeds. Within crop types choices must be made between alternatives, such as wheat or barley. Selecting a species of crop affects future selections of crop group and crop species. Decisions must then be made between crop cultivars as this influences costs, income, and future crop options. Effects of current crops on future gross margins are important in this case. Crop cultivars are selected for a number of reasons: tolerance and resistance to disease; length of growing season; tolerance of frost and waterlogging; resistance to lodging; and growth rate where weed competition is important.

Previous crop sequence: yield, cultivation

The effect of previous crop influences yield and inputs for alternatives in the current year. The previous crop sequence effects are shown in soil structure and disease, weed and fertility status. All of these affect expected gross margins. For example, a paddock that has been cropped continuously to cereals for a number of years is usually very different in fertility status to one which has had several years of legume pasture. Yield and input requirements for cereal crop in the next year in two such paddocks will be quite different.

Previous crop yield influences crop residues (and self-sown crops) and soil fertility in the current year. Nutrient removal in the previous year has to be considered when determining fertilizer requirements in the current year. Nutrient removal varies with crop yield and treatment of crop residues. Crop residues have implications for grazing, for number and types of cultivations, and for chemical use in the current year. Previous crop yields and residues influence current year crop decisions, and current year crop yields and input requirements for alternatives vary accordingly.

The paddock history of cultivation determines soil status such as tilth and 'hard pans'; disease; susceptibility to erosion; chemical requirements; and time of sowing. Different crop sequences could involve different numbers and types of cultivation. Crop sequences which include crops in which chemical control of weeds is limited might require numerous cultivations for weed control. Combinations of cultivations and chemicals are important in determining yield expectations and these also affect expected costs both in the current and future years.

Fertilizers and chemicals

Great advances have been made in research to find the correct types, blends, and rates of fertilizer for various soil and crop types. This, combined with advances in both soil testing, and the quality, range, form and availability of, tailor-made blends of fertilizer have transformed the process of fertilizing many crops to a precision operation.

Chemicals used in previous crops influence expectations about weed, disease and pest levels in the current and future years. Also, the effects on future crops of expected current year chemical use must be considered when making the current year decisions.

Expected weeds, disease and pests

Past weed, disease and pest levels help determine crop possibilities, and the input and yield expectations for the current year. Regrowth from previous crops is a weed. Weed seeds, disease-affected grain, and insect damage all influence quality of the grain and the price. Extra handling, storage, cleaning and grading costs can arise.

There are technological advances of weed and pest control. Thousands of weedicides and pesticides are tested annually. The ones made available to farmers create new horizons for cropping. Intelligent use of weedicides and pesticides enables the cropping phase of a sequence to be lengthened without reducing yields, although additional cost is incurred in most cases.

Soil

Soil characteristics set limits on crop possibilities. Soil features to consider are pH; structure; erosion; incidence of water logging; water-holding capacity; stored moisture; and fertility status. The soil characteristics affect crop options; expected yields and machinery; contractor; fertilizer and chemical costs. Soil moisture at planting affects seeding rates and fertilizer needed. Many of the technical considerations discussed above are evident in the soil condition at time of sowing. It is only then that final decisions about crops can be made.

Development of new varieties

With new facilities and breeding techniques and the development of plant variety rights and large, worldwide commercial plant breeding organizations, cropping farmers can probably expect a supply of higher yielding, disease-resisting crop varieties to be available over time.

Machinery

Advances in machine and plant design aid the farmer in a number of ways:

- planting, weed control, and crop harvesting are completed more quickly;
- sowing and harvesting are more precise and efficient; thus there is better germination and less loss at harvest;
- capital investment in plant leads to replacement of labour.

Developments in tillage methods

Soil disturbance through mechanical methods of tillage is essential to crop production, making soil conditions suitable for germination, seedling establishment, crop growth, and weed control. Scientists and producers have devised changes in approaches to tillage practices in order to:

- protect soil from wind and water erosion;
- maintain soil structure;
- increase the flexibility of the cropping system;
- counter problems of rising chemical, fuel and machinery costs.

The major change in the use of tillage has been to produce crops with less cultivation. Zero and minimum tillage are management practices in which there are no (or relatively few) cultivations during the non-crop phase. Weed control is achieved by herbicides, depending on weed type and growth. The next crop is sown directly through whatever crop or weed residue remains on the soil surface.

With reduced or minimum tillage most weed control uses herbicides or subsurface cultivation, but the overall number of cultivations is reduced. Reduced tillage disturbs more soil and buries more crop residue than zero-till operations, but significantly less than conventional practices. The major advantages of reduced cultivation are less damage to soil structure; less risk of erosion; and reduced compaction from repeated tractor operations. The reduced tillage techniques need to produce similar profits to methods which involve more cultivation.

Soil fertility

What do we mean by soil fertility? A soil is fertile if it has the following features:

- adequate nutrients;
- a structure which encourages vigorous root growth and which retains moisture;
- absence of weeds;
- low levels of harmful micro-organisms such as viruses, bacteria, fungi, and larger harmful organisms (nematodes and insect larvae);
- a high population of desired micro-organisms such as nitrogen-fixing bacteria and earthworms;
- little or no erosion.

In Australia's cereal cropping zones, nitrogen and phosphorus are the elements most commonly deficient in soils.

Continuous cropping of the same area of land usually leads to a decline in crop yield through loss of soil structure, depletion of nutrients (especially nitrogen), an increase in weeds and often a build-up of harmful fungi, bacteria, microbes, and insects. It can also cause erosion.

The traditional method of maintaining soil fertility on crop farms has been to mix a legume–pasture phase with the crop phase. The commonest legumes used are clovers, medics, and lucerne. A vigorous legume phase builds up soil fertility. It improves nitrogen levels, soil structure, suppresses weeds, reduces harmful micro-organisms (disease break) and renders the soil less prone to erosion. Now in predominantly cereal cropping areas grain legumes play a large role in the cereal crop sequence, maintaining and improving soil fertility.

A crop following a legume (or ley) phase reduces fertility, although not always to its pre-ley level. The amount of nitrogen fixed by a legume varies with soil type, the vigour and type of the legume pasture stand, the existing level of soil nitrogen, the efficiency of nodule-forming bacteria, and the extent to which the high nitrogen dry matter is harvested, be it as hay, seed or livestock. Then much of the nitrogen is removed and some of the nitrogen fixed by the legume does not become available to a following crop, because it is lost into the air or leaked, or is stored in a way which is not accessible to crops.

Some of the advantages of ley farming systems are:

- increasing soil nutrients;
- forage production;
- increasing crop yields;
- better soil erosion control;
- improved weed control;
- lengthened grazing season in drier areas.

Fertility is maintained or built up by chemical and mechanical means. Stable systems which contain no legumes or animals in the rotation have been developed by using:

- fertilizer (especially nitrogen) to maintain the nutrient status;
- stubble retention to improve the structure and reduce erosion;
- sprays, cultivation and alternating winter and summer crops to reduce weed competition;
- chemicals and rotating cash crops to prevent build up of harmful micro-organisms.

The decision on which system is appropriate is governed by soil type; cropping history; rainfall distribution; relative prices or animals and crops; and costs of sprays; fertilizers; machinery; and fuel. There is no universal 'best' system. The unique situation of each farm determines the degree of emphasis given to the two broad methods of maintaining fertility.

In essence:

- a cropping sequence need not involve using a legume during the resting phase between crops;
- substitutes which perform similarly to a legume phase usually work in practice, but their profitability relative to legume leys has to be judged, with all relevant factors considered.

Table 5.1 has a summary of the ways chemical and mechanical methods can benefit soil fertility.

Role of ley alternatives

Table 5.1: Role of ley alternatives

influence on the soil of continuous cropping	mechanical and chemical means which can help offset the influence of continuous cropping
depleting soil structure and increasing erosion	special stubble mulching machinery, anti-run-off contour banks, strip farming
decreasing the amount of nutrients	chemical fertilizer
decrease of organic matter	retaining stubble and applying extra N
increase in disease-causing organisms	chemical pesticides, fungicides, and bactericides

In Table 5.2 are listed the main variables in a cropping activity affecting yield which can be manipulated by the farmer.

Table 5.2: The main variables affecting crop yields

A virtually complete control	B moderate degree of control	C little or no control
species	moisture stored in seedbed (with fallow)	time of sowing (other crops)
variety	soil structure	frost
plant population (seeding rate and row spacing)	other diseases	moisture at harvest
fertilizer	time of sowing (some crops)	moisture during growth (except irrigated crops)
most insects	length of sowing period	wind
degree of grazing	date of harvesting	flood
hail (via insurance)		large scale plagues of insects (e.g. locusts)

Column A contains variables over which the farmer, with the aid of labour, machinery and chemical technology, has greatest control. Column B gives those factors over which the farmer has varying degrees of control. The variables possibly beyond managerial control are shown in column C. There are also varying degrees of uncertainty about price depending on the crop. The operator of a cropping enterprise thus shares many of the problems of the gambler or the business executive who has to make decisions although there is some uncertainty. So the 'what if' way of thinking about crop decisions is relevant.

The following information is needed when farmers' consider crop sequences for particular paddocks:

- minimum period of ley phase needed to restore adequate fertility;

- minimum period of break between similar crops with similar disease-hosting qualities and vulnerability to diseases;
- maximum period of crop phase given the likely fertility;
- feed supply for animals from crops in the sequence;
- gross margin from crop phase in immediate year of concern;
- gross margin (GM) from ley phase, e.g. stock, hay, pasture seed, agistment;
- maximum period of crop phase, assuming sound technical use of fertilizers, herbicides and insecticides;
- gross margin from crop over successive years assuming proper technology;
- whether fallow is needed to grow an acceptable crop.

Further factors governing decisions about crops on a particular farm are the likely pattern and amount of rainfall, the likely incidence of frost, and the existing farm machinery type and capacity. Also, there are the labour supply, grain storage and handling facilities, and both the paddock size and lay-out of the farm to be considered.

Many of the factors which determine crop yield are outside the control of farmers. At market farmers are faced with 'take it or leave it' prices. The weather, especially rain, has a far more important influence on yield than any other factor. Weather conditions can double or halve the expected crop yield. Market conditions can do the same to prices offered.

Financial and economic considerations

Price expectations

Expectations about product prices for given yield estimates in current and future years are important in determining expected gross income for specific crops.

As price estimates change, so the relative profitability of alternative crops and crop sequences change. Where yield and input cost estimates are similar for alternative crops, relative price levels and uncertainty are the keys to crop choice. After yield uncertainty, price is one of the most uncertain elements involved in crop choice. This is usually influenced by factors beyond farmers' control.

Crop gross margin

Expected crop gross margins combine expected yield, price and variable costs for crop alternatives. Activity gross margin is the income from sales of output plus unsold or consumed stocks produced minus money spent on variable costs for a given year. A gross margin for a crop comprises gross income (yield by price), assuming that output is sold in the year when the crop is produced less variable costs. Activity gross margins are usually expressed as gross margin per ha.

Variable costs of crops are mainly:

- pre-harvest or growing costs, establishment costs: seed, fertilizer, water, labour, sprays, and machinery running costs (fuel, oil, repairs);

- harvest costs: casual labour, machinery running costs, harvesting materials;
- marketing costs: direct costs of storage, processing, transport, and selling costs;
- machinery costs: repairs and maintenance costs. Part of depreciation can be treated as a variable cost. This suggests that the cost is a result of use-depreciation. Depreciation cost can also be because of time and obsolescence. This cost is an overhead cost occurring whether the machine is used or not. One workable convention is to allocate repairs and maintenance as a variable cost of the crop, and as a proxy for some of the depreciation as a result of use of the machine. The rest of the depreciation is treated as an overhead cost.

Calculation of gross margin per ha of a cash crop

Table 5.3: Gross margin—wheat 1,000 ha

income	$
2 t per ha at $130 per t × 1,000 ha	260,000
total gross income	260,000
variable costs	
seed 60 kg per ha at 20¢ per kg × 1,000 ha	12,000
chemicals $25 per ha × 1,000 ha	25,000
fertilizer $25 per ha × 1,000 ha	25,000
crop insurance	6,000
machinery costs per hr	
(hrs of use—other plant 4 ha per hr = 250 hrs)	
—tractor 1 hr per ha cropped = 1,000 hrs)	
fuel and lubricants average 20 L per hr at 40¢ per L = $8 per hr × 1,000 ha	8,000
repairs and maintenance	
tractor $5 per hr × 1,000 hrs	5,000
header $5 per hr × 250 hrs	1,250
other machinery average $2 per hr × 250 hrs	500
tyres $2.50 per hr × 1,000 ha	2,500
batteries 10¢ per hr × 1,000 ha	100
total variable cost	85,350
total gross margin	174,650
gross margin per ha	175

Two alternative crops with the same or similar expected gross margin can have markedly different gross margins per dollar of cash cost.

Example

	crop A $	crop B $
GI	200	400
VC	100	280
GM	100	120
GM per $ cash cost	1	0.43

Where cash availability (working capital) is a limiting factor expected gross margin per dollar of cash cost is important in annual crop decisions. Here, too, is the notion of loss if the crop fails. The higher the growing costs, the greater the potential loss when the crop fails.

A crop might be chosen because it is expected to produce a relatively higher 'worst-case' gross margin than other feasible crops. Such a strategy could suit farmers who are possibly going to be unable to meet all immediate financial needs if losses occur in the coming year. On the other hand, some farmers might select crops that have the chance of producing maximum gross margins 'in the right year', and they gamble on the current year being 'the right year'.

Gross margins in crop decisions

At first sight the application of the law of diminishing returns to the problem of declining yields suggests that an area be cropped until the gross margin falls to the gross margin from the alternative crop or restorative pasture phase. However, the expected gross margins of individual phases of the sequence alone, such as wheat or lucerne, are not sufficient information on which to base decisions. The relative lengths of alternative crop sequences, and the size and timing of gross margins of each phase of a sequence, have to be considered to validly evaluate alternatives.

The effects of one crop in one year on another crop in another year have to be counted. These effects might be of benefit, such as providing a disease break or nitrogen, or it might be harmful, such as depleting nitrogen, or adding to yield reducing or cost-increasing populations of disease-causing organisms, weeds or crop regrowth. If comparing the profitability of different farm plans involving different crop and livestock combinations, returns from whole sequences are compared, not single segments of a sequence.

If it is assumed that each segment of each sequence were going to be present on the farm in each year, then the annual total gross margin (TGM) per sequence-ha is the figure to use to compare with alternative rotations.

Example

Crop sequence:
1 ha wheat followed by 1 ha peas. In any year total crop area is sown half to wheat and half to peas.
wheat GM per ha = \$180
peas GM per ha = \$220

$$\text{annual GM per sequence ha} = \frac{\$180 + \$220}{2}$$
$$= \$200$$

It is incorrect to believe that full cycles of sequences necessarily happen in practice. The calculation that 'this' is better than 'that' for 'these' set of yields and price is used at the time the decision is made to follow a given plan of action. It might not happen. Once a sequence is underway, as prices and seasons change, new sequences start.

There is often some flexibility within the biological constraints which set some of the rules for sequences. It is important to recognize this when comparing the profitability of other sequences. As well, in sums evaluating crop and sequence GMs, there is one key thing to recognize. When all the sequences are not present on the farm in each year, then the time effects on cash flows will influence the value of returns. The choice of starting point for series of sequences of activities and cash flows significantly affect the resulting expected NPV of the sequence. Also, any major differences in overhead costs which apply to other sequences have to be fully taken into account when making comparisons (a partial budget might be needed). In particular, any difference in machinery needs and operations or implications for other activities such as livestock have to be counted when comparing profitability per sequence–ha.

Analysis of simple 2-phase sequences when all components are present each year

An area of land with a crop and pasture ley sequence of four parts pasture and six years' crop would have two-fifths of its area in ley and three-fifths in crop, rather than having the whole area under ley pasture for four years and crop for the next six years. Similarly, a farm following a five-years' pasture, three-years' crop sequence over the whole farm would have five-eighths of its area under pasture and three-eighths of its area under crop. To calculate the gross margin per typical ha after a sequence has been set up, multiply the gross margin per ha of the ley phase by the proportion of the area devoted to ley. Add to it the gross margin per ha from crop multiplied by its proportion.

Example

GM ley per ha $60 (5 years in 8)
GM crop per ha $200 (3 years in 8)
$(60 \times 5/8) + (200 \times 3/8) = $37 + 75
annual GM per ha per year from rotation = $112

In this example, if the total cropped area were 400 ha, then 250 ha would be devoted to ley and 150 ha to crop, thus giving an annual sequence TGM of:
ley (250 ha $\times$ $60) + crop (150 ha $\times$ $200) = $45,000

Sequences in tabular form

A five-year legume, three-year crop sequence over the whole of a 400-ha area can be shown in tabular form. If the soils of the crop area were all suited to ley and crop, and paddock sizes all similar, then in this eight-year sequence each area would be carrying a particular stage of ley or crop. The same piece of land would have ley for five years and crop for three years. The eight-year cycle for the farm as a whole is shown in Table 5.4. L1, L2, etc., refer to years 1 and 2 ley and so on. C1, C2, C3 refer to years 1, 2, and 3 crop and so on.

Table 5.4: Eight-year, whole farm rotation

year	paddock							
	1	2	3	4	5	6	7	8
1	L1	L2	L3	L4	L5	C1	C2	C3
2	L2	L3	L4	L5	C1	C2	C3	L1
3	L3	L4	L5	C1	C2	C3	L1	L2
4	L4	L5	C1	C2	C3	L1	L2	L3
5	L5	C1	C2	C3	L1	L2	L3	L4
6	C1	C2	C3	L1	L2	L3	L4	L5
7	C2	C3	L1	L2	L3	L4	L5	C1
8	C3	L1	L2	L3	L4	L5	C1	C2

At the start of year 2 the following events take place:

Area 8 (which has been cropped for three years) is sown to ley. It will remain in ley for five years. Area 5 (which has carried ley for five years) is ploughed up and sown to crop.

Area 6 is cropped for the second time, and area 7 cropped for the third time in a row. Areas 1, 2, 3, and 4 remain in lucerne which advances in age by 1 year. A similar process is repeated at the start of each of the next six years.

Effect of fallow

If a long fallow has to be used to grow reasonable crops, the land has to be set aside for nearly a whole year without producing anything except perhaps some short periods of grazing of unwanted grasses and other weeds. This means that the GM per ha devoted to crop has virtually to be halved, i.e., one fallow ha and one crop ha are needed to produce each crop. Proportionate reductions can be made for shorter fallow. A short fallow period might permit crop residues (or pastures) to be grazed for some of the year, or even a crop to be grown on the same land each year. Since proportionately less area is available for ley land, the contribution of ley income (e.g. stock, hay) per ha decreases.

For example, assume a ley, fallow, and crop sequence on a number of paddocks of a farm. Remember though it is not usually the case of having whole crop sequences over the whole farm. It is more useful to think of paddock-by-paddock analyses, with different sequences applying to groups of paddocks. Thus:

0.33 of the paddocks in this sequence are medic or clover
0.33 of paddocks in this sequence are in fallow
0.33 of paddocks in this sequence are in crop
GM per ha for ley is $45
GM per ha for fallow is $5 from intermittent grazing
GM per ha for crop is $200
the annual GM per ha per year:
$(0.33) (45) + (0.33) (5) + (0.33) (200) = \$82.50$

The profitability of a cropping sequence depends on the GM of the crop phases, the GM of non-crop restorative phases, and the relative lengths of the various phases of the sequence. Techniques designed to make the pasture, clover or lucerne as productive as possible in the early life of the ley phase are critical. A poor ley crop does not add to the ensuing crop, other than to provide a break, and it does not earn much income from grazing either.

The economic reason why some farmers choose to crop continuously is that there are some major costs associated with beginning a legume-based ley system, which many farmers are unable or unwilling to meet. The GM from the ley phase in the first two years of the establishment of the ley phase may be less than the GM from further cropping, even though the land is low in nutrients, poorly structured and, perhaps, both weedy and partly eroded. Low comparative value of the ley phase can be either because not enough effort is made to get vigorous legume stands established, or because crops are more valuable.

The farmer who is short of cash is forced, by economic reasons, to adopt a legume–ley sequence only when the expected GM from the crop is less than the GM of the legume–ley in its first year. We can show that a crop–ley sequence is often more profitable per ha per year than continuous cropping in the medium term. But farmers short of funds could well sensibly choose to continue to crop the land for a further period rather than adopt a crop and ley rotation, although continued cropping might run counter to longer term principles of conservation of soil and soil quality. The more urgent the need for funds, the more farmers tend to crop the land. Usually, where they can, cropping farmers plan their current cropping activities with an eye to the effects of the current plan on future returns and not just to the expected income in the current year.

Alternative crops and crop plans have different levels and timing of cash costs and returns. Farmers' cash position and the expected flows of cash in and out during the year can influence crop decisions. Farmers with high cash reserves might act very differently from farmers whose year's operations are financed from borrowings. Alternative crop plans have different effects on the level and timing of expected peak debt and the timing of receipts to cover cash outlays (e.g. to reduce overdraft). Full payment from some buyers might not be received until some considerable time after the crop is delivered, while full payment for other crops and buyers can be almost immediate. (In some unfortunate cases, no payment is received at all.)

If the sole criterion for crop selection were to make most expected gross margin in the current year, then the annual crop selection process would be clear-cut. In judging the lack of a role of the technique known as linear programming in annual crop selection, Mauldon concluded that:

> In cropping regions the pattern of production is so definitely seasonal that alternative cereal crops compete for the same factors of production at around the same times of the year. Thus, the most profitable activities can be selected on simple gross margins estimates.
>
> (Mauldon 1958, p. 195)

Sound as Mauldon's comments are, when future implications of this year's decision have to be considered, the analysis becomes more complex. One development, the computer spreadsheet, makes it possible for analysis of farm management decisions on issues such as crop sequences to be made fuller, more easily, than before. By making budgets on the spreadsheet, the worth of a current crop plan, with some allowance for the effects of time and specific technology, can be assessed fairly quickly. That is, due weight can be given to the possible implications for yields, costs, and returns of chosen crops in chosen paddocks in crop plans, both now and in the near future.

Effects of time on net returns from sequences

In the case where not each component is on the farm in each year in the same proportions, or where different paddocks will record different crop performances for the same crop the usual measure annual GM per sequence–ha is limited.

The better measure of the worth of alternative sequences having different patterns of cash flow, but covering the same length of time, is the net present value of the stream of net cash flow, discounted at an appropriate rate. To compare the economic worth of crop sequences involving different time lengths it is possible to use annuities. An annuity is an annual sum equivalent to the NPV of a cash flow (for more on NPVs and annuities see Chapters 2 and 9). As well, when expected activity gross margins vary according to each paddock or crop area, then the choice of starting point for a series of sequences of activities and cash flows will significantly affect expected NPV of the rotation. Suppose there are two crop sequences with streams of net cash flow, as follows:

sequence A

year	1	2	3	4
NCF stream $	100	50	50	300
5% discount factor	0.9524	0.9070	0.8638	0.8227
PV sequence A $	95.24	45.35	43.19	246.81
NPV $	430.59			
annuity $	121.43			

sequence B

year	1	2	3	4
NCF stream $	100	100	150	(starts again)
5% discount factor	0.9524	0.9070	0.8638	
PV sequence B $	95.24	90.70	129.57	
NPV $	315.51			
annuity $	115.86			

There are two ways to compare the expected returns from these two sequences with these two streams of cash flow of different lengths and amounts. One way would be to pretend that the two sequences were run a number of times until an equal number of years was reached, and to compare the overall value of each complete sequence. That is, the four-part sequence A was repeated three times over 12 years and the three-part sequence B was repeated four times over 12 years. Then the total 12 years' return could be compared. This method however becomes unwieldy and unrealistic.

The alternative is to use the annuity method. At 5% discount rate sequence A over four years has a net present value (NPV) of $430.59. The three-year sequence B has an NPV of $315.51. Sequence A's NPV is equivalent to $121.43 per year ($430.59 × 0.2820 annuity factor). Sequence B's NPV is equivalent to $115.86. The conclusion is that sequence A offers higher returns than sequence B. Implicit here is the presumption that sequence B would continue and start again in year 4, and the crops in the cycle would perform at the same level. If something different were to happen in year 4 instead of sequence B this would have to be counted instead. Then, the NPV of a series of activities over the given number of years has to be estimated and compared.

The discount rate used to estimate the NPV and annuity represents the alternative earnings if the money spent on cropping this land were used in another way on this land, such as implementing another crop sequence. If one crop sequence promised a return of, say, 8% per annum, then 8% would be used to discount alternative crop sequences. Another way to think of the discount rate is as representing the cost of borrowing the money to grow the crops. This is similar to seeing the discount rate as the return you would forego if you used money in the bank to grow the crop.

Compare the following alternative sequences in this example:

year	1	2	3	4	5
area 1 sequence	wheat	barley	canola	lupins	(start again)
area 1 sequence	barley	peas	wheat	(start again)	
area 1 sequence	wheat	wheat	medic	medic	medic

In this case the crops are grown in sequence on one area. Not all the components of a sequence are on the farm in any year. Annual gross margin per sequence-ha cannot be used because the crops grown on the farm are different each year. Even if all sequences were on the farm in the same year, care would have to be taken to allow for the build-up and depletion effects on yields and gross margins at different phases of the sequence, e.g. wheat in year 3 of the barley and peas wheat sequence could be expected to have a different gross margin to wheat in year 2 of the wheat, wheat, medic sequence. As well, paddocks differ.

The economic outcomes of the sequences could be compared using the format shown in the table on the following page.

The tradition of 'rotations as routine' have been partly taken over by technological changes. It is possible to substitute more activities and techniques within any particular phase of a cropping sequence. Chemicals can substitute for some cultivation; or a nematicide can be used with cereals instead of a break crop for cereal cyst nematode control; or grain legumes can be grown instead of pasture to maintain soil nitrogen levels. In the late 1980s emphasis was on treating the pasture component of an activity sequence as a crop in its own right.

year	1	2	3	4	5	6
crop	wheat	barley	canola	lupins	(start again)	
GM						
NPV at 5%						
annuity						
crop	barley	peas	wheat	(start again)		
GM						
NPV						
annuity						
crop	wheat	wheat	medic	medic	medic	(start again)
GM						
NPV						
annuity						

Crop sequences: paddock by paddock over time

Different crop sequences structured around different land types on the farm, and which are run out of phase with each other, have a number of advantages: the yield and crop health benefits of technically sound sequences of crops; the advantage of spreading the risks for cash flow fluctuations as a result of season or price effects across a number of crops; and the benefit of flexibility from being able, in any year, to exploit opportunities which arise for profit by changing planned crop sequences.

The specific technical status of different areas on most farms means that the potential of crops ought to be assessed for sequences on areas, over time, and for whole farm crop mixes in any year because the annual crop mix has to meet economic, financial, and risk criteria.

Take as an example a farm which has four paddocks, A, B, C, D, each of 100 ha. Soils in paddock A and B are heavy clay-loams, suited to sequences of grain legumes and cereals continuously, e.g. wheat, lupins, wheat, peas. In the first year paddock A might have wheat and paddock B might have lupins or peas.

Paddock C has lighter, sandy loam soils. This paddock can be cropped to cereals and grain legumes as long as a canola crop separates two cereal crops, and a legume crop follows two cereal crops, e.g. wheat, canola, barley, lupins.

Paddock D is also sandy loam and has less crop disease problems than paddock C. It is well suited to a sequence involving at least three legume crops followed by two wheat crops and a barley or oat crop. In this paddock three years of clover ley is included in the sequence. However, it is probably unwise to sow paddock D to clover for three years' grazing unless some thought is given to where equivalent grazing will come from when this paddock is under the crops which follow the ley (assuming the farmer is not going to trade-in and trade-out stock). The paddock might have to be divided, with half under ley and half under crop at any time. On the basis of highest expected gross margins crops are then selected. The crop plan for the first year and the ensuing future might look as follows:

year 1		year 2		year 3		year 4	
A	B	A	B	A	B	A	B
wheat	lupins	peas	wheat	wheat	lupins	peas	wheat
C	D	C	D	C	D	C	D
barley	½ clover	lupins	½ clover	wheat	½ clover	canola	½ clover
	½ wheat		½ wheat		½ barley		½ wheat
crop areas (ha)		crop areas (ha)		crop areas (ha)		crop areas (ha)	
wheat 150		wheat 150		wheat 200		wheat 150	
lupins 100		lupins 100		lupins 100		peas 100	
barley 100		peas 100		barley 50		canola 100	
clover 50		clover 50		clover 50		clover 50	

The crop plan for year 1 is the plan which is of most interest. It is technically sound for the first and ensuing years. Depending on whether relative prices and expected gross margins changed, some substitution between crops would occur. If wheat prices rise before sowing more wheat might be grown instead of barley in paddock C; or peas might be substituted for lupins in paddock B.

The main point is that paddock sequences over time have to be looked at in relation to their implied expected TGM for the whole farm in any time, most importantly of course, in the current and forthcoming year. The sequence requirements are then matched with, and adjusted to meet, requirements to do with overall returns and riskiness.

Running technically sound crop sequences on a number of different crop areas, out of phase with each other, over the whole crop area, can appear to be a sequence which is run across the whole farm. For example, a crop area A (wheat, pasture, fallow), a crop area B (pasture, fallow, wheat), and a crop area C (fallow, wheat, pasture), would result in one-third of the total crop area of wheat, pasture or fallow. However analysis should be based on the wheat and pasture yields, costs and returns relevant to each distinct crop area, not 'whole farm' wheat and pasture yield, costs and returns, because variations between different crop areas can be great.

Summary

Important economic and financial aspects of cropping crop sequences (which do not involve changes in capital used on the farm) include the following:

- the expected current year and near-future year's cash expenditure, income and net cash flow, before overheads, on an area by area basis, and on a whole farm basis;
- the expected range and size and frequency of fluctuations in net cash flows before overheads from a particular sequence of crops and pastures, on an area and a whole farm basis, over the period of the crop sequence;
- the expected present value and annuity of the series of net cash flows from both the current year and near-future years, for areas and for the whole farm crop plan;

• the sensitivity of the above criteria to changes in product prices.

Avoid having cropping decisions subject to 'rigid' technical needs, such as a requirement for every crop single phase of a crop sequence present in each year. In such cases there is less scope to exploit market or seasonal conditions favouring a crop or crops which could be fitted into a phase of the planned crop sequence.

Gearing and credit

Gearing (debt-to-equity) ratios of the farm business can be an important influence on current year decisions about crops. Farmers might plan a crop program aimed at meeting given debt-servicing needs, depending on whether the season is to turn out 'average', 'good' or 'poor'. Alternative crop plans have different effects on beliefs about debt servicing with different seasons. Plans may be chosen with minimum debt-servicing capability needs as one of the decision criterion. Access to credit is also important. For highly geared farmers, availability of short-term bank credit might set limits to crop plans in the current year.

Tax

Many farmers, like most business operators, are averse to paying income tax. Extreme examples are demonstrated where higher long-term profit is not aimed for, just to avoid paying extra income tax, or, in making other less rational decisions about such things as machinery investment. Tax, particularly provisional tax, in some years, can greatly affect the cash position and so choices about alternative crop plans. In some years when a large taxable income is predicted there is a spending spree on high-cost crops and items such as extra fertilizer, fuel and weed control, simply in order to reduce immediate taxable income.

Part 2
Vegetables

These are the major types of commercial vegetable production:

1 Broad-area crops are usually grown with other broad-area cropping enterprises, or sometimes with livestock, e.g. potatoes, onions.
2 Market gardens produce mainly for fresh consumption markets, with some going to food processors.
3 Vegetable growing for processing can be both intensive and excessive. Intensive crops include cauliflower, broccoli, celery, brussels sprouts, beetroots, and cucumbers. Extensive crops include peas, beans, sweet corn, and potatoes.

The main features of commercial vegetable production are the high capital investment in land and machinery, and labour costs, and the need to make and implement major decisions rapidly. The crop is usually perishable. Pest, diseases, and bad weather can quickly and markedly reduce potential crop returns. Harvesting usually has to be completed within a limited and specific time. Many production and harvesting operations have a large and intensive labour input. This creates special needs for skilled management of labour, which is, in many ways, the key to success. Vegetable growing, using many alternative crops and combinations of crops, is an opportunistic activity; more so than cropping systems which have limited crop options, prescribed production patterns and relatively long production cycles; e.g. grain production.

Growers of fresh vegetables share the following production, harvesting, and marketing-decision problems with broad-area grain producers:

- which crops, and combination of crops?
- which variety of crops?
- what husbandry practice for each crop?
- when to plant?
- how best to use permanent labour?
- where and when to employ casual labour?
- how best to ensure timeliness of operation, such as sowing, weeding, disease control, spraying, and harvesting?
- how to use labour and specialized machinery for maximum efficiency?

These are special problems of importance to the vegetable grower:

- how to obtain the best technology to maximize profits in a highly intensive, risky and disease-prone production system;
- where and how to sell the produce;
- what to do with the produce if prices are low;
- generally, storage is not possible;
- what will be the likely price at harvest;
- what crop to plant after the present crop has been harvested (often, three crops per year are grown on the same field);
- whether to plant all of the crop at the same time or to stagger plantings.

Vegetable growers face some major uncertainties which make planning difficult:

- the price of produce sold varies often daily and from the corresponding periods of one year to the next;
- yields vary seasonally, often because of managerial expertise and not because of climate and disease;
- planting and harvesting times alter considerably if there is bad weather, and there are implications for other crops which are planned;
- the amount and timing of labour needs similarly varies with the timing of operations and the size of the harvest.

Management and planning for vegetable holdings

It is crucial that the technical needs for a possible new activity are fully understood and met. Also, when expansion is a possibility there is the chance that the extra crop area can stretch resources, especially labour and management, to the point where total production is reduced. Delays, inadequate seedbed preparation, moisture stress because of delayed irrigation, or poor crop husbandry at critical periods, can reduce the return from a larger area to below the return from a better managed smaller area.

Figure 5.1: The sequential decision process in vegetable production

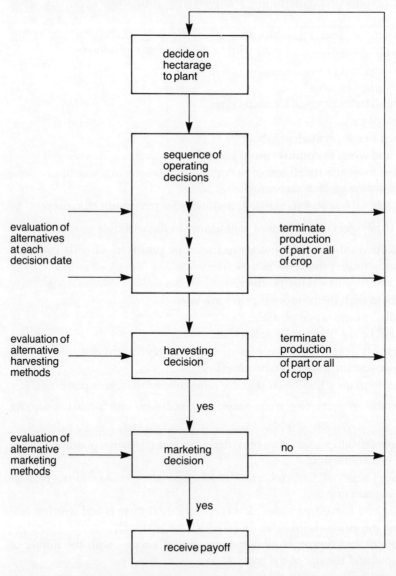

Source. A. N Rae, *Stochastic Programming, Utility and the Solution of Sequential Decision Problems: With Application to Horticulture*, unpublished PhD thesis, University of New England, Armidale, 1971.

The management decision problems of vegetable production can be shown as a stage-by-stage, decision process (Rae 1971). This is shown in Figure 5.1. According to Rae, the critical management task of a vegetable farmer is to 'link the decisions for all crops growing at the same time. This reduces resource bottlenecks.'

Some planning tools

Budgeting lets the manager 'experiment' with different plans on paper. Planning vegetable enterprises, as other agricultural production, uses partial, gross margins and development budgets, as well as parametric and break-even budgets. Plans need to be flexible and to relate mainly to short-term decisions and actions, using all the information available.

Gross margins and crop combinations

Gross margins alone do not indicate the best enterprise combinations on an individual vegetable holding; GMs are a guide to choosing crop activities if other factors such as produce price stability, yield variability and technical and management needs are well thought out.

Crop diversification can reduce fluctuations in total income. Crops with different growing and marketing seasons can be combined so that possible low returns from one crop are compensated by good returns from another crop. An example of the different effects of various combinations of crops with gross margins variations is shown in Table 5.5. If the vegetable grower plants the whole 10 ha to tomatoes, which has the highest gross margin, total gross margin is expected to fluctuate between $15,000 and $5,000, and average $10,250.

Table 5.5: Crop combinations and total gross margins

crop	year 1 $	year 2 $	year 3 $	year 4 $	average $
tomatoes GM per ha	1,000	500	1,500	1,100	1,025
potatoes GM per ha	500	800	300	600	550
10 ha tomatoes TGM	10,000	5,000	15,000	11,000	10,250
5 ha tomatoes TGM	5,000	2,500	7,500	5,500	5,125
5 ha potatoes TGM	2,500	4,000	1,500	3,000	2,750
TGM (5 ha tomatoes + 5 ha potatoes)	7,500	6,500	9,000	8,500	7,875

If half of the land were planted to potatoes and the other half to tomatoes, the variability of TGM is expected to fluctuate from $9,000 to $6,500, and expected average $7,875: variation is less, but so too is expected average TGM. This is the cost of stabilizing the expected income from the 10 ha of vegetable land.

Flexible production and marketing plans which can be altered at short notice help to reduce losses and make it possible to cash in on opportunities as they arise. Flexibility in enterprise depends on the type of crop. Changes in vegetable crops can be made more readily than changes to longer term crops such as berry or stone fruits. Whether a crop is perishable, and how long it can be stored, also affect flexibility. Storable crops allow more flexibility in harvesting and marketing decisions. So also do crops having alternative end uses. Some products can be used for the fresh or processing market, some products might have an end use even if damaged.

Investment in fixed capital resources affects flexibility of a business. A cheap hothouse gives more business flexibility than an expensive glasshouse. A poorer production performance in the cheaper hothouse would then be the cost of flexibility. With mixed intensive enterprises, possibly costly side effects not accounted for in the economic analysis of particular crops need to be assessed, such as future extra weeds, effect on soil structure, yields of subsequent crops.

Marketing

Vegetable growers have different ways of selling their products. Produce might be purchased by marketing boards or co-operatives, sold fresh to wholesalers, or retailers, sold direct to customers, or sold for processing. Growers decide about packaging, grading, storage and sometimes, pricing. There is a strong incentive for vegetable growers to know how their markets work, and to have some positive ideas about near future and longer term price levels. Prices of fresh vegetables vary a lot as a result of perishability, seasonal production patterns, variability in areas grown and yields, and a fairly fixed demand.

Fresh vegetables are sold mainly through central markets in centres with large populations. Production for processing is often based on contracted prices for certain quantities and qualities. These prices are more stable but they are generally lower than fresh market prices. A flexible marketing strategy, using some contractual arrangement; and growing seasonal produce where there is a price advantage, and selling to a number of fresh produce outlets, can reduce problems caused by wide price variations. Meeting a specialist product or quality market can also help stabilize prices and raise average prices received. But this strategy requires high levels of management, more specialized labour, and investment in facilities such as cool stores and processing equipment.

Estimating future prices

The following flow chart and check list shows the main steps involved in forming judgements about future prices for products such as vegetables.

This is a procedure for estimating market price of a farmer's product.

1 Define the harvest or sale period:
From . . . . to . . . .
2 List the varieties and choose the most suitable.
3 Consider the market possibilities and choose the best place and method.
4 Having chosen likely markets, do the following flow chart.

Extract A:

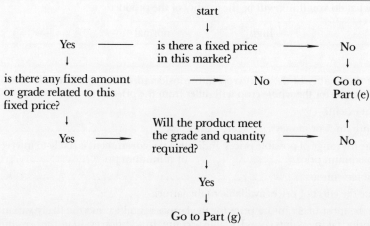

(e) Investigate past prices. Try to recall what the prices for an average quality product were during the past three seasons.

	1 season ago	2 seasons ago	3 seasons ago
price			

Explain if possible, in terms of supply and demand, the reasons for the prices being what they were during the past three seasons.

	price 1 season	price 2 seaons	price 3 seasons
Supply was the main reason (specify details)			
Demand was the main reason (specify details)			
Both supply and demand were 'abnormal' (specify details)			

(f) Estimate future price: estimate, from as many informed sources as practicable, whether supply will be greater, smaller or about the same as either last year or some 'normal' (base) year.

Estimate likewise whether the demand is likely to increase, decrease or remain stable, relative to a base year.

Decide what the net effect of the supply and demand (above) will have on the future price when the product is going to be sold.

Estimated future price, at time of sale for average-quality product

. . . .

(g) Adjust price for quality: Does this expected price depend on the quality or grade?
If yes: what do you think will be the quality of the product?

	high	normal	low
%			

Taking the quality of the total crop into consideration, do you think the average price obtained for the whole crop will differ from the price in (e) above?

To what extent?

Difference (in % or money): ....

(h) Estimate the range of possible prices: Indicate if the government is likely to intervene with maximum price .... or minimum price ....

Other interventions: ....

Estimate the effect of prices available to the farmer.

(i) Decide the most likely future price for the farmer's product and the likely variation of this price, taking points (f) and (g) into account. In addition evaluate the possibility of the following prices occurring:

	% chance
Most likely future price	
Pessimistic future price	
Optimistic future price	

Estimate the period for which the most likely price estimate will remain valid: e.g. six months, one year, two years.

	net financial outcome %	chance %
Most likely	1,000	60
Pessimistic	600	25
Optimistic	1,300	15

If pessimistic outcome: How seriously will this affect the total finances of the farm? (Very seriously/seriously/not seriously).

What action(s) can be taken if the pessimistic outcome occurred?

If optimistic outcome: What effect will this have on the total finances of the farm? (Great benefit/moderate benefit/little benefit)

What action(s) can be taken if the optimistic outcome occurs?

Decisions on crop production and harvesting

Crops have growing and harvesting and marketing costs. It is useful to separate pre-harvest costs, and harvesting and marketing costs. As an example, assume that there are two crops, one of which (crop A) has high harvesting and marketing costs (labour, storage, processing or transport), but low pre-harvest costs. Crop

B has relatively low harvesting and marketing costs but high growing costs. With average yields, the total variable costs (pre-harvest, harvesting and marketing) are the same. In Table 5.6 are shown the relevant costs per ha.

Table 5.6: Per ha costs

	crop A $	crop B $
pre-harvest costs	10	20
harvesting and marketing	20	10
total variable costs	30	30

If only the total variable costs were considered the wrong conclusions would be drawn. Since both crops have a total variable cost of $30 a farmer might think that there is no difference in the amount of money which would be lost if the crop failed to grow to maturity. But in many cases crops reach a stage close to harvesting, and then cannot be harvested because of unfavourable weather, damage caused by insects and disease, or because there is no market. In such cases, the farmer loses only $10 per ha with crop A, but $20 with crop B.

Deciding whether to harvest a crop

The main economic factors which determine whether or not a crop should be harvested are the expected harvesting and marketing costs, and expected gross income, or costs, or income from the crop residue if the crop is not harvested.

Sunk costs are sunk. The fact that money has already been spent on growing (i.e., pre-harvest production) costs is not relevant at this stage to the decision of whether or not to harvest. This is true even when the total variable costs are more than the total gross income as this situation then calls for minimizing losses rather than maximizing profits. Imagine if there were no extra costs incurred when the crop is not harvested, such as from having to chop it up and work it into the soil, or if no income could be earned from the unharvested crop from, say, feeding it to animals. The rule then is that the crop should be harvested if the gross income from the sale of the crop exceeds the costs of harvesting and marketing.

When there is either a cost or an income associated with the unharvested crop this rule has to be modified. A farmer might face the following situation, because of a fall in prices of a perishable vegetable crop.

1 Pre-harvest growing costs $10 per ha.
2 Harvest and market costs $30 per ha.
3 Expected income $25 per ha.
4 Extra cost of disposing of crop residue if crop not harvested $10 per ha.

If the farmer does not harvest the crop, net costs are $20, i.e., 1 + 4. If the farmer harvests the crop, net costs are $15, i.e., 1 + 2 − 3. So the farmer is better off by $5 to harvest in this case, even though the harvest and marketing costs exceed the expected crop income. As the $10 growing cost is common to both calculations, it can be ignored. Hence the statement made above that growing costs are irrelevant to the decision at harvest time of whether or not to harvest. A rule can be deduced from this example: if the cost of disposing of the unharvested crop (4), exceeds the harvest and marketing costs minus the income from the sale of the crop (2 − 3), then the crop should be harvested, regardless of the amount of money spent on growing costs, i.e., if 4 exceeds 2 − 3, then harvest.

The next example deals with the case where there is income, rather than costs, associated with not harvesting the crop. Where the unharvested crop can be used for fattening animals, say,

1 Harvest and market costs, $30 per ha.
2 Expected income, $35 per ha.
3 Income if not harvested but fed to animals, $15 per ha.
gain from harvesting, $5 per ha (2 − 1);
gain from not harvesting = $15 per ha.

Here, the rule is: if the income from selling the crop minus the harvesting and marketing cost (2 − 1) is less than the income from the unharvested crop residue (3), then the crop should not be harvested, i.e., if 3 exceeds 2 − 1, do not harvest.

Part 3
Pastures

Pasture paddocks in grazing areas are continually getting better or worse. Pasture improvement involves applying fertilizer and chemicals, and usually introducing better plant species into soils of suitable type and nutrient status. The aim is to increase both the quality and quantity of seasonal feed available to livestock. Investment in pasture improvement is a process carried out in many ways. There are periodic bursts of increased investment in pastures in response to related phenomena: increases in the actual and expected profitability of grazing activities, and increases in the funds left over for investment.

A general picture of the pasture improvement process, typical of many parts of Australia, is given in Figure 5.2.

In Stage A, superphosphate and grass and legume seed are applied to the native or run-down pasture which has been sprayed with chemicals and heavily grazed. Superphosphate supplies phosphorus (P) and sulphur (S) to the plants. Given a satisfactory strike of the applied pasture seed, the legume will dominate the pasture. Grass production is low at this stage, largely because of the low soil N. As the legumes build up the N status of the soil (stage B), increasing amounts of nitrogen become available to the grasses in the pasture. The grasses can then compete more vigorously with the legume for moisture, light, and nutrients. Gradually the grasses become dominant in the pasture (stage C).

The production and composition of the pasture then depends largely on the species of plants, the climate, and grazing intensity and frequency.

Figure 5.2: Pasture improvement process

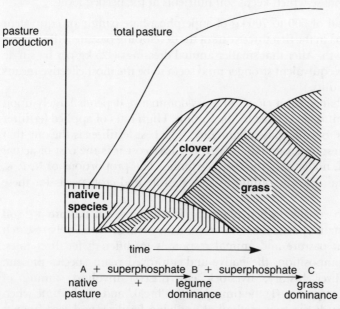

Source. Lazenby, A. and Swain, F. G. (eds), *Intensive Pasture Production*, Angus & Robertson, Sydney, 1972.

At the legume-dominant stage of the pasture improvement (B), the pasture produces much more than the native pasture did, and it is of far better quality, because of the much higher protein content of the legumes. At stage C the grass-dominant pasture generally out-yields the clover-dominant pasture of stage B, especially in winter growth. Factors such as pasture quality, seasonality of production, pasture persistence and resistance to adversity, digestibility, and the risk of animal disorders, are important when assessing the value of various plant species and of clover–grass balance in a pasture.

Fertilizer

Maintaining soil fertility is the key to persistent, consistent pasture production. The major fertilizer deficiencies in Australian soils are N, P, S, potassium (K) and to a lesser extent molydenum, copper, and zinc.

N is the most important plant nutrient. In a pasture, well-nodulated legumes produce N which can become available to the soil and the grasses. Up to 50–100 kg N per ha per year can be added to the soil if it is not 'harvested'. Not that all this N ever becomes available to plants. P, S and trace elements deficiencies are overcome by adding superphosphate and trace elements. The aim of a fertilizer program is to rectify quickly soil nutrient deficiencies and then to maintain a stable and appropriate grass–legume balance. In run-down or unimproved pastures there is usually a noticeable response to initial superphosphate applications.

There are two distinct phases in fertilizing pastures:

- a development phase, usually needing a high rate of superphosphate, where soil nutrient levels are built up;
- a maintenance phase which keeps soil nutrients at the needed levels.

Usually, a total of 600 to 700 kg of superphosphate (single or equivalent stronger mix) per ha in the first three years of the developing pasture will produce rapid pasture growth. After that smaller annual dressings (125 kg per ha single superphosphate or equivalent stronger mix) seem to be the most effective means of maintaining fertility.

The rate of change from clover to grass dominance depends largely upon the rate at which nitrogen is fixed by the legume. High rates of applied fertilizer hasten the process towards grass dominance. The best fertilizer is the one that gives most plant response per dollar. With fertilizer cost it is the cost of actual nutrients required, not simply the cost per tonne. The proportions of N, P, K, and S need to be assessed according to soil, pasture and crop needs for these nutrients.

Key things to consider when planning fertilizer use on pasture are soil type and nutrient status, particularly P levels and the trend in these levels; research information about pasture and animal responses to different fertilizer rates; present pasture composition; the native and improved plant species present, and weeds; fertilizer history; livestock enterprise(s) involved; timing of applications with respect to (1) the timing of the 'break' and (2) the time when extra feed is required; cheapest method of applying fertilizer and seed finance available; priorities for rationing the superphosphate (and hence the fertilizer budget) among various pasture types.

As a general rule these are the priorities for top dressing:

1 Newly sown improved pasture which is still in the development stage.
2 Established pastures.
3 Top-dressed native pastures which have some legume content.
4 Low fertility, unsupered native pastures with little legume content.

If funds are available such pastures as 1, 3, 4 above will show dramatic responses to large superphosphate applications, provided that a good legume base can be established. Ultimately the effectiveness of any pasture fertilizer program is determined by the total animal production turned off the improved area. The costs and returns of fertilizer programs are spread over a number of years. The economics of fertilizer programs depends on fertilizer prices, pasture establishment costs, the expected plant response (which relies on the existing super bank and the state of the existing sward), and livestock prices.

Pasture development decisions

Read this section and refer to Chapter 9, 'Analysis and Planning', which gives a sample budget for evaluating pasture development decisions.

The term 'pasture improvement' covers a continuum of actions and degrees of change, from clearing scrub and fully preparing a seedbed for a mixture of pasture species to aerial sowing or spray–grazing and minimum tillage, or direct drilling, to simply pasture topping to control seed set, with unnumerable combinations and permutations of these techniques in between.

In appraising pasture development the method is to compare the expected profitability of the land without improvement versus the expected profitability with improvement.

Budgeting methods of appraisal need estimates of costs and returns. Estimate the capital costs of different methods of pasture establishment, and the annual pasture maintenance costs. The choice between different pasture establishment methods might be dictated by some obvious factors or there might not be much choice involved in deciding whether to go for traditional seedbed pasture establishment, aerial-sown pasture, chemicals and direct drilling. Sometimes it is whether or not the land can be cultivated. Other times the decision can be more complex and subtle, such as when comparing, say, a more expensive, slower, longer life, and ultimately more productive method (full seedbed) with a quicker, cheaper and less productive and shorter life method (chemical and direct drilling).

If capital is a more severe restraint than land then more expensive pasture establishment methods (in many ways the ideal), might not be best. The best decision when there are short-term cash constraints is to opt for the method needing less cash but which gives a satisfactory increase in carrying capacity. To decide on a development project the following questions need to be resolved:

- are there any alternative on-farm investments which could give greater returns?
- are there some more profitable alternative off-farm investments for which finance is available?
- how much capital is needed to put into this pasture development?
- how vital is the extra improved area going to be to the whole farm financial position and performance?

Costs

Pasture establishment costs include all initial costs such as clearing, timber poisoning, spraying, initial fertilizers, ploughing, sowing, seed, fences, initial grazing losses, water facilities, fixtures, and labour. Another cost is an allowance for possible failure of the pasture to establish. Then, there is an annual pasture maintenance cost for each year after establishment: annual fertilizer costs, and weed control measures such as periodic spray topping.

Returns

Realistic estimates of likely increased returns are an important part of pasture development project appraisal. Estimate

- the extent and rate of increase in carrying capacity in dry sheep equivalents (dses) or livestock months (lsms);
- the proportions of different types of animal production which will be turned off the pasture;
- a range of prices and yields from these different types of livestock.

It is necessary to assess:

- the time it might take to reach the steady state;
- the rate of build-up in carrying capacity;
- any loss of grazing or extra feed purchases, compared to the current situation;
- other methods of pasture improvement.

The expected extra feed which will be produced and the type and class of stock which it will support has to be estimated. This is measured in dses or lsms. Suppose one-quarter of the extra feed, measured in dse, will be used by autumn calving cattle and the rest used equally by spring lambing Merino ewes and spring lambing crossbred ewes. Thus a typical dse of feed would comprise one-quarter cattle feed, three-eighths Merino ewe dse and three-eighths crossbred ewe dse.

An area of some contention is how to estimate the lift in carrying capacity because of improved pastures. Increased stock carried can be assessed as increases in dses or livestock months (lsm) of grazing capacity, remembering that as stocking rate increases so too will many other factors change such as pasture quality and quantity, labour needs and risk costs such as supplementary feeding requirements.

The way in which surplus feed is used affects estimates about the ultimate lift in carrying capacity. As well feed quantity and quality affect the animal outputs produced. The true annual gain from pasture improvement is the sum of all the quantity and quality increases in output from the whole activity, not just number of head carried but all changes in productive performance. Alternatively, stopping some adverse effect, which would otherwise have happened, such as declining productivity, counts as a gain with the improved pasture.

Net cash flow

A discounted net cash flow budget for the pasture development period is done for the life of the pasture. An example pasture improvement appraisal is explained (see Chapter 9). The revolution in budgeting made possible by the computer spreadsheet has changed a few of the restrictions on farm financial analysis for decision making, planning, and project appraisal. There is less reason now not to attempt to take some formal account of the effects of time and risk on the outcomes of an investment. The development–budgeting procedure is relatively straightforward. It involves forming a 'sketch' (sometimes called a 'model') using numbers, of the technical processes involved in establishing, maintaining, and grazing the pasture.

The technical basis of the 'sketch' has to be well understood. Judgements are needed to build, manipulate, and interpret farm management budgets. Good judgement is the critical, and difficult, part of decision making. A sketch of the pasture development process, using numbers, involves the decision analyst making judgements about such things as:

- the likely life of the pasture;
- the likely rate of increase in pasture quantity and quality;

- the initial fertilizer needed (a capital cost, like establishment costs);
- the annual maintenance fertilizer requirements (an annual operating cost);
- the rate at which animal, fertilizer, and other maintenance costs might increase according to the stocking rates achieved;
- the cost of buying in extra stock for the improved pasture;
- the ranges, and worth, of levels of animal production performance, according to stocking rate achieved;
- the added risk costs associated with higher stocking rate (e.g. increasing drought feed costs can be a result of increased stocking rate);
- any changes in overhead costs as a result of intensification;
- significant effects on the rest of the farm's operations;
- the salvage value of the initial capital investment in land preparation, fertilizer, pasture species and stock;
- the rate of return which the project has to make to be worthwhile;
- the tax implications;
- any capital gain in real terms.

When evaluating a pasture development proposal it is useful to look at a range of possible livestock returns, as well as the different costs of alternative pasture improvement methods. In reality, factors other than just economic performance, such as a wish to improve the farm, are also usually part of the decision about pasture improvement.

Extra production has to be assessed not as more of the average of existing production but should be assessed as the 'new' level of performance from all stock which can be expected from the more intensive farming system.

Unmeasurable aspects of the project need to be listed and judged, including effects on other activities in the farm business, and of the project in reaching non-monetary goals.

The risks involved need to be looked at closely. Budget the results of various scenarios for key variables, and, in particular, do some break-even analyses. If the project passes the economic development budget and risk–break-even tests then a finance (nominal cash flow) budget is needed.

The cash flow budget contains expected cash flows, yearly or quarterly, over the life of the project, or at least for the critical early years. This is done in nominal (i.e., future, inflated) dollars to find out the likely size and timing of peak debt and the extent of borrowings needed. An important aspect of the cash flow budget is to allow carefully for stocking the developed pasture, either through cash purchases or through retained stock and thus reduced animal sales. Pasture improvement projects can run into trouble if lack of liquidity prevents full use of the increasing feed supply. This danger is commoner than is usually recognized.

Some common mistaken beliefs

A view held is that $ per dse spent on improving the supply and quality of grasses and clovers on-farm can be compared validly with the $ per dse that would need to be spent on buying additional land, pasture and other

improvements. This is invalid. Improved pasture and land and other improvements are different assets, with different lives, providing different services.

It is often believed that the costs of time taken for pasture development
to reach the maximum state of development can be generally overlooked. Time
costs can be very important, especially differences between alternative ways of
improving pastures.

The risk of pasture failure is critical, including the differences in risk
between different ways of establishing pastures.

The dynamic effect of stocking rate on pasture production is also important.
Pasture production is a function of stocking rate and in turn stocking rate is
also a function of pasture production.

Part 4
Trees

The term 'tree crop' is used here to include orchards, woodlot plantations, and
vineyards. Tree (plantation) crops have a number of common biological and
economic features.

Biological features

Each crop has a limited life and so it has to be re-planted. There is usually
a time lag (in years) between planting and the sale of product. There is a
succession of harvests from the time of first harvest until the end of the useful
life of the crop. Such harvests need not be annual; thinnings from pine
plantations may occur in years 8 and 15, and harvest at year 25. Fruit tree
harvesting is usually annual. Insect, weed control, and fertilizing have to be
performed annually to protect or to promote the growth of a crop. Also, there
is harvesting and transporting of produce.

Economic features

Plantation crops have initial capital costs followed by annual overhead and
variable costs. During the period between capital invested for establishment and
the first harvest, costs, yields and prices are not known for certain. The periods
to initial pay-off vary. These are longer with a pine plantation than for an
orchard activity. So, the expected values for final timber cuts are less certain
than for fruit crops, pulping wood, and thinnings. To illustrate the main cost
associated with plantation crops consider an orchard activity.

1 The initial capital costs of establishment:

land preparation	irrigation (plant and lay-out)
tree purchase	shedding
planting	buildings
tracks and roads	machinery
fencing	plant

2 The annual overhead or 'fixed' costs, which have little or no effect upon the level of yields:

depreciation   administration
rates and land tax   insurance
permanent labour   interest
repairs and maintenance   fire control
to fixed structures

3 The variable costs.

In the early years of the life of a stand there may be no variable costs associated with production. However, these costs relate to output once the stands become productive so the pre-harvest costs of irrigation, sprays, and pruning in the early years are responsible for the level of yield once the stand begins production and are variable costs related to output.

A list of the main pre-harvest variable costs is given below. Direct harvest and marketing costs are deducted from gross income.

pruning   green cover crop (if used)
disposal of prunings   wiring and propping (if necessary)
fertilizer   cultivation
sprays   vehicle costs
                                      casual wages

The economic analysis for tree crops is discounted cash flow analysis. The same technique is used for a pasture improvement example (see Chapter 9). The NPV of future returns minus future costs is estimated using a discount rate which reflects the opportunity cost of the investment funds.

Replacing tree crops

An interesting economic question concerns the replacement time of tree crops. As a tree crop ages, after a certain time, the annual yield declines. There is a break-even yield and net return at which it is more profitable to re-plant and to wait for the new crop rather than to suffer the results of declining yield from the existing crop.

For example, if the expected net revenue after tax per ha next year from the existing crop is $125, and the average expected net revenues per ha from the full next cycle is $180 per year, then re-planting would seem worthwhile, at least for part of the stand.

Cash flow factors are critical here. Usually replacement of a small portion of an activity regularly is sensible, from the view of continuing to earn sufficiently large, regular net cash flows.

It is necessary to discount net cash flows when appraising projects with a life longer than a couple of years (for more on discounting see Chapters 2, 9). The rule for replacement considering the diminished value of distant cash flows is that the perennial crop should be replaced when the extra net revenue (after tax) from growing it for one more year from the present cycle is below the highest present value annuity of expected net revenues (after tax) from the next cycle. The annual cash flows or net revenues received from a semi-perennial crop are not even; they are negative in the early years and positive in later years.

By discounting to present value, an uneven stream of net revenues can be converted to an even stream which has an equivalent lump sum present value.

For example an NPV of, say, $60,000 from an uneven stream of net revenues per ha received over 20 years, with a discount rate of 5%, is equivalent to receiving an even stream of $4,800 net revenue per year for 20 years (from annuity whose present value is 1, Table D in Appendix, factor 0.0812). The discounted present value of $4,800 received each year for 20 years is $60,000 (from present value of an annuity, Table C in Appendix, factor 12.4622), even though the nominal cash receipts over the period are 20 × $4,800 = $96,000 (see Chapters, 2, 9, for more on present values and annuities).

The rule is to compare the expected return from another year of the existing stand with the annuity expected from a new cycle. The choice of the optimum re-planting time depends on assumptions made about yields, costs and prices perhaps 20 or 30 years ahead, as well as on the rate of interest chosen for discounting.

Use expected money values rather than crude average in calculations involving replacement time. In practice, because of the uncertainty associated with expected future returns, replacement decisions are based in part on the replacement rule outlined above, although more weight is placed on practical and immediate considerations. Replacement is a continuing process, with a proportion of the tree crops being replaced on a regular periodic basis even when all trees are all of a similar age, i.e., to have more even flows of all cash over time.

Farming trees

In a farming context, one relevant tree crop analysis is of the option of establishing a stand of pine trees on an area which is currently devoted to crops or livestock. Care needs to be taken to get the comparison right. A partial development budget (as in Chapter 9) is the technique used. Attention has to be paid to establishing the full reduction in whole farm annual operating profit and eventual net worth with a *removal* of an area of land from production of crops and livestock, and the full addition to future whole farm operating profit and net worth from the *addition* of the tree crop. Thus it is necessary to estimate the economic and financial effects on the existing, remaining farm activities of a reduction in a portion of these activities.

Importantly, all the ways in which a tree crop replacing a grazing or cropping activity affects the flexibility of future responses to future changes need to be considered even though this limitation on, or loss of, future options is difficult to put an economic value on.

The assumptions behind discounted cash flow need to be well understood (see Chapter 9). An assumption underlying an NPV is that capital markets enable the investor to borrow and lend at the discount rate used in the analysis in a way which satisfies his or her requirements. If this were so and there were no uncertainty associated with future outcomes, there would be no adverse cash flow implications involved with a change from a farming activity to a tree activity which promises to be more profitable.

So, as well as economic (NPV) analysis, financial cash flow analysis is critical. In practice, dealing with cash flows and risk are largely what farm management is about. The reduction in whole farm operating profit associated with replacing a farm activity with a tree plantation means a reduction in current and near-future farm net cash flows. Even if the potential tree plantation promises a better eventual economic return, farmers' needs and preferences might be for cash-in-hand and more immediate wealth over some more distant, and thus, by definition, more uncertain cash flows and net worth. This partly explains farmer reluctance to invest in trees even if occasionally on conventional analysis a change to trees might appear to improve profitability of the current farm plan. The validity of recommendations based on analysis can be better appreciated if the underlying assumptions are well understood. Usually it is problems with liquidity and flexibility which make investment in tree crops, other than for shelter and aesthetics, relatively unattractive to farmers.

There are other reasons also for reluctance by farmers to invest in tree crops. Often analyses of tree crops on farms represent incomplete with–without and before–after comparisons and fail in a number of ways:

- to capture fully the effects of a reduction in the size of existing activities on the operations and profitability of those activities and the whole farm;
- to use the most appropriate discount rate;
- to fully capture the effects on cash flows and liquidity of such a change;
- to represent how such a change affects the exposure to risks, in particular, failing to adequately capture the riskiness associated with the more distant returns of the pine tree crop than those from farming.

When contemplating a change in farm plan, the correct discount rate to use is the expected marginal return from alternative possible changes. Returns from new investment in pines have to be compared with returns from extra investment in existing activities.

'Agroforestry' refers to a combination of tree crops and other farm activities. The objective of such joint production is to exploit any complementary effect and to achieve a greater TGM and operating profit from the two activities than from either activity alone. The scope for combining trees and pastures is limited mainly to benefits from the use of shelter belts and aesthetics. It seems that the proportions of trees and pastures which produce good saleable quality trees produces poor pastures. Alternatively, the proportions of trees and pastures which produce good pastures result in poor quality tree production. To assess agroforestry fully, budgets are required in which such effects are accurately represented and all extra costs of various tree and crop mixes are included. Agroforestry seems unlikely to play a large part in modern Australian farming.

5

Questions for discussion

1   Consider two legume-based crop rotations (sequences) in an area you know. Could these sequences be replaced by chemical and mechanical methods of maintaining fertility and using no legumes, e.g. sprays, minimum till, more nitrogen, stubble retention, etc.?
    Why? Why not?

2   The way to analyse the economics of crop sequences is to find the total gross margin for all the years of the sequence, and divide it by the number of years. This gives the average annual GM per ha per year for the whole sequence. Just calculating the individual GMs for each phase of the sequence does not tell us much. Why do we say this?
    What about the NPV–annuity equivalent approach?
    Is it only 'theoretical'?

3   If you manage a sown grass–legume pasture correctly, it should not have to be ploughed and resown for at least 20 years (ignoring using the area for cash cropping).
    Do you agree?
    Do you have to plough the pasture because it has 'run down'?
    Why has it 'run down'?

4   Consider the economic techniques described in the 'pastures' section for planning a pasture development project. Would they help convince you to act?
    Why? Why not?

5   Is using the flow chart and check list for estimating next year's prices for, say, a vegetable crop, better than just relying on the two 'gs', 'gutfeeling' and 'guesstimation'? (Perhaps you need to use each.)
    Discuss.

6   How might you decide whether or not to harvest a vegetable crop?

7   How useful in practice is it to discount the expected returns from a plantation whose main benefits do not occur for 40 years? Justify your answer.

8   'A plantation should be replaced when the extra [marginal] revenue from leaving the existing stand for one more year is just less than the annuity value of putting in a new stand.'
    What does this mean?

5
Further reading

Barnard, C. S. and Nix, J. S., *Farm Planning and Control* (2nd edn), Cambridge University Press, Cambridge, 1986.

Boehlje, M. D. and Eidman, V. R., *Farm Management*, John Wiley & Sons, New York, 1983.

Castle, E. N., Becker, M. H., & Nelson, A. G., *Farm Business Management—The Decision Making Process*, Macmillan Publishing Company, New York, 1987.

Edwards, R. G., *Evaluating Crop Sequences for Farm Management*, unpublished MAgrSc thesis, School of Agriculture, University of Melbourne, 1989.

Lazenby, A. and Swain, F. G. (eds), *Intensive Pasture Production*, Angus & Robertson, Sydney, 1972.

Mauldon, R., 'An Introduction to the Application of Linear Programming to Farming Problems', *Journal of the Australian Institute of Agricultural Science*, 24(3), 1958, pp. 191–198.

Rae, A. N., *Stochastic Programming, Utility and the Solution of Sequential Decision Problems: With Application to Horticulture*, unpublished PhD thesis, University of New England, Armidale, 1971.

Rae, A. N., *Crop Management Economics*, Crosby Lockwood Staples, London, 1972.

6

Horsepower and Hidden Costs: Machinery

In this chapter the topics discussed include machine costs, comparing sources of machinery service, replacement policies, and new or used machines.

Apart from buying land, the purchase of farming machinery is often the major decision a farmer has to make and can involve an investment of more than $250 per ha ($100 per acre). Here, we outline the principles and explain aspects of machinery economics and the factors which are important when making decisions about machinery.

The detail of applying these general principles to any specific farm situation varies greatly. The values which individual farmers attach to each factor relates to the specific farm.

Machine costs

In any machinery operation there are a number of types of costs involved. The costs of owning a machine are the 'fixed or overhead costs' and include depreciation, insurance, registration, shedding, and interest on the capital invested. The capital invested in the machine has an 'opportunity cost', as the money could earn interest in another use. These costs are incurred whether the machine is used or not.

The second category of costs are 'variable costs', the direct running costs which include fuel, labour, tyres, lubrication, batteries, repairs, and maintenance. These costs are fairly constant per hour of operation and consequently vary with the hours of operation. Expense for repairs and maintenance per hour generally increases as the machine ages. A proportion of repairs done on machines is usually as a result of the age of the machines as well as their use.

The third category of machinery costs are 'penalty costs' or 'timeliness costs'. The lack of timeliness of operations can incur a cost to the machine's owner in the form of weather losses at harvest, poorer yields, or a poorer quality of product, than the farmer would have achieved with better timeliness of the key machinery operations.

Tax effects on costs

Tax reduces some costs. Suppose the tax rate is 35 cents in the dollar and a machine's annual overhead and variable costs is $1,000. Each dollar of expenses deducted from taxable income represents a saving of 35 cents in tax; thus the $1,000 machine cost becomes:

reduction in taxable income: $1,000;
tax saving from reduction in taxable income: $1,000 × 0.35 = $350;
actual overhead and variable cost: $1,000 − $350 = $650.

Depreciation and interest

Most capital items depreciate in value from wear or obsolescence. A depreciation cost has to be counted to get the true cost of the business operations in 12 months. The simplest way to estimate annual cost of using capital items over 12 months is the straight-line method. In this method we assume that an item loses value by the same amount each year. Suppose a machine would cost $60,000 to replace now, and it is expected to last five years and then be worth $10,000 real dollars. The depreciation cost is $60,000 minus $10,000, divided by five, which is $10,000 per year. The method used to determine how depreciation is worked out depends on why it is being done. The annual depreciation charge can be based on either the real market value (or real replacement cost), or the expected replacement cost at the time of replacement. From these values deduct the expected salvage or trade-in value, in real or future dollars as appropriate.

An example of estimating depreciation when calculating profit (using current cost accounting), straight-line method, i.e., analysing the cost of machine to the business in any year:

$$\frac{\text{current market value (or current expected replacement cost)} \ \ less \ \ \text{expected salvage value in current \$}}{\text{years}}$$

An example of estimating depreciation when doing some financial planning:

expected future replacement cost in future $ − salvage value in future $
= future sum required × sinking fund factor (see Chapter 2)
= annual depreciation amount to set aside for machine replacement

There is also the diminishing balance method of calculating depreciation, calculated for each year by multiplying the replacement value of the machine in each year by the estimated annual percentage rate of depreciation. This method causes more of the total depreciation cost to fall earlier in the machine's working life rather than in the later years. By using expected replacement cost as the basis for the annual depreciation allowance the manager of the business is making provision to meet the inevitable cost of replacing equipment, at some future time. The sums can be done in present or nominal terms for economic comparisons between alternative machines, but they are in nominal terms for financial planning.

It is difficult to estimate the annual depreciation cost when it is not known how long the machine will last, or what it will cost to replace it. We have to make some guesses about the market value, replacement cost, salvage value, and the possible working life of the machine. The future replacement cost of a machine could be more or less, in real terms, than the new present price. The machine will be more technologically advanced, and better, and may not be more expensive in real terms. One approach is to use present cost as a guide to the future expected replacement cost. But we recognize that the farmer will probably be trading-up to a more sophisticated, perhaps more powerful, model. Similar reasoning applies to guesses about future salvage value. Current trade-in prices of similar equipment after similar working life is a guide here.

J. G. Blomfield (1982) of the Queensland Department of Primary Industries surveyed farmers to get their estimates of the value of their farm machinery. The results are shown in Table 6.1.

Table 6.1: Farm machinery depreciation (proportion of current to new value)

	age (years)												
	1	2	3	4	5	6	7	8	9	10	11	12	13
2-WD tractors	0.88	0.78	0.69	0.61	0.54	0.48	0.42	0.37	0.33	0.29	0.26	0.23	0.20
4-WD tractors	0.91	0.79	0.69	0.60	0.53	0.45	0.34	0.30	0.26	0.23	0.17	—	—
headers	0.80	0.70	0.61	0.53	0.47	0.41	0.36	0.31	0.28	0.24	0.21	0.19	0.16
conventional combines	0.75	0.67	0.60	0.53	0.48	0.42	0.38	0.34	0.30	0.27	0.24	0.21	0.19
chisel ploughs	0.76	0.67	0.59	0.52	0.46	—	0.35	—	—	0.24	0.21	0.19	0.16
scarifiers	0.80	0.75	0.70	0.65	0.61	0.57	0.54	0.50	0.47	0.44	0.41	0.38	0.36

Source. J. G. Blomfield, *An Economic Investigation of Farm Machinery*, Queensland Department of Primary Industries, 1982.

Interest

'Is interest on the capital you have put into buying a machine, rather than putting that capital into the bank to earn interest, always counted as one of the fixed costs of owning a machine?' The answer is 'it depends'. For instance, take the situation where the farmer is trying to decide whether to buy a machine, lease it, use contractors, or hand the entire operation over to sharefarmers. It would be necessary to take account of the 'opportunity' interest cost of the capital tied up if you were to buy the machine instead of adopting the other options.

Once the farmer has decided which option is economically best, financial analysis is done. Then, opportunity interest cost is not one of the fixed machinery costs. If the farmer is paying interest on the machine then it will be part of the financial (cash flow) planning and one of the ways the available annual cash surplus before interest is used.

When considering economic and management aspects of machinery, first work out the total annual costs, i.e., what it costs each year to acquire the services of the machine. If the machine is owned then the total annual costs include the fixed costs of ownership and the running costs. There is also the cost called 'untimeliness cost' or 'penalty cost', although this is difficult to assess. If the machine is leased then the total annual costs are running costs, lease costs (after tax), and timeliness costs.

Suppose a farmer buys a $100,000 machine which is expected to last five years. Its replacement in five years' time is expected to be the same real cost as the present, and after five years it is expected to get $40,000 for the old machine in the present dollar terms. Also, suppose the farmer's money could be earning 5% real return elsewhere. The annual depreciation and interest costs of the machinery are calculated below.

The depreciation cost:

$$\frac{\text{future replacement cost now} - \text{expected salvage value at end of life in current \$}}{\text{years}}$$

$$= \frac{100,000 - 40,000}{5} = \$12,000$$

The interest cost is tricky because the value of the capital tied up in the machine is unknown. It depreciates every year and there is a range of values you could use for the machine. Thus, charge the 'opportunity' interest cost against the average value of the capital tied up in the machine over the life of the machine. If the budget is being done in real (current) dollars, then the current value plus expected salvage value in current dollars, divided by two, is the average real value of capital to use. A real interest rate is then charged against this. Alternatively, if the budget is in nominal terms then current value and nominal salvage value divided by two gives the average nominal value of capital tied up. A nominal interest rate is used.

In this case the sums are in real dollars. The average value of the capital invested:

$$\frac{\text{current value} + \text{salvage value in current \$}}{2}$$

$$= \frac{\$100,000 + \$40,000}{2}$$

$$= \$70,000$$

A real interest cost of 5% is charged, i.e.,

interest $= \$70,000 \times 0.05$

$\qquad = \$3,500$

total depreciation plus interest is

$\$12,000 + \$3,500 = \$15,500$

A better method of estimating the annual depreciation and interest cost is this. We are investing $100,000 in a machine for five years, at the end of which we will get $40,000 in present dollars for it. From the earnings from the use of the machine we want to recover the $60,000 in lost capital plus interest. That is, we want to recover the depreciated capital and allow for the interest cost on that capital over the five years.

This approach uses the amortization or capital recovery factor. Suppose a farmer were to borrow $60,000 from the bank at 5% real for five years. Each year the farmer has to give a certain amount to the banker to repay the principal (capital) and also pay the annual interest. There is the table called 'annuity whose present value is one' (Table D in Appendix). In the body of the table, there is a 'factor' of 0.2310, for five years and 5% interest. This number lets you work out how much you have to pay per year. So $60,000 × 0.2310 sums to $13,860 to repay all the principal and interest on the loan every year over the five years.

Capital recovery of the investment in the machine uses the same ideas. If the farmer wants to allow for the $60,000 of capital lost over the five years ($100,000 − $40,000), then allowance for a cost of $13,860 per year has to be made. This covers the lost capital and the 5% real interest on it. As well, even though the farmer will get $40,000 of the capital back at the end of the machine's life, there is also the interest cost of having that $40,000 capital tied up in this way each year for the life of the machine. So, the farmer has to allow for a cost of $40,000 × 0.05 = $2,000. The total depreciation and interest cost of owning the machine is thus:

$60,000 × 0.2310 amortization factor = $13,860+
$40,000 × 0.05 interest on salvaged capital = $2,000,
= $15,860.

This is a bit more than the previous estimate of $15,500.

This information, about depreciation and interest costs, and other relevant annual costs like insurance, shelter, registration, direct running costs, timeliness losses, and tax effects, form the basis for comparing alternative sources of machinery services and types of machines. The calculation of depreciation and interest are for comparing the costs of different machines, or different forms of machinery services.

If you have made the decision on the basis of real terms, and are working out the cash flows for the five-year period, the constant dollar sums have to be adjusted into future dollars. That is, the expected effects of inflation have to be added on, otherwise there will not be enough inflated (nominal) dollars available when these are needed. The expected replacement price of the machine is adjusted to its expected inflated future value. In this case it is $100,000 × inflation of, say, 8% for the five years. That is, from the 'compound growth' table in Table A in Appendix, $100,000 × 1.4693 = $146,930, say, $150,000. This suggests that the farmer might need about $150,000 to replace the machine in five years' time. There is also the salvage value of $40,000 in present terms. If salvage value keeps up with inflation the farmer will get $40,000 × 1.4693 = $58,772, say, $60,000. The farmer will need about $150,000 − $60,000 = $90,000 to replace the machine.

This is where you use the 'sinking fund factor' (see Table F in Appendix). You use the market rate of interest here, say, about 13% (5% real plus 8% inflation). This gives $90,000 × 0.1542 = $13,887. If you set aside about $14,000 each year and invest it compounding at 13%, the $90,000 needed will have accumulated when the time comes to replace the machine. This can be checked using the terminal value of a unit annuity (Table E in Appendix). In this case it is for $13,887 at 13% for five years which comes to $13,887 × 6.4803 = $89,992, say, $90,000.

So far the focus has been on working out the total annual costs (operating, fixed, and penalty for untimeliness and standard of work) associated with owning a piece of machinery. The total annual costs are then used to compare alternative sources of machinery services or alternative machines. The idea here is that the machine with the lowest annual total cost is the most profitable.

The annual cost of owning a piece of new machinery is calculated as follows:

1 Find out the current capital cost of the machine.
2 Estimate its 'most likely' working life. *Note.* People change their machines over when they can afford it. This could occur within a shorter or longer time than the 'most likely' machine life.
3 Estimate the expected capital cost of the machine and the 'most likely' time of replacement, in real dollars. There are no set rules for this. Some machines will cost less, in real terms, in future, even if they were exactly the same as the present machine. Also, technological change embodied in new machines means that for quality of product and speed of operation some will be cheaper in future, in real terms, than they cost at present. Other machines, doing the same task as current machines will increase in real cost. A safe guide in making this estimate is to assume that the present machine will cost the same to replace in real terms as it costs now. We will use this assumption.
4 Estimate the expected trade-in value, in real dollars, of the machine at the end of its 'most likely' working life. A guide to this is the current price that machines of similar quality are bringing.
5 Subtract 4 from 3 to get the amount which is expected to be needed to replace the machine; this is the capital which is lost over its life.
6 From the expected replacement sum needed, estimate the annual cost of recovering the 'lost' capital and allowing for the interest foregone by having this capital tied up in this use for the life of the machine; use Table D in Appendix, annuity whose present value is 1. This is equivalent to the equal annual sum which will fully repay the principal and interest of a loan over a number of years. It is also known as the 'amortized value' of a lump sum.
7 Calculate the cost of interest foregone on the capital which is salvaged when the machine is sold.
8 Calculate the expected other fixed costs of registration, insurance, shelter.
9 Add the costs from 6, 7, and 8. This is the total annual capital, interest and other overhead costs of owning a machine. We call this 'annual ownership cost'.

10 Once a form of machinery service is chosen, then the expected future inflation rate must be considered in financial planning. To work out how many dollars to set aside each year so that you are able to replace the machine, calculation of a sinking fund then needs to be done in nominal (inflated dollars).

If the costs of alternatives are distributed over time differently, then simple comparisons of annual costs will not necessarily be valid, because of effects of time on the value of money. Estimate the expected lifetime total costs for the machines. Discount the total costs over the machine's lifetime to the net present value (NPV), called in this case net present total cost (NPTC) (see Chapters 2 and 9 on discounting and NPV). The NPTC for a machine kept for 10 years is the annual cash flows for each year discounted to their NPV, in the following way:

Net present total cost

$$
NPTC = \frac{\text{initial capital cost} + \text{operating (overhead and variable costs but not depreciation)} + \text{penalty costs (if possible)} - \text{tax savings} - \text{salvage value}}{(\text{discount rate})^{\text{no. of years}}}
$$

Example

year	1	2	3	4	5	6	PV
	initial + capital cost	operating + costs	penalty costs	− tax savings	− salvage value	discount rate $(1 + r)^n$	$\frac{(1+2+3+4+5)}{(6)}$
1	xxx	xxx	xxx	xxx	—	x	xxx
2	—	xxx	xxx	xxx	—	x	xxx
—	—	xxx	xxx	xxx	xxx	x	xxx
year n (end of machine's life)							NPTC

The machine with the lowest NPTC for its lifetime service is the best choice. NPTC can be expressed as an amortized annual cost, i.e., the annuity whose present value is one. This is the annual sum which, if paid each year for the life of the machine, is equivalent to the stream of costs (including interest) which sum to the NPTC. The machine with the lowest amortized annual cost (annuity) is the least costly investment. If one machine has a shorter life than another then the implicit assumption with this method is that the 'cycle' is repeated, i.e., the machine with the shorter life is replaced with one with the same annuity for costs.

Annual usage

The annual use or the annual output of a machine determines the relative unit cost of a large or small machine. A large tractor has an annual overhead cost of \$6,000 and a smaller one \$3,000. If the smaller tractor works 300 ha of cultivation, its overhead cost per ha is \$10. If the larger tractor cultivates 800 ha the overhead cost per ha is \$7.50. However, if it completes 1,000 ha of cultivation, the overhead cost per ha will drop to \$6.

Overcapitalization

At some stage in their farming lives, most cropping farmers face the charge that they are overcapitalized in machinery. 'Overcapitalized' refers to a situation where annual machinery ownership costs are high relative to the value of production from the asset. Remember timeliness and risk when considering excess capacity and excessive costs, and the operator's attitude to such risk. Farmers' attitudes to leisure and their dislike of sitting on tractors 20 years on and, keeping up with the neighbours, are only a part of the story for what might seem to be a gross overinvestment in machinery.

Break-even costs for ownership and contract

The less a machine is used, the higher the fixed costs per unit (per ha or per hour). As the machine is used more, the fixed costs are spread over more hours or ha, so the per unit costs are lower (see Figure 6.1).

Figure 6.1: Cost per ha as area cropped increases

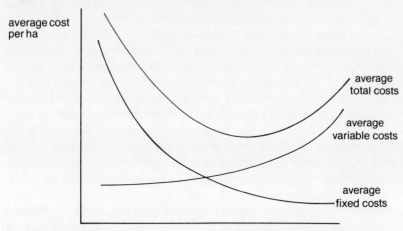

Break-even costs and areas

It is not economic to own expensive machinery which has little annual use. Below some level of machinery use it is cheaper to pay a contractor to carry out the task. Alternatively, above a certain level of machinery it is cheaper to own the machine than to hire contract services (see Figure 6.2). The break-even time per year for owning medium-sized tractors is usually 600 to 700 hours.

Figure 6.2: Break-even costs; contract vs owning

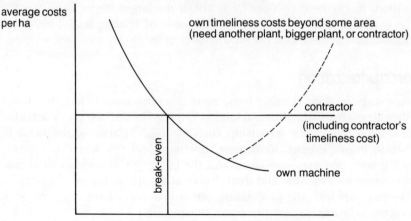

Replacement policies

The farmer with a large profitable operation tends to trade frequently and to keep equipment fairly new. The operator with a farm of medium size might run equipment until it is nearly worn out before changing it. An operator of a small farm may buy used plant and wear it out or hire contract services. One factor in the decision on when to replace machinery is the least average annual cost, the components of which are the relative levels of overhead and variable costs and annual hours of use over the machine's life.

Similar reasoning applies to the timing of the replacement of a machine. In theory, if a machine were to be replaced by an identical one then it should be kept long enough to achieve the lowest amortized average annual cost. To find this out, estimate the cumulative net cash flows and amortized annual cost, for a range of numbers of years for which the machine might be kept. This gives an initial guide about how long to keep a machine. A further guide for when the suggested replacement time is getting close is the total annual costs of owning and operating the machine for another year compared with the amortized annual cost which is expected to apply over the life of a new machine.

In practice, the best time to replace a machine depends on the current and expected near-future financial circumstances of the business, and the arrival of new technology. Often it is most useful to ask 'Is it worth keeping the current machine for another season?' This involves looking at the net changeover costs (including taxation implications) and the current liquidity of the business. Some assessment is made about the probable annual costs for the likely life of the replacement machine. This is then compared with the likely cost of keeping the present machine for another year. Generally, machine replacement is an opportunistic decision. If need be, the economic life of machinery can usually be extended considerably if times are tough. That is, higher operating costs may be incurred but new and higher ownership costs deferred temporarily.

The least average cost principle of replacement has the assumption that no newer models, with substantially lower operating costs, or greater speed or efficiency of operation, appear on the market. If such were the case, the change would be made if expected future costs (including costs as a result of untimeliness) of the machine fell below the unit costs of the existing machine. The changing relationship of overhead and variable costs as machines age results in varying costs per hour of operation from year to year (assuming annual output is constant). The tax laws have a major effect on optimum time of replacement. Where there is little difference in annual average cost of ownership over a certain range of years, the decision to replace is (quite sensibly) based on a good year or improvements in machine design.

These are the key factors involved in machine replacement:

- tax advantage (see below);
- a good salesman with new gimmicks on his model (especially comfort);
- available funds (a good season);
- expected advantages from better timeliness or performance;
- obsolescence.

Theoretically, the best time to keep the machine is until the total cost per ha per year ('average total cost') is about a minimum.

Rates of machinery costs

Having decided which costs are to be included decide the rates at which they are to be charged. The rates vary for the individual farm because of variations in the physical conditions of soil; topography; and most importantly in the standard of servicing under which the machine will operate. These will affect its operating cost and length of useful life of the machine. Some examples of cost rates as approximate guides are given below. There are lots of such rules of thumb held by farm workers and in agricultural engineering and machinery fields.

Depreciation (straight-line method) % of current new price

self-powered machinery	18
complex, non-powered	12
simple, non-powered	7
storage (shed) costs	1–2

Standard recurring costs as percentage of new price

Mechanical repairs and maintenance per year for a machine at about 'mid-life'; these costs will vary with age:

self-powered machinery per 1,000 hrs 5% to 8%, e.g. tractor repair and maintenance costs 8% of new price per 1,000 hrs
complex, non-powered per 1,000 hrs 5% to 8%, e.g. power take-off header
simple, non-powered per 1,000 hrs 2% to 5%, e.g. cultivator, air-seeder

lubrication:

complex machinery per 1,000 hrs 1%

simple machinery per 1,000 hrs 0.5%

tyres

   replace rear tractor tyres every 3,000 hrs

   replace front tractor tyres every 4,000 hrs

new battery every 2,000 hrs

Machinery work rates

Fundamental to assessing machinery costs is estimates of work rates which can be calculated using the following formula:

work rate in ha per hour

$$= \frac{\text{width} \times \text{speed} \times \% \text{ field efficiency}}{1,000}$$

where:

width is implement width in metres

speed is speed of travel during operation in km per hr.

Percentage field efficiency is actual work rate as a percentage of the theoretical work rate. Theoretical field efficiency is the work rate which could be achieved when the machine is operating at the best speed it can and covering the maximum width. Field efficiency is the actual or practical work rate achievable after allowing for failure to use the full width of the machine, turning time, stopping for loading and unloading, making adjustments and other stoppages. Field efficiency is 75% to 90% of theoretical work rate, depending on operation. From Blomfield (1982), in Table 6.2, are some theoretical work rates for a range of operations in a range of areas of Queensland. The different work rates reflect different scales of operations and size of plant, as well as different types of cropping.

Table 6.2: Theoretical work rates for farm machinery

Implement	Average ha per hr for a number of different cropping systems (early 1980s)	ha per hr
chisel	width (m)	6.37
	speed (kph)	6.4
	work rate (ha per hr)	4.08
disc plough	width (m)	4.91
	speed (kph)	5.3
	work rate (ha per hr)	2.60
disc harrows	width (m)	3.82
	speed (kph)	7.3
	work rate (ha per hr)	2.79
wheeled offset	width (m)	3.83
	speed (kph)	7.0
	work rate (ha per hr)	2.68

Implement		ha per hr
sweep plough	width (m)	6.83
	speed (kph)	6.3
	work rate (ha per hr)	4.30
scarifiers	width (m)	7.03
	speed (kph)	5.9
	work rate (ha per hr)	4.15
tined harrows	width (m)	10.50
	speed (kph)	9.1
	work rate (ha per hr)	9.55
roller	width (m)	10.14
	speed (kph)	9.6
	work rate (ha per hr)	9.73
inter-row cultivators	width (m)	4.58
	speed (kph)	7.4
	work rate (ha per hr)	3.39
conventional combine	width (m)	6.39
	speed (kph)	6.0
	work rate (ha per hr)	3.84
pneumatic combine	width (m)	9.46
	speed (kph)	7.9
	work rate (ha per hr)	7.47
row-crop planter	width (m)	5.13
	speed (kph)	7.2
	work rate (ha per hr)	3.69
header	width (m)	5.88
	speed (kph)	6.9
	work rate (ha per hr)	4.06

Source. J. G. Blomfield, *An Economic Investigation of Farm Machinery,* Queensland Department of Primary Industries, 1982.

What form of machinery service?

Most farm management plans involve using machinery services: we concern ourselves first with the question of what is the best way of acquiring machinery services. To start, it is necessary to determine, from the proposed physical farm program, what machine service will be needed, with provision for a small amount of overcapacity to cope with unforeseen events.

When the amount and types of machine service have been decided for a particular farm plan, e.g. tractor services, harvesting, cultivation and sowing services, the farmer should ask these two questions:

- need machines be bought at all, or can the services be provided by contractors, sharefarmers, lease, hire or machinery pooling?
- what are the capital costs, risks, and running costs of each type of service?

The various types of service listed in the first question must be available in the district; as the alternative is to buy the machinery. The problem then becomes one of the farmer providing machinery services as cheaply and reliably as possible. Then, a few calculations and comparisons are warranted.

Machinery syndicates or multi-farm use are another form of machinery ownership. Such syndicates spread the capital cost of ownership among several users. These are becoming more popular for using machinery where timeliness is not too critical, or where timing is discretionary e.g. fencing.

Costs of alternative sources of machinery services

When the decision (i.e., ownership of machinery or not) is not self-evident, the following points have to be clarified:

- the annual use to be made of the machine;
- likely changes in costs of contract versus ownership, e.g. contract prices might decline relative to ownership costs as more contractors compete for work;
- the value of timeliness of the operation;
- the value of quality of the completed service;
- the return which can be earned through alternative investments;
- the approximate opportunity cost of the operator's own labour force at the time the machine would be operating;
- the rate at which income tax is being paid.

The traditional 'cost accounting' type of approach to providing farmers with information on their machinery decisions uses only such measures as overhead costs, running costs and, on occasions, interest on capital. It generally takes little or no account of timeliness, standards of operations, the opportunity cost of capital, and, very important, the effects of tax.

In the following example we have incorporated these features as well as identifying the factors that underlie the choice of machinery services.

In choosing between alternative sources of machinery services these are the key questions to consider:

1 What amount of machine services will be needed?
2 What financial reserves and credit do I have access to?
3 Given the answer to 2, what are the implications for my equity position of financing the different machinery service options which I have, i.e., what is the range of sizes of investment which I can consider and still keep to what I feel to be a 'safe' equity position.
4 Of the financially feasible options, which gives the most 'profit'? This involves estimating the annual (overhead) cost of owning; the direct costs of the different forms of machinery services; any costs involved with the quality and timeliness of operations; 'opportunity' interest cost of the capital tied up in this way, and the tax implications of it all.

The first step in choosing between alternative sources of machinery services is to calculate and to compare the annual ownership cost of each. To compare them these figures must be expressed in the same dollar terms. In the following example the method is to do the sums in real dollars when comparing alternatives. The following example is about choosing the form in which machinery services should be acquired. The farm is an 800 ha grain farm in the north-west plains of New South Wales. A five-year crop sequence is followed: two years of winter crop (wheat, barley, beans), two years of summer crop (one sorghum, one sunflower) and a total of one year of fallow spread over the five years. In any year it is expected that there will be 320 ha of winter crop, 160 ha of sorghum, 160 ha of sunflowers, and 160 ha of fallow.

Four ways of acquiring machinery services are to be considered:

1 Owning all cropping equipment, but with contract carting to silos.
2 As for (1) but with contract harvesting instead of owning a header.
3 Having all operations done by contractors.
4 Sharefarming, with one-third of gross income going to the owner and two-thirds share going to the sharefarmer. Sharefarmer to pay all the growing and operating costs.

The relevant costs are the annual capital recovery (depreciation), opportunity interest and other overhead costs; the variable costs and the penalty costs for each means of acquiring machinery services. The decision about sources of machinery services is based on the expected best after-tax return from the alternatives. In all cases it is intended that a stubble-retention cropping system is carried out and good modern equipment is used.

The cropping plant required is as follows (see Table 6.3, p. 230), in 1991 dollars.

The capital recovery and interest charge is calculated as:

([replacement cost − salvage value] * amortization factor at 4%) + salvage value × 4%

The real cost of owning a $125,000 header, which is expected to have a trade-in value of $45,000 in five years is $19,768 per year. That is, there is $80,000 capital used-up or 'lost' over the five years, plus 4% real interest cost incurred on this capital, plus 4% real interest cost on the $45,000 capital recovered as trade-in value.

The difference is not large between the options: the contract option(s) involves paying for the contractor's labour, and so what the owner–operator does with labour becomes relevant. If, say, the operator does those tasks which would involve hiring some labour if the machinery were owned instead of contracted, and a saving on casual labour costs is made worth, say, $3,000, then the total gains from contracting also includes the $3,000 saved.

The decision as to which source of machinery to use is made after all of the pertinent other factors are considered.

The comparison in Table 6.5 is not strictly comparing like to like until a value is placed on any labour and capital which would be released for alternative uses by the contracting options. Importantly, any difference in income or costs owing to timeliness needs to be considered. If it is too difficult to put a figure on this factor, then the comparison indicates that the contract option would have to achieve timeliness gains over the performance of the own-all option. The likelihood of this occurring has to be evaluated. Some of the 'other' relevant factors in this decision are listed in the following Table 6.6.

Table 6.3: Annual 'ownership' cost of farming plant ($)

(800-ha crop farm—the plant is bought today and all sums are in real (1991) dollars)

	1 capital cost today's (1991) $	2 expected life (years)	3 expected capital cost at time of replacement (in 1991 $)	4 expected trade-in value (in 1991 $) the current price of similar machines	5 depreciation (capital lost) (3–4)	6 annuity for capital recovery plus interest	7 interest on capital salvaged	8* total annual depreciation plus interest cost
4-WD tractor	67,000	5	67,000	22,000	45,000	10,107	880	10,987
chisel plough (7 m)	15,000	10	15,000	4,000	11,000	1,356	160	1,516
air seeder and cultivator	30,000	10	30,000	8,000	22,000	2,712	320	3,032
precision planter	15,000	10	15,000	3,500	11,500	1,418	140	1,558
inter-row cultivator	4,500	10	4,500	1,250	3,250	400	50	450
mounted harrows	2,000	5	2,000	700	1,300	291	28	319
boom-spray	12,000	5	12,000	6,000	6,000	1,347	240	1,587
field bins	5,000	20	5,000	500	4,500	331	20	351
second-hand truck	10,000	10	10,000	1,500	8,500	1,048	60	1,108
slasher (7.5 m)	10,000	10	10,000	1,500	8,500	1,048	60	1,108
header (7.5 m)	125,000	5	125,000	45,000	80,000	17,968	1,800	19,768
Total	295,500		295,500	93,950	201,550	38,026		41,784

* The figure in 8 is the capital which is 'lost', multiplied by the amortization factor for 4% real return and life of machine plus salvage value 4 × 4% real interest cost, i.e., annual opportunity cost for the capital which is tied up but not lost.
Note. The high annual cost associated with the large items, the tractor and header.

Table 6.4: Direct and overhead costs to farmer of growing 640 ha of crop on 800-ha example farm, using alternative sources of machinery services (in 1991 real $)
Note. Figures are approximate

	own all machinery	own all cultivation machinery, but contract harvesting	all operations done by contract	sharefarming (one-third owner two-thirds sharefarmer)
	$	$	$	$
variable costs				
seed and fertilizer	15,650	15,650	15,650	
tractor and implements	13,000	13,000		
sprays	14,500	14,500		
harvesting	4,000			
contract costs				
plough			18,500	
cultivate and plant			28,500	
sprays and spraying			16,500	
harvest		23,000	23,000	
total variable costs	47,150	66,150	102,150	0
overhead costs				
insurance	2,700	1,100		
shelter	1,000	500		
ownership (from Table 6.3)	41,784	22,016	0	0
total overheads	45,484	23,616	0	0

Table 6.5: Costs of alternative ways to acquire machine services (real 1991 $)

	own-all, no borrowing for machinery	own-all, all borrowing for machinery	own but contract harvest, no borrowing for machinery	own but contract harvest, all borrowing for machinery	all contract	sharefarm
A gross income	140,000	140,000	140,000	140,000	140,000	46,200
B variable costs (Table 6.4)	47,150	47,150	66,150	66,150	102,150	—
C overheads (Table 6.4)	45,484	45,484	23,616	23,616	—	—
D total cost before tax (B + C)	92,634	92,634	89,766	89,766	102,150	—
E tax aspects						
gross income	140,000	140,000	140,000	140,000	140,000	46,200
cropping expenses	47,150	47,150	66,150	66,150	101,150	—
depreciation	33,160	33,160	17,160	17,160	—	—
interest (real)	—	7,779	—	4,379	—	—

continued

	own-all, no borrowing for machinery	own-all, all borrowing for machinery	own but contract harvest, no borrowing for machinery	own but contract harvest all borrowing for machinery	all contract	sharefarm
F taxable income	59,690	51,911	56,690	52,311	37,850	46,200
G tax payable (F × 0.25 cents in $)	14,922	12,978	14,172	13,078	9,462	11,550
H measurable benefit (A − D − G)	32,444	34,388	36,062	37,156	28,388	34,650

Table 6.6: 'Other' aspects of getting machine services

source of machinery service	own-all, no borrowing	own-all, all borrowing	own but contract harvest, no borrowing	own but contract harvest, all borrowing	all contract, no borrowing	sharefarm
measurable benefit (item H from Table 6.5)	$32,444	$34,388	$36,062	$37,156	$28,388	$34,650
other effects						
untimeliness cost	less than contracting	—	higher than with 'own-all'	—	higher than with both of the ownership options	same as with the 'own-all' option
probable size of untimeliness costs in 'normal' year compared to 'own-all'	—	—	e.g. 5% reduction in product	—	e.g. 10% reduction in product	—
what effect on debt-servicing ability and survival if untimeliness causes a large loss in gross income in one of the next couple of years?	—	—	e.g. could survive or serious	—	e.g. could survive or serious	—
equity and cash flow effects, i.e., ability to borrow for other uses and implications for repayments, costs, and cash flow	—	interest could have large effect	similar to 'own-all'	interest could have large effect	ability to pay contractor	depends on yield

continued

source of machinery service	own-all, no borrowing	own-all, all borrowing	own but contract harvest, no borrowing	own but contract harvest, all borrowing	all contract, no borrowing	sharefarm
after-tax value of earnings of any labour which is freed or of any labour costs which are saved by the labour which is 'freed'	none	—	may be some	—	yes, depends on situation, e.g. could be half a person-years	yes, could be as in 'all-contract' case or more
after-tax value of earnings of any capital which is 'freed' or of any capital costs which are saved by the capital which is 'freed'	none	—	yes, e.g. interest earned on average value of header, $85,000 at 3% after tax = $2,550	—	yes, e.g. interest earned on average value of machinery capital, $194,725 at 3% after tax = $5,842	yes, as in the 'all-contract' option
direct costs lost if total crop failure	base amount	—	same as 'own-all'	—	higher than own-all	none
overhead costs if total crop failure	base amount	—	less than 'own-all'	—	none	none
income foregone if very good year	no	—	no	—	no	could be significant
what other tax effects have you not counted	—	inflation will affect interest rates and tax paid	—	inflation will affect interest rates and tax paid	—	—

Estimates of annual ownership costs of capital equipment are used when comparing alternative machines to see which would be the more profitable one to own, and in comparing different ways of acquiring machinery services.

However, these figures are for the 'most likely' year. In years worse than this, the annual header ownership costs are incurred regardless; contracting harvesting expenses might be less in years of poor crops.

A further point to consider is if 'own-all' is the most attractive option, then the next set of sums to do is to compare the header ownership options within this option. The annual ownership costs for different 'own-all' options should be investigated. These will vary a great deal. As well, any untimeliness costs associated with the cheaper ownership options needs to be assessed.

A final factor which could act against the 'own-all' option is if the real interest rate exceeds 4%. The higher the interest rate, the more favourable the contract option might become. This depends on how competitive contract services are and how contract rates might change as interest rates might change.

The best decision in a comparison of options for acquiring the services of machinery might depend on the key 'other' factors such as outlined in Table 6.6. The key factors could be: (1) the effect on gearing and debt servicing (2) the expected size and likelihood of the untimeliness costs (3) the ability to withstand the effects of a bad outcome in any year (4) the realistic value of the other uses, if any, of the farmer's labour and capital if any is saved or not used in the cropping activity. Although the size and the likelihood of many of the other factors cannot be predicted accurately they have to be considered, and the relative advantages and disadvantages have to be balanced by the decision maker.

For example, a cropping farmer might go for the 'own-all' option as the best bet because the farmer might have doubts about employing sufficiently good contractors on time and could not afford to risk a significant loss of income in the next few years, and did not have other farm activities.

Further factors influencing choice

In general, the machines whose services are the most economic to obtain by methods other than ownership are those which:

* have a low annual use on the farm;
* require a large investment (e.g. earth-moving equipment);
* perform operations in which timeliness is not crucial.

When the decision of buying or hiring machinery is not self-evident, the following points have to be clarified:

* the annual use to be made of the machine;
* likely changes of cost of contract versus ownership, e.g. contract prices might decline relative to ownership costs as more contractors compete for work;
* the value of timeliness of the operation;
* the value of quality of the completed service;
* the rate at which profits can be earned through alternative investments;
* the approximate opportunity cost of one's own labour force at the time the machine would be operating;
* the rate at which income tax is being paid.

The type of service chosen depends upon the availability of capital and the rate of interest the owner decides to charge on it. The interest rate used should be the after-tax return which the capital could be earning were it invested in the best alternative; on some farms this can be as high as 20% real. A high opportunity rate of interest frequently favours services other than ownership.

Machinery syndicates

The main advantages of machinery syndicates are that they reduce the overhead cost of machine ownership, frequently allow more profitable use of limited capital funds, use otherwise idle machine capacity, and make available machine services which would normally be unavailable to the operator. Disadvantages are fear of arguments and being imposed on, especially in relation to maintenance, allocation of repair costs, order of machinery use. As well, there is uncertainty as to whether work of the desired quality will be carried out, and on time.

Another form of multi-farm use of machinery which is gaining popularity is where the machine remains the private property of one individual who hires out the idle capacity for a fee. The fee is often on a non-cash basis, with the user being obliged to return an equivalent service with some other machine. In future there may be a greater use of contract services for machines whose capital cost is significant. However, costs from inconvenience and untimeliness can significantly reduce the attractiveness of syndication to many farmers.

Deciding on size of machine

At some time most farmers face the problem of what size of machine they should buy. This decision often is the result of their personal preference, their economic position, and sales pressure. The logical criterion in the decision of how large a machine should be is that it should be large enough to get all important field operations completed well, on time; and that there is enough work to keep the per ha overhead costs down to a reasonable level.

The requirements for labour and machinery in other enterprises, the value placed on completing the job on time, and interaction of soil and weather variables, will all determine the total hours of work on which a tractor can be used over the year. Consequently, if the yearly work program is to be completed, a tractor of minimum capacity for the farm would theoretically use all the available days to complete the program. In practice, however, every season is different and some slack to handle emergency work, or work unaccounted for, or extra workings or re-sowings has to be allowed for in budgeting annual hours of use.

Looking only at overhead costs, the longer the machine's service life, the cheaper its overall costs of operation. However, variable costs must also be considered: over time these remain relatively constant per hour of use with the exception of the repair and maintenance and tyre component.

Steps in the process of deciding on size are to estimate:

- importance of untimeliness, and what this may be for different-sized machines;
- the approximate number of hours each size of tractor would take to complete the job;
- the proposed work program, and how many labour hours will be required;
- the cost per hour (exclusive of labour and interest costs) of each tractor;
- different hours of use for machines of various sizes;
- availability of funds;
- the approximate rate at which funds would earn income if invested in other farm activities.

The conditions which favour the use of a large machine are large risk from weather or untimeliness; high rate of income tax; high labour costs; high annual hours of use and low opportunity interest rates on capital.

The economics of the decision depends mainly on these factors:

- the cost associated with failure to perform the operation on time, i.e., the value of timeliness of operation;
- the value of labour saved (if any) by the larger machine;
- the difference in the annual overhead cost of the large and small machines;
- the annual hours of use the machine is likely to be put to;
- the level at which income tax is being paid;
- the availability and alternative uses of capital.

This reasoning is an application of the least-cost principle.

Timeliness

The value of timeliness of operations should be the first consideration when choosing the size of machinery as loss of income from this source alone can more than cover the extra cost of a high capacity machine in the first year. This particularly applies to the operations of weed control, sowing and harvesting. By comparing the relationship between the cost of untimeliness and the added overhead costs of larger capacity machines, a definite minimum capacity can be decided upon. The remaining factors (listed above) will determine optimum size.

These are the major operations with high penalty costs for untimeliness:

- time of fallowing: delays mean less moisture stored, hence lower crop yields;
- speed of working fallows: weeds have less chance to transpire moisture if killed quickly;
- time of sowing: delays lead to lower yields from either weed competition or loss of moisture;
- harvesting: rain damage, shaking, and hail loss.

Many managers of cropping enterprises try to have a machine capacity so that every operation is completed within 10 to 14 days. Thus they recognize the cost of untimeliness and are prepared to pay a price to minimize it. So the criticism that many farmers are overcapitalized in machinery has to be viewed with consideration of timeliness sometimes, though exposure to risk that can be increased by having the capacity to get all of the crop in quickly. This can mean that all of the crop is at a vulnerable stage at the same time, possibly susceptible to being hit by a single bad frost or a short burst of hot weather.

Capital investment to offset weather risk

In most districts larger machine size or capacity is regarded as an insurance against unfavourable weather conditions. The amount of additional money which should be invested for this purpose depends on crop requirements and on the opportunity interest rate chargeable on the extra capital, and, most important of all, the number of hours for which the machine will be used each year. Investment in extra machine capacity ties up funds for years. When contemplating investment in a margin of machine capacity as an insurance against operational delays, assess the value of timeliness for the additional future income expected to result from purchase of the machine.

A farmer thinks that with a certain $100,000 machine no major losses from untimeliness will be incurred in most years. However, with a smaller $75,000 machine the farmer estimates that in, say, four in 10 years, about 10% to 15% more yield will be lost than with the larger machine. The reasoning then is to assess if the value of losses saved are likely to be more than the opportunity of having $25,000 extra tied-up cost in the larger machine.

In reality, some losses because of weather are inevitable, but large-capacity, efficient harvesting machinery can reduce this risk to the minimum, at the price of higher running and overhead costs.

Increasing overheads: saving labour

This decision is dependent on a comparison of the costs of labour and capital. Farmers commonly invest in larger capital equipment to cut down an increasing permanent wage bill. When large machines are substituted for smaller machines, extra overhead costs are incurred, e.g depreciation, interest. These extra costs are partly offset by reduced labour costs. The important consideration is whether the value of the labour saved by the larger machine is sufficient to offset its higher costs.

In some cases the labour-saving dollars may be surpassed by the extra high fixed costs of larger machines. But if the annual hours of use are high, the labour costs saved on a larger machine will usually outweigh the additional overhead costs. The amount and thus the value of labour saved can be calculated by estimating the difference in hours of operation required by the two machine sizes to complete the job. Approximate hours of labour saved can be estimated by using a labour hour to machine hour ratio of 1.25 to 1 for small areas and for large areas 1.1 to 1. Some dramatic increases have been achieved in areas cropped per labour unit. This has come about largely through farmers trading-up to significantly larger plant.

New or used machines?

Is it cheaper to purchase new or used machinery? These are factors in this decision:

- the relative purchase price of new and used machines;
- investment allowance on new machinery;
- the expected rate of depreciation;
- the opportunity cost of capital;
- cost of time lost because of mechanical failure;
- obsolescence;

- the associated overhead and variable costs;
- income tax rate;
- the expected period over which it is intended to use the services of the machine.

The costs of acquiring machinery services in farming are difficult to identify accurately as there are a number of best-guesses. Nevertheless these costs can vary a lot between basically similar farms because of different standards of machinery management and also the results of good and bad machinery investment decisions. However, these costs are crucial. With big investments such as machinery it is worth doing a few calculations of your own, and not simply rely on the dealers (or coveting thy neighbours' plant).

6

Questions for discussion

1   How do you work out the total annual cost of owning a farm machine?

2   When is interest counted as a cost in machinery decision, and when is it not?

3   Untimeliness of operations (fallowing, sowing, harvesting) can be very costly. Can you put a money value on it for a farm you know? How do you get over the problem: by using large capacity plant; hire; use contractors to take up the 'slack'; sharefarming; syndicate a larger machine; or other strategies?

4   Consider the differences in total annual costs (running costs, untimeliness, interest, depreciation, etc.) between buying a good second-hand tractor and a new one? What costs are likely to differ the most?

5   What different machines, which farmers do not have now, will some have in five years' time? These will be needed to help them keep up with advances in cropping technology.

6

Further reading

Barnard, C. S. and Nix, J. S., *Farm Planning and Control* (2nd edn), Cambridge University
Press, Cambridge, 1986.
Boehlje, M. D. and Eidman, V. R., *Farm Management*, John Wiley & Sons, New York,
1983.
Calkins, P. H. and DiPietre, D. D., *Farm Business Management: Successful Decisions in
a Changing Environment*, Macmillan Publishing Co. Inc., New York, 1983.
Castle, E. N., Becker, M. H., & Nelson, A. G., *Farm Business Management—The Decision
Making Process*, Macmillan Publishing Company, New York, 1987.
Whan, I. F. and Hammer, G. L., 'The Cost of Delay in Harvesting Wheat', *Review of
Marketing and Agricultural Economics*, 53(1), 1985.

7

They Don't Make It
Any More:
Buying and Leasing Farmland

A t some time most farmers and many business people buy, sell, and lease
farmland. The decision to buy land is the biggest single business decision
a farmer ever makes. When should the farmer buy more land? Could it
possibly be worth that much to the farm family? How much should we, could
we, and would we pay for this land? And, most important of all, is the time
right? These are the searching, worrisome questions that haunt farm buyers
and their families before they commit themselves to a large, long-term debt,
often of 20 years or more. As well as haunting farmers at various stages in their
career, the question of the value of the farmland has been a worry to economists
for centuries. In this chapter ways of thinking about land value and of buying
a farm are dealt with. Practical applications of these ways of thinking are
explored; the question of leasing land is also investigated.

Just as the land market is remarkably complex, so, too, are the ways of
thinking about it. Though we deal at some length with the concepts of the
value of land and the theoretical maximum offer prices, the major practical
aspect of how much to pay for land is about timing. One of the most important
factors in success in farming is the price you pay to get into the game. Price
paid for farmland relative to longer term prospects for operating profits and
capital gains is the primary consideration. An interesting aspect is the price
asked during a current down-turn, or at the start of a recovery when some farmers
leave farming, compared with what the land could be worth if reasonable
expectations about future commodity prices were to eventuate. Good timing
is the crux of the land purchase game.

One of the major benefits from using the methods outlined in this chapter
for valuing farmland is that, done properly, these methods should make it

obvious when a price is unrealistic. By taking explicit account of all the known, measurable factors affecting the value of farmland, unrealistic prices become obvious. This alone could save some farm buyers a lot of trouble in the future. The main reason for farmers 'going broke' is unwise land purchases.

Ways of thinking about farmland value

Farmland is a fascinating resource. First, 'they don't make it any more' and it is not a mobile resource. It is durable and varies greatly in type, quality, and uses. Importantly, people regard land as more than a factor of production. Thus the word 'value' of land, has many meanings in everyday farming language. Farm landowners if asked the value of their land may answer:

- the price they paid for it;
- the price they would like to receive for it at sale;
- the amount they would be prepared to pay for it if they had to buy it now;
- the sum they would like adopted for rates, land and capital gains taxes.

Despite this, all landowners have as a reserve price the minimum price they would be prepared to accept for their land. Similarly, all potential land buyers have some offer price, which is the maximum price they would be prepared to pay for a particular parcel of land at a given time. So we need to look at the factors that determine the offer and reserve prices which land buyers and sellers have.

The basic economic influence on offer and reserve prices is the profitability of owning agricultural land. Both offer and reserve prices of prospective land buyers and sellers depend on their expectations about future profitability and prospects for capital gains. Other factors which underlie the respective prices include present financial position; availability of finance; taxation; the alternatives to buying or selling land; and non-pecuniary aspects of owning farmland.

Capital involved in farming

Farmers manage substantial assets. A grain grower farming 1,500 ha can have \$200,000–\$300,000 tied-up in plant, and own land worth \$1 m. Farmers controlling such large capital resources should ask the following question, and review the answer, at regular intervals: how should I manage my resources to obtain the most (1) annual income, and (2) capital gain? The answers are found by assessing relevant alternative investment opportunities; of which these are the chief:

- on the present farm;
- in another farm in a different area;
- in shares, bonds or banks;

- in urban, industrial or recreational real estate;
- education for their children (and perhaps themselves).

Most farmers have developed considerable skill in managing agricultural resources. They usually wish to continue living the way they do, and where they do. Staying in agriculture is often the most attractive course. Where off-farm investment looks more profitable, farmers invest some of their resources off-farm. Many farmers have considerable off-farm investments. Ultimately the values placed on rural life and to some extent on being one's own boss are usually important considerations. Further, there usually is a close inter-relation between the farm household and the farm business. Decisions affecting the household cannot be made independently of the farm business. Farming differs from many businesses as the farm family's investment in physical capital (land, etc.) and human capital (skills, interests) are intimately related. As well, the farm usually represents part of the farmer's 'superannuation' or retirement fund.

The movement in selected Victorian and New South Wales' land prices in the post-war era, in nominal and real terms (i.e., in values corrected for inflation) is shown in Tables 7.1 and 7.2. The apparently spectacular increase in land values is not so significant when inflation is taken into account. Thus the rise in wheat land prices in nominal terms from $154 per ha in 1967 to $1,000 per ha in 1991 in the Wimmera (see Table 7.1) reduces to $175 dollars when the purchasing power of the 1967 dollar is deflated (see Table 7.2).

Table 7.1: Some examples of prices per ha of improved farmland expressed in nominal dollars, i.e., dollar values as at the year quoted

	years							
	1960	1967	1971	1973	1980	1988	1990	1991
wheat								
Wimmera (Vic.)								
(black soil)	128	185	148	222	600	750	1,100	1,000
north-west plains (NSW)								
(black soil)	90	136	109	148	450	1,000	1,250	1,200
Spring Ridge (NSW)						880	1,400	1,300
dairying								
Gippsland (Vic.)	494	741	618	988	2,000	4,500	5,750	6,000
Goulburn Valley (Vic.)								
(irrigation)	780	988	865	1,235	2,400	5,000	6,500	7,000
Taree (NSW)						2,500	3,500	4,000
grazing and mixed farming								
Western District (Vic.)	188	250	200	297	750	1,400	2,200	1,750
New England (NSW)	160	198	160	220	600	1,100	2,000	1,600
Northern Tablelands								
(Tenterfield) (NSW)						700	1,050	1,000
near-city grazing								
Romsey (Vic.)	221	370	395	586	1,500	3,750	4,500	4,250
orchards								
Shepparton (Vic.)	3,700	4,200	4,450	4,695	4,900	18,000	20,000	18,000

Table 7.2: Some examples of prices per ha of improved land in areas similar to those in Table 7.1, but converted to 'real' terms in 1967 dollars by the Consumer Price Index, i.e., corrected to take part account of inflation

	years							
	1960	1967	1971	1973	1980	1988	1990	1991
wheat								
Wimmera (Vic.)	154	185	137	181	214	175	206	175
north-west plains (NSW)	—	136	101	121	161	233	234	210
Spring Ridge (NSW)	—	—	—	—	—	204	262	228
dairying								
Gippsland (Vic.)	595	741	572	810	714	1,050	1,078	1,052
Goulburn Valley (Vic.) (irrigation)	940	988	800	1,012	860	1,162	1,219	1,228
Taree (NSW)	—	—	—	—	—	581	657	701
grazing and mixed farming								
Western District (Vic.)	226	250	185	239	270	325	412	307
New England (NSW)	193	198	148	180	215	255	375	280
Northern Tablelands (Tenterfield) (NSW)	—	—	—	—	—	163	197	175
near-city grazing								
Romsey (Vic.)	266	370	366	480	536	872	844	746
orchards								
Shepparton (Vic.)	4,553	4,200	4,120	3,848	1,750	4,190	3,752	3,157
Consumer Price Index (a fairly crude measure of inflation, as it affects farmers) Base: 1967 = 100	83	100	108	122	280	430	533	570

Land prices are not determined by present income per ha, but by the expected future net income per ha. In essence, land values reflect the expected incomes and capital gains which result from their management and control, after the potential purchaser has made some allowance for the uncertainty of prices and yields in the future.

Subsidies and tax concessions and the pressure of urban demand for land close to cities or for recreation and hobby farms were important considerations in many sectors of the agricultural land market in the post-war era. In the future subsidies and tax concessions will have much less influence. Also, periodic rises in capital value of farmers' land increases borrowing power which is used to expand holdings; this partly accounts for much of the demand in the land market.

Land values can rise or fall in real terms over time. For example, many properties in the wheat zones of Australia rose in real value during the late 1970s and early 1980s, and then declined in real value because of falling wheat prices. Similarly values for land for growing wool rose markedly during the wool boom of the late 1980s, then fell from high levels once wool prices fell in the early 1990s.

Much land is bought for production potential and security of wealth rather than its immediate productivity. Buyers see scope for increasing output and income by implementing technological advances. The retiring farmer or landowner who sells farmland reaps the benefits of technological advance. That is, if technological progress over time lifts the potential productivity and profitability of farm production, then this will be reflected in land values. The main point in discussions about land values is this: whatever happens to profitability of production, be it a sustained rise in produce prices because of increased demand from a new market; or protection and assistance granted to farmers by governments; *it will all end up in the land value.*

Land values reflect mostly the incomes and capital gains which are expected after the potential purchaser has made allowance for the uncertainty about future prices and yields. The demand for land for recreation and country living and part-time farming accounts for a rapidly increasing proportion of the number of sales of farmland, albeit very small 'farms'.

Buying farmland

Farm buyers have different motives for buying: it is a way of life; profits; capital gain; is a hedge against inflation; is security; a form of speculation; and a hobby. Value a prospective buyer places on a farm incorporates such a range of matters, only some of which are economic factors. Here we concentrate on the economic aspects of farm purchase.

Physical aspects such as location are important: state of housing; proximity to other landholdings or important services; improvements to pastures, buildings, water supplies, fencing; proportion of tree cover; and soil types; these are hard to value and are valued differently by different buyers.

Before proceeding with plans to expand farm area, look at the potential of further development of the existing area. Sometimes it is possible that the benefits expected to flow from farm expansion can be achieved better by developing and diversifying the existing holding. Farmers often find that until their own farms are reasonably well developed, investment in developing the existing farm will bring greater returns than buying more land under good management. Each case has to be judged on its particular merits, because so many factors are involved.

Once the decision has been made to buy farmland, the first aspect to consider is the area in which the available farm for sale is situated. Investigate, from as many informed sources as time permits: the history of settlement; climate; likelihood of drought; incidence of floods, fire, and other natural disasters; present land-use and agricultural production systems; crop yields, and stock-carrying capacities; recent past and forecast trends in the industry; educational facilities; employment opportunities and the expected influence of urban growth; mining developments; and national parks.

Knowing the number of times a particular farm was sold in recent years; its access; location; the state of the house; the structures and improvements help determine its appeal for the buyer and family. How much money might be needed to bring the structures up to a standard which suits the would-be purchaser must be assessed, too.

See Chapter 2 for a check list of agricultural and financial features. It was stressed that a farm had to be analysed before it could be planned. In any analysis of a farm, the present situation and the potential for change and for development, as well as restraints on (and risks of exploiting) this potential, must be considered.

Land value

There are a number of ways of calculating how much to offer for a parcel of farmland. In essence these methods are how much a bidder:

- should pay;
- could pay;
- would pay; and
- might have to pay.

What should I pay? Income capitalization method

The heading 'what should I pay?' refers to the economic value of the investment; the expected after-tax returns on the investment, made up of annual operating returns and expected capital gains, if any.

Theoretically, one way to calculate how much an investor should pay is to use the method 'income capitalization' or 'asset valuation method', or variations of these methods such as the net present value of the investment. The essence of this approach is that the value of an asset depends on the future streams of net income which the asset is expected to give, and the rate of return on the investment which the would-be buyer needs.

The present value (PV) of a future stream of income earned by an asset is the sum of the future income flows discounted to the PV by the required rate of return (see also Chapters 2 and 9). The PV then represents the amount which should be paid for the asset, because, if this amount were paid, and the income stream received then the required rate of return will be earned.

Example

An asset promises a stream of net income for three years as follows:

year	1	2	3
amount	$100	$100	$100
discount factor at 5%	0.9524	0.9070	0.8638
PV	$95.24	$90.70	$86.38

where

$$PV = \frac{\text{income stream}}{(1 + i)^{\text{no. of years}}}$$

i is the discount rate (i.e., required rate of return)
total PV of net income stream is $272.32

Therefore if an investor requires a return of 5% on the investment, then up to \$272 should be paid for the asset which promises this stream of \$100 net income for three years. If \$272 were paid, then the investment yields the investor the 5% specified. The 5% required return is also 'the capitalization rate'.

When calculating the PV of income streams in perpetuity the formula for PV,

$$PV = \frac{\text{net income stream}}{(1+i)^{\text{no. of years}}} \text{ reduces to } \frac{\text{net income stream}}{(i)}$$

If an asset promised a constant net return (after all costs including tax) forever of \$100 per year, and the investor's required minimum real rate of return (opportunity cost) were 5%, then the asset would be valued at $\frac{\$100}{0.05} = \$2,000$.

That is, if the asset were purchased for \$2,000, and a net income of \$100 every year were earned, then the investor receives 5% return on the investment. The value \$2,000 is the 'productive value' of the asset.

$$\text{productive value} = \frac{\text{net return to the asset}}{\text{capitalization rate}} = \frac{\$100}{0.05} = \$2,000$$

The assumption of the income stream going in perpetuity might not be unrealistic. The next buyer at some future time will similarly assess the PV of the future income streams.

Now, using the income capitalization method the value of all the farmland improvements, stock, plant, and machinery, i.e., 'walk-in, walk-out; (WIWO) value, can be derived by capitalizing the operating profit after tax which is expected to be produced by the whole bundle of assets.

To value farmland, the expected net returns to the land alone would have to be separated from the return to the land and the associated investment in plant, stock, and improvements. Thus, in theory, to value farmland alone, the return to use should be after deducting from operating profit an interest return to the non-land capital such as the improvements, machinery, and stock.

$$\text{value of land alone} = \frac{\text{after-tax net return to land (after deducting return to non-land capital)}}{\text{after-tax capitalization rate}}$$

But, in practice, it is very hard to allocate a return to non-land capital to derive a return to the land alone. Care has to be taken with valuing non-land capital. Some of the capital invested on the farm might have little realizable market value if the owner were to sell it as an independent item. This is because capital is sunk into a specific use such as a shed or a bore, and this has little value other than as part of the whole farm business. But, a prospective buyer still values the services of such assets in any offer price.

To estimate operating profit per ha and capitalize it gives the value of all the land and improvements, plant and stock WIWO. Then the realizable worth of the non-land assets such as machinery and stock can be estimated and deducted from WIWO value. The remainder of the WIWO value is the implied worth of the land and fixed improvements.

Note. The value of the machinery and stock to use is the value of machinery and stock services needed to earn such an operating profit, not necessarily the value of those particular assets on the farm in question.

Example

operating profit (return to land and improvements, plant and stock) = $100 per ha
capitalization rate = 5% real
total assets value = $2,000 per ha WIWO
value of non-land capital needed to earn the operating profit (plant + stock) = $500 per ha
value of land and improvements at 5% capitalization rate
= $2,000 per ha − $500 per ha = $1,500 per ha.

The value using the income capitalization method is very sensitive to the measurement of the expected net income stream and to the required rate of return used.

Example

operating profit	$100	$100	$120	$120
capitalization rate	0.04	0.05	0.04	0.05
capitalized value	$2,500	$2,000	$3,000	$2,400

This simple use of the income capitalization method is not very informative about how much to pay for some land. The expected future net income stream(s) used has to reflect any expected changes in net income over time. Expected capital gains, related to any changes in net income over time or independent of net income, have to be taken into consideration.

Some comments on the income capitalization method

How should values estimated by the various income capitalization methods be interpreted? The income capitalization method works very well for valuing government bonds or the assets of some non-farm businesses; it is less useful when it comes to valuing farmland. Thus values derived in this way are treated as giving only a range of 'fixed points' for the potential buyer to focus on.

Studies which have attempted to assess the implied rates of capitalization of farmland by farmers from buying prices and income streams usually find the implied rates of capitalization are extremely low. This means 'apparently' high values for farmland. Problems arise with valuations of assets and with estimates of annual net returns because estimates of operating profit, net farm income, and net return to land include a range of imputed values; capitalizing net cash returns per ha usually gives a more realistic estimate of land values because the cash figures are more objective than guesses about non-cash items such as depreciation and the operator's allowance.

The goals and objectives of farm families are important in land values.

The land purchase decision can involve long-term objectives. Some farm families wish to continue farming because they love it, know it, and do it best. Often they wish to increase the size of their holdings to enable heirs to continue farming, and also to build-up an adequate-sized 'superannuation' for retirement. Thus short-term alternative rates of earnings from a similar-sized investment might never come into the decision. This is possibly why apparent capitalization rates used by farmers often seem low.

Even when the income capitalization method is relevant to a decision about land value, anomalies are found: rising land values at times coincide with apparent falling net returns per ha. This could be explained by expectations about a future recovery of profitability, and partly by expectations about inflation and by changes in the real cost of borrowed money. The availability of credit to farm buyers affects their bidding power. Thus the usual relationship explaining land values and capitalization rates (where value = net cash return over required rate) might not be as accurate as a relationship between land value, capitalization rate, and net cash flow plus some allowance for the access which bidders have to credit.

With the income capitalization approach, some say 'deduct the rate of expected annual capital gain from the required rate of return, and capitalize returns with that figure'. This is incorrect. If 2% capital gain p.a. is expected, then it is 2% each year of a different base value. It is necessary to assess the effects of capital gains on offer prices on a year-by-year basis. The same applies to incorporating effects of inflation on operating profits or land values. Inflation means a variable stream of future cash flows, and so to estimate land value a planning horizon needs to be set.

A variation on the simple income capitalization approach: the present value method

The earning potential of farmland is more realistically valued once expected annual cash earnings and the expected capital gains are treated as part of farmers' total returns. If a planning horizon for the valuation of the asset in question can be defined, then the expected changes in annual net returns and eventual capital gains can be accounted for by discounting the future returns and gains to NPVs. The NPV is the current amount which could be paid for the asset, and could still earn the required rate of return.

With no inflation, the PV of land is determined by the current PV of its net earnings after tax. However, often the land and other assets are expected to increase in value at the general inflation rate. This tends to happen if the farmers' net returns keep up with inflation, i.e., maintain their real value.

Once there is inflation or it is anticipated, then the value of land, stock, and plant has to be estimated using nominal values. The capitalization method cannot be used as it is based on constant future earnings. A distinct planning horizon has to be used because a varied series of earnings is involved, and the standard NPV, project analysis approach, is applied.

In essence the approach is to say 'If I pay this amount for the land, and it earns $Z amount each year, and the returns and land, plant and stock value grow by this percentage each year, with land, plant and stock worth $Y at the end of a time, what is the land worth in NPV terms?'

In effect the internal rate of return (IRR) of buying the land at a particular price is calculated, with land price being varied to give an IRR equal to the required rate of return. This gives a theoretical 'should pay' price estimate, which is valid only if there were no uncertainties about the various parameters in the calculation.

The land value is found by trial and error, working out the PV of the future operating profits plus the PV of future capital gains for each of a number of possible land prices. Remember, the value of any given percentage annual capital gains depends on the initial land price, and vice versa.

The aim is to find the land price and WIWO value which is equal to the PV of future operating profit plus the PV of capital gains, all minus the opportunity cost of having capital tied up in this investment, for given conditions of inflation, capital gain, etc. When the land price which meets this criteria appears higher than the market or asking price, as can happen with some combinations of assumed profits, inflation, capital gains, and discount rate, then find the discount rate which equates the PV of the future earnings to possible land prices. That is, find the IRR of the investment, if you were to pay the current market, or asking, price. An example is given below.

Present value method of land valuation

The PV method of assessing land value is, in essence, standard project analysis, with the focus mainly on the initial asking price for land.

Example A

planning horizon:	20 years
expected annual after-tax operating profit per ha:	$40 per ha
expected average annual inflation rate:	3.5% per year
required after tax real rate of return:	2% per year
after-tax nominal discount rate:	5.57% per year (0.035 + 0.02 + [0.035] (0.02))
expected real gain in land value	0% per year
expected nominal gain in land value:	3.5% per year
land is salvaged in year 20, after growing in value at 3.5% per year	
machinery and stock are salvaged in year 20, after periodic replacement, and after increasing in value at the annual rate of inflation over this period	

year	1	2	3	4	. . .	20
cash in						
operating profit per ha	40	41.4	42.85	44.35	. . .	79.59
land salvage						2,985
machinery + stock salvage						696
cash out						
asking price land per ha	1,500					
machinery + stock per ha	350					
NCF	−1,809	+41.4	+42.85	+44.35		+3,760
net present value	+49					

Interpretation

If the investment promises a positive NPV at the required rate of return and for the given assumptions and initial asking price, then the investment has earned at more than the required rate. This is so in this case, thus the purchase of the land at the asking price of $1,500 per ha represents good value. Alternatively, if the NPV were negative, then the asking price for the land is too high—the returns are not there to justify this price. The land price at which NPV is zero represents the maximum land price which could be paid, and the required rate of return still be earned, if all the other assumptions were to be 'true'.

The above analysis (example A) can be reorganized (example B) to compare explicitly the initial WIWO investment (asking price of land plus cost of machinery and stock) with the PV of the expected operating profits, plus the present value of expected land capital gains, minus the opportunity cost of having capital tied-up in land and stock and plant over the time. The WIWO price which equals the PV of the investment, under the given conditions, is the theoretically 'correct' price to pay.

Example B

initial WIWO

land	$1,500 per ha
machinery + stock	$350 per ha
WIWO	$1,850 per ha

PV of investment

operating profits PV = $654

PV of the investment in land = $1,009 (after capital gains from land and after discounting for opportunity cost of capital tied-up in this use)

PV of the investment in machinery and stock = $235 (after keeping up with inflation and after discounting for opportunity cost of capital tied-up in this use)

NPV of investment = $1,898 ($654 + $1,009 + $235) present value of earnings and salvage value minus $1850 initial cost of land, machinery, and stock, i.e., $49 NPV at the 5.57% discount rate.

If PV of the investment (earnings plus salvage values) is greater than the initial WIWO value of the investment at the asking price for land, then, if the assumptions are realistic, buying the land at the asking price gives a rate of return more than the required rate of return. The land is good value at this price. When the PV of investment is less than the initial WIWO value of the investment at the asking price for land, then, if the assumptions are realistic, buying the land at the asking price gives a rate of return less than the required rate of return. The land is not good value at this price.

But when the PV of investment is equal to the initial WIWO value of the investment at the asking price for the land, then the asking price represents the maximum price which could be paid and the required rate of return still be earned, given the assumptions.

To draw more useful information from this method you need to use the computer spreadsheet. The key variables can be changed easily to explore other likely scenarios, providing information to help form judgements about how much to pay for land.

Buying and developing land

When the land in question is to be further developed, such as by further investment in pasture or animal improvement, then the standard development budget is done (see Chapter 9), except the focus is more on the price paid for the farm. The additional investments and increased operating profits are included in the appropriate years, and the land and improvements, stock and plant are salvaged at the end of the planning period. The rate of return and the NPV of the project is assessed for a range of land values.

A practical application of the PV method of valuing land is given later in this chapter. With some combinations of the key parameters a land price can be defined which equals the value of the expected stream of operating profits and the capital gains and salvage values. At other times the parameters are such that if they were to hold true, then in theory it would appear that a much higher price than the asking price could be paid, before the price exceeds the value. Again, this is found when the sums are done on the spreadsheet. Land values sometimes appear to be much higher than land prices because the capital gains depend on the initial price used, and value is extremely sensitive to the discount rate used (as in the capitalization method). Remember that the assumed rates of OP, capital gain, inflation, and interest rates might or might not happen. When this result occurs look again at the rates which have been assumed, and work out the implied IRR at the current asking price, i.e., use a higher required rate of return.

It is more sensible to say 'If I pay the asking price of $2,000 per ha I get a rate of return slightly above my required rate' than to say 'the asking price is $2,000 per ha but according to all of my criteria it appears I could pay up to $4,000 per ha for the land and still earn my required rate of return'. With this method if we are estimating a maximum offer price; it is only the case if all of the assumptions were to hold true. In reality, the estimated price paid for the land is but one more piece of information; one point to fix on and to consider, amongst other bits of information.

So far we have discussed deriving some economic values for what a buyer, in theory, should pay for some land. This is useful information as a starting point. However, more practical information is needed.

The key to success is to be able to buy-in at considerably less than theoretical 'should pay' prices, and thus get good value. If the timing is right, when current expectations are well below reasonable medium to longer term expectations and the buyer is 'cashed-up', then land can often be obtained at a price which lets the buyer survive the variability of returns which occurs around the expected average returns. Remember that 'average' outcomes rarely happen in any particular year.

Two particularly practical bits of information are 'What is the current market value of similar properties in the area?' and 'How much could I pay for the land given the relevant financial constraints?' In practice current market prices and what can be financed, are the keys in decisions about how much to bid. All of the methods outlined in this chapter are worth using, particularly as they help identify prices which would not really be economically sensible, given reasonable expectations about the future levels of key determinants of land value.

Market value

The market value method is the commonest used, and a useful approach; the amount the buyer ultimately pays. The potential buyer needs to explore the market prices current for similar types of properties. Adjust the known figures for a number of important factors:

- the method and conditions of the sale. When a seller provides vendor finance at below market rates, the sale price has to be adjusted to an equivalent market price without vendor finance, or to an equivalent market price under the terms of the proposed sale of the land which is being considered for purchase;
- the differences in the sizes of the properties; the type and state of improvements (especially house); the possible uses for the house; the management history (well-farmed and maintained or run-down and neglected); the different types and state of the soils, pasture, and topography;
- the different timings of the past sales compared to the present;
- changes in expectations about future commodity prices, inflation, interest rates, and the related local and international economic conditions.

Such adjustments are critical but they are also hard to make. Only serious sales are worth looking at. The adjusted market value gives some indication of what a potential buyer might have to pay for a property. In a similar way to the income capitalization method, the market value method yields further information to use in the decision, but it is also only an approximate guide.

The term 'market value' is ambiguous; in a downturn in commodity prices when a proportion of farmers with too little equity and too high debt to service are in financial trouble, many declare they will get out if they can get their price. Often a price is mentioned which represents good buying value, given the longer term prospects of the industry.

However, sometimes few buyers are sufficiently cashed-up and they and their potential financiers do not have the confidence about the immediate- and medium-term outlook to buy, despite the attractive asking price. Thus little or no land changes hands at this asking price. Eventually, a market price is formed and sales take place, some time later. This is when both buyer's expectations and cash positions have picked up, and financiers are a bit keener. The market price formed might be 12 months or more later, and it is usually higher than the earlier asking price. It is often still considerably less than the prices ruling before the down-turn. A market price is only a market price when a sale takes place.

What I could pay

The financial feasibility of investment in farmland, at various possible prices for the land, is the key to appraising the land price a particular potential buyer could offer. In any year the farm family needs enough cash to meet operating expenses; living expenses; replacement costs; taxes; and interest and principal payments. The annual cash surplus has to be worked out after all the sources of cash have been accounted for and have been met, but before new interest and principal payments. This shows how much debt could be serviced, for various types of loans and terms of loan servicing.

To estimate financial feasibility is simple. First, expected annual cash surplus before new debt is estimated, and it is the potential amount available to meet annual interest and principal repayments. This surplus represents an annuity available to meet the annual payment (interest and principal) on an amortized loan. For example, 100 ha of adjacent crop land is under consideration. Suppose the expected annual cash surplus which could be devoted to servicing new debt is $21,000, from all sources including the 100 ha, after all cash uses to farm the extra land and before new debt servicing. To be cautious let us say that two-thirds of this sum can be expected to be available in any year; so, say, there should be $14,000 available. This sum is a nominal value and it is expected to increase at the annual rate of inflation over time. Therefore the debt terms are calculated using nominal, not real, interest costs.

The amount of an amortized loan serviced by this sum is given by the PV of an annuity (Table D in the Appendix). With no initial deposit, $14,000 per year could service a 10-year loan, at 15% interest, of $14,000 × PV factor 5.0188 = $70,263.

As a check on this the annuity factor needed to service a debt of $70,000 is given by: the annuity factor for 10 years at 15%, 0.1992 × $70,263 = $13,996 annuity. The buyer could offer up to $\dfrac{\$70,000}{100}$ = $700 per ha for the 100 ha of land, because the debt can be serviced with the expected annual cash surplus. When some equity capital is available the financial feasibility of an investment is assessed as follows:

$$\begin{matrix} \text{price} \\ \text{could pay} \end{matrix} = \begin{matrix} \text{equity capital} \\ \text{available} \end{matrix} + \left(\begin{matrix} \text{cash surplus available} \\ \text{to service debt} \end{matrix} \times \begin{matrix} \text{factor for present value} \\ \text{of an annuity} \end{matrix} \right)$$

If enough money for $200 per ha is available in equity capital, then in the example given above $700 + $200 = $900 per ha could be paid for the land. Whether it should be paid though is another question. The spreadsheet is used to derive a schedule of maximum financially feasible prices per ha with various interest rates; loan maturities; annual cash surpluses; and equity capital available.

What I would pay

There still remains those benefits of land ownership which are unable to be measured and can include the fulfilment of some deep-seated intrinsic wants. Or it may be the benefits of being close to the existing holdings. As most farmland is sold in parcels to neighbours, the effect of proximity and competition between neighbours on purchase prices of particular parcels of land can be marked. Another attribute of land value, again difficult to assess, is farmer's preference for longer term wealth over short-term to medium-term operating profits, probably something farmers are as much, or more, interested in as profits. Wealth, and thus equity, is valued in part for the security it provides as it reduces risk by reducing gearing and therefore increases liquidity.

As well as what a buyer 'should pay' on purely economic considerations, and what a buyer could pay on practical grounds of cash available, many non-economic and non-financial considerations also play a part in determining what a buyer would, and may have to, pay for a parcel of farmland.

Estimating land value in practice

Initial steps in estimating land value include the following:

* the operating profit over recent years should be the first financial information sought. Where farms have wide fluctuations in annual operating profit, the purchaser needs low debt to avoid financial trouble. Operating profit has to meet the returns to capital, both owners and creditors, and also cover operator's labour and management costs. Moreover the annual cash surplus, after family living expenses, has to be enough to meet tax; interest on borrowed funds; principal repayments; and new capital investment (in the absence of extra borrowings).

Having calculated the operating profit for the past two to three years the next steps should be taken:

- compare the three to four years' yields from crops and animals on this farm with those of the better-than-average farms in the district;
- explain, preferably with the help of an unbiased adviser experienced in the district, the reasons for any large differences in yields of the farm under review;
- determine whether simple improved management techniques, which include newer methods, could significantly improve yields of the activities presently being run;
- estimate the operating profit which could reasonably be expected from simple changes in techniques. *Note*. At the present stage, without outlaying capital or large new investment in major development;
- calculate the operating profit which should result by running the activities which the purchaser thinks most suitable for the farm, if he or she were running it without any further development;
- compare the profit figures of the two systems and select the one, or a combination of the better elements of each, which will give the highest expected long-term pre-development operating profit;
- obtain an estimate of the market value from recent sales of similar types of farms from a range of sources, taking account of necessary adjustment;
- draw up a table showing:
  the price which the seller is asking, and the range of values quoted by the various sources listed above;
  the capital cost of buying the necessary stock and plant to run the farm in the manner proposed;
  the estimated operating profit as a percentage of the total capital value or WIWO value of the proposed farm investment. A range of combinations of possible returns to capital for a range of expected operating profits and expected capital values can be estimated;
  the amounts which the buyer could pay once all sources of cash surplus available for debt servicing are considered and borrowing ability is added to available equity.

Suppose that the farm has potential for development through clearing, pasture improvement, cropping, and a small amount of low cost irrigation. Before any decision is made about buying the farm, it is necessary to estimate if investment in development would be worthwhile. This is done by using partial and development budgets (see Chapter 9). Then offer prices are derived with adjustment for the capital investment necessary to develop the land.

The procedures outlined above are useful first steps in appraising the economics of a farm investment. A purchaser should run through these procedures for a number of farms on offer. It is not usual for a buyer to take the first farm he or she looks at.

Note. If a purchaser selects a farm, after taking the above steps, he or she should then work out a detailed year-by-year development cash flow budget to look at a range of financial possibilities before a final decision is made.

Adjusting land price for financing by vendor

Favourable finance is where the effective interest rate is less than market rates. If the land sale transaction involved favourable financing, the sale price has two components:

- value of the property; and
- the value of the favourable finance.

If sale terms include an interest rate less than market rates then the purchase price overstates the real value of the property.

The equivalent cash value of a land purchase deal is equal to the initial deposit (or down payment) plus the true 'value' of the sum of the principal and interest payments which are to be made under the favourable conditions. Suppose the current market interest rate is 12%. A farmer buys 100 ha at $1,000 per ha, a total cost of $100,000. The terms of purchase are 20% down-payment, and the balance over five years at 10%.

To find out the cash equivalent value of this deal, amortize the $80,000 'loan' over five years at 10% (annuity whose PV is one factor, 0.2368). The annual principal and interest repayment is $80,000 × 0.2368 = $18,944.

The 'correct' PV of an annual payment of $18,944 over five years, if 12% is the current market interest rate, is $18,944 × 3.6048 (PV of an annuity) = $68,289.

The cash equivalent value of this deal is $20,000 down payment + $68,289 = $88,289.

The adjustment for favourable financing is the difference between the nominal cost and what the terms and conditions of financing make the land really cost. In this case the amount paid is $100,000 or $1,000 per ha and the cash equivalent is $88,289 or $883 per ha. Adjustment for favourable financing is $11,700 or $117 per ha.

There is a further consideration on calculation of land value. If it is planned to finance the investment by borrowing, then the interest payments are tax deductible. This affects the after-tax returns which can be expected, and thus the offer price which could be paid. Using the after-tax interest rate is adequate as long as the tax savings amount to cash available to service the debt at the time required. To calculate the actual after-tax annual returns the annual interest payment for each year of the loan which is taken out can be worked out, or average interest based on the average loan over the life of the loan can be used.

If an after-tax interest rate of 10% is used in the above example, then $14,000 per year could service a 10-year loan of $14,000 × PV of annuity factor 6.1446 = $86,000.

Further, the required rate of return (r) will be a weighted average of the cost of equity capital and the cost of debt capital. To the extent that equity capital has a higher cost than debt capital because interest on debt capital is tax deductible and equity capital is at greater risk, then the offer prices with debt finance will be higher than the case with no debt finance.

The scope for development of a property also plays a large part of the land value story. Valuation needs to be done for the situation before and after development, with the after-development value adjusted by the expected costs of development to arrive at a value of the land before development.

Purchasing a well-developed mixed animal–crop farm

The hypothetical farm is 30 km from Gunnedah, in the north-west plains of New South Wales. There is no influence for subdivision from urban demand. It is a viable unit of 800 ha. It runs sheep and cattle, and produces both winter and summer crops. Rainfall is 625 mm (25 inches), two-thirds of which falls in spring, summer, and autumn; one-third falls in winter. Details are given in Table 7.3

Table 7.3: Details of example farm

600 ha arable red-brown earth
200 ha undulating to hilly non-arable, native grasses and legumes

crop		
crop sequence on arable land	4-yrs lucerne, 4 yrs crop	
crop sequence	150 ha winter crop (wheat, oats, barley, canola)	
	150 ha summer crop (sorghum, sunflower)	
crop phases on land currently growing crops	3 crops in 4 years (1 winter, 1 sorghum, 1 sunflower, 1 fallow)	
carrying capacity	non-arable 200 ha × 5 dse = 1,000 dse	
	lucerne on arable 300 ha × 8 dse = 2,400 dse	
total dse = 3,400		

stock		
stock composition	80 cow units (2 bulls) 1,830 Merino ewes (joined to BL) 46 rams	
dse rating	1 self-replacing cow unit	15
	1 ewe unit	1.2
total dse	cattle = 80 × 15	1,200
	ewe unit = 1,830 × 1.2	2,196
	total	3,396
capital cost of stock	cattle	
	80 cows × $450	$36,000
	20 replacement heifers $250	$5,000
	2 bulls × $1,500	$3,000
	total cattle	$44,000
	sheep	
	1,830 ewes × $20	$36,600
	46 rams × $100	$4,600
	total sheep	$41,200
	total stock capital	$85,200

continued

plant

		$
capital cost of plant (new and second-hand)	$400 per ha × 300 ha	120,000
total plant and stock	$120,000 + $85,200	205,200

gross margins

gross margins from stock	cow unit	250
	ewe unit	30
	80 cow units × $250	20,000
	1,830 ewe units × $30	54,900
	total gross margin from stock	74,900
gross margins from crops	winter crop per ha	180
	summer sorghum per ha	250
	summer sunflower per ha	200
average annual gross margin from crop phase (3 crops in 4 years 1 wheat, 1 sorghum, 1 sunflowr, 1 fallow)	$180 + 250 + 200 + 0 = \dfrac{630}{4}$	157
total annual GM from crop phase	300 ha × $157	47,100
total GM from stock and crop (TGM)	$74,900 + 47,100	122,000

overhead (fixed) costs

total wages: operator and permanent staff		45,000
pasture fertilizer on 200 ha (1 year in 3)	annual cost $20 × 200 ha	4,000
vehicle running		9,000
annual depreciation of vehicles, plant, and machinery	⅙ of $120,000	20,000
repairs to structures		1,000
depreciation structures		3,000
total insurances (not crop)		1,500
rates and land tax		3,500
accountant		1,000
administration and sundries		2,000
total overheads (OH)		90,000

operating profit (before tax)

TGM − OH	$122,000 − $90,000	32,000
after tax @ 15%	$32,000 − $4,800	27,200 ($34 per ha)

We will now estimate the maximum that a purchaser can afford to pay for the land and the fixed improvements (Table 7.4).

Table 7.4: % return on total capital for range of land values

1 $ price per ha	775	875	975	1,065
2 total land price	620,000	700,000	780,000	852,000
3 value stock	85,200	85,200	85,200	85,200
4 value plant and machinery	120,000	120,000	120,000	120,000
5 total land, stock, plant, and machinery (2 + 3 + 4)	825,200	905,200	985,200	1,057,200
6 most likely operating profit after tax	27,200	27,200	27,200	27,200
7 % return on total capital (⁶/₅ × 100)	3.3	3	2.76	2.58

The information in Table 7.4 refers to land valued in perpetuity and it is a starting point, but it does not tell us a lot. Depending on the rates of return which are relevant, and the guesses you make about the operating profit, you can come up with a wide range of values, which are uncertain too. What is more, no consideration has been taken of the expected inflation or the possibility of any expected real and nominal capital gains. Yet these will be part of the seller's asking price and the buyer's offer prices; and hence part of market price.

If the effects of inflation are expected to be neutral on operating profit (i.e., operating profits retain their real value), and if no real capital gains are expected, then we know that around $775 to $1,065 per ha will give returns of around 2.6% to 3.3% real, after tax, per year for land held in perpetuity. However, if real and nominal capital gains are expected, or inflation is expected to affect costs, returns or land values differently, then these effects ought to be included in the estimates of land value. To do so requires the net present value method of estimating land value.

The calculation is done in nominal terms, and can be done on a per ha or whole farm basis. This method is an application of the standard investment appraisal techniques using discounting. Assume that there are no non-economic benefits associated with the land. If the asking price for land, plant, and stock is greater than the calculated PV of operating profits plus capital gains at the required discount rate, less the opportunity cost of the capital invested, then the asking price is too high. The maximum price which a buyer could offer for the land (assuming the estimated operating profits and land capital gains are already 'risk-adjusted') is the asking price which equals the PV of profits and capital gains. A trial-and-error approach is needed, until this figure is found. There is no other simple way because the size of capital gain depends on the initial price paid, and so on. The calculations are more manageable using the computer spreadsheet. An example follows.

Example Farm

planning horizon: 20 years

operating profit after tax:	$34 per ha
required real rate of return after tax:	2.5%
expected inflation rate per year:	3.5%
expected interest rates, and required discount rate, is approximately 6.0% (2.5% real and 3.5% nominal)	

Strictly speaking, to get 2.5% real return with 3.5% inflation requires market rates of interest of $0.025 + 0.035 + (0.025)(0.035) = 0.0609$. So the discount rate used is 6.09%.

Operating profits after tax are expected to more than keep up with inflation because of some expected new market opportunities and cost reducing advances in technology, and are expected to grow at an average of 4% p.a. in nominal terms. Land and improvements will also gain 0.5% real p.a. (for various different reasons), and stock and machinery will increase in value only at the average rate of inflation.

The following calculations are done:

operating profit after tax per ha growing at 4% nominal p.a.

value of land in year 20 if $1,100 is paid today for it and it grows in value at 4% nominal (0.5% real) p.a. Stock and plant grows in value at 3.5% p.a.

the PV of the 20-year investment in land, stock, and plant using the asking WIWO price and the required discount rate

the sum of the PV of OP and the PV of the investment in land plant and stock gives the PV of the whole investment

the PV of the whole investment is compared to the asking WIWO value today. If the discounted future earnings exceed the asking WIWO, then at this required rate of earning (discount rate) the investment is worth more than is being asked at this point.

When these sums are solved it is found that, with a 20-year planning horizon, at a required earning rate of 2.5% real, the asking price ($1,100 per ha) could, if paid, result in the required rate of return of 2.5% after tax being earned, plus more than this because the NPV is + $95, i.e., the value exceeds the price. In fact, under these conditions $1,390 per ha could be paid and the required return would be earned.

$1,390 per ha is the maximum the buyer should pay for the land, if there were no uncertainty about the assumed values of the key parameters. At a price greater than $1,390 per ha the price exceeds the value. At a price less than $1,390 per ha value exceeds price and the buyer is getting 'good value' for his or her purchase.

To be on the safe side, what if operating profits were to be less than $34 per ha. For these assumed conditions of inflation and real gain and required returns, at $28 per ha operating profit the 'break-even' land price is $1,090 per ha. At $25 per ha operating profit, the buyer could pay only $940 per ha.

What if the assumptions about real gains in operating profit and land value are unrealistic, and no such gains were to occur. Then at $34 operating profit, $1,100 per ha land-asking price equals land value. At $28 per ha operating profit, $860 per ha land price equals land value. At $25 operating profit per ha, $745 land price equals land value.

The buyer might decide to act on a conservative but safe $30 operating profit per ha, no real gains in operating profit on land, and stick with a minimum required return of 2.5% after tax. With these conditions, $945 per ha is the value of the land.

Financing the purchase of the farm with different levels of equity

Suppose real capital gains were expected, and a lower real return was acceptable, and thus $1,200 per ha was paid for the farm. An example assuming 80% equity is given.

Example

Land value based on expected 3.5% per year inflation affecting operating profit and land value

	$
land (800 ha × $1,200 per ha)	960,000
stock, plant, and machinery	205,200
total (including extras)	1,180,000
debt (equity at 80%)	236,000

The aim is to calculate whether a debt of $236,000 incurred now can be serviced over the next 15 years by a current operating profit of $25,600, which is expected to increase in nominal terms at 3.5% per year. If inflation is lower than this, so will be interest rates. It is also possible that operating profit might not increase in nominal terms at the rate of inflation or it could be much more or much less than $25,600 or its future equivalent. One way to calculate how much debt can be serviced is to calculate how much debt the $25,600 operating profit could service, if it were all cash and all available to service debts, and if it did not increase at 3.5% per year with inflation.

In this case, the debt amortization factor for a 15-year loan at 7% nominal interest rate = 0.1098. Annual repayment = $236,000 × 0.1098 = $25,913. At 80% equity the expected operating profit would not quite service the $236,000 debt in year 1. Later, it could if it increased with inflation. Also, the interest component in year 1 of $16,520 could create a tax saving of $3,000 to $4,000, depending on the marginal tax rate.

If the borrower is confident that inflation will affect interest rates and operating profit similarly (i.e., operating profit increases at the inflation rate) then the debt-servicing ability can be calculated on the basis of the current (real) operating profit and real interest rates, as follows:

amortization factor, 15-year loan at 4%, real interest rates = 0.0899
annual debt-servicing charge = $236,000 × 0.0899 = $21,216.

Thus if operating profit increases with inflation, the debt could be serviced.

Here, the operating profit is assumed to equate to cash flow. For this to be so, depreciation would have to be matched by cash expenditures on replacements and investment out of cash flow, operator's allowance would match cash drawings, and any non-cash income would need to be in near cash form, i.e., readily saleable.

Interest paid is a tax deduction, so each year tax would be less than shown and cash surplus greater. Interest paid in each year differs, and the tax saving will be higher earlier in the loan when interest payments are greatest. Average interest paid is average debt by interest rate, i.e.,

$236,000 × 0.55 = $129,800 × 0.07 = $9,086
Average tax saving at 20 cents in the dollar tax rate is $1,817.

Calculating break-even equity

(with operating profit increasing with inflation)

Real annual operating profit after tax: $25,600
assume a 15-year-loan is involved
$25,600 per year for 15 years has a PV at 4% real interest rate of $25,600 × 11.1184
(PV of annuity factor) = $284,631
that is, an annuity of $25,600 real would service a debt of $284,631 over 15 years
at 4% real. Break-even equity is $1,180,000 − $284,631 = $895,369

break-even equity % is $\dfrac{\$895,369}{\$1,180,000} = 75.9\%$

Thus, with equity at 75.9%, no cash would be left after meeting loan
repayments. However, remember we have allowed $25,000 per year for living
costs of the owner–operator. Drawings can be less than this if need be. Also,
the tax deductability of interest has not been included, which will add a bit
to cash surplus. However uncertainty surrounding the cash surplus and
operating profit of $25,600 might mean that break-even equity should be
estimated on the basis of say $20,000 cash surplus and operating profit. This
would mean:

$20,000 per year would service a debt of $20,000 × 11.1184 = $222,368

This implies an equity of $957,632 and an equity percentage of 81.2%.
The break-even with an operating profit not keeping up with inflation
is $25,600 × 7% PV of annuity factor = $25,600 × 8.8271 = $225,974. Thus a debt of
$225,974 could be serviced; an equity of $1,180,000 − $225,974 = $954,026;
a break-even equity of 80.8%. It would seem that 80.8% would be the minimum
equity which could be managed, assuming the real value of operating profit
is maintained.

Essential questions an intending buyer of rural property needs to consider:

- What are realistic costs of production, including full allowances for labour
  and management; maintenance of the property and plant; allowance for
  depreciation on improvements and plant, stock replacement rates; insurance;
  and administration expenses?
- What are reasonable maximum and minimum annual operating profits from
  the intended purchase?
- What is the probable cost of stock and plant? Add this probable cost to the
  possible cost of the land. Also add the necessary amount of working capital
  and minimum net earnings.
- What rates of return apply with various purchase prices?
- What is the PV of the purchase, at a range of land prices, and discount rates?
- How much cash equity can be put into the new property, and its stock and
  plant?

- What loans will be needed and what terms and rates of interest will apply?
- What annual debt-servicing commitments are likely?
- Is enough money available from all sources without incurring too much debt on present land and other assets?
- At which time of the year are these payments due?
- Does the expected operating profit give attractive returns for the equity in the property?
- What are the tax implications?
- Will purchase of the property increase or decrease the overall soundness of family business undertakings?
- Is there a likelihood of buying this property at a lower price than that assumed for the previous calculations?
- Would some other property be a better buy, taking all things into account?

It is difficult to know all the reasons why land buyers pay the amount they do for any parcel of land, but there are two major considerations: the future income the land is expected to produce and its prospects for increasing in capital value. Rate of return on capital is at least part of an analysis of what the land might be worth to a buyer. The potential for development warrants detailed analysis before any land is bought.

Leasing and sharing farmland

Some generalizations about leasing and sharing can be made, though each case is unique in finer detail. Leasing and sharing arrangements deal mainly with the issue of each party being rewarded fairly, both for their respective contributions and for their relative share of the burden of risk. When leasing land, the landowner usually provides land and fixed improvements. With sharefarming the landowner puts in land and fixed improvements, and, in some cases, a variety of other inputs as well. Sometimes an agreement will involve a mix of cash lease and sharing some of the costs and income. For tax purposes the landowner or lessor in a cash lease agreement does not qualify as a primary producer, whereas the landowner in a sharefarming arrangement has primary producer status.

A lease or sharefarming agreement has to set out how production and income will be shared; what resources and expenses will be put in; what improvements are to be undertaken; any special conditions relating to such things as annual fertilizer applications; movement of livestock onto the property; restrictions on crop sequences; and repair and maintenance of improvements. With a cash lease, the lessor takes none of the risk; the lessee bears nearly all of the risk. With sharefarming the risk is shared in proportion to the share of costs contributed and the crop yield.

Tradition and custom play a role in the numbers and obligations used in leasing and sharefarming agreements. In different areas there are different standard 'rules of thumb' or generalized starting points for negotiation, with adjustment made for the circumstances of each case. Sharefarming agreements reflect the different expected productivity of different pieces of land. Land area A might be expected to yield $400 gross income per ha and land area B might be expected to produce gross income of $300 per ha. Sharefarming costs in both cases might be $200 per ha. The sharefarmer of land area A would need to receive half of the crop to cover expenses and the sharefarmer of land B would need to receive two-thirds of the crop to cover expenses.

There are several methods of calculating how much to offer to lease some land. One method is based on the prospective tenant's ability to pay. This involves calculating the expected net income from production left over after all the non-land expenses have been met. That is, the amount of money expected to be left after all the operating costs, depreciation of capital, and the labour and management costs of the tenant, and the opportunity cost of any capital inputs of the tenant.

Example

(with no inflation expected) $

expected gross income from 500 ha	170,000
less	
• operating costs	90,000
• depreciation of tenant's capital	10,000
• tax	10,000
• labour and management reward needed by tenant	25,000
= opportunity cost of tenant's capital,	
say, $150,000 at 4% real	4,500
total costs	139,500
= maximum tenant could offer	30,500 ($61 per ha)

The residual $30,500 is the maximum, before risk is considered, which the tenant could pay for the lease if the expected outcome happened. This method gives the maximum lease payment the tenant could pay and still expect to receive a market return on all his or her inputs to production.

Another method is to work out the amount the landowner needs to get a market return on his or her contribution to the business. This involves estimating the minimum lease payment needed to cover the landowner's annual costs.

Example

(with no inflation)

Required real operating return after tax, on land and improvements worth $1,000 per ha is 3% per year (1% real capital gain after tax is also expected).

	per ha $	500 ha $
so the required earning rate is 3% after 25% tax, i.e.,		
4% needed before tax	40.00	20,000
depreciation on improvements per ha	5.00	2,500
repairs and maintenance costs of improvements per ha	2.00	1,000
property rates and land taxes	5.00	2,500
insurances	1.00	500
minimum lease payment to landowner		
(before income tax)	53.00	26,500

In this case, if the gross income were certain, the maximum the tenant could pay would be around $30,500. This is true if the opportunity cost of his or her capital and labour, and management skills, are real ones and the tenant would consider seriously putting capital, labour, and management skills into some other use. If this is not so, and the tenant would accept a lower return to personal capital, labour, and management, then more than $30,500 could be offered for the lease. However, as gross income is uncertain, the tenant would probably offer a lower bid than $30,500 to lease the land.

The minimum the landlord could accept is $26,500. Again, this is true if the landlord regards the after-tax opportunity cost of capital in the land as truly being 4% after tax. That is, the capital would be re-invested to get 4% elsewhere if there were not 4% return in this use. If this is not the case and the landlord is interested in the land for other reasons as well and would not re-invest the proceeds from sale of the land to get 4% elsewhere, then the landlord will have a lower minimum offer which he would accept.

The amount which is agreed on is a complex amalgam of supply and demand of lease land and potential lessees. The motives and required rates of return of lessors and lessees are important here. So too is risk. These factors all change 'theoretical' maximum offers and minimum requirements greatly.

If inflation is expected the figures will be different. The same sums are done for each year of the proposed lease using nominal (inflated) numbers. For instance, expected inflation will change land values; interest rates; required returns; gross returns; and operating costs.

In theory it could be expected that lease agreements would include an allowance for expected inflation; lease payments would increase at the expected rate of inflation, and the real returns to both lessor and lessee would remain constant. In practice, this rarely happens. Possibly the uncertainty surrounding prices and yields is so great that the effect this has on reducing the lease price below what would be paid if there were no uncertainty tends to overshadow concerns about the next couple of years' inflation rates.

With leasing and sharing arrangements it is expected that higher risk will be associated with higher expected returns, and lower risk with lower returns. From the tenant's viewpoint, sharefarming has less risk associated with an undesirable outcome than does leasing. The amount of 'rent' eventually paid with sharing varies as yields and prices vary. With leasing, the amount paid is constant regardless of the yield and price outcomes. If prices fall then the sharefarmer gets a higher return from sharing than from leasing, because the cost of the share 'paid' to the landowner also declines. With leasing, the tenant pays the full lease even though the prices received fall below the expected price. Thus the portion remaining and going to the tenant is less than with the share arrangement.

From the landowner's view, with sharefarming he or she might retain more control over the operation of the farm than is the case with the cash lease. Also with sharing, as the landowner is taking a share of the risk, 'on average' returns should be higher. If prices rise, with sharing the landowner gets some of the benefit, whereas with leasing the landowner can miss out. The lease agreement tends to lag behind an improved price or yield outlook.

From the tenant's view the cash lease might mean that over time the rent is lower than with sharing, because the tenant is taking all of the risk. Also the tenant has full control (subject to the conditions of the agreement), and reaps all the returns to his or her own managerial skills. When prices rise the tenant gets the benefit, in the short term at least.

For the landlord, leasing has the advantage of providing a risk-free income for the coming year, and any capital gain. The landlord need not know much about farming, be involved, or take decisions. Also, compared with most sharing arrangements, with leasing, less capital input is required from the landlord.

Length of lease is always tricky. Ideally what is needed is 'short lease but long tenure'. This means that appropriate flexibility is needed to meet the landowner's need to be able to finish an unsatisfactory arrangement. At the same time it should give the lessee the incentives needed to farm with the long-term productivity of all the farm's resources in mind. Short-term leases require strict conditions to be made about the addition of any improvements or fertilizer and maintenance of existing improvements. Deciding on compensation for the carryover effects of fertilizer can be a problem; sometimes the landowner pays for the annual fertilizer and receives a proportional share of output in return.

Leasing non-land assets can be attractive, depending on the tax laws and the tax rates of the time. Lease costs are usually a tax-deductable expense. Leasing is also a way of reducing the amount of initial capital investment to acquire the services of an asset. For financial analyses, a leased asset can be shown as an asset in the balance sheet, and the PV of the lease obligations can be shown as a debt. This captures the important effect of the leased asset on the liquidity of the business.

Items which should be mutually agreed upon in a lease include (from Gibson, Powell, & Makeham 1986):

1 The area of property and the amount of plant involved.

2 The number of livestock involved, if any.
3 The amount of rent to be paid, when, and how it is to be paid, and if there is to be any provision for review of amount paid.
4 The dates for commencement and termination of the lease.
5 The amount of notice required from either party for termination of the lease.
6 Whether there will be an option to renew the lease or to buy the land at the termination of the lease; the price to be paid for either of these alternatives; and the amount of notice needed to take up either of these alternatives.
7 Any restrictions as to the number and type of livestock.
8 The level of repair and maintenance work to be undertaken, and how much of the cost will be met by either party.
9 Who will pay for and carry out weed and vermin control.
10 The cost sharing or compensation to the lessee for any capital improvements.
11 The type, amount frequency, and cost-sharing arrangements of fertilizer applications.
12 The area of cropping permitted.
13 Who is to pay rates and taxes.
14 Who is to pay for insurance.
15 The right of entry of the lessor.
16 The procedure in the case of a need for arbitration.
17 Any other items relevant to the particular circumstances such as removal of timber, soil conservation works, use of buildings, etc.

Leasing example

Here we will examine the issue of leasing land from both the lessor's and lessee's angle (Table 7.5). The farm is 400 ha, and valued at $875 per ha. The expected real and nominal capital gain is 8%. The lease cost is 5% of the capital value of the land and the lease is for five years. The lease cost is based on a commonly used 'rule of thumb'.

Table 7.5: Costs and income for lessor

costs per ha	$	
rates and land tax	6	
depreciation	3	(4% of 75)
insurance	0.50	
repairs	2	(½ of 4)
½ weeds and vermin	1	
superphosphate ½ of $30 per ha	5	(every 3 years)
	17.5	

continued

income per ha	$
rent 5% of 875	43.75
rent − costs = 43.75 − 17.5	26.25
tax at 10% on 26.25	2.62
after-tax net income from rent	23.63
cash gain from leasing 23.63 + 3 depreciation	26.63
real capital gain over 5 years' inflation 5%, real gain 3%	
(875 × 1.1593) − 875	139.39
annuity whose terminal value is one factor	0.1883
annual capital gain 139 × 0.1883	26.17
tax on capital gain at 25% marginal rate	6.54
after-tax annual capital gain	19.63
total annual increase in wealth	
from rent	23.63
from capital gain	19.63
	43.26
total annual increase in wealth 400 × 43.26 (rent and capital gain)	17,304
gain from rental income only 23.63 × 400	9,452

Table 7.6: Costs and returns for lessee

	$
lease payment—5% of $875 × 400 ha	17,500
350 ha stock (cattle and sheep)	
50 ha mixed crop—all contract	
money for stock purchase all borrowed at 13.5%	
value of stock (22.50 dse × 6.25 dse per ha × 350 ha)	49,219
vehicle—average value $10,000 − interest at 8.5%	850
(A)—gross margins	
stock 350 ha × $15 × 6.25 dse	32,812
crop 50 ha × $140	7,000
total gross margin	39,812
(B)—costs	
lease rental	17,500
R & M structures	800
all vehicle costs (except interest)	1,600
½ super costs	2,000
½ weeds and vermin	400
administration and sundries	700
casual labour	400
livestock and crop insurance	1,000
interest on livestock = $22.5 × 6.25 × 350 × 0.085	4,184
interest on vehicle	850
total costs	29,434
(A − B)—operating profit before tax	10,378
less tax at average rate 15% of operating profit	1,557
= gain (labour and management) after tax	8,821

This preliminary analysis is based on an arbitrary assumption that the lessee pays a nominal 5% of the capital value of the land. The lessor receives $17,304 reward, and the lessee, $8,821 reward after interest. This is not much of a reward for the efforts and risks which the lessee takes. The lessor receives an attractive reward from nominal capital gain as well as a reasonable return from the lease payments. The lessee might aim to negotiate a lease on a more favourable basis.

Break-even lease price

What is the break-even lease price, given that the lessee specifies that he or she wants $12,000 reward for his or her effort and management?

reward to management and labour (RML)

RML = (after tax OP + annual lease price paid in old agreement) − X

where X is the break-even agreement annual lease price

$12,000	=	$8,821 + $17,000 − X
$12,000	=	$25,827 − X
X	=	$13,827
X % of land value	=	$13,827

$$\frac{\$13,827}{\$350,000} = 3.95\%$$

Lessor

1 Leasing (real terms)

annual net gain from leasing =

(land value per ha × area × required interest rate % of land value) − costs

$$= (\$875 \times 400 \times 0.0395) - \$7,000$$
$$= \$13,825 - \$7,000 = \$6,825$$

less tax at 15% of operating profit   = $6,825 − $1,023 tax

annual net gain after tax from leasing = $5,802

2 After-tax capital gain at 3% real = $7,852
   (from Table 7.6 $19.63 per ha × 400 ha)

total annual gain

from leasing	=	$5,802
from capital gains (real)	=	$7,852
total	=	$13,654
total per ha	=	$34
% real return per ha	=	3.9%
plus 5% nominal capital gains	=	8.9%

The lessor receives $13,654 reward, the lessee, $13,827 reward.

What is a fair thing?

What a fair thing is depends on who you are, the lessee or the lessor. The lessor is receiving a real return after tax which is about 20% better than the risk-free, after-tax return he or she would get elsewhere, such as in a bank. The lessor is getting a market interest return on the capital he or she contributes, and the $12,000 he or she has valued his or her labour and management as being worth. The risk of yield or price falls has been shared to some extent by the lessor paying half the superphosphate and weed and vermin control costs.

Yields and prices could fall a lot compared with the expected level or they could also rise a lot. The scope for getting another couple of thousand dollars out of the landlord as further 'insurance' would depend on many factors including the personal relationship; the history of the leasing agreement; competition from other potential lessors; supply of alternative leaseland; and so on. Probably this agreement is close to a 'fair thing', although the ultimate agreement will depend on the horse-trading which takes place.

7

Questions for discussion

1 We provided for any real or nominal annual capital gain component in our guide to the maximum price you should bid for land. Do you think that it is realistic to do this?

2 Our method estimating a maximum bid price has several components:
(a) estimated (from knowledgeable sources) market selling price;
(b) estimated after-tax operating profit assuming attainable better than average management;
(c) a guess at likely future capital gain;
(d) a guess at likely future inflation rates.
We are 'estimating' and 'guessing' quite a lot of important things.
Can you suggest any other approach to the problem?
What are your views on how to decide how much to offer for land?

3 Choose a block of farmland and estimate how much debt it could service if you farmed it.

4 Rules of thumb about leasing charges, such as 5% of capital value, are rough and ready. Are a few more sums needed?

7

Further reading

Barry, P. J., Hopkin, J. A., & Baker, C. B. *Financial Management in Agriculture* (3rd edn), The Interstate Printers and Publishers Inc., Illinois, 1986.

Boehlje, M. D. and Eidman, V. R., *Farm Management*, John Wiley & Sons, New York, 1988.

Calkins, P. H. and DiPietre, D. D., *Farm Business Management: Successful Decisions in a Changing Environment*, Macmillan Publishing Co. Inc., New York, 1983.

Castle, E. N., Becker, M. H., & Nelson, A. G., *Farm Business Management—The Decision Making Process*, Macmillan Publishing Company, New York, 1987.

Gibson, A. L., Powell, R. A., & Makeham, J. P., 'Private Leasing of Grazing Land in NSW, 1984', *Farm Management Report No. 14*, Department of Business Management and Agricultural Economics, University of New England, Armidale, NSW, 2351.

8

Who Bets?
Risk

arming is a very big gamble. All risk has a cost. Risk is almost the major player in the farming game, and it is the factor least recognized and least understood by those who are not farmers. At some time risk brings undone the best laid plans of everyone involved in farming; from new entrants not appreciating the full range of possibilities; to agricultural scientists and advisers wondering why potential yield is not maximized or why the latest yield-increasing trick is not being adopted rapidly; to farm financiers; to prophets; and to farmers who suffer a bit of bad luck sometimes increased by bad management.

This chapter deals with risk in farm management, although aspects of the riskiness in farming have been dealt with in each chapter of this book. Of risk there are two key points: risk comes into all aspects of farm management, and all risk involves an unavoidable cost in adverse outcomes or in costs incurred to reduce or avert the consequences of risky outcomes.

Risk is conventionally classified into two types: business risk and financial risk. Business risk is the risk any business faces no matter how it is financed. It comes from production and price risk, uncertainty, and variability. Business risk refers to variable yields of crops, reproduction rates, outbreaks of disease, climatic variability, unexpected changes in markets and prices, changes in government policies and laws, fluctuations in inflation and interest rates.

Financial risk refers to the gearing ratio of a firm and the operation of the principle of increasing risk. In this chapter we focus mainly on business risk, bearing in mind that its effects are worsened by financial risk.

Decision making in farming, as in all forms of business, involves making a choice among possible alternative actions. It is one of the most important activities which a farm manager has to carry out. Decision making is management that cannot be ignored or postponed; failure to take decisive action, when a choice is possible, is itself a choice (decision). The outcomes are just as real (and so either as good or as bad) as those resulting from an overt decision and action by the decision maker.

Since the 1950s much research, field testing time, and money has been spent in trying to assist decision makers, mostly in the business world, to handle the problem of decision making under risk. The main outcome of these studies has been procedures to help them to approach a decision problem in a systematic manner. In practice, it often just involves getting decision makers contemplating the range of likely outcomes of their choices and attaching money values and probabilities to these outcomes, before they make their final choice.

The primary benefit from a formal approach is that decision makers have a better chance of making the right decision. This is done by ensuring that all relevant data is considered and that a consistent, logical, and realistic process is used to select the action or set of actions most likely to reach the goal(s). These goals must first be defined clearly.

We distinguish a 'good' decision from a 'right' decision. A good decision is a rational decision under the circumstances. In a rational decision, each of the relevant factors involved in the decision are given degrees of importance and likelihood, usually subjectively, often mostly unconscious. The weights given reflect the decision-maker's beliefs, founded on experience and information obtained about alternatives. As well, a good decision is consistent with the decision-maker's preferences. As most decisions are made in the face of uncertainty, there is no guarantee that a good decision will be the right decision. That is, decision makers might act rationally, using formal decision-making methods, but they have no control over the outcomes.

For instance, instead of selling a crop for $50 per tonne, a farmer might have decided to store the crop in the prospect of getting $70 in one month's time. Information and experience leads the farmer to assign a 90% chance of getting $70 per tonne the following month, but only a 10% chance of getting $40 per tonne the following month. As a result of some unusual factor in the market, the actual price received is $40. Thus, the good decision has had a bad outcome, so ultimately it was not a right decision.

The techniques we outline help the decision maker to focus on all the options and to weigh appropriately all the factors involved in, and consequences, of a decision, thus a decision is taken with more knowledge of options and outcomes. However, these methods do not replace intuition or experience.

We stress that a risk is a dominant factor in Australian farming life and this risk shows itself in the need for farmer–decision makers to gain extra returns for taking extra risks. The returns needed increase as the risk increases. Take, as an example, an investor happy to receive 14% nominal return annually on government bonds before tax, he or she would want more than this from a riskier investment before it became an attractive option. The extra return the investor would need is a 'risk premium'; 'the interest rate is proportionate to the risk'. This is an axiom often overlooked by naive investors.

The trade-off between risk and expected profit is illustrated in Figures 8.1 and 8.2, where the risk of several investments is reflected by movement up the vertical axis; higher profits are measured along the horizontal axis.

Figure 8.1: Risk versus return

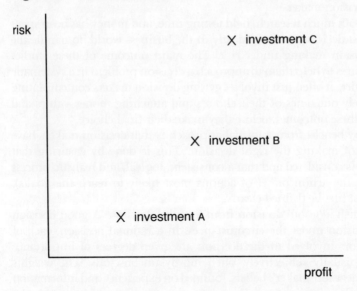

Suppose a number of alternative investments could be represented as follows:

Figure 8.2: Risk versus returns and risk-efficient choices

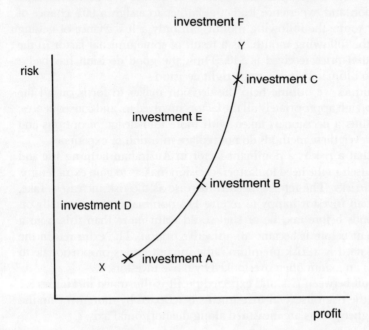

In Figures 8.1 and 8.2 risk is shown to increase at a faster rate than profit. Without knowing anything about an individual farmer's attitude to risk, it would be safe to say that any rational investor, given a choice between two projects of different risk and the same expected profit, would prefer the lower risk option. These options are indicated in Figure 8.2 along the line XY. Investments shown along this line are called the 'risk-efficient' or 'risk-dominating' choices. The choices which promise the same profit but have more risk (DEF) are called the inferior or 'risk-dominated' choices. Which of the investments A, B, C is 'best' depends on the specific case and psychological make-up of the investor.

Anyone planning to make a change on a farm knows that the final outcome will probably not be precisely that which is hoped for, even if it is thought most likely to happen. Numerous different outcomes are possible. The investor has to think about these others too. There are a couple of ways of doing this formally. There is the use of personal probabilities and there is the use of 'what if' scenarios using budgets (sketches or models) built into the computer-based spreadsheet, and weighed up in terms of how likely they are to happen.

Probability

It is useful to understand probabilities when making decisions on proposals which are risky. Probabilities are strengths of belief about an event happening, and these are expressed as a rating from zero (no chance) to one (certainty).

A farmer putting in a wheat crop might know that the price will not be affected whether the yields are high or low. Yield and price are independent, because the farmer sells on the world market and world prices are not affected whether the farmer and all fellow farmers have good yields or bad yields. The farmer might believe that regardless of yield in six months' time, there is, when the harvest is ready for sale:

- a good chance of getting $200 per tonne;
- a good chance that the price will be a relatively poor $150 per tonne;
- less chance of getting a top price of $250 per tonne;
- less chance of getting $100 per tonne.

The farmer might refine these beliefs as follows:

- four chances in 10 of getting $200 per tonne;
- four chances in 10 of getting $150 per tonne;
- one chance in 10 of getting $250 per tonne;
- one chance in 10 of getting $100 per tonne.

Probabilities can be stated as the odds of an event happening. An event might be thought to have a probability of occurring of 0.4; i.e., four chances in 10 of it happening, and six chances in 10 of it not happening. This is a 6 to 4 against chance (odds). If it were thought to have 0.6 chance of happening and 0.4 chance of not happening, then this would be a 6 to 4 on chance (written as 4 to 6 against), i.e., it is less than 1 to 1, an even money or 50:50 bet. To convert odds to probabilities this is the formula:

$$\frac{1}{1+ \text{odds}}$$

Thus, odds of 10 to 1 = 1 chance in 11 $= \dfrac{1}{1 + 10} = 0.09$ probability

Odds and probabilities can be put into budgets. It is not easy to do but sometimes it is of value to try to estimate the odds of possible outcomes happening, such as prices, yields, costs. The odds for the most likely outcomes, and also for worst, poor and good results can be estimated.

Expected value

Another thing to do is to work out expected values of possible outcomes. If there are 100 tickets in a lottery and the prize is worth $5, then each ticket has an expected value of ($5) by (0.01) chance of winning. The expected value of a ticket is five cents. In this case there are 100 possible winning tickets, each with a one in 100 chance of winning, each with an expected value of five cents. The expected value of buying all the tickets is $5.00. Expected value is worked out as the sum of a series of possible outcomes such as 'good', 'most likely', 'poor' seasons or prices. These are then multiplied by the probability of them happening, as estimated by the decision maker. Instead of using a single value for yield, say, 2 tonnes per ha, probabilities can be used to work out an expected value for yield.

Table 8.1: Expected value of yield

No. of years in 20 yrs it is expected to happen	probability	×	yield t per ha	=	expected value
2	0.1		0.5		0.05
6	0.3		1.0		0.3
8	0.4		2.0		0.8
3	0.15		2.5		0.375
1	0.05		3		0.15
					1.675 t per ha

If the most likely figure were used it would be 2 tonnes per ha. If outcomes were what had happened in the past 20 years then the expected value of yield over this period would be 1.675 tonnes per ha. Expected value is more useful than historical (original) average because historical average relates to a unique past, never to be repeated exactly, while expected value relates to what is believed might happen in the new, different, and unknown future.

The expected value, a composite figure, captures the situation which would apply if all the chances came at once; it is what you would get, on average, if you made the same investment a large number of times, and the probability distribution of outcomes remained stable. If this were true then profit over time will be greatest if the alternatives having the highest expected money values

(EMVs) are always chosen. It is an approximation; it is a 'most likely' figure, fine-tuned by the chances of the other less likely outcomes occurring. It is more informative than the 'most likely' or the historical 'average' level. Averages are about the past. Expected and most likely values allow more explicitly for new developments which may affect future events.

There are a number of limits to the usefulness of EMVs. These are apart from the general limits to the usefulness of probabilities in agriculture associated with the relatively small number of the main 'events' (seasons, prices, yields, investment decisions) involved in a farmer's career, when the 'laws' of probabilities work best over a large number of 'events'.

Care is needed when yield and prices are correlated. This could happen when products are sold mostly on the domestic market, and if one farmer has a big yield it is most likely that many of his fellow producers will also produce a lot. The result will be that the price will fall because supply has increased a lot relative to what may have been expected, and relative to demand. In such a case the big yield achieved by an individual farmer will be correlated with a relatively lower price than the price which can be expected when yield is less. Here expected revenues $(Y \times P)$ from the various scenarios need to be estimated.

As choices increase and sequential decisions become possible, the expected value of the outcome of an action at an earlier time (e.g. storing product instead of selling it) cannot be calculated until the expected value of the outcome at the later time (e.g. selling now or after storing for a while) is estimated. Obviously, with more than a couple of choices and possible sequences of action, this method of using EVs quickly becomes intractable, at least for the simple techniques used in farm management. Dynamic programming, a technique designed for these sorts of problems, has many possible real world and research uses, but no practical farm management applications.

Whether an expected value of an important item suits the decision maker depends on the person's make-up—on his or her attitude to taking risks— depending on this, and whether the outcome is adequate to meet all needs, the farmer will decide whether or not to 'bet'. The expected value is a good figure to use in the decision if you can live with a very bad result or do not desperately need an improbably high result. As a cynic would put it 'expected value would be a fine basis on which to run your life if you were to live forever and only the final outcome mattered'.

Probabilities and farm management analysis

Good business is all about information, judgement, and luck. The key to the 'quality' of decisions is the quality of the information available. In farming much is unknown and uncertain, thus the quality of the information is often unavoidably poor. Possibly, people overstate the chances of outcomes which they know most about or have experienced recently. They may not be good at guessing the chances of events which are not very likely but these could still upset their plans. The estimates people make about probabilities are affected by the information they have. Often this is not a lot. There is the phenomenon, known to anyone who has ever been to a racetrack, where the winner appears, after the race, to have been more likely to win than it did before the race.

Also, sometimes people's estimates of probabilities violate the rules of probabilities, and add up to more or less than one. Even more important, the significance of the outcome to people's financial or personal affairs can govern the probabilities which they attach to outcomes. Someone who is thinking of a last-ditch investment which, if it succeeds, will make them, and if it fails, will ruin them, may well overstate the chance of success. This occurs because the alternative is too bad to contemplate, realistically. In contrast, another person might err in the opposite direction. For similar reasons, some risky investments are not considered. The reason is that the probability of an unfavourable outcome, and the ensuing consequences, exceed some critical level. A further limit on the ability of anyone to assess probabilities is that all previous sets of circumstances which the decision maker can draw on for information, are unique, as will be any future situations. All this makes guesses about probabilities, by necessity, rough.

A part answer to the question about how well people handle probabilities is to explain the gamblers' fallacy. If you had a fair coin and you were to toss it a lot, you would expect half heads and half tails to show. Say, after a number of tosses, there have been more heads than tails. Then you might back tails in the hope that some kind of a divinely ordained correction factor might come into play.

The problem here is that you would be mixing up two things. There is the undeniable truth that ultimately 50% heads and 50% tails will happen, but only after a very large number of tosses. The reality is that as the percentage of heads and tails approaches 50% each, the absolute difference between the number of heads and of tails, or winning or losing bets can still be very large. This is because a large number of tosses would have had to have been held.

The 'gambler's fallacy' occurs because the 'law of averages' or 'the correction factor' works only over a very, very large number of events and so the probability for each single toss of the coin remains the same. Many of the events about which farmers have to assess probabilities are like this. For practical purposes, the probability of a good season following a bad season is the same as the chance of a good season following a good season, or a bad season following a bad season. The coin does not remember.

Various complex computer techniques can be used to put probabilities on as many prices and yields as possible. Then these are combined into estimates of the full range of a large number of the possibilities for farm income. However, there is always the 'many probabilities' problem. Once many probabilities are combined to take account of many possible variable events occurring, the combined estimate is often no better than what the decision maker could have guessed at first, intuitively.

Further, while probabilities are used to give a more realistic measure than single value estimates, when using probabilities the probability of the probability problem arises. More problems arise because the assumed relationships between the uncertain variables of an activity are also uncertain. Often, to do anything sensible with probability distributions, one needs to assume that they are independent, which is not always realistic.

It is more useful, in practice, to test the sensitivity of results to changes in critical variables, using the 'what if' approach. Probabilities are then useful in a general way to help assess whether the changes and outcomes which are particularly interesting and important, are likely to happen.

Finally, note carefully one important proviso with using probabilities in farm management analyses. This proviso relates to the relatively few 'events' in the relevant planning period, in terms of the numbers of seasons, prices, product buying and selling decisions, major investment decisions and such like which will be experienced. Relate this phenomenon back to the gambler's fallacy (the fallacy is the notion 'that the coin remembers'). The small sample of 'events' means that good or bad 'luck' about important variables in farming life have a more significant effect over success or failure than is the case where 'probabilistically rational' decisions are made by players in a game where the uncertain and variable events can happen a lot, such as dealing in the money market; it is all about the quality of the information. With farming there are generally too few events for whatever information we have about probabilities to be highly useful. Therefore the decision techniques which incorporate probabilities in a formal way, such as EMVs and joint probabilities, are of limited usefulness. We say, be aware of probabilistic ways of thinking about outcomes but do not try to make too much of 'the odds' because the events are too few, and the information too poor.

We prefer to explore 'sketches' of possible outcomes, saying in effect, if you do 'this', and 'this' happens, then the ultimate outcome(s) will be like 'this'. The decision maker then weighs up all the information. Alternative budget scenarios and break-even budgets are invaluable techniques to add information to this decision process.

Break-even budgets, scenarios, and sensitivity testing

To test the sensitivity of a budgeted outcome, the factors affecting the outcome of a particular project or activity need to be listed. Then the effect of a change in these factors needs measuring. This will show the sensitivity of the result to variations in the performance of key variables. Break-even budgets can be done to show the levels of key factors at which the proposed change in farm plan produces a result as good as the current set-up. Then, the odds of the critical level of the critical variable happening can be assessed. If break-even figures are such that the decision maker is willing to go on with the proposal, then the change has a good chance of being a good decision. The decision makers need to spend some time doing homework before they take the final step.

Doing 'what if' sensitivity testing and break-even budgeting is worth doing. The computer spreadsheet allows for this sort of testing to be done quickly and relatively simply. Once critical levels of key variables are identified, such as the break-even yield or price, or the gearing rate at which debt can be serviced, the decision maker can weigh up how serious it would be if the poor outcomes happened, also considering the chances of such outcomes happening. A farmer might say 'it's the price of wool which is the most critical thing. As I can see from the break-even budget, if wool hits 'x' cents per kilogram, I'm in big trouble. But I don't think that it will, but I'll have a look at a couple of other possible outcomes.' That is the advantage of break-even budgeting. Then the farmer might say, 'balancing the consequences of that outcome happening with what I reckon are the chances of that happening, it will be all right. We will do it.' In practice, considering risk when framing farm budgets involves lots of 'what if this happens?' types of budgets.

The computer spreadsheet is a great tool for experimenting with numerous 'what if' situations. Especially those which could wreak havoc with an investor's confidence if they were not tested. It also shows directions for contingency planning.

Budgets are no more reliable than the data and the judgements that go into them. Often much of the data which is used may be very uncertain. Sensitivity testing and break-even budgeting do not solve the problem of uncertain data, but they do tell the farmer what might be the outcome if and when prices, costs or rates of performance vary from the 'most likely' levels.

Thus sensitivity testing and break-even budgeting are the most practical ways of bringing risk into the budgeting and decision-making processes. Again, we simply end up saying to the decision maker: 'these are possible outcomes. How do these outcomes, and the chance of them happening, fit with your objectives, your financial position, your personal make-up and your ability to bear risk?' This is not as bad as it may first appear. The whole budgeting process needs just enough information about likely profitability and risk to let a good decision be made. In many cases the answer may be fairly obvious, for many reasons which have to do with the objectives, needs, financial position and make-up of the investor. It is not true to think that all prospective investments require detailed analysis of risk.

When a range of outcomes is possible, where the costs of inputs or the prices and yields of outputs are likely to vary, which is almost always, then any number of budget scenarios can be looked at, using the spreadsheet. In many activities or projects, the net profit depends on the values of just two or three key parameters. Sensitivity analysis using budgets on the spreadsheet can show:

- those parameters (yield, prices or costs) which have the greatest effect on net profit;
- the extent to which the size of the net profit is sensitive to a change in the value of one or more of these parameters.

In a crop production activity, the size of the net profit or gross margin (GM) might depend mainly on the yield (Y) and the cost of fertilizer (F) used. This could be because the price, after deducting harvesting and marketing costs, the 'net price' (Pn), is known with considerable certainty, and the pre-harvest variable costs (V), other than fertilizer (F), are unlikely to vary greatly.

These relationships can be expressed in the profit equation below:

GM per ha $= Y \times Pn - V - F$

Substitution of values for Y, Pn, V and F allows the sensitivity of the gross margin to changes in these likely values to be tested. The range of gross margins that come from the sensitivity test gives a basis for deciding on the amount of fertilizer to use. The data from sensitivity tests further stimulates the decision maker to focus on the need to use proper crop production techniques, in this case, proper fertilizer use. Also it stimulates the decision maker to take timely actions to achieve the expected result.

The variability of total outcome can be looked at. This method focuses on the total picture, and incorporates some probabilities. A budget using most likely single values is done first. Then the expected annual profits or the annual net cash flows is worked out. After that, the possible variation around the most likely figure is estimated, together with the percentage chance of these happening. The farmer next has to specify contingency plans (i.e., what action the farmer has planned) should an outcome other than the most likely outcome happen. The example below shows one format for considering the total variability.

outcome: % chance of it occurring
(A) most likely outcome
net financial outcome (50% chance)
(B) pessimistic outcome
net financial outcome (35% chance)
(C) optimistic outcome
net financial outcome (15% chance)

If outcome B: i.e., pessimistic outcome:
1 How seriously will this affect the farm finances?
• seriously;
• not seriously.
2 What action(s) will be taken if the pessimistic outcome occurs?

If outcome C: i.e., optimistic outcome:
1 What effect will this have on the total finances of the farm?
• of moderate benefit;
• of little benefit.
2 What action(s) will be taken if the optimistic outcome occurs?

The issue arises: given that the computer spreadsheet makes it easy for many scenarios to be explored, how is the decision maker to go about assimilating lots of information, making it coherent and usable?

The key is to focus on the important variables in a budget. Not all the numbers are equally important. Take the example (shown in Table 8.2) where operating profits on a dairy farm are crucially dependent on the feed per ha and milk produced each year, and the price per kilogram of butterfat (or per litre of milk).

Feed produced is measured in cow days (cds). A cow day is about 15 kg dm of good ryegrass and clover pasture. Between 300 and 330 cds of good pasture per cow will be required for the year. One ha of irrigated improved pasture on the farm could produce 10 to 12 tonnes dm per ha per year. The average production of butterfat per cow is expected to be 180 kg per year (4,000 L of milk). The price received could be $5 per kg (23.5¢ per L), $4.50 per kg (18.8¢ per L) or $3.50 per kg (16.5¢ per L). Farm pasture area is 120 ha. The farmer has a base cowherd of 300 and has plans to lease some more. The farmer decides 320 cds of feed is likely to be required per cow (see Table 8.2).

Table 8.2: Scenarios for gross income from 120 ha of pasture

dm		10 t per ha	11 t per ha	12 t per ha
cds of feed produced and available after losses		667 per ha	733 per ha	800 per ha
cds per 120 ha		80,040	87,960	96,000
no. of cows at average production 180 kg butterfat per head				
cow days required per cow	330 cd	242	266	291
	300 cd	267	293	320
amount of butterfat (kg) produced				
cow days required per cow	330 cd	43,560	47,880	52,380
	300 cd	48,060	52,740	57,600

The farmer feels cds required would be nearer 330 cd than 300 cd. So 'guesses' 320 cds.

	10 t per ha	11 t per ha	12 t per ha
no. of cows	250	275	300
butterfat (kg)	45,000	49,500	54,000

Table 8.3: Prospective total gross income for cows requiring 320 cd per year

dm	10 t per ha	11 t per ha	12 t per ha
cds of feed produced	667 per ha	733 per ha	800 per ha
cd per 120 ha	80,040	87,960	96,000
no. of cows (320 cd)	250	275	300
kg of butterfat produced	45,000	49,500	54,000
price per kg of butterfat	$	$	$
$5.00	225,000	247,500	270,000
$4.50	202,500	222,750	243,000
$3.50	157,500	173,250	189,000

Looking at Table 8.3, the farmer feels that the production will be nearer 10 to 11 tonnes per ha than 11 to 12 tonnes per ha. This puts gross income in the range of $247,500 to $157,500. The farmer feels that milk prices will be nearer $4.50 to $5.00 per kg than $3.50 to $4.00 per kg. This puts gross income in the range of $247,500 to $202,500.

Looking closely at the 10 to 11 tonnes per ha, $4.50 to $5.00 per kg ranges, the farmer settles on an expectation of feed production nearer 11 tonnes per ha than 10 tonnes per ha, and a price nearer $4.50 per kg than $5.00 per kg. The farmer finally settles on an expectation of gross income of about $220,000.

Information about scenarios can be presented in the form of a matrix as in Table 8.3, and interpreted as described above. However, once more than two variable parameters are varied it becomes complicated. Some variable parameters can first be combined into possible outcomes, just as feed tonnes per ha and cds required were combined into possible levels of butterfat production. Production and prices were then presented in a matrix. Remember though the law of compounding and its effects when making several guesses.

A third variable parameter can be presented for interpretation, for example, wheat yield and price and interest rate on $100,000 debt.

Table 8.4: Wheat income for 500 ha

wheat prices per t	Yield		
	1 t per ha	1.5 t per ha	2 t per ha
	$	$	$
$100	50,000	75,000	100,000
$150	75,000	112,500	150,000
$200	100,000	150,000	200,000

Table 8.5: Wheat income after interest

$ per t	1 t per ha			1.5 t per ha			2 t per ha		
	income	interest	income after interest	income	interest	income after interest	income	interest	income after interest
	$	%	$	$	%	$	$	%	$
$100	50,000	8	42,000	75,000	8	67,000	100,000	8	92,000
		10	40,000		10	65,000		10	90,000
		12	38,000		12	63,000		12	88,000
$150	75,000	8	67,000	112,500	8	104,500	150,000	8	142,000
		10	65,000		10	102,500		10	140,000
		12	63,000		12	100,500		12	138,000
$200	100,000	8	92,000	150,000	8	142,000	200,000	8	192,000
		10	90,000		10	140,000		10	190,000
		12	88,000		12	138,000		12	188,000

The farmer feels the most likely ranges are $150 to $200 per tonne, but nearer $150 per tonne; 1 to 1.5 tonnes per ha but nearer 1.5 tonnes per ha; and 10% to 12% interest rates but nearer 10%. The farmer settles on an expected gross income after interest of around $110,000.

Practical aspects of risk management

Farm incomes will be uncertain—that is for certain—farm operators know that, over time, they will experience booms and busts, high prices, low prices, good seasons, droughts, market collapses, market changes, government policy changes.

Booms and busts

Booms create chances to reduce debt, modernize plant, broaden the range of
investments, and to improve and expand farm area. Busts often feature falling
product prices and unstable land prices. With enterprise and well-reasoned
strategies, farmers can reduce the variability of their incomes, exploit booms,
survive busts, even exploit them, too. Remember the old saying: 'optimism
involves an intellectual flaw'. This is most apt during a boom. The same can
be said of pessimism in a bust.

Poor decision making often comes from either being too optimistic or too
pessimistic about the future. Decisions go wrong because at the time the decision
was made the financial considerations and beliefs were for the short term. That
is, the over-optimistic assumption is made during booms that good times will
continue at that level for a long time; or an over-gloomy outlook was taken
and the predicted events did not happen. While this is patently obvious, it is
surprising how short-sighted some farmers can be, whether in good or bad times.
Short-sightedness, however, is an expensive handicap. The commonest case of
poor decisions is where land is purchased at too high a price relative to any
reasonably expected long-term trend in product prices. This could be because
in budgeting to justify the price, a commodity price has been assumed which
is far too high and also unrealistic for the longer term. One reality of farming
life is that success depends on buying-in at the right price.

In good times it is common for farmers to convert cash surpluses into
updated plant. Such action is often essential, but a reflex 'buy a new tractor'
mentality should not prevail at the expense of considering alternative use
of funds.

Diversification is usually seen as a wise management strategy to reduce the
problems of variability of yields, prices, and income. Those areas of Australia
which readily lend themselves to produce a range of commodities are often the
most desirable areas to farm. However, many farmers are not in this situation, so
their chances to diversify are limited. Appropriate diversification can make up for
fluctuations in commodity prices. This effect can be even better where production
cycles can be changed rapidly, e.g. in cereal production, which is more rapid
than cattle production. However, diversification can make income variability
greater if the various activities are affected by similar seasonal and market forces.
In this case, prices and yields move in the same direction at the same time.

It can still be argued that if one takes the attitude of making most profit,
despite fluctuation, diversification might not be the best option. Remember,
in business in general, one of the commonest causes of failure is expansion
out of fields which are known and the outcome is successful, into a field which
is unknown. This is usually highly risky and, not surprisingly, often leads to
failure. This phenomenon is true of all businesses, from the largest to the smallest.
Diversification has its merits, as well as specialization, or at least, diversification,
within the general area of genuine expertise has merit.

If the equity is low, it seems sensible to use high incomes to lift equity
and so (hopefully) survive the next fall in profits. Given a current high equity

position a number of options are available to the farmer. An extra 20% to 30% of land can be added to the existing farm when the pressure goes off the boom, or during a bust at the start of the inevitable recovery. Modern stock-handling facilities can be used to carry more stock per unit of labour. Investment in proven technology to further intensify the production process and, as a result, increase the value of the whole farm in another option.

Flexibility in financial structure is one of the keys to surviving and even exploiting economic downturns. A flexible cost structure is an advantage in coping with adversity. It is important during good times to reduce commitments to those fixed costs which cannot be cut readily during the next recession. Cost structures with some flexibility reduce the extent to which temporary income falls threaten long-term profitability and farm survival.

A reserve of liquid assets and income-producing off-farm investments is commonest, and a valuable stand-by. The ideal off-farm investment is one which produces income regularly and it also provides capital gains. Although it is best to invest in some area of the economy which is a growth area, in practice, this is not easy. It is essential to make full use of experienced professional advisers here.

Devices to stabilize and equalize incomes can also help. There will almost certainly be more emphasis in future on farmers' own ability to use voluntary stabilization and equalization devices. Financial instruments and income equalization deposits are examples. Such devices can help producers attain some stability of income. Apart from diversification into conventional agricultural enterprises, scope also exists to engage in small-scale, intensive, innovative activities. Planning for the next setback should take place during a current boom. It is commonsense to consider how to best use the cash surpluses of booms to help survive the inevitable busts.

Some specific measures to cope with income variability

Now, we will discuss some of the measures available to help farmers reduce income variability (i.e., to keep net profits at a fairly stable level) in the inevitable price and climate variability.

Means of reducing income variance include:

- yield insurance: hail, flood, fire, and sometimes frost insurance, can be obtained for some crops. Livestock is more difficult to insure. The premium is in proportion to the risk borne by the insurance company;
- adoption of sound crop and animal production techniques: an explanation of why one farmer makes a success of an activity in a given area and given time while the neighbour makes a loss, is that the first farmer paid proper attention to the basic husbandry techniques needed to produce the crop or animal product. The successful farmers pay attention to good cultural techniques, operations done on time, proper depth and spacing of seeds, timely drenching, using sprays and fertilizers correctly, and preparing a good seedbed. The use of good methods and techniques as a means of reducing the effects of risk is often not given enough attention;

- producing products for which there is a guaranteed price: for some commodities, government marketing boards or co-operatives guarantee the minimum prices; the producer has the choice of growing these products and thus reducing the income variance. In some years income would be higher if products for which there was no fixed price were produced;
- diversification: diversification can be of value when there is price- or weather-induced production variability. On the other hand specialization has obvious advantages as resources (including related managerial skills) can be devoted to growing the product which gives the highest return. Where the relationship between two activities is competitive, the inclusion of the less profitable activity in the farm plan is usually not warranted, unless for biological reasons, such as in crop rotations;
- keeping borrowings to a level where they can be serviced: the ability to service debt depends on the level of the annual cash surplus which comes from the year's operations, before deducting interest and principal payments. The higher the annual cash surplus, the higher the debt that can be serviced and the lower the critical equity percentage needed for the viability of the farm business.

Alternatives to increasing productivity of existing activities

A number of alternative courses of action should be considered by those to whom directly increasing productivity of activities is not attractive, not feasible or not the solution to their problems.

Tightening the belt and hoping for the best; for some, this course of action is not as silly as it sounds. If both the farm income and the equity are moderately high, the occasional boom year, combined with prudent use of income equalization deposits, and off-farm investments, should make up for periods when conditions of trade are not particularly favourable.

Changing the mixture of enterprises is an area where there can be scope for increasing income. People who are prepared to analyse the relative profitability of their various enterprises, and take action using the best information they can get on market prospects, are likely to 'win' at the game.

Introducing new enterprises, both farm and non-farm, with care at the trial and early adoption stages, can be worth following. Money spent on investigating new, maybe innovative, enterprises can often be more rewarding than increasing the productivity of the existing ones. These new ones need not necessarily be farm enterprises.

Syndicate either land, or machinery, or stock (or all of these). With current technology and management practices it is feasible to run the equivalent of 6,000 to 8,000 dse per person in many areas, and sometimes considerably more with 'low maintenance' systems. Similarly, with some casual labour, plus contract cartage, 600 to 700 ha of crop per person is not unusual.

Buy more land, especially in a recession. This option depends on the price and availability of the land; the operator's present equity; and access to credit on favourable terms. Adding about 20% more land to a moderately sized (not large) property employing two people is often a more attractive proposition than investing in measures to increase productivity on the existing area.

Investigate off-farm investments. Although there have been a number of disasters in the 1980s in property, share and financial investments, some off-farm investments have been sound. The key word in this proposed option is 'investigate'. The services of competent financial advisers are basic to success here.

Another option is to sell out and move to an area where land is cheaper but production per ha only slightly less; alternatively, sell out and leave agriculture. This option will be favoured by different types of people at different times of their lives such as the person who wishes to retire, or wants to start a different business.

Of the 160,000 commercial farmers in Australia, about 30% have little debt and another 40% have less than 10% debt on their total assets. These people, and the growing numbers of part-time farmers and hobby farmers from urban centres, continue to be the main buyers of the land of those wishing to leave agriculture.

Lease the property. Although commercial leasing of farmland is not a common practice in Australian agriculture, it is an option for people who are not keen to increase productivity themselves, but who wish to retain the farm in the hope that the rate of capital gain will at least keep pace with, or perhaps outstrip the rate of inflation. It also can provide the younger, well-trained, energetic, potential new entrant to farming, who has limited capital, with a chance to use funds more fruitfully than by tying them up in the purchase of land.

Climatic and yield variability

On animal farms, there are five ways of reducing the harmful financial and physical effect of uncertainty about the future:

1 Keep the equity high; do not over-borrow. Keep the equity in the property (using realistically conservative market values) high enough to allow access to further funds. These can be used for re-stocking, re-planting, or for minimum purchase of feed to keep the basic breeding herd or flock in good condition. In general, the equity percentage should not drop below around 85% in safer grazing and cereal areas. This 'rule of thumb' figure is not absolute, because the level of net surplus disposable income, after tax, and living expenses, will also affect the safe lower limit of equity. For more intensive production with greater control over environment and with some market security such as contracts for sales, higher gearing is sometimes possible.

2 Build into each yearly budget a contingency sum to allow for unexpected costs or reduced income. On an animal property this is usually done by making an allowance for drought, say $1 to $2 per year per sheep and $10 per year per head of adult cattle. The allowance, if not used in the current year, can be invested in readily cashable investments against the day that it will be needed.

3 Opportunity buying of grain, storing it for use in the expected difficult period, and selling it when the difficult period has passed. There is usually benefit in buying grain virtually off the header and then selling most of it near the end of the danger period, which is near the end of winter in many areas.
4 In years of good profit, invest only some of the surplus in the property and then only in those activities which are expected to show at least 10% to 15% real return after tax on the extra (or marginal) invested funds. It is often a good idea to invest the rest in safe off-farm investment in areas which have no relation to agriculture, but where the securities are readily negotiable and yielding a safe interest return, showing a sound prospect of capital growth.
5 Keep animals in good health and in at least forward store condition, so that they are always saleable at reasonable prices. Also, be sufficiently flexible to be prepared to sell some stock and re-stock later. Rarely do post-drought stock prices rise to prohibitively high levels; also, with the exception of special stud animals, there are few animals which are so unique in their physique and performance that they cannot be replaced with others of comparable quality.

On crop farms, income fluctuation resulting from climatic variability can be reduced by diversification and by having the plant capacity, technical knowledge, access to working capital and labour to permit a quick and flexible response in land use as each seasonal opportunity presents itself.

Where there is a chance of a total crop failure, say, once every five years, an allowance of one-fifth of the total pre-harvest variable crop costs can be added to each year's planned costs, and the money put into interest-earning investments which can be readily converted to cash. If this precaution is taken there will be, in general, funds available to meet pre-harvest costs in the year following one of crop failure.

When a crop activity fails during the early or middle part of the year it is often still possible to follow it quickly with another, thereby compensating for the loss of the first activity. The manager needs to be prepared by knowing the technical requirements of the next activity, and have made arrangements to obtain quick access to the inputs (seed, labour, etc.) needed, otherwise he or she would not be in a position to make a successful change of plan.

Comments on high equity and off-farm investments, made above in relation to animal farms, apply with equal strength to crop farms.

Price variability

There are a number of specific financial management methods of coping with the uncertainty and variability of commodity prices and interest rates. The main ones are forward contracting of sales of commodities, forward interest rate agreements, use of futures markets for commodity sales and interest rates, and purchasing the right to sell foreign currency or the right to borrow at particular interest rates, 'options'.

These techniques can enable hedging against adverse movements in prices and interest rates by enabling producers to shift risk on to other willing traders and 'lock' into particular prices and interest rates which are deemed satisfactory.

These forms of risk avoidance, like all measures ameliorating consequences of risk, have costs. With forward contracting and futures, the costs are administrative costs, as well as costs incurred if a producer happens to be 'locked out' of beneficial effects such as a rise in commodity prices or a fall in interest rates. With options, the cost is the cost of buying the right to sell or to borrow, and any associated futures trading costs.

Buying on interest rate option, a 'cap', gives the right to borrow at a particular rate for a certain time. This protects the borrower from a rise in interest rates while allowing the borrower to take advantage of any fall in interest rates, i.e., the option does not have to be taken up. A variation on this is the right to borrow at a range of borrowing costs between, say 12% to 15%, a 'collar', and it costs less than the 'cap' method.

The fascinating details of how futures markets for agricultural commodities work is not dealt with here, but we do briefly describe the essential features of futures markets. The essence of futures trading is in the operation of two markets: the physical commodity market; and a market in future contracts to deliver or accept standard amounts of the commodity. The two markets are related, thus the risk of a price fall faced by a producer can be shifted through the market in futures contracts to someone to take this chance.

The producer of a commodity can contract to deliver, in future, the standard commodity (i.e., sell a futures contract) at a certain price. Then, when the time comes the physical commodity is sold at whatever the market price is and the futures contract to deliver is cancelled by buying back a contract, done at the time the product is sold. At this time the contract price and the market price are similar. So if a market price for the physical product is received which is lower than the expected price at the time the futures contract was sold, then this means that the futures contract can be bought back for less than it was sold for. Thus a 'loss' on the physical market is offset by a 'profit' on the futures contract selling and buying. The net result is that, roughly, the initially hoped-for price is received, albeit in a roundabout way. This is called a 'hedging' to ensure a particular price is received.

An advantage of using futures contracts is that only a small proportion of the total value of each contract has to be deposited to conduct the transaction. A disadvantage is that if you have sold a contract and prices rise, meaning you will have to pay more to cancel out the game (i.e., you will make a potential loss on futures), then you will have to make good these potential losses until you sell the physical commodity and close the futures contract. Thus a reasonable bankroll will be needed to conduct your futures operations. Commodity futures are seldom used by farmers in practice, but this might increase as marketing becomes deregulated such as the wool market. Forward contracting and currency and interest rate futures and options might be used more frequently in the future, though these markets will suit the circumstances of only a small number of farmers. For instance futures contracts for bank bill interest rates are highly standardized, with all contracts having a face value of $500,000 for 90-day contract periods, corresponding to the financial quarters. Also, a good deal of short-term liquidity can be needed for successful hedging on futures markets.

Drought

Here we look at some of the decisions farmers face during a drought, and some strategies they can adopt to thwart the worst intentions of 'Old Man Drought'.

There is no one definition of 'a drought', although there is general agreement that it is 'a severe water shortage'. The existence of a drought depends on many factors other than annual average rainfall. Rainfall distribution, evaporation, farm activities and their needs, all determine if a farm is in drought. This fact has important implications when planning drought strategies.

Farm activities in any area evolve, over time, to fit the varying climatic conditions of the area. For animal enterprises, the breeding, mating, stocking, weaning, and feeding management strategies evolve. For cropping, the types and varieties of crops grown, crop sequences, tillage practices, timing of operations and harvesting systems are all adapted to suit the climate. Drought is not simply a severe water shortage, but an abnormal severe water shortage.

A practical definition of a drought for a grazier is when the usual feed supply, including fodder normally conserved for feeding, cannot meet the feed demand at the 'normal' stocking rate. The grazier is then forced to make a decision. The point at which he is forced to make this drought-related decision is a good definition of the start of a drought. Drought is related to stocking rate. The higher the stocking rate the greater the chance from suffering from drought. A 'grazier' with no stock would never suffer drought.

During a dry spell, the chance of it continuing and developing into a drought forces farmers to start thinking about drought options and tactics. This is hard and trying, as any decisions taken then affect the scope for later actions. However, once a drought is recognized, decisions and actions to keep its costs low have to be taken.

Drought strategies

Surviving a drought depends as much on actions taken in previous years as on action taken during the drought. An important part of preparing for drought is to exploit good years. The aim is to improve the financial ability of the farm business to withstand the certain future drought. As well as aiming to be financially 'secured' against drought, commonsense dictates that good year dollar surpluses should be invested in adequate water supplies, and perhaps fodder reserves. The ultimate effect of drought is to reduce equity through loss of income, cost of feed, loss of livestock and increased debt.

The ability to survive drought is determined by the level of equity at the start of the drought and the drought strategies adopted. If equity is around 100% then drought is unlikely to reduce this to below about 70%. If equity at the start is only about 70%, it can easily be reduced to below 50%. Credit-worthiness plummets, and the possibility of ruin becomes a fact. The usual drought management options are to cull and sell some stock, agist stock, sell all stock, and feed stock. In practice, some combination of all these options is used. Drought strategies centre on decisions about whether to sell stock, feed stock or some combination of the two.

Important factors in the sell and feed decision:

1 Expected length of drought.
2 Cost of feeding.
3 Expected cost of replacement stock relative to selling prices.
4 Income from the stock not sold.
5 Use of the money from sale of stock.
6 Interest rates.

Feeding

Feeding ensures that stock will survive the drought, but the economic survival of the farm business is the objective. The costs and returns of feeding, and feeding at various levels, must be carefully weighed.

If feeding is opted for, the choices are feeding with any fodder reserves already on the property, purchase of fodder, or agistment of stock.

Here are some general points on drought feeding:

* agistment is usually a good proposition, if it can be found. It is usually the cheapest of the drought options (especially if freight costs are reduced by government drought-assistance schemes);
* the irregularity of droughts means that extensive fodder conservation measures are not usually economic;
* feed properly. That is, feed at a level which will ensure that the stock remain saleable products. Survival feeding is a dangerous game.

Drought management of stock needs a sound grasp of the feed requirements of different classes of stock. As well, the technical aspects of preparing and feeding various types of rations have to be mastered. During a drought, state departments of agriculture and feed firms provide all the technical information needed to carry out effective drought feeding.

Selling

Sale prices tend to decrease as a drought progresses; more stock is on the market and their condition deteriorates . Furthermore replacement costs tend to rise as the drought period lengthens and replacements become more scarce. If costs of replacing stock exceeds the selling price, as usually happens, then the stock owner faces a capital loss. If the farmer sells stock, there is a capital loss and forfeit of future stock income until replacements are bought.

Essentially, the decision between selling and feeding depends upon the relative costs of feeding and replacing the stock. The drought strategy maxim: 'Sell, prepare to repent, but sell early' generally holds good. Early sale can help avoid the trap of having both a heavy feed bill and greatly depreciated stock values plus heavy stock losses, i.e., feeding your business into trouble. The problem is how to estimate when a dry period is going to turn into a drought, and if it does, how long will it last?

If culling and selling, it is only worth keeping those stock which have a good chance of surviving and will be the most valuable when the drought breaks. It is commonsense to reduce stock numbers by heavily culling aged and inferior stock, and selling non-breeders in preference to breeding stock. On mixed properties cattle should usually be sold before sheep. Effective stocking rate can be reduced by not mating. The price of fat stock tends to rise during drought. So there comes a time when it can pay to feed stores up to fat condition, provided that the working capital is available.

Drought recovery

A vital aspect of farm management in drought is recovery afterwards. A complete technical and economic reappraisal of past practices is a first step towards some post-drought planning. Such plans aim to restore lost equity, increase income, and reduce future vulnerability to drought.

Management's decisions when the first rain falls have to deal with such issues as:

- is the rainfall sufficient to act on it? i.e., 'Do I sell now or hold onto stock and feed them?' If a farmer considered the drought had an 8 in 10 chance of ending in a month but a 2 in 10 chance of lasting beyond the month he or she would probably decide to hold on to stock and feed;
- can the present farm plan produce the gross margin needed to cover overheads and service existing and new debt which might need to be incurred?

The farmer then needs to detail specific aspects including:

- sources and amount of extra funds, including carry-on finance;
- technical basis of the plan for the immediate future;
- a development budget;
- equity positions before, during and at the end of plan of repayment.

Usually governments widely recognize, and readily act to alleviate problems caused by drought. Consequently there are numerous drought-assistance schemes which are usually quickly made available. In some cases some of the assistance received means the drought is seen as a thinly disguised blessing. However in future it is likely that more of the onus of responsibility for dealing with droughts will be shifted from the taxpayers and returned to those to whom it belongs— the risk-taking private entrepreneur—the farmer.

Drought assistance provided to the under-prepared managers severely disadvantages those well-prepared managers. Take the case of farmers who have incurred costs to hold appropriate feed and cash reserves, and hope to sell good young replacement stock to others at the end of the drought. The prudent ones are penalized by the subsidies given to the under-prepared farmers. This lets the latter carry their stock through the drought.

The obvious uncertainty of droughts makes farmers aware of the need for forward planning. Alternative drought strategies must be assessed taking into account the affected farmer's conviction about how long the farm business can survive a continuing drought; and how much longer the farmer believes that the drought will continue. Drought-affected farmers need to weigh up the major possible consequences of taking different actions, and their chances of occurring, before deciding to take a specific action.

It is impossible to keep all these options in one's head and make a decision. There is no alternative but to put pen to paper if farmers are to give themselves a fair chance of success. There have been many attempts to derive analytical tools and techniques to aid farmers' decisions in droughts. Most of these tools can give only general analyses with useful insights for general, not individual, drought policies and strategies. There can be no specific prescription for drought survival and recovery. Drought decisions will ultimately be based on individuals' situations and experience, and on their judgements of the situation. Having high equity and significant off-farm investments and income sources remain the most prudent steps to take.

8

Questions for discussion

1   Explain what the term 'probability' means. How might you use probabilities in analysing a farm management option?

2   Like it or not, farm decision makers are conscripts to gambling and to weighing up 'the odds' in decision making. What is meant by this statement?

3   Identify sensible strategies to help a farm business to survive:
    (a) a short-term collapse in the market, for a major commodity;
    (b) a sustained rise in interest rates;
    (c) a serious drought;
    (d) the long-term cost–price squeeze in farming.

8

Further reading

Anderson, J. R., Dillon, J. L., & Hardaker, J. B., *Agricultural Decision Analysis*, Iowa State University Press, Ames, Iowa, 1977.

Barry, P. J., Hopkin, J .A., & Baker, C. B., *Financial Management in Agriculture* (3rd edn), The Interstate Printers and Publishers Inc., Illinois, 1988.

Boehlje, M. D. and Eidman, V. R., *Farm Management*, John Wiley & Sons, New York, 1983.

Calkins, P. H. and DiPietre, D. D., *Farm Business Management: Successful Decisions in a Changing Environment*, Macmillan Publishing Co. Inc., New York, 1983.

Castle, E. N., Becker, M. H., & Nelson, A. G., *Farm Business Management—The Decision Making Process*, Macmillan Publishing Company, New York, 1987.

9

Will We Give It A Go?
Analysis and Planning
for Change

▬

W̶e now turn to the crux of the decision process: the choice between alternatives. Farmers often make investment decisions intuitively. These can be based on past investment decisions which have worked out well, despite difficult cost-price trends. The purpose of this chapter is to demonstrate how such a choice can be made systematically so that the decisions reached have a good chance of proving successful. We try to be a bit more precise than the farmer who told us:

A good bit of that plan had a fair bit of promise, a fair bit had some good bits in it, a little bit looked a bit suspect, but overall the plan was a bit of all right.

This chapter has two parts: Part 1. Introduction to key (theoretical) aspects of techniques used, and the way of thinking about analysing and planning a change to how the business is operated; Part 2. Practical applications of main techniques of analysis, and some discussion about interpreting farm management budgets.

Part 1
Introduction to ways of thinking about analysing and planning a change

Making decisions about changing the way a farm is operated has a series of steps. Problems, or needs for action, have to be recognized; the nature of the problem or need, and its effects on other aspects of the business, have to be identified and then defined accurately; courses of action chosen have to be feasible according to both the decision-maker's objectives and the technical needs and constraints; analysis of the economic and financial feasibility has to be done. The unmeasurable aspects of the decision have to be weighed up. After these are complete a decision can be made and the intended steps have to be carried out well. As the results are never exactly as expected, the program then has to be monitored, controlled, and revised for unexpected developments, as they occur.

Sometimes farm profits can increase if prices received increase and costs stay the same, but this is not something over which farmers have control, and cannot be of a long-term nature anyway. Farmers increase profits by improving the quantity or quality of their output by spending on variable costs, keeping overheads relatively constant, or they can spend on both overheads and variable costs, and change the structure of the business. Usually an increase in capital investment, or a change in the nature of capital invested, is involved when changes are made.

These essential economic criteria are used in evaluating a change to a farm plan:

- net return on the capital invested after tax is paid and risk allowed for in the sums;
- net cash flow for either the life of the project or until some steady state is reached;
- break-even criteria for the 'new' versus the 'old' or another option;
- effects on debt and equity as shown in the farm balance sheet, currently and over time.

There are two broad types of change, simple and complex. The essence of a simple change is that it is straightforward and quick. The changed farm plan is reasonably fully operational within a year, or two years, at most. A simple change could involve replacing one activity with a similar one—barley with wheat—in a particular paddock, or changing from Dorset Horn rams to Southdowns. When making a simple change not as many detailed steps in analysing are needed as for more complex changes. A budget for one year's operations will usually suffice. This is the common partial budget.

Complex change usually takes a fair amount of time, and has a number of significant implications for the way all of the farm operates, as related activities and choices in the business are affected. Most often, a significant change involves relatively large investment, several years to be fully operational, and causes important changes in the way the farm now operates. This is so when a decision is made to improve an area of low producing pasture, to install some irrigation, to purchase and develop more land, or to change cropping sequences or time of lambing and calving.

Before managers can make a sound choice between two or more alternative farm plans they need to know how the alternatives are likely to compare in terms of profitability, and risk, and other less clearly defined aspects as well. If a small adjustment to the present farm organization is proposed, the structure and arithmetic of the budget is relatively simple. However, if a major re-organization of the farm business is under consideration, a considerable amount of arithmetic will be involved. Budgeting is the most powerful tool which a farm manager can use to improve decision making. We will discuss the logic and procedures involved in budgeting in some detail.

The first need in preparing reliable budgets is a sound knowledge of the technical aspects of agriculture and of the situation of the specific farm. It is no use dreaming up numbers to put in the budget and then expecting the answer to mean anything. Relevant farm records can be a help in putting numbers on the present position as these show the use of inputs of labour, machinery, fuel, seed, fertilizer, feed and so on, in relation to the levels of output of crops and livestock of the present system. This information will usually need to be supported by technical data from other sources such as neighbouring farmers, and experimental plots. Then estimates must be made of the input costs and product prices which are thought to be relevant to the planning period to which the budget relates.

In earlier chapters we have described briefly the basic planning tools including gross margins; partial and whole farm budgets; break-even budgets; gain from extra capital; cash flow budgets; and using discounting to adjust future dollars back to their equivalent values at the present.

Here, we show how these techniques can be used for planning and decision making, focusing on budgeting in the commonest planning and decision problem facing any farmer of whether or not to adopt a new activity (or project). The physical and technical aspects of the project have to be right, and judgements about the market prospects and expected prices have to be sound. Tax implications have to be explored and accounted for. Often most important of all, the human and intangible aspects of the project, have to be given the appropriate weighting in the decision. Net returns, opportunity interest cost, risks, and prospects for capital gains or losses, must all be considered.

Deciding on a new activity or project

Before farm operators adopt a new activity, or expand an existing one, they need to take into account some or all of the following points:

- market prospects for the new or extra products;
- human aspects, the skills required, ability to carry out a plan, ability to cope with the risks;
- physical and technical aspects of making the change;
- likely inflation in the future;
- the 'compared with what?' criterion; also, 'with-without' or 'before-after' criteria;
- interest rates to use in economic and financial analyses;
- activity gross margins and gross margins analysis;
- change in profit after tax, assessed on partial or whole farm basis;
- break-even budgets;
- outcomes for different scenarios;
- amount of extra capital investment needed to bring about the change;
- gains after tax expressed as a percentage of the extra capital invested;

- net cash flow over time expected to result from the change;
- net present value and internal rate of return of the investment;
- taxation aspects;
- expected change in assets and debts over time;
- risk and variability associated with the change;
- related effects on the rest of the farm business;
- intangibles.

Look at these points systematically to permit valid comparisons between alternative changes. They are all discussed and demonstrated in various parts of this chapter.

Market prospects

The decision maker needs to investigate, from as many sources (people and publications) as practicable, the likely demand and the range of possible prices for the product, especially at the time it will be available for the market. If possible, the decision maker should find out what might be the likely increase in supply of the product from other producers. After giving due weight to these factors, reasonable assumptions can be made about the prices to expect. As far as possible the decision maker has to determine when and how to sell the product(s) resulting from the change.

Human and social aspects

Although a planned change might look attractive on both economic and technical grounds, the expected result could be thwarted because of human and social obstacles. It is vital that the farmer and the employees have the required skills and knowledge. If they do not, could they acquire them? Many projects look attractive on paper and fail because the people doing them lack the ability to carry them out. A common reason for good ideas not being put into practice is that the skilled and reliable labour essential to the plan is not available. The values of the people involved, the attitudes to work, a sense of what is fair, the wishes of the people to obtain too large a share of the benefits, or levels of expectations, might also partly frustrate the problem. So the farmer has to assess whether these factors are likely to cause trouble, what steps can be taken to avoid them, and at what likely cost.

Physical and technical aspects

The physical aspects to consider are whether the resources are available (labour, soil type, water, animals, pasture, machinery) to carry out the change, or whether extra resources have to be obtained. Technical needs to make a success of the plan could include specific types of fertilizer, specific animal husbandry techniques, and the methods of growing, harvesting, and marketing. To ensure that all relevant aspects of the change are accounted for, a detailed physical plan of the land, machinery, crops, and types of animals has to be drawn up. Make some allowances for inefficiency in the early stages of the change, especially if the farmer is unfamiliar with the new activity. We stress that the physical and technical bases of operation need to be sound so that the economics is sound, and time spent on budgeting and other financial calculations is valuable.

Inflation and the numbers

Judging alternative projects to determine which is better or best, involves choosing the numbers to use in the budgets. If inflation is anticipated over the life of the proposed change make some allowance for this in the economic evaluation and financial planning of the change. One method is to use current (real) values for all costs and prices, rates of return and interest; this done, and a project chosen from the alternatives, then the financial or cash flow budgets need to be expressed in nominal (inflated) dollars. Financial budgets must be in nominal terms, otherwise they would understate the amount of nominal dollars needed to fund the project in future. A case can be made for another approach: doing the economic evaluation in nominal terms. This way the financial budget is automatically done, the returns are comparable to market rates and also it is easier to get the interest deductions from taxable income right. Some examples and explanation follow. First, an example budget is given using real terms. The cash flows of a project in current 1991 dollars are expected to be as follow in Table 9.1.

Using all real dollars and real rates of interest to compare projects is making the implicit assumption that the real costs and prices do not change relative to each other over the life of the project. When projecting current values for costs and receipts forwards, it is assumed that the current relationships between product returns and input costs remain the same in the future as they are now. If this assumption is invalid, which is possible given past inflation of farm costs compared with prices received, then the analysis can be done in appropriately adjusted real dollar costs and prices.

Table 9.1: Real cash flows

year	cash in	cash out	annual net cash flow	cumulative net cash flow
	$	$	$	$
1991	200,000	1,000,000	−800,000	−800,000
1992	500,000	600,000	−100,000	−900,000
1993	1,000,000	600,000	+400,000	−500,000
1994	1,000,000	600,000	+400,000	−100,000
1995	1,000,000	600,000	+400,000	+300,000

NPV %	$	benefit:cost ratio discount rate %	$\left(\dfrac{\text{PV benefits}}{\text{PV costs}}\right)$
5 real	135,400	at 5	1.045
7 real	81,900	at 7	1.029
10 real	12,200	at 10	1.005

real internal rate of return
10.6%

Another adjustment to consider is a possibility of technological gains over time reducing some costs. Inevitably, there have to be guesses in all this. Using inflated (nominal) dollars you have to guess what will be the future inflated values of the costs and prices.

Table 9.2: Cash flow budget in nominal terms with 10% inflation

year	cash in	cash out	annual net cash flow	cumulative net cash flow
	$	$	$	$
1991	220,000	1,100,000	−880,000	−880,000
1992	605,000	726,000	−121,000	−1,001,000
1993	1,331,000	798,600	+532,400	−468,600
1994	1,464,100	878,460	+585,640	+117,040
1995	1,610,510	966,306	+644,204	+761,244

NPV

real discount rate %	rate of inflation %	real interest (r)	+ +	+ inflation (f)	+ real interest × inflation + (r) (f) =	= nominal discount rate	NPV $
5	10	0.05	+	0.10	+ (0.05) (0.10) =	0.155	135,400
7	10	0.07	+	0.10	+ (0.07) (0.10) =	0.177	81,900
10	10	0.1	+	0.10	+ (0.1) (0.10) =	0.21	12,200

nominal internal rate of return
21.6%

benefit:cost ratio discount rate %	$\left(\dfrac{\text{PV benefits}}{\text{PV costs}}\right)$
at 15.5	. 1.045
at 17.7	1.029
at 21	1.005

The returns on capital and discounted economic analysis (NPV, IRR, B:C) of this project, in Table 9.1 above, are worked out using 1991 dollars and real discount rates. To use nominal (market) interest rates, which include the expected inflation for the period between 1991 and 1995, is wrong because the dollar values have not been inflated for the same period. The dollar values used are all 1991 dollars. This implies that expected inflation over this period is zero. If this were the case interest rates would not have an inflation component in them.

If inflation were expected to be 10% per year for the next five years then you can either use current dollars and real interest rates for the analysis or all nominal dollars and interest rates. As shown in Tables 9.1 and 9.2, the answer is the same.

A point to remember is that if an expected return on capital is calculated in real dollars, then the return is a real return. It is not to be compared with market rates of interest as the opportunity cost of this use of the capital. This is because the market rates of interest is made up of the percentage real return which investors hope to get, and the expected rate of inflation and an allowance for risk. Only if the return on capital were calculated using nominal dollars is the return on capital comparable with the market rates of interest for uses of funds with similar riskiness.

Further, care is needed with comparisons of returns on, say, a financial investment which does not increase its value over time with inflation with another investment such as land which might keep up with inflation. For example, with 10% inflation, 10% return on a fixed deposit just breaks even in real terms, whereas 10% return from land which also appreciates at 10% means a total gain of 20%. With 10% inflation this amounts to 10% real gain.

If projects were compared in terms of NPV, IRR, and B:C ratio on the basis of budgets in real terms then once a project is chosen the financial planning has to be done in the future dollar terms. If inflation of 10% per year were expected, it would be necessary to inflate the future cash flows by the expected 10% per year, and use nominal interest rates. The real cash flows from the budget in Table 9.1 then becomes the nominal cash flows as shown in Table 9.2.

When preparing the nominal cash flow budget as above, for financial planning, it is necessary to decide what inflation rate to use. The decision maker has to use the rate of inflation which he or she most strongly expects will apply. It is wise to check out the experts' views, although they are wrong often because it is impossible to forecast the level of important economic variables without contributing to actions which will ensure that the prophecy does not happen.

If the actual rate of inflation over the life of an investment exceeds the expected rate on which market rates were formed, then the investor has earned a lower real return than anticipated when making the investment decision. When this happens, borrowers on fixed interest loans gain, and lenders lose. Borrowers repay their principal and interest with cheaper dollars. During unexpectedly high periods of inflation real interest rates can turn out to be negative. But, if inflation turns out to be less than expected, lenders get a higher real return on their lendings than they had planned. Then the real cost of borrowing to fixed interest borrowers is higher than hoped for, and they lose out.

If inflation exceeds the market rate of interest then negative real returns to the fixed interest lender will result. This happened during the 1970s. When interest rates reflect inflationary beliefs, then only unexpected changes in the inflation rate will benefit a borrower or a lender. This depends on which way the inflation rate goes. In competitive markets changes in the expected rates of inflation are built into changes in the nominal rate of interest. The mechanism by which this happens is 'arbitrage'.

Arbitrage is the process whereby people with an eye to the main chance buy and sell, or invest and speculate, to take advantage of perceived discrepancies between markets. In this way any gap between the ruling rates of interest and current expectations about future rates of inflation are acted on. Thus market rates of interest tend to change. This reflects the change in the beliefs about inflation held by the market participants. In practice, barriers to such market adjustments mean that it is not safe to assume that, with inflation, market rates of interest will correctly incorporate inflation, or that they will do so quickly enough to ensure that a real rate of earning is maintained (in the short term).

But, there is a little bit more to it. Our discussion of real and nominal dollars and interest rates is simplified. There is a real chance that the present capital value of a productive asset itself has some premium for expected future rates of inflation. This means, in practice, that attempts to put all values into real terms, so as to derive measures of the relative fruitfulness of uses of resources which mean anything, are a bit rough. This is true if the capital values we are talking about also include a part which can be put down to beliefs about future rates of inflation.

It is best to do all the sums in either constant or future inflated values but it may be that capital values used are still something of a hybrid of real and nominal values because expectations about future inflation are built into current capital valuations.

Compared with what? Returns on capital

When doing a budget, the key question is 'With what do I compare the results?' There are two related criteria for evaluating a proposed action; there are the questions 'Am I better off after the action, all things considered?' and 'Is this the best of the several, possible actions I could take?' The focus in this chapter is on analysis of choices in order to make the best choice of what to do from the several possible options. We have to take care to compare like to like.

A simple approach is to compare the expected annual profits of alternatives, in an expected 'steady state' or 'average' year even though the investments will have a life longer than one year and might take some time and expense to get to this stage. In some cases comparison of the annual profit in an average year as a return to capital will be adequate to indicate which option is likely to be more profitable once all things are considered.

Some people who do partial budgets express return on capital invested as a percentage of the average value of the capital invested. This gives a higher rate of return than when the initial capital is used as the denominator.

We can only compare like to like. So a return to capital in one use can only be compared to an equivalent type of measure of return and of capital in another use. This has a number of implications:

- the measure of return and capital in the different uses must be in the same 'types' of dollars and interest rates. That is all in real, or all in nominal terms;
- the period involved has to be comparable; returns and capital need to be for the same time, such as a year;
- the value of capital which is used can be a problem. Sometimes returns are calculated and expressed as a return on the initial capital invested. Other times, returns are expressed in terms of the average capital invested over the life of the investment.

Example

investment A	
initial investment	$1,000
annual profit before depreciation	$200
salvage value of the initial investment after five years	$500
depreciation per year	$100

$$\text{return on initial capital} \quad \frac{\$200 - \$100 \text{ depreciation}}{\text{initial capital } \$1,000} = \qquad 10\%$$

$$\text{return on average capital} \quad \frac{\$200 - \$100 \text{ depreciation}}{\text{average capital } \dfrac{(\$1,000 + \$500)}{2}} = \qquad 13.3\%$$

These two measures of return, on initial capital and on average capital, can be compared to the same measures of the profitability of another project having the same life. Comparisons between alternative investment on the farm are reasonably straightforward. It becomes more confusing when a financial investment is the alternative choice being considered.

A common yardstick for comparing the profits from an investment on the farm is what the money could earn safely in a bank. However, comparing the returns from an investment of capital on the farm to a financial investment of a different type such as money in the bank is a bit tricky. We have to take care to account for all the differences. For example, money invested in some long-term use on the farm is usually subject to an annual depreciation (though farm net returns allow for this), and also there might be (though farm net returns allow for this) capital gains arising from the investment, nominal and real, whereas the initial sum invested in the bank is not subject to depreciation or capital gain (see Table 9.3).

Table 9.3: Money in bank versus investment on-farm (no inflation)

money in bank with no inflation year	1	2	3	4	5
initial investment	1,000				
return 5% per year (not compounding)	50	50	50	50	50
capital recovered at end					1,000

investment on-farm with no inflation year	1	2	3	4	5
initial investment	1,000				
return before depreciation	150	150	150	150	150
depreciation $\left(\dfrac{\$1,000 - \$500}{5}\right)$	100	100	100	100	100
return after depreciation	50	50	50	50	50
capital recovered at end from salvage					500
(plus depreciation sums if invested in farm or depreciation allowance account)					

continued

comparison between these two investments
initial investment in bank	$1,000
initial investment in farm	$1,000
average investment in bank	$1,000

average investment in farm $\left(\dfrac{\$1,000 + \$500}{2}\right)$ $750

annual simple interest % return p.a. on initial (and average)

investment in bank $= \dfrac{\$50}{\$1,000}$ 5%

annual return on initial capital invested on farm $= \dfrac{\$50}{\$1,000}$ 5%

annual return on average capital invested on farm $= \dfrac{\$50}{\$750}$ 6.6%

Table 9.4: Money in bank versus investment on-farm (with 10% inflation)

money in bank with 10% inflation

year	1	2	3	4	5
initial investment	1,000				
return 15% per year	150	150	150	150	150
capital recovered at end					1,000

investment on-farm with 10% inflation
(affecting returns and capital values)

year	1	2	3	4	5
initial investment (subject to some inflation)	1,000				
return before depreciation	150	165	181	200	220
depreciation (including inflation is $\dfrac{\text{replacement value} - \text{salvage value}}{5}$	100	110	121	133	146
return after depreciation	50	55	60	67	74
capital recovered at end (salvage)					730

(plus depreciation sums if invested in farm or depreciation allowance account)

comparison between these two investments
initial investment in bank	$1,000
initial investment on-farm	$1,000
average investment in bank	$1,000

average investment on-farm which in this case means average nominal

investment, with an expected inflation of 10% is $\dfrac{\$1,000 + \$730}{2}$ $865

annual simple interest % nominal return on initial (and average)
investment in bank 15%

annual nominal return on initial capital invested on-farm in year 1

$= \dfrac{\$50}{\$1,000} = 5\%$ plus 5%

   maybe 10% inflation of initial capital investment on the land;
   a total of 15% return 15%

annual nominal return on average capital invested on-farm in year 1 $= \dfrac{\$150}{\$865}$ 17.3%

The value of capital and net returns is confounded by the effects of inflation. Capital invested could be wearing out (depreciating in value) and yet at the same time be appreciating at replacement values because of the effects of inflation. By using the approach of valuing assets at their current or replacement value to the business, the depreciation sum also contains some effects of inflation.

The question remains: can the annual return on the investment on the farm be compared to the annual return on the initial $1,000 if it were put in the bank? The farm return in this case is an annual and not a compound return, so the bank return has to be in simple, not compound terms also. The simple return in the bank is 5% real per annum.

Is it the return on the initial capital invested on the farm or on the average capital tied up in the farm project which should be used? When comparing farm projects, it does not matter as long as the same measures are used. The rankings come out correctly. Some analysts prefer to use average value of the capital invested as the yardstick. They argue that although $1,000 was invested in the first year, in the second year there is less capital invested because of depreciation. The alternative view is that the $1,000 initially invested is tied-up in that use until some of it is eventually salvaged, and so the more informative sum to focus on is the initial investment. The average value of capital proponents argue that the depreciation sum deducted from profit each year is used in the business to either save interest or to earn interest. This implies that the depreciation sum is cash. This is not always so. When the income figure includes non-cash items then profit after depreciation need not necessarily equate to cash. Further, even if depreciation did equate to cash, some of this could be used for consumption and not be available for use in the business. We conclude that the issue of using average value of capital or initial value to either express returns as a percentage of, or to charge opportunity interest against, reduces to a number of propositions, as follows:

- if comparing on-farm alternatives it does not matter whether average or initial value of capital is used, as long as you are consistent and compare like to like;
- if you wish to compare a farm investment with a financial investment off the farm, use annual profit after depreciation on the initial value of capital plus capital gains to compare to the annual simple return from the initial capital if put in a bank;
- correct analysis requires that you do a discounted cash flow budget for the whole life of the investment, working out net present value, internal rate of return, and benefit–cost ratio.

Many people include interest as a cost in a budget; others calculate return before interest, which is then compared to opportunity earnings from using the same capital elsewhere. Let purpose, logic, and consistency dictate method.

Interest costs

In doing budgets to appraise the economic worthiness of alternative proposals, the fact that the capital involved is relatively scarce and has a number of alternative uses, has to be acknowledged. Budgets for financial planning require you to examine what actual interest payments will be coming due, and when.

The important question is 'What interest cost to include in budgets?' A good starting point is the idea of opportunity cost. The objective of investment decisions usually is to make best use of limited funds. The cost of capital needs to be posed on earnings foregone by using the capital in this way and not in some other way. This opportunity cost of capital can be allowed for in a couple of ways. If we are not using discounting methods of budgeting, then the return to capital in one use can be compared to what it could earn in another use (i.e., opportunity cost) to see which is better. Using discounting techniques, the future net cash flows are discounted by the opportunity interest cost.

One test rule used to decide on what interest cost to include in budgets is the opportunity cost of the capital the farmer has or could borrow, for on-farm or for off-farm investment. This assumes the farmer is willing to consider both investment options. For instance, consider a well-developed farm where the farmer is using all of his or her own funds. The relevant interest rate to use in budgets could be the current market interest rate (real or nominal depending on whether the budget is being done in real or nominal terms) which is available for safe investments for a similar amount of funds and for a similar period. A farmer on an under-developed property is in a different situation. In this case, investment on the farm could earn a much higher return on extra invested capital than, say, the cost of borrowing, or the market rate for investing in government bonds.

Let us say that a farmer was weighing up a number of alternative investments, one of which was farm development which has a fairly high return. The above reasoning implies that the opportunity cost to use in evaluating alternative, similarly risky investments, other than the farm development option, is the high return the farmer could receive on the investment in developing his farm.

It is always difficult to know what is the true opportunity cost of capital: it is valid to use a weighted average cost of capital where the capital comes from a number of different sources of finance. In economic theory, the interest cost of funds which you borrow (from competitive markets, not at concessional rates) is close to the opportunity cost of those funds. Competition between borrowers for funds to carry out the most rewarding projects makes it so.

Imagine numerous borrowers with a range of investments in mind, each which is of a particular size, type, length, risk, and a particular return. These investors have to compete to get funds. They bid up interest rates as they compete to get funds for their project. Thus interest rates come to approximate the opportunity rates of return which are available from projects in the economy. It is valid to regard the interest you pay for borrowed funds as being close to the range of opportunity costs of those funds.

Alternatively, the opportunity cost of the owner's equity capital is an estimate of the rate of return which could be earned by that capital in other investments. Usually investment funds are made up of a mix of borrowed and equity capital. Hence the overall opportunity cost of capital can be made up of (1) the opportunity cost of borrowed funds (interest cost is an approximation of this in competitive markets); and (2) the opportunity cost of equity capital (which can be a guess, based partly on market rates of earning of alternative investments, with some consideration given to the differences in riskiness and prospects for capital gains).

For practical purposes, the opportunity cost of capital can be estimated like this: the average proportion of debt capital multiplied by its cost, plus the proportion of equity capital multiplied by your guess about the opportunity cost of your own capital.

Suppose 40% of capital is borrowed at 10% nominal interest, and 60% of the owner's own capital is used in a project, and this has a nominal opportunity cost of 12%. This is the weighted average nominal cost of capital:

10% (0.4 of capital) + 12% (0.6 of capital) = 4% + 7.2% = 11.2%

Risk premium

There is also the riskiness of the project to consider. To allow for the fact that one investment might be more risky than another, then an investor might say, 'I would be happy with 5% real return, from the safer investment, but I would want to be looking at 10% real return from the risky one. This will cover me for the chance that it might fail.' For a risky investment one approach is to add a bit onto the safe opportunity interest rate. Instead of a safe 4% to 5% real return after interest and tax, an investor might make the project pass a 10% real rate of return after interest and tax, before going on with it. That is 'adding a risk premium'.

In doing calculations of net present value, a risk premium can be added onto the discount rate. Increasing the discount rate automatically reduces the value of the more distant returns. This emphasizes the fact that the more distant in the future a return is expected, the more risk there is attached to the chance of it ever happening. The risk premium notion is arbitrary. It depends on the decision-maker's attitude to risk. Also, someone in a strong financial position might be able to tolerate some risk, others less favoured may not.

Some decision analysts do not advocate the approach of adding risk premium onto required rates of return of discount rates. They say 'fudge the net cash flow figures of the risky project with risk allowances, but try not to mess around with the discount rates'. So instead of a risk premium an alternative method is to manipulate the expected costs and returns to meet the aim of allowing for risk. Another test is to analyse the project over a conservatively reduced life.

Where do we stand on all this? We like to first put risk allowances into the sums in the budget, such as drought-contingency sum, or an inflation allowance on costs greater than on prices received, and test out some less than most likely outcomes, such as poor and worst yields and price, or crop or pasture failure in the early years of a project. Then, test the worth of the project over a less than most likely life is worth doing. Later interpret the rate of return, evaluate the relative safeness of the return in the alternative investment (which the discount rate refers to) with the riskiness of this project, given that a number of allowances are built into the project analysis to enable the farmer to reduce the consequences of some of the possible risky outcomes. Do the discounting using the realistic alternative earning rate and cost of borrowings, and then compare the riskiness.

For example 'I can get 5% real return, safely in the alternative use. This project promises a positive NPV at 5% discount rate, and earns 10% real return (IRR), after I have put in some allowances to cover me for when things go awry. With the allowances I have made in the calculations, the margin of 5% over the safest option looks near enough for me.'

A final general point: the rate of interest paid for capital is determined by many things. Like all issues in economics there is no one simple explanation for the existence of, or size of, rates of interest. Interest rates have much to do with the relative scarcity of funds and the relative productivity of those funds. These are also affected by people's preferences between present and future consumption, their wish to be financially liquid, and expectations about inflation. As government policies affect the supply of and demand for money, they affect its price. There is also a strong link between the country's balance of payments on current account deficit and exchange rate position, and interest rates. Roughly, for Australia, if the balance of payments or current account deficit increases, there is pressure for the exchange rate to decline and interest rates to go up, and vice versa. Other factors permitting, this all happens so as to balance the external accounts, and also it reflects government policies to control inflation and to affect domestic demand.

Tax

(see also Chapter 3)

There is always a tax angle in any business decision. Returns or gains have to be assessed after tax. The expected extra tax liability incurred after the investment is made must be taken into account. Extra income tax payable is estimated on the basis of extra income minus extra tax deductions coming from the project. These are extra operating costs, depreciation and interest. Any new capital gains tax burden incurred has to be brought in as well. Tax payable on extra taxable income is calculated as follows where:

- extra income (Y) − tax relevant costs including interest paid during year (TC)
  = extra taxable income (TY) × the average-marginal tax rate (T rate)
  = tax payable (TP)
  i.e., Y − TC = TY × T rate = TP

Once tax is deducted, the return to capital is an after-tax return and it has to be compared with other after-tax returns. As interest payments on actual borrowings are tax deductable like operating expenses, it is sometimes said that the current interest cost to use should be the cost after tax. We say, to keep it simple, a tax deduction is of a different nature from a borrowing or an opportunity cost, and it is usually more accurate to calculate the tax implications of a proposal separately and for each year, using a separate tax schedule. Using a tax-adjusted discount or interest rate implies that the tax advantage is constant throughout the life of the project, which is not the case.

For the appropriate marginal tax rate to use see the discussion in Chapter 3. For most farmers the appropriate marginal tax rate will be between 15% to 25%.

Partial budgets

A common technique used for evaluating relatively simple changes to a farm plan is the partial budget. For major changes in organization or structure of a farm it is usually best to use a whole rather than a partial budget.

The partial budgeting way to evaluate a decision involves comparing the after-tax net return of the added activity to the activity being replaced. Normally, in choosing alternatives, we would reduce these down to two or three realistic options, on the basis of obvious reasons, objectives, constraint. We can then analyse and compare these alternatives. A partial budget is used to assess a proposed change within the overall plan, and thus it shows only the extra expenses and the extra revenue resulting from the change. The net profit or loss can be expressed as an annual percentage of the extra (or marginal) capital involved, giving a preliminary basis for comparing with other alternatives. Only those parts of the business which are affected by the change form part of a partial budget, whose format is designed to capture the changes occurring at the margin. All the favourable aspects of the change are balanced against all the unfavourable aspects, and as many as possible of these are given a dollar value. The format most commonly recommended is as follows:

favourable (gains)	unfavourable (losses)
extra income	extra costs
reduced costs	reduced income
total (A)	total (B)
net gain measured (A − B)	net loss (B − A)
other considerations, pluses and minuses	

This format is confusing, and has too much of the 'recipe' approach to it.

The major imperative with learning and doing farm management analyses is to understand the reasoning behind the numbers and the budgets. Therefore we present a less stylized approach to budgeting. Here persons doing the budget must understand the logic well, making up their own format which suits the particular question being investigated. The stylized or rigid approach can be too restrictive and give the appearance that all that you need to do is to 'fill in the boxes'. The full aspects of a particular question might not be included or explored or even understood. 'Recipe' approaches are attractive to people not familiar with the economic reasoning behind farm management analyses, and this can be detrimental to good decision analysis.

The types of sums which should be in any partial budgeting analysis are as follows. Note, though, this is not a recipe, but an indication of the logical flow of the sorts of things to consider in such an analysis. The focus is on identifying the gains currently coming from an existing activity and comparing these to the possible gains from a new investment on the farm which might replace the existing activity.

Steps in partial budgeting

1 Establish a clear picture of the proposal or alternative to be considered.
2 Determine the relevant physical information and assumptions on production and prices, etc.
3 Identify any changes in capital requirements.
4 List changes in costs and income over time.
5 Establish the return on the extra capital invested and compare the result with other opportunities for investment.
6 Evaluate any changes in asset values over time.
7 Take account of intangible factors which cannot be considered in the budget, e.g. risk.

present activity	proposed activity
A revenue (foregone if change made)	C revenue (gained if change made)
B cost (avoided if change made)	D cost (incurred if change made)
E gain from present activity	F gain from proposed activity

G difference (gain from change F − E)
H other gains/losses which can be given a dollar value
I total gain (G + H)
J average marginal tax rate (e.g. 0.25)
K extra taxable income (from taxable income schedule. Might be different to calculated gain in G)
L gain after tax from proposed activity I − (K × J)
M capital required for proposed activity
N capital released from ceasing present activity
O net capital investment required (M − N)

P extra return after tax on net extra capital $\left(\dfrac{L}{O}\right)$

Q capital gain aspects
R risk analyses
S other considerations (non-monetary)

Permanent labour costs are not usually included in a partial budget unless:

• extra permanent labour has to be employed;
• the opportunity cost of existing permanent labour is known (i.e., the value of the work it would otherwise be doing).

The partial budget captures the economist's way of thinking: a bit more of this, a bit less of that, am I better of? Partial budgets can be used when considering:

1 Adding a new activity, by substituting some of the resources used in one activity for the new activity, e.g. cattle for sheep.

2 Adding to an existing activity by intensification, e.g. pasture improvement.
3 Replacing an existing machine with a better one.

The commonest way of using a partial budget is to express the change
in profit as a percentage return on the additional capital invested. This is done
for when the effects of the change are realized and the plan is fully operational,
taking no account of the effect of time or of the costs incurred between initial
set-up and steady state, such as income foregone over time from the replaced
activity. Therefore, if the change is complex and involves more than a year
or two, the partial budget is inappropriate. Net cash flow analysis and
discounting is needed. This is sometimes called a 'development' or discounted
cash flow budget.

With a partial budget, if extra capital is involved in the change then extra
costs include the opportunity cost of this extra capital, i.e., the rate of return
it could earn in another use. If capital is released then it could be that there
is some scope to invest it and earn interest on it. Also capital gains tax on
new investment needs including. If the change looks to be worthwhile so far,
the risks involved and the financing of the change then need more study.

Analysts often carry out partial budget analysis in too restrictive a manner.
Because of the nature of farm activities, and the complex relationships within
a farm business between the resources used in various activities, partial budgets
can fail to show the real situation. All budgets are attempts to estimate future
reality. The more complete the picture, the better. For this reason whole farm
analysis is often needed, with as many of the linkages between activities accounted
for as possible. Thus comparing before and after whole farm budgets using
the spreadsheet is better than the traditional partial budget as the spreadsheet
enables inclusion of the dynamic effects of changes which cause other changes.
If prices fall, for example, then it is likely that some costs such as chemical
or fertilizer application will also be deferred or reduced; or a use of funds such
as consumption will also be reduced. If yields fall then some harvesting costs
change. Linked results within and between activities, caused by changes in prices
and yields, can be captured well in whole farm profit and cash budget scenarios
on the spreadsheet.

Expected gain from marginal capital after tax and interest, in the steady
state, is a useful preliminary screening device for selecting developments. If the
expected percentage return is high, then the development warrants further study.
If it is low, it can usually be rejected and an alternative development studied.

If one activity is being replaced with another and no extra capital is required
(the capital released from one activity is sufficient to set up the alternative activity)
then a net gain after tax and risk represents increased earnings on the same
amount of capital invested. If extra capital is invested then the net gain after
tax and risk using partial budgeting is the extra return on the extra capital.
The new activity has done as well as the old activity. The 'old' return on the
old capital has been covered, and the net gain or surplus is extra return on
the new, extra capital. This indicates only whether the new use of the resources
involved is better than the old use.

Partial budgeting is used to tell if there is a net gain or loss from change.

It does not necessarily show whether this change is the best thing to do, because it does not identify the return on all the capital involved in the activity. It only shows the gain from extra capital invested.

The gain calculated in a partial budget is not the true return to capital, because much of the capital involved in production is not included in the analysis. Only the capital which changes is considered. The investment in the farm and most of the plant is not in question. The correct interpretation of a 15% gain from the investment is that it is a result of adding more capital to existing capital. Suppose the farmer is not concerned with the return to total capital, and is not considering selling up and moving all his or her capital out of the farm business. Then it is valid to compare the gain from adding 'new capital' to existing capital in the farm, with the return from using the same amount of 'new capital' in another use, on the farm or elsewhere, i.e., return on extra capital on the farm compared with return on the same amount of extra capital if used elsewhere.

If return to total farm capital is of interest then a whole farm budget, not a partial budget, is necessary. Importantly, if there is a gain from replacing an existing activity without investing any extra capital, then overall return to capital will have risen. Suppose the gain expressed as a percentage of the extra capital added to the farm is greater than the average return to all the capital in the farm before the change. Then, after the change the new average return to total capital will be better than it was. If return to total capital is of concern steps will have been taken in the right direction.

If safe returns in alternative investments are 10% nominal each year, comprising 5% inflation plus 5% real, and safe after-tax returns are 7% nominal and 2% real, then it would usually not be wise to invest in a new farming development unless the real gain on the extra capital was around 15% to 20% nominal (10% to 15% real) before tax. This implies returns of 10% to 13% nominal after tax (5% to 8% real return after tax). There are a few reasons for this:

- new capital is added to existing capital on the farm which might be earning a relatively low return: good returns from extra capital invested raises the average return to all the capital invested in the business;
- the risks involved;
- the need (often) to pay back principal on loans from the extra net cash flow.

Risk and variability

(also see Chapter 8)

Once something is started, other developments are set in train, some of which change the situation that first existed. Different sets of associated problems have to be dealt with. The variable weather and changeable agricultural markets means that no farm plan is likely to work out exactly as expected. So it is necessary to work out what would happen if prices or yields or interest rates were worse or better than expected. The percentage change (or probability) of these events happening should also be specified.

Cash flow budgets

There are two aspects to cash flow budgets; a farmer does a cash flow budget
to keep an eye on the periodic flows of cash out of and into the business. This
differs from the cash flow budget we refer to when evaluating a change in farm
plan where the flows of cash associated with an investment on the farm are
used to evaluate the profitability of the investment. This is a 'discounted cash
flow budget', and it is used to work out the economic worth of the planned
change. Then a financial planning budget is done to assess the amounts of
borrowings, peak debt, and cash surpluses possibly involved if the project is
undertaken. Both discounted cash flow budgets and financial planning cash
flow budgets are explained below.

Discounting techniques: NPV, IRR, B:C ratio

Discounting has been explained briefly in Chapter 2. To recapitulate: a project
with a positive NPV at the required discount rate is earning at that rate plus
some more. With projects involving the same capital and using the same discount
rate, the one with the highest NPV is the most profitable.

There are two critical assumptions which users of net present value (NPV),
internal rate of return (IRR), and benefit–cost ratios (B:C) should be aware of
when interpreting the results: that capital markets are perfect, and that investors
can borrow and lend their cash during the life of the project at the same rate
of interest and can get all the money needed during the life of the project at
the required rate; that positive net cash flows not withdrawn from the project
during the life of the project can earn at the same rate as the project. This
is the 'reinvestment assumption', that as long as capital, including interim
earnings, is still in the project, it has to be earning at the project rate for the
overall rate of return or discount rate to be earned.

Were capital markets perfect, the investor could borrow and lend at the
market rate of interest. By doing so the flows of cash which the NPV sum
represents could be adjusted to a pattern of cash flows which suit the investor.
Remember the sum we call NPV is a lump sum at present worth the same
as a series of flows of cash at various times in the future, discounted by the
chosen opportunity interest rate.

The second assumption 'users of net present value make is about
compounding. Underlying the NPV idea is the notion that the present values
are what they are, and are equivalent to the future values, because the present
value sums could grow at compound opportunity interest rates to the value
of the expected future cash flows of the project. This is the reinvestment idea.
Positive net cash flows not withdrawn from the project have to continue to
earn at the same rate as the project in order that the overall rate of return on
the capital in the project is maintained. This might not be so because a high
earning rate in a project might not be matched by equally high alternative
earning rates outside the project and enabling the retained cash surpluses to
continue to earn the same high rates as obtained within the project.

The higher the discount rate used, the more profitable the project has to
be to pass the positive NPV test. This is so because a high discount rate means:

1 A high preference for current consumption of income versus future consumption.
2 The existence of potentially highly profitable alternatives.
3 An allowance for risk is sometimes built into the rate used.

If these conditions exist, the project has to promise to be the more profitable for it to be as worthwhile as the current consumption or the alternative investment opportunities which are given up for it. A high discount rate means that only the most profitable and shorter term uses of funds will pass the positive NPV test. Long-term projects often fail the test because, at high interest rates, the present value of distant future sums of money rapidly become worth very little. Even at moderate interest rates, returns due more than about 25 years in the future are almost worthless in present value terms.

Internal rate of return

A related measure of profitability is the internal rate of return (IRR). The IRR is that interest rate which just balances the present values of cash receipts and cash outlays. Put another way, IRR is the discount rate which makes the discounted net present value equal to zero. With the IRR method, an investment is considered worthy if the IRR exceeds the interest cost of using the capital in this way. The IRR can be thought of as being a bit like the average annual return on capital invested in the project.

Whilst the annual return on capital, as it is usually worked out, is like a snapshot of one year in the life of an activity or project, the IRR is based on a movie of the project's life and the rate of return refers to the return over the whole life of the investment. The IRR can be interpreted as the maximum interest rate which a business could afford to pay for the funds to carry out the project and not lose any money. If the operator of the business did borrow all the funds at the IRR rate, then all costs are being met and the capital would be properly rewarded, but there would be no net earnings above this. A decision rule is to accept projects in which the IRR is greater than or equal to the opportunity cost earning rate, i.e., the discount rate which would be used if you were calculating the NPV of the project.

Using the IRR it is not necessary to specify an opportunity cost interest rate before doing the calculations. At one level, IRR is a straightforward measure. It is a fairly practical statistic and it gives some idea as to whether a project is worth undertaking. At a rigorously theoretical level the IRR comes in for serious criticism. Depending on the pattern of the cash flows, it is possible to come up with a number of IRRs. This can occur where there is a major cash outflow incurred some time later in the life of a project. In such cases it is best to rely on the NPV approach. The interest rate at which the NPV is positive is compared with the needed rate of return. If NPV is positive at the needed rate of return then there is no problem with multiple IRRs.

A further difficulty with the IRR is the reinvestment assumption mentioned earlier. In essence it is the same as in the NPV calculation but the rate at which reinvestment occurs is not the opportunity cost rate as is the case with the NPV method. Instead it has to be at whatever is the IRR rate. The problem with the IRR is that the reinvestment opportunities on which the calculation of present values are built might not be available in practice. Hence the IRR is a flawed tool. The IRR method gives sensible results only when the estimated IRR is similar to realistic opportunity cost and reinvestment rates which are available.

Conflicts between NPV and IRR

It is possible for two projects being compared to give conflicting results. That is, a project with a lower NPV than another could have a higher IRR than it. If you cannot do both projects, then there is a dilemma. Depending on the rates the investor can get, use of the IRR could lead to the project being chosen that is not the best one for net gain. If faced with a contradiction between the NPV decision rule and the IRR decision rule it is best to accept the project yielding the highest NPV. But you will need to use the discount rate that realistically approaches the return which could be had from alternative uses of the funds.

There is no way of knowing, with either method, whether the project will let the investor meet his or her wishes for consumption and saving over time. It is only if these needs and wants are met that the project is strictly the best one to do. The reinvestment assumption means that the IRR is only a good guide when the IRR rate relates to actual opportunity earnings available. The IRR is the maximum interest which the project could pay if it had to, which is handy to know.

If IRR and NPV give conflicting results for two alternative projects requiring different amounts of capital, then as the IRR indicates the earning rate of each dollar invested, the IRR can be used if it is a realistic number. Alternatively, you can look at the difference between the capital needs and the difference between the NPVs of the respective projects. Work out the extra return implied to be earned by the extra capital required for the project that needs most capital. Compare this to the opportunity cost of the capital. If the extra capital used in the larger investment earns more than the opportunity cost, then it is the better choice.

To sum up the NPV–IRR choice: NPV is best. Have a bet each way: use both. The more information the better. Interpreting information is the key to good decision making. Just be aware of the limitations of each method. The IRR indicates the break-even earning rate of capital, but it does not give the absolute size of the total earnings. It is vice versa for NPV, but it does not tell precisely how well the capital is being used. NPV is good for valuing assets. The IRRs, if sensible, can be used for decisions about allocating capital between alternative uses.

Benefit–cost ratio

The ratio of the discounted present value of benefits to the discounted present value of costs is called the benefit–cost ratio. If this ratio is greater than one, at the required discount rate, the project is earning more than the required rate of return. Benefit–cost ratio is commonly used in social benefit–cost analysis, which is simply investment analysis carried out from the perspective of spending public money. That is the economic and non-economic benefits and costs to society at large are analysed. The magnitude of the benefit–cost ratios of alternative projects can be compared at the same discounted rate. The project with the largest ratio, greater than one, is the most profitable.

The main point to note is that any results, NPV, IRRs, or B:C ratios, can carry with them a false impression of precision. The NPV, IRRs and B:C ratios are only as accurate as the estimates of cash flows and the assumptions are accurate. These can turn out to be considerably different in practice. The errors in cash flows can greatly exceed minor differences in NPV, IRRs or B:C ratios, making minor differences in rankings according to these criteria insignificant in practice. Too much precision should not be attributed to the ranking criteria; they are not as good as that.

Life of project and salvage value

You have to make a guess about the life of a project and the salvage value at the end, aiming to err on the short side. There is usually little point assuming a project life longer than, say, 15-20 years. Beyond this, at reasonable discount rates, discounting reduces cash flows to very little.

One way to handle the problem of what project life to assume is to pretend that the investment is sold some time after the project has reached a steady state and cash flows have stabilized. After an arbitrary time the project is assumed to be cashed and the salvage value goes into the final year's cash receipts.

There are a number of options for handling salvage value. The method to use depends on the type of appraisal being done, and the type of assets involved. Some assets will decline in value over the life of the project, or might not have any other use, and so might only be worth scrap value. Other assets will maintain or even increase their value over the life of the project.

An expected salvage value, based on current relative worth of similar items, has to be placed on the major assets involved in the project. Again, it is probably wise to err on the conservative side in these estimates. They are difficult to guess. Some specialized investments will have only scrap value or salvage value.

Thus the results of project appraisal have to be interpreted carefully. An unrealistic salvage value, or too much reliance on the salvage value as a factor in evaluating financial success, can mean that the expected success of the investment does not happen.

Choosing the length of the project life can have a big effect on its NPV. Where a project is repeatable, such as a plantation, you need to compare the expected profitability of another year of the existing activity with the expected average profit for each year of a new cycle or life of the activity. Again you need to work out the equal amounts of money which, if received each year of the cycle, will equal the NPV of the production from the whole cycle, i.e., the amortization figure or 'annuity equivalent'.

Projects involving different lengths of time can be compared. There are several approaches. One way is to compare the NPV of the longer project with the NPV of the shorter project as well as the return from the succeeding use of the capital once the shorter project finishes. The comparison has to be on the basis of the same number of years. This only works if the projects are easily divided into discrete lives.

Another way is to run out cycles of the projects until a common total number of years is involved; a three-year-project and a four-year-project could be compared in terms of a 12-year-cycle involving four runs of one project and three runs of another project. This is not usually a sensible approach because in practice this is unlikely to happen.

The most sensible way to compare two projects with different lives is to convert the NPV of each into its annuity equivalent. That is the amount that, if earned each year in the life of the project, would sum, at the interest rate used, to the NPV of the project. The project with the highest annuity equivalent is the most profitable. For example, there are two projects, one for three years with an NPV of $10,000 at 5%, and another for four years with an NPV of $11,000 at 5% discount rate. The three-year project's NPV of $10,000 has an annuity value of $3,672 at 5% interest (annuity whose present value is one, factor 0.3672). The four-year project with an NPV of $11,000 at 5% interest has an annuity value of $3,102 at 5% (annuity whose present value is one, factor 0.2820). The shorter project is the more profitable, though this annuity approach has the assumption that the shorter project begins again and the cycle continues. If this is not sensible, then the profitability of the use of the capital which follows should be estimated. This approach is also used to compare different sequences of crops (see Chapter 5).

If the investor has some other criterion such as to break-even as soon as possible then no discounting technique will satisfy this criteria. Pay-back period, which gives no idea of economic worth of a project, would meet this criteria.

Different amounts of capital

There is also the problem if the two projects compared involve using different sums of capital. In economic theory the decision rule on how to make most profits is to choose the project or activity with the greatest return on capital, then the next best, and so on. As long as projects are not mutually exclusive it would pay to keep 'picking off' the most attractive investments, NPV and all other things considered. If comparing two projects involving different amounts of capital but applying the same discount rate, then the one with the greater NPV adds most to total profits and this should be chosen first as long as all the other criteria of an investment are met.

But theory does not take full account of the degree of 'lumpiness' in allocating large sums of investment capital in practice. It is not simply a matter of $5,000 here, $550,000 there, and $1 m. to that one. That would only be so if you had exactly $1,555,000 to invest now and all investments could start immediately. In practice, the size of investments is partly governed by the available surplus funds and borrowing ability. In most cases, for a number of reasons, it is likely that you would look at a couple of alternatives of similar size.

Net present value does not indicate what the return to capital is but the relative size of NPVs at the same discount rate indicates which has the higher rate of return. Therefore, net present values of two projects can only be compared if the same amount of capital is involved. To more accurately compare investments involving different amounts of capital, the return per dollar invested has to be compared. The internal rate of return does this, as long as it is a sensible IRR, i.e., feasible, given the reinvestment assumption. When comparing projects involving different amounts of capital, NPVs can be misleading.

Example

	project A	project B
investment	$100,000	$1,000,000
interest rate	5%	5%
NPV	$20,000	$15,000

The project B has a lower NPV but absolute earnings are higher, i.e., equivalent to 5% return of $1 m. plus $15,000. Alternatively, the ratio of benefits to costs for different projects can be compared. The B:C ratio indicates which investment has the highest return to capital. The highest B:C ratio represents the highest return to capital, regardless of the amount of capital invested. However, significant differences in NPVs of two projects can show up as very small differences in the B:C ratios.

Timing of cash flows

There is the problem of timing as flows of cash occur at many different times in one year, and yet they are discounted on the basis of annual earning rates. For ease, it is necessary to make a guess about the timing of the cash flows within each year. It does not matter whether you assume that all cash flows occur on the first or the last day of the year, but you have to be consistent. If cash flows are assumed to all occur on the last day of the year, then start discounting from year 1. If the start of the year is when cash flows are assumed to occur, then the first year's net cash flow is not discounted because it is already in present value terms. Also, cash flows can be done in half-yearly, quarterly or even monthly terms if these effects seem significant but, usually, yearly is good enough. The computer-based spreadsheet is a help in this.

Depreciation

Depreciation costs are often a problem. In discounted cash flow (DCF) analysis depreciation is not deducted as a cost because the total capital costs are included when they are incurred. This is different from working out annual farm-operating profit where costs of replacing capital items which wear out are charged progressively over the life of the capital items. With DCF analysis the full capital costs are entered in the year in which they are incurred. Net cash flow is reduced in that year by the total amount spent to buy the piece of capital equipment. At the end of the project's life the expected remaining value of the equipment (salvage value) shows up as cash in. NPV is the discounted sum of all flows of cash in and out. Instead of annual depreciation of capital, the capital invested is counted as a lump sum when it is incurred, which hopefully is recovered when the cash inflows occur. The NPV calculation covers both the return of the capital and a return on the capital. To include depreciation is to count the cost of the capital invested twice, once as the initial capital investment and second as an annual depreciation cost.

Financial cash flow analysis

Two developments showing a similar return on extra capital investment do not mean that they are equally attractive. For example, the total farm annual net cash flows before borrowing (cash received less cash spent in a year, excluding loans needed), which should result from adopting each of two developments are shown below (see Figure 9.1).

Development A has large cash deficits in the early years, but high positive cash flows from about the third year on. Development B has only a small deficit in the early years but a lower positive cash flow from about year 3 till year 6.

The cash flows shown are those before borrowing, i.e., they indicate the amount of money that has to be borrowed in early years if the farm is to remain solvent. With development A, this may be too large for the banks to consider, and so even though the medium-term prospects are good, the farmer might find it hard to obtain finance. Even if the borrower could obtain a loan, markets or seasons might be adverse in the first or second year. Then the farmer could find that the needs for loans far exceeds the estimates. This could lead to bankruptcy or at least severe financial problems.

Figure 9.1: Cash flows from two projects

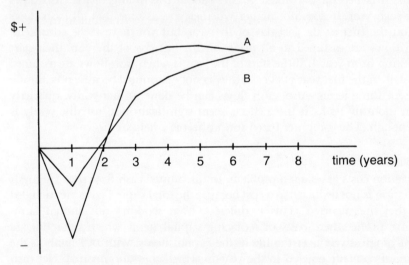

With development B, the risk is relatively low, but so are the profits in years 3, 4, and 5. Net cash flow from year 6 onwards is similar to that of development A. Choosing which development to accept will depend on:

• the farmer's attitude to risk;
• access to credit;

- credit terms;
- the value attached to an early rather than a late pay-off;
- the relative size of the positive and negative cash flow of the two developments.

Before a rational choice can be made between the two developments the farmer should know both the return on extra capital, and the pattern of pre-loan net cash flows. For an example of a cash flow budget for economic analysis and financial planning see Table 9.5.

Capital aspects

Even if the plan is physically possible and leads to an expected improvement in profit, a loan could be needed to put the plan into effect. The amount of extra capital needed should allow for any sales of plant, livestock or other assets no longer needed if the plan is carried out. Any new overheads such as permanent labour, shelter, registrations, and insurances need to be counted.

Movement in assets and debts

A new activity often uses borrowed money. The increase in debts means higher interest charges and principal repayments. At the same time the investment should raise the value of a farm. However, spending $1,000 on improving a farm is no guarantee that its market value will increase by $1,000. Sometimes it can increase by more, sometimes less.

When a new development is taken on, it is usually worth working out the expected change in value of assets and debts over its first four to five years. There are three main reasons for this:

- to avoid the possibility that the level of debts will rise too high in relation to the assets. If debts become relatively high, there is danger of financial problems;
- to assess the likely change in net worth (or equity) as a result of the project;
- to work out any capital gains tax which may arise, if relevant.

Depending on the conditions of ownership, increase in net asset worth and market value can be a valuable benefit from an improvement or intensification program.

Intangibles

There will always be factors difficult to quantify in decisions on whether or not to go ahead with changes. These factors include the farmers' own preferences, values, and ambitions. A satisfactory decision is possible only after the intangibles have been taken into account.

If the proposed activity gets a 'pass' on the criteria of gain on extra capital, net present value, expected capital gain and the 'other' considerations, the business structure and financial aspects of the proposal need to be looked at, along with intangible factors.

Part 2
Practical applications of budgeting
for analysing changes

Example partial budget

The objective of a partial budget is to find out the profitability of a new activity compared to an existing activity (once the new activity is fully operational, i.e., when it reaches the steady state). A partial budget can be used for new activities which are fully operational in a short time, say, one to two years. Otherwise, a partial development budget is needed.

A farmer who runs a mixed grazing and cropping operation is considering replacing a 50-ha dryland grazing activity with an irrigated–cropping activity. Currently 3,750 dse is run on 500 ha of pasture and there is the machinery for the growing and harvesting of the 50 ha of irrigated crop. However, the intention is to replace the existing old tractor for a slightly larger new one. This change can be implemented and fully operational in the second year. In total, 500 ha on the farm will be cropped after the change, i.e., with the extra 50 ha of irrigated crop. There is a transition period during the first year in which sheep returns will be reduced and returns from the new activity will not have started. These factors need to be included in the decision, but, first of all, it is sensible to do a partial budget to see if the new activity compares satisfactorily with the existing one, once it is fully operational. The budget is to be done using the current values of the costs and returns which are expected to apply, i.e., real dollars and interest rates. By using real values the assumption is that inflation which could occur will affect all costs and returns equally, although this might not always be true. The partial budget is as follows:

present activity (sheep grazing)	$	proposed activity (irrigated cropping wheat–soya bean)	$
A revenue (foregone if change made)		C revenue (gained if change made)	
50 ha × 7.5 dse per ha × 5 kg wool per dse		25 ha wheat × 4 t per ha × $130 per t	13,000
at $4.50 per kg net	8,438	25 ha soya bean × 2.5 t per ha	
cast for age dses at $8 per dse		× $200	12,500
for ¼ of flock per year	750		25,500
total	$9,188	D costs (incurred if change made)	
B costs (avoided if change made)		crops variable costs:	
$13 variable costs per dse × 375		seed, fertilizer, chemicals, crop	
dse (includes $5 per dse		insurance, etc., at $160 per ha	8,000
replacement costs)	4,875	tractor and implements	
supplementary feed costs		running costs:	1,250
$2 per dse	750		

continued

present activity (sheep grazing)	$	proposed activity (irrigated cropping wheat–soya bean)	$
activity related overheads	1,000	water costs $18 per ML × 300 ML	5,400
none			
share of pasture average annual maintenance costs for 50 ha at $20 per ha		overhead costs: tractor, plant, storage equipment depreciation, insurance, registration	750
total costs	6,625	irrigation plant depreciation $15 per ha	750
E gain from sheep activity	2,563	irrigation bay levelling and layout at $20,000, with a life of 10 years, with a salvage value of 25% at end of 10 years. Annual depreciation is $20,000 − $5,000	1,500
		10	
		total costs	18,650
		F gain from crop activity	6,850

difference is (F − E) = $6,850 − $2,563 = $4,287

G other gains or losses which can be given a dollar value

H tax on extra taxable income comes from taxable income schedule. Extra taxable income may differ from what is calculated as gain because of different depreciation rates of machinery or different livestock values or accelerated depreciation of water and soil conservation measures and so on. An estimate is made. In this case extra taxable income from change to cropping = $4,287. If the extra capital that is required is to be borrowed, then the extra interest is deducted from taxable income. Because the budget is in real dollars, real interest is charged. This will understate the interest deduction if inflation occurs and nominal interest rates are higher than this. If inflation occurs and affects prices and costs equally the nominal gains will be correspondingly greater. In this case, extra capital invested in the irrigation activity is $47,000 less $5,625 received from sale of surplus sheep from the old activity (from point J). If all the capital is borrowed then interest paid in the first year will be on a total net investment of $47,000 − $5,625 = $41,375. The interest paid, and the tax deduction, will be less in later years as the loan is reduced. Suppose an eight-year loan is taken out for, say, $41,000. The average borrowings in any year is $\frac{\$41,000 + 0}{2}$ = $20,500. So, use the interest paid on the average debt as the annual tax deduction. At 5% interest this works out to be = $1,025. Also, there is extra interest paid on higher working capital for cropping. Working capital (overdraft) over the year can be estimated as activity cash costs. Extra working capital is simply the new activity cash costs less the old activity

cash costs, which is $16,400 − $6,625 = $9,775. This is adjusted by a factor of 0.55 to allow for the fact that the costs, and overdraft, is distributed through the year, and not all incurred on the first day. Thus $9,775 × 0.55 × 5% real interest = $269.
taxable income if capital is borrowed is $4,287 − $1,025 − $269 = $2,993
average marginal tax rate 20¢ in $1
if capital borrowed extra tax payable is $2,993 × 0.20 = $599
if no capital is borrowed, then extra taxable income is $4,287 and tax payable is $857

		$
I	total gain (if all capital borrowed) $4,287 − $599 (tax)	3,688
	total gain (if no capital borrowed) $4,287 − $857 (tax)	3,430

J capital aspects:	$
capital recovered from sale of surplus sheep 375 × $15	5,625
this activity's share of extra capital invested in cropping plant (10% of $70,000 new tractor)	7,000
extra capital invested in irrigation plant	15,000
extra capital invested in storage equipment	5,000
extra capital invested in land preparation for irrigation	20,000
total capital invested in irrigation activity	47,000
net extra capital $47,000 − $5,625	41,375

Note. Sheep are valued at average annual capital value because of the 'revolving' nature of this capital.

K interest cost of all of the extra capital investment in cropping
calculated on the initial value of the net extra capital invested

	$
extra initial capital invested in irrigation activity	47,000
capital currently invested in sheep	5,625
net extra capital invested is $47,000 − $5,625	41,375
interest at 5% on extra capital invested due to irrigation activity	2,069

This can be seen as the low risk opportunity cost of the capital if all extra capital comes from the owner.

L other costs, not annual, but initial costs associated with the change are for establishing the new activity but these do not form part of the steady state annual costs. However, if these initial costs are large, or if the steady state is not reached within a couple of years, then a partial budget for the steady state is not adequate. Instead a partial development budget should be used. In many cases there is extra taxable income in the first year on sale of capital items such as stock or machinery. In this particular example sheep are sold. The difference between sale and book value is taxable. This extra tax is incurred only in the first year and not in the other years. Therefore, leave this extra tax out of the steady state assessment, but still estimate it because it could have implications for the early cash flows. Here the surplus sheep are sold at a $10 per dse difference between the book and the sale value. Taxable income is ($10 × 7.5 × 50) = $3,750. This amounts to an extra $750 tax payable in the first year, and is to be kept in mind in weighing up the decision.

M compared with what?	$
net extra initial capital investment	41,375
net gain after tax (all borrowed)	3,688

net gain after tax (all borrowed) as a percentage of net extra initial capital invested

is $\dfrac{\$3,688}{\$41,375} \times \dfrac{100}{1} = 8.9\%$. This is not return on all capital invested in the activity

(only extra capital: we have not counted land, for instance) but it is the extra earned by the extra $41,375 invested in this use. If no borrowings are involved and the farmer uses all his or her own capital, then the net gain after tax is $3,430, i.e., a gain of 8.3% from the extra capital invested. This has to cover an opportunity interest cost on the extra capital of 5% or $2,069. After tax this is $2,069 × 0.8 = $1,665 (or 5% × [1 − tax rate of 0.2] = 4% after-tax return).
net gain with no borrowings is $3,430 − $1,665 = $1,775.
net gain from irrigation activity (all borrowed) over sheep activity, after tax and opportunity interest on initial value of extra capital invested is $3,688 − $1,655 = $2,033.
The irrigated cropping in the steady state shows a most likely gain of approximately $1,800 to $2,000 over the sheep activity, depending on how the change is financed. An extra $41,375 is invested, and the gain after tax is 8% to 9% of this sum. If the farmer had this sum 4% or around $1,600 after tax could fairly safely be earned in a financial institution. The most likely gain from the change is $1,800 to $2,000 above opportunity cost.

N other considerations:

- riskiness of cropping returns vs. sheep returns;
- capital gains prospects;
- income tax might be paid on sheep sales;
- skills, labour supply.

Riskiness:
The before-tax break-even income from cropping (yields and prices) is assessed as follows:

	$
gain from crop activity	6,850
gain from sheep activity	2,563
balance	4,287

break-even income (yields and prices) required is:
income 'x' = sheep gain $2,563 + crop costs $18,650 + opportunity interest cost $2,000

crop income 'x' =	23,213

To break even with the sheep activity the crop income has to be $23,200. There are numerous combinations of wheat and soya bean yields and prices which could go to make up a gross income from cropping of $23,200. Many possible scenarios can easily be checked if the budget is done on a computer spreadsheet. However, as sensible decisions have to be able to be made without resorting to the computer spreadsheet we have used simpler methods. The following assessment for riskiness merely involves using a calculator; as follows:

Various combinations of wheat and soya bean yields and prices which would make a gross cropping income of around $23,200 (break even) can be calculated.

Break-even combinations of wheat yields, wheat prices, soya bean yields, soya bean prices for 25 ha of wheat and 25 ha of soya bean

	most likely	possible	comment
	$25,500	$23,437	
t per ha wheat	4 t per ha	3.75 t per ha	good chance (less than most likely yield)
$ per t wheat	$130 per t	$130 per t	most likely price
t per ha soya beans	2.5 t per ha	2.5 t per ha	most likely yield
$ per t soya beans	$200 per t	$180 per t	good chance (less than most likely price)
overall: break-even—a reasonable bet to get at least this			
	$25,500	$23,425	
t per ha wheat	4 t per ha	4 t per ha	most likely yield
$ per t wheat	$130 per t	$125 per t	good chance (bit less than most likely price)
t per ha soya beans	2.5 t per ha	2.3 t per ha	good chance (bit less than most likely yield)
$ per t soya beans	$200 per t	$190 per t	good chance (bit less than most likely price)
overall: break-even—a reasonable bet			
	$25,500	$21,000	
t per ha wheat	4 t per ha	4 t per ha	most likely yield
$ per t wheat	$130 per t	$110 per t	highly likely (much less than most likely price a minimum price would expect)
t per ha soya beans	2.5 t per ha	2.0 t per ha	a minimum yield
$ per t soya beans	$200 per t	$200 per t	most likely price
overall: not enough, but very high chance as wheat price is highly likely, and soya bean yield is a minimum			

Interpretation

The key to interpreting budgets is to decide which numbers in the budget are the most important ones. After all, not all numbers in a budget are of equal importance.

In this case, the critical numbers are wheat yields and prices, soya bean yields and prices, wool prices, the cost of irrigation water, and the relative size of variable costs associated with each activity. The farmer has considered these numbers. Looking at the yield and price possibilities, the farmer might conclude that the most likely result is that the cropping activity would be better than the sheep activity.

The farmer also knows that in the next few years water prices for irrigation will increase significantly, and so a water price has been used in the crop budgets which is higher than the current price. The costed water prices will reach this level in about two to three years' time, but the farmer knows it could happen earlier than this. The farmer might think that for the next few years the most likely wool price is not going to improve above the $4.50 net used in the budget for the sheep activity, or the cfa prices. The farmer recognizes that the cropping activity has higher cash costs associated with it, and thus more significant losses if there is a crop failure than is the case with, say, a dry spell affecting the sheep activity. But, the farmer thinks that the irrigation, and mastery of the technology is sufficient to reduce the chances of major crop failures.

On balance, the farmer might think there is a reasonable chance that the change will make the farm family sufficiently better off, everything considered. In the first year the extra tax cost associated with the sheep sales will be more than offset by extra depreciation on the investment in the tractor, storage equipment, and land preparation for irrigation.

Capital gains aspects
There will not be any implications for capital gains. The land is expected to keep up in value with inflation, whether it is used for cropping or grazing. The farmer hopes for small real gains over time, but is not counting on them.

Financial aspects
This proposal is economically sound. The extra return exceeds the earnings from the replaced activity and exceeds the amount similar resources could earn in the alternative uses the farmer would consider. It has also to be financially feasible as well. While the project will more than pay for the annual overhead and variable costs, and extra interest, the farmer has to be able to arrange the extra borrowings and extra working capital for the cropping activity. The sheep activity had cash costs of around $6,600 and the cropping activity has cash costs which would come to more than $16,500 (i.e., only the cash costs, not the depreciation costs). Also, as a new tractor is being bought for the whole farm, this too has to be financed. In this case the new activity earns enough cash to service extra overdraft interest resulting from higher working capital requirements. Also, the capital released from the sheep sold, after tax, goes a long way toward meeting the new activity's share of the capital investment in the new tractor.

Other things
The farmer is satisfied about the labour implications of the change. There is no tax problem from selling the old tractor as any extra tax on the difference between book and market values, will be more than offset by the depreciation on the new tractor.

What else is there to consider?

Table 9.5: Budgeted net cash flow for pasture development

	year 1	2	3	4	5	6	7	8	9	10	11	12
extra dse	−1	5	9	9	9	9	9	9	9	7	5	3
extra income												
extra wool 5.5 kg greasy $4.50 per kg greasy	0	25,988	49,116	51,572	54,151	56,858	59,701	62,686	65,821	53,754	40,315	25,399
cfa sales												
¼ flock at $8 per dse	0	2,100	3,969	4,167	4,376	4,595	4,824	5,066	5,319	4,344	3,258	2,052
salvage of livestock at 100%	3,150									9,308	9,773	10,262
salvage of pasture improvement at 25%												16,697
total extra cash in	3,150	28,088	53,085	55,740	58,527	61,453	64,526	67,752	71,139	67,405	53,346	54,410
extra costs												
initial capital costs:												
land preparation at $75 per ha	15,000											
fertilizer year 1 $80 per ha, year 2, $50 per ha	16,000	10,500										
seed and sprays at $40 per ha	8,000											
extra stock at $15 per dse												
other establishment costs:												
loss of grazing in first year 1 dse per ha at $15 per dse	18,900	13,230										
gross margin	3,000											
effect of other activities?												
extra annual activity costs												
sheep variable costs at $8 per dse	0	8,400	15,876	16,670	17,503	18,378	19,297	20,262	21,275	17,375	13,031	8,210

continued

Table 9.5 (continued)

year	1	2	3	4	5	6	7	8	9	10	11	12
extra dse	-1	5	9	9	9	9	9	9	9	7	5	3
sheep replacement purchases ¼ at $15 per dse		4,725	7,442	7,814	8,205	8,615	9,046	9,498	9,973	7,757	5,540	3,324
pasture maintenance fertilizer at $15 per ha	0	0	3,308	3,473	3,647	3,829	4,020	4,221	4,432	4,654	4,887	5,131
pasture maintenance: topping, etc. $5 per ha	0	1,050	1,103	1,158	1,216	1,276	1,340	1,407	1,477	1,551	1,629	1,710
extra overhead: permanent part-time labour $4,000 from year 2	0	4,200	4,410	4,631	4,862	5,105	5,360	5,628	5,910	6,205	6,516	6,841
extra risk cost: supplementary feed at $1 per dse per year from year 4	0	0	0	2,084	2,188	2,297	2,412	2,533	2,659	2,172	1,629	1,026
total costs before tax and interest	42,000	47,775	45,368	35,828	37,620	39,501	41,476	43,550	45,727	39,714	33,232	26,243
annual net cash flow before tax and interest	-38,850	-19,688	7,718	19,911	20,907	21,952	23,050	24,202	25,412	27,691	20,115	28,167
tax payable (from tax schedule)	-1,767	1,025	3,884	4,389	4,924	5,505	6,136	6,819	7,560	6,521	6,025	4,564
A *Economic analysis*												
annual net cash flows after tax	-37,083	-20,712	3,833	15,522	15,983	16,447	16,914	17,383	17,852	21,170	14,089	23,603
B *Financial analysis*												
cumulative net cash flow after tax	-37,083	-61,680	-63,524	-53,398	-41,776	-28,579	-13,648	3,182	22,090	36,811	46,105	48,442
total interest on cumulative deficit or surplus	-3,885	-5,677	-5,396	-4,361	-3,249	-1,982	-553	1,055	2,859	4,978	5,693	7,427
cumulative net cash flow after interest and tax	-40,968	-67,357	-68,920	-57,759	-45,026	-30,561	-14,201	4,238	24,949	41,789	51,789	55,869

net present value of annual net cash flows after

internal rate of return %	0%	105,001
	5%	56,444
	10%	26,841
18.3%	15%	8,333
	20%	-3,465

continued

Table 9.5 (continued)

year	1	2	3	4	5	6	7	8	9	10	11	12
extra dse	−1	5	9	9	9	9	9	9	9	7	5	3
C Tax schedule												
tax relevant income:												
extra wool												
5.0 kg greasy												
$4.50 per kg greasy cfa sales	0	25,988	49,116	51,572	54,151	56,858	59,701	62,686	65,821	53,754	40,315	25,399
¼ flock at $8 per dse	0	2,100	3,969	4,167	4,376	4,595	4,824	5,066	5,319	4,344	3,258	2,052
total extra tax relevant income (A)	0	28,088	53,085	55,740	58,527	61,453	64,526	67,752	71,139	58,097	43,573	27,451
minus tax relevant costs:												
initial pasture capital costs deducted at 10% per year for tax	4,950	4,950	4,950	4,950	4,950	4,950	4,950	4,950	4,950	4,950		
stock replacement purchases ¼ at $15	0	3,938	7,442	7,814	8,205	8,615	9,046	9,498	9,973	8,144	6,108	3,848
annual activity costs	0	8,400	15,876	16,670	17,503	18,378	19,297	20,262	21,275	17,375	13,031	8,210
extra interest:												
interest on annual cash flow before tax	3,885	1,969	−772	−1,991	−2,091	−2,195	−2,305	−2,420	−2,541	−2,769	−2,011	−2,817
interest on cumulative deficit or surplus from start of year												
total extra tax relevant costs (B)	8,835	22,965	33,664	33,795	33,907	33,926	33,846	33,655	33,339	25,491	13,447	4,631
extra taxable income (A − B)	−8,835	5,123	19,421	21,945	24,620	27,527	30,680	34,097	37,801	32,606	30,126	22,820
average marginal tax rate 20c per $												
extra tax payable	−1,767	1,025	3,884	4,389	4,924	5,505	6,136	6,819	7,560	6,521	6,025	4,564
D Interest schedule												
interest on money borrowed during year (i.e. interest on annual net cash flow before tax)	3,885	1,969	−772	−1,991	−2,091	−2,195	−2,305	−2,420	−2,541	−2,769	−2,011	−2,817
	0											
interest on cumulative cash deficit or surplus from start of year	0	3,708	6,168	6,352	5,340	4,178	2,858	1,365	−318	−2,209	−3,681	−4,611

Summary

If the most likely outcomes occurred the farmer would gain $1,800 to $2,000 per year more from the cropping than the sheep activity. The yields and prices required to break even with this change have a good chance of being achieved. Unless some other use of $41,000 and the 50 ha on the farm can be found which promises an annual gain after tax of more than $1,800 to $2,000 above the earnings from the old activity and the interest cost or opportunity cost of the extra capital, then the irrigated cropping is the best use of the farmer's capital.

Example: Partial discounted cash flow budget

A farmer is considering improving 200 ha of low producing pasture. An economic budget is done which shows the profitability in terms of net present value and internal rate of return. A financial budget is done showing the annual and cumulative net cash flows which are expected. Both budgets are in nominal terms, see Table 9.5.

Details of partial development budget

- inflation of 5% per year is assumed. This affects all prices received and costs equally;
- all dollars and interest rates are nominal;
- output is extra above the 'do-nothing different' option;
- cfa sales = $2 per dse per year;
- salvage value of livestock is 100% of the initial capital cost. The flock is self-replacing, and the average value is maintained in nominal terms by the annual cycles of culls, births and replacements;
- salvage value of pasture improvement is in nominal terms, and so represents the worth to the business of the improvement which remains at the end of the period being analysed;
- fertilizer in year 1 and 2 is regarded as a capital cost as a bank of fertilizer is being built up;
- excess stock are sold in first year as carrying capacity declines;
- extra stock are bought in years when carrying capacity increases;
- loss of dse per ha and thus gross margin is incurred in first year as stocking rate declines. This is not a cash cost though. It shows up in the financial cash flow budget as income foregone;
- replacement stock are bought in each year;
- a risk allowance is included in the form of a supplementary feed allowance which increase with increases in stock carried. This would increase more than proportionately as stocking rate increases;
- NPV is calculated on the annual net cash flows after tax. Interest is not included in the cash flows for the NPV calculation as the discounting procedure is the way of allowing for interest costs;
- to work out tax, interest paid each year has to be known;
- interest paid each year is based on the cumulative deficit carried forward plus any annual deficit for that year. The annual deficit is approximated as an

overdraft accumulated over the course of the year, spread evenly through the year. Thus interest is not charged on the full overdraft, which would be the case if the full overdraft was incurred from day 1 of the year. Instead, interest is charged on the total annual deficit, multiplied by 0.55. This gives the average overdraft over the year, if it were incurred evenly through the year;
- interest is earned on cumulative and annual cash surpluses;
- total interest paid during the year is worked out on the NCF (net cash flow) before tax in any year. Tax is then worked out and a cumulative NCF after tax and interest is derived.

This cumulative NCF after tax for one year becomes the opening balance for the following year. Thus interest on the tax component (if any) of a cumulative deficit in one year is paid in the year following the levying of the tax bill.

Financial analysis
- for tax purposes, depreciation of the initial capital expenditure is included as per the tax laws, but this depreciation is not an annual expense of the project;
- for financial analysis the cash flows are worked out for cash in and cash out including interest and tax payments.

Interpretation
Using a 15% after-tax discount rate, for the most likely array of prices, yields and rate of increase in carrying capacity, the project promises a positive NPV. A positive NPV at the required discount rate means that the project has earned more than the rate of return used as a discount rate. The IRR is 18% after tax. Further, as the budget is done in all nominal terms, the earning rate is a nominal rate. An inflation rate of 5% has been assumed. If real after-tax earnings from very safe investments are expected to be 3% after, say, an average of 20% of profit going to tax, then this implies market rates of around 3% real + 5% nominal = 8% after tax, and about 10% before tax. There may be more riskiness with the farm investment earning 15% return after tax, with a positive NPV, and 18% IRR, compared to the off-farm investment promising 8% after tax. Note that some allowance for risk has been built into the budget with a supplementary feed allowance which might or might not be needed each year.

A comparison such as the one above is valid if the farmer had the money and would consider investing it off the farm in a bank. If the farmer is borrowing all the money then the interpretation is slightly different. In this case the 15% return with a positive NPV, or 18% IRR after tax, has to be compared with the after-tax cost of borrowing the capital.

Another case, say, where the farmer has put in half the funds and has borrowed half, then the appropriate opportunity cost (discount rate) to compare with is the weighted average of the oportunity cost of the farmer's own funds and the cost of the borrowed funds. For example, the farmer believes he or she could pick up a similarly risky 12% after tax in the share market and has to pay 9% after tax to borrow the capital. The weighted average opportunity costs is $0.5(12) + 0.5(9) = 10.5\%$.

What if the farmer would not consider investing anywhere but on the farm? The appropriate opportunity cost then is what other investments on the farm could earn. His or her response to this project which earns a bit more than 15% after tax (an IRR of 18%), is that nothing else on the farm would do better than this. That is, the farmer's intuition that this project was potentially good has been borne out by the analysis.

In this case the opportunity cost is really what the farmer thinks he or she could get elsewhere in another use on the farm but the potential earnings have to be enough to justify the riskiness the farmer feels is involved. Somehow the returns in the good years have to be enough to cover the poor returns or losses which occur in other years; this is particularly so with the chance of a poor start to the project in the first couple of years.

Another angle which the farmer needs to consider is that this is a partial analysis. These returns are more than what would be earned from the existing activity continuing as it is. The assumption is that the present level of spending, on the old activity would enable the current profitability (i.e., the 'compared with what?' in this budget) to continue at the same level in the future.

In practice, the profitability of the existing activity could decline in future despite the current levels of spending on, say, pasture maintenance, e.g. pasture quality might decline owing to a lack of persistence of various species, no matter what is done. Certainly in this budget the cost of such a decline is built in to the later years of the new pasture. There are two possible interpretations of the extra production per year, resulting from the investment in pasture improvement: production above the existing level; or production composed of replacing a decline in production in future years to bring production up to current levels, plus some extra production on top of that.

For example, an extra 9 dse per ha in year 4 could imply a stocking rate of 12 dse per ha (existing 3 dse per ha + extra 9 dse per ha). Or, an extra 9 dse per ha in year 4 could imply that the 100 ha is actually carrying 10 dse per ha altogether. That is, the current 3 dse per ha would have declined to 1 dse per ha due to ageing of the pasture. Therefore the extra 9 dse per ha due to improvement lifts the total to 10 dse per ha. Either way, the interpretation that spending the money now gives an extra 9 dse per ha in year 4 is correct.

The project is sensitive to a fall in the wool price to $3.50, with the most likely yield and rates of increase in carrying capacity, when the IRR falls to 5%. Negative NPVs are found when the rate of increase in carrying capacity is markedly slower than the most likely, and the low wool price prevails. However, this is an unrealistic scenario because if the planned pasture improvement were not achieved in the early years, further steps would be taken to cut any losses and save the situation. With confidence in the likelihood of the most likely outcomes prevailing, the investment in the pasture improvement looks well worthwhile, returning over 15% after tax per annum.

Once a project passes the test of economic profitability, the financial feasibility has to be assessed. In this development the peak debt is around $70,000 and it occurs in year 3. The net cash flows become positive in year 8 under the most likely circumstances.

A further indicator of the viability of the investment is the life of the improved pasture. In this case it is set to decline after nine years, despite annual maintenance. In reality if this is unlikely, then the investment will perform better than indicated in the budget. A key test is 'how does it look after the first few years?' The further into the future the numbers are projected, the more uncertain they are. Often the first four to five years are sufficient to look ahead to, in development budgeting.

Using gross margin budgets in planning a change

Change usually involves changes in overheads, and thus a partial budget, not gross margin budgets, is required. If gross margins budgeting is appropriate, the first step when planning with gross margins is to examine each activity to see whether the existing gross margin could be improved by using better technology or management. If activity A promises a gross margin of $30 and activity B a gross margin of $20, it is wrong to simply infer that the most profitable step to take would be to implement activity A at the expense of activity B. A simple change in technique, e.g. a new drench or plant variety could lift the GM of activity B to $35, whereas activity A could be at that best achievable level of technical performance.

Calculating gross margins is a simple, direct technique, and an essential first step in any form of farm budgeting and planning. A farmer needs to identify production and planning constraints, and to budget activity incomes and variable costs. The procedure is to first select the activity with the highest gross margin per unit of the assumed most limiting resources (often, but not always, land), and then expand this activity to the maximum level permitted by the planning constraints. Other activities are introduced in order of decreasing gross margin per ha until further increases in total gross margin cannot be achieved without exceeding the constraints imposed by the resources available for this activity. Then the activity with the highest gross margin of all the remaining availability activities is introduced until it too meets a restraint, and so on.

Cases where it would be unwise to adopt the activity with the highest gross margin without further investigation would be where no labour of the quantity or quality to handle the activity was available, or where capital was limited. To illustrate this latter limitation, assume that a farmer had access to only $30,000 of credit and that he or she has to decide between activities A and B, which perform as follows:

	activity A	activity B
	($ per ha)	
gross margin	300	200
capital needed	600	300

If the farmer adopts activity A, then $600 is needed for every ha. Since the farmer has access to only $30,000 credit for capital investment, he or she can have 50 ha of activity A. This will give the farmer a gross margin of 50 ha × $300 = $15,000. To adopt activity B, the farmer can have 100 ha of this activity, which will produce an annual total gross margin of 100 × $200 = $20,000. For this farmer, activity B should be the one to choose. Thus it is necessary to consider both the gross margin per ha and the capital investment needed per ha, and thus gross margin per $100 capital, before deciding which activity to choose.

Enterprise relationships cannot always be considered independently. For example, the complementary use of land with crops and livestock, or the feed provided by a cereal stubble for a sheep activity. If this is not considered, then the GM of the cereal activity is understated, and the GM of the sheep activity is overstated.

Gross margins do not include overhead costs or costs which are constant for all the enterprises being considered or compared. But undue emphasis cannot be placed on a distinction between fixed and variable costs, because all costs are variable in certain situations or for particular periods, and very few farm operations can be considered as occurring in complete isolation. As overhead costs are not taken into account, gross margins should only be used when enterprises being considered can be carried out within the existing resource structure (land, labour, and capital) on the property.

The linearity assumption means that expanding the use of a resource in a high return enterprise produces constant extra product and returns. Where there are diminishing returns at the margin, maximum profit combinations of activities will be determined by the principle of equal–extra returns.

What should be included in a budget depends on the purpose of doing the budget. When estimating activity GMs to estimate total gross margin for the business, do not include interest (which is not a variable cost) on, say, livestock. There are lots of different bits of capital invested in an activity, such as land, improvements, plant; it makes little sense to include interest on one of these bits of capital, the livestock. Usually when interest is found in a GM budget it means that the analyst should be doing a full partial budget, and the comparison being made using GM budgets will be invalid.

It is common to express GMs per $100 capital when comparing activities. Associated with this approach is the common comparison between GM per unit of capital invested in sheep versus the GM per unit of capital invested in cattle. (It is also common to conclude from this that sheep are more profitable than cattle.) While this may well be true in many cases, care is needed as there are some problems with this comparison.

The size of the GM and the amount of capital invested in stock at any time are linked. The main link is that if the GMs from, say, cattle were expected to be high over some time, the capital value of the livestock will reflect this expectation and will rise as the price of both production and breeding stock increase. Care is needed when interpreting estimates of GM per $100 capital because of the subjectivity of estimates of capital value of animals, and, often, ambiguity about the period to which the GM estimate and the capital values refer.

When it is found that cattle GM per $100 of capital invested appears much less than the sheep GM per $100 capital it is also partly because not all the complementary and supplementary benefits of the cattle have been counted. There will be benefits from the cattle activity from the cattle's effect on pasture composition and feed quality, as well as benefits from different labour demands or from risk-spreading.

An example of benefits associated with labour demands from having a mix of activities is where a farm could run more stock as feed is available, but there is no spare permanent labour during busy times. Cattle could have a lower total requirement for labour, and this could occur at different times from the sheep activity. Thus cattle could be added to use the surplus feed, without any extra labour being employed. Then, although sheep could show a higher GM in the existing plan, in farm management analysis the focus has to be on changes at the margin. In this case an extra sheep would require extra casual labour which should go in the gross margin for the marginal sheep. The GM for the extra sheep will be lower than the average of the existing flock. It is this GM of the potential sheep which should be compared with the GM of the cattle activity which could be expanded without extra casual labour.

For the above-mentioned reasons simple comparisons of sheep and cattle GMs, and others, can be misleading. This is especially so when GMs are not cited in the context of a particular farm situation. GMs have to be related to particular decisions on particular farms involving particular time periods. They also have to be expected marginal GMs not average GMs of an activity.

Another comparison often made is between cropping activities and livestock. However, the cropping activity GM includes only use depreciation of the machinery (in the form of repairs and maintenance), and the livestock activity GM includes all depreciation of the livestock. If changes in capital are involved, then the gross margin is not the correct tool. A partial budget is needed for such comparisons.

The practical implication of all this is that usually when debate or queries arise about the validity of the GM in decision analysis, then the GM is not the correct technique. Almost always, in such cases, what is needed is partial and whole farm budgeting, not simple GM analysis. Often GMs are asked to do far more than they were intended for or are equipped to do. Widespread misuse of the GM concept and technique has lead in some quarters to the gross margin earning the unflattering title the 'gross illusion'. But, the gross margin budget can be a useful tool, provided it is properly understood and used in the appropriate situations.

Planning mixed farms

It is not what you do but how you do it. This is the essence of deciding what activities to run on a farm. To analyse what activities to have on a mixed farm you need to consider what the relationships are between activities; what does each activity need in the way of land, labour, and capital and all the other inputs; what returns can be expected from each activity; and what is the variability of these returns? The commonest method of comparing the returns and costs from activities used is gross margins per ha. GM per ha is only one indicator of the contribution of an activity to whole farm profit. Activities need other resources, too, such as labour at different times of the year; working capital; capital investment; machinery. The key to farm profits is to make best use of all the resources.

The first step in planning activity mix on a farm is to establish the likely activity GMs using current technology, and then consider the following:

1 Is there scope to lift the GMs by changes to the technology and the management?
2 If an activity were to be expanded what might be the marginal GM? The

average GM of the existing activity is only relevant as a guide to what the marginal
GM of the expanded activity might be.
3 What resources are available?
4 What resources are needed by each activity?

Having considered these questions the decision maker is in a position to
devise a farm plan, using the type of thinking best represented as 'a bit more
of this, a bit less of that, what is the effect on the total?'

An example will illustrate this type of thinking for farm planning.

Example
A mixed farming business, i.e., the farmer intends to have a mix of crops and
livestock to spread some income risks.

the farmer has 1,000 ha of land available	1,000 ha
non-arable improved pasture	600 ha
arable land	400 ha
cost of pasture maintenance per year	$20 per ha
labour available per year	4,000 hrs
labour required for cropping	3 hrs per ha
labour required per ewe unit per year	1 hr
labour required per cow unit per year	5.5 hrs
feed produced per ha of pasture per year	100 lsms
feed required per ewe unit per year	18 lsms
feed required per cow unit per year	175 lsms
GM wheat or lupins per ha	$170
GM barley or lupins per ha	$120
GM per breeding ewe and followers per year	$30
GM per breeding cow and followers per year	$250

The farmer has enough machinery to crop the 400 ha and intends to have a
mix of crops and livestock, and has access to working capital through a bank
overdraft facility which does not limit any of the activities. Capital is available to
fully stock the property with sheep or cattle. The pasture cost is common to the
grazing activities, and so these can be ignored for the livestock activity comparisons. The pasture cost and pasture production figures are expected to apply with
a reasonable mix of sheep and cattle, although the precise mix has to be decided.

In this example annual feed available and feed required for the breeding
stock is the measure used. In practice the feed supply and demand would be
broken down into sub-periods to reflect different supply and demand through the
year. In this case the feed supply of 100 lsms per ha per year is one which matches
the feed demands for pregnancy, lactation, growing of young stock and so on.

	annual feed supplied per ha	annual feed demand per ha	annual SR per ha
sheep (ewe unit)	100 lsm	18 lsm	5.5
cattle (cow unit)	100 lsm	175 lsm	0.57

Gross margin

	GM per ha $	GM per hr labour $
wheat and lupins	170	57
barley and lupins	120	40
sheep (ewe unit)	165 ($30 × 5.5)	30
cattle (cow unit)	142 ($250 × 0.57)	45

The planning process involves choosing the activity with the highest GMs for the key resources, in this case land and labour. The 400 ha arable land will be used for growing wheat and lupins at a GM of $170 per ha and $57 GM per labour hour.

This leaves the non-arable land to be allocated to the grazing activities. Because there are only two choices the situation can be represented clearly on a diagram.

Figure 9.2: Feasible combinations of sheep and cattle

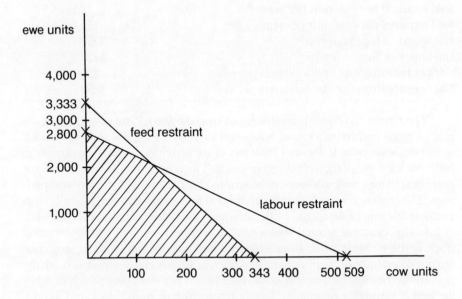

There is enough feed to run 3,333 ewe units $\left(\dfrac{600 \text{ ha} \times 100 \text{ lsms}}{18 \text{ lsms}}\right)$. There is enough feed to run 343 cow units $\left(\dfrac{60,000 \text{ lsms}}{175 \text{ lsms}}\right)$ or, some combination of sheep and cattle can be run. These two maximum points define the feed restraint on each activity.

There is enough labour to run either 2,800 sheep (i.e., 4,000 hrs − 1,200 hrs for crops leaves 2,800 hrs. Thus 2,800 hrs at 1 hr per ewe unit = 2,800 ewes) or, there is enough labour to run 509 cattle $\left(\dfrac{2,800 \text{ hrs}}{5.5 \text{ hrs}}\right)$.

On the diagram in Figure 9.2 the hatched area represents the feasible combinations of sheep and cattle, given the feed and labour supply, and each activity's needs.

The objective of planning now is to choose the combination of sheep and cattle which gives the highest total gross margin. The farmer is not interested in the all cattle or the all sheep options. Furthermore, the GMs, pasture production, and labour availability can only be achieved by a mix of the two activities. As well, the farmer wants a mix of the two activities for reasons of income stability and risk-spreading. On the basis of the farmer's intimate knowledge of the farm, the judgement is made that the pasture production, and GMs, and labour requirements would be valid for anything from 1,000 ewe units and 240 cow units to 2,200 ewe units, and 140 cow units.

For this example the TGMs of various combinations of sheep and cattle can be worked out by hand, deriving the highest TGM by trial and error. The method is analogous to the method called 'linear programming' (LP) using a computer (Table 9.6).

Table 9.6: Gross margins planning table

plan no.	activity	GM per unit	TGM	available lsms	lsms used	surplus lsms	available labour (hrs)	labour used (hrs)	surplus labour (hrs)
1	2,200 sheep	30	66,000	60,000	39,600	20,400	2,800	2,200	600
	109 cattle	250	27,250	20,400	19,075	1,325	600	600	0
	TGM		93,250						
	surplus					1,325			
2	2,000 sheep	30	60,000	60,000	36,000	24,000	2,800	2,000	800
	137 cattle	250	34,250	24,000	24,000	0	800	753	47
	TGM		94,250						
	surplus								47

The reasoning behind the numbers in Table 9.6 is as follows.

In plan 1 the 2,200 ewe units produce an activity TGM of $66,000, and consume 39,600 of the 60,000 lsms available. This leaves 20,400 lsms available for the cattle. The 2,200 sheep use 2,200 hours of the 2,800 hours of labour, leaving 600 hours of labour for the cattle activity. The surplus 600 hours of labour would enable 109 cow units to be run, which would give an activity

GM of $27,250. Total gross margin would be $93,250 and there would then be a surplus of 1,325 lsms of feed, enough for 74 more ewe units or another 8 cow units. Given the nature of the estimates of labour requirements, there would be enough slack in the system to run these extra animals. But, even if this were not the case, with plan 1, if each extra 18 lsms of feed could be used by extra sheep this would add up to $30 to TGM. The addition to TGM by an extra ewe unit is the 'marginal value product'. An extra ewe unit would require an extra hour of labour. If extra labour could be hired for $10 per hr, one could confidently hire some help.

Alternatively, operating plan 2 with more cattle, no surplus feed, and a bit of surplus labour, it could be possible to buy in extra feed and run more stock. An extra 175 lsms of feed enables an extra cow unit to be run, which will add up to $250 to TGM (depending on the effect on the production from the existing stock). The addition to TGM by an extra cow unit is called the marginal value product of an extra cow unit.

There are many combinations of sheep and cattle which are feasible, and in this case many combinations in the 1,000 ewes and 240 cow units or 2,200 ewe units and 110 cow units ranges will yield about $90,000 TGM. The higher cattle numbers free some labour, which could be put to other productive uses, such as more pasture improvement or, if the farmer is aged, an easier time or more leisure.

Total gross margin is maximized once all resource constraints are taken into consideration. The applications, strengths, and limitations of the LP technique for planning a farm is dealt with fully in many texts. For more discussion of the history and limitations of LP for farm management see Chapter 10. In essence, LP has been tried and found wanting for most farming situations in Australia. The exception where LP is enormously valuable is in feed-mix analyses. For farm planning, in practice, budgeting techniques such as partial, creep, and development budgets which allow greater flexibility for changes to be explored, and which better allow all aspects of the picture to be considered, are more useful methods for practical decision analysis and planning.

The risks and the uncertainties in farming are great; often the options are few; the assumptions about linearity unrealistic; and the TGM of many different plans are often very similar. Thus sophisticated LP analysis for farm planning is too limited in scope for most practical farm management (though it is a useful research tool). However, the 'programming mentality', whereby activities are expanded until restraints are met, and the focus is on use of all resources, not just land, is essential in devising farm plans which make good use of all resources to give as good a TGM as can be had, all things considered.

Partial and creep budgeting

Partial budgeting involves changes in which many of the resources available are relatively fixed: such as the available permanent labour; machinery; improvements; and working capital. However, the point of exploring changes is to see if the existing resources, and new resources, can be combined to increase operating profit. Of particular interest is how returns to an activity change as the size of an activity changes; as well, how are returns in other activities affected?

With crops, constant returns could result from increases in area, up to the limits of fixed factors such as machinery and working capital or, until some proportion of various crops is reached which changes significantly the risk and thus the risk costs faced. Constant returns as crop area expanded would mean that crop technical aspects and gross margins are an adequate basis for selecting crop mixes. Indeed, this is probably the best use of the gross margin. When the tractor and air-seeder are at the gate of the paddock, the crop decision is based on technical aspects and the expected crop gross margin from this paddock, given the way the season and markets are shaping up.

Changing animal activities is more complicated, because changes in stocking rates of an activity changes the profitability per ha from the activity. As well, these affect many other aspects of the farm, such as related activities; labour requirements; working capital; timing of operations and so on.

The technique of 'creep budgeting' (Cocks 1964) is an elaboration of partial budgeting. In it more emphasis is put on all possible limiting resources, first looking at the current whole farm plan, investigating technical aspects, and expected future returns from each activity at their current levels. The aim here is to see if simple changes can be made to increase the profitability of activities. In particular, the purpose is to ensure that no obvious surplus capacity exists of key resources such as particular land types; machinery; and permanent labour. Once a full capacity whole farm plan and expected operating profit is arrived at, the 'programming attitude' comes into play, using creep budgeting when a couple of alternative whole farm budgets are tested in which one activity, or a portion of it, is substituted for another activity at the margin. This is done with close attention to the effect this has on all the resources such as land; feed; labour; and working capital machinery.

Cocks (1964) developed what he called 'creep' budgeting, which involved two main steps:

1 Develop 'full capacity' plans where no enterprise can be increased, i.e., some resource is limiting. Most advisers have found that when they first arrive on a farm rarely is it operating at full capacity. The process of developing 'full capacity' involves expanding the most profitable enterprise determined on the basis of the expected first limiting resource. During this stage the implementation of technological changes takes place to the stage where all enterprises are operating reasonably efficiently.

2 The next step involves substituting one enterprise for another at the margin (using gross margins and partial budgeting techniques) and taking into account any possible labour and capital limitations.

This procedure allows for the 'marginal effects' of expanding enterprises, e.g. lower crop yield with increased crop area, or lower wool cuts per head with increased stocking rates. At the same time budgeting of changes in resource restrictions can be undertaken to evaluate possible longer term changes. In the changing farm environment where technical and economic aspects are continually changing, this procedure is a continuing process.

Experience shows that optimum activity mix might not be as important as the level of technical efficiency in carrying out a plan, and avoiding excessive investment in high cost inputs, particularly machinery and labour, within the chosen plan.

Financial analysis of machinery acquisition

A farmer wishes to get the services of a $60,000 tractor. The alternatives are to lease it, use hire purchase, or borrow and buy it using bank bills. These comparisons follow.

Leasing

Table 9.7: Leasing a $60,000 tractor, 30% tax rate, four years

year	lease payment at end of year	residual (25%)	tax saving (30%)	effective annual cost	16% discount factor	net present cost (NPC)
0	−17,600	—	—	−17,600	—	−17,600
1	−17,600	—	+5,280	−12,320	× 0.8621	−10,621
2	−17,600	—	+5,280	−12,320	× 0.7432	−9,156
3	−17,600	—	+5,280	−12,320	× 0.6407	−7,893
4	−17,600	−15,000	+5,280	−9,720	× 0.5523	−5,368
						−50,638

The annuity equivalent is $50,638 × 0.3574 = $18,098

The tax saving is lagged by a year; it is subtracted from the lease payment and the residual to give the effective annual cost. Next, the present value (net present cost, NPC) of the lease payments are calculated using a bank interest rate of 16%.

The annuity equivalent of the $50,638 is worked out using the 'annuity whose present value is one' for 16% over four years (see Table D in the Appendix). The factor for this is 0.3574. The annuity equivalent of the annual cost of $50,638 over four years is $18,098.

Bank bill

This is a form of 'interest only' loan for 180 days at a time, which will be 'rolled over' each time for the four-year-period. Then the farmer has to pay the $60,000. It will cost 19% per year (see Table 9.8).

Table 9.8: Bank bill finance for a $60,000 tractor, 19% interest for four years

end of year	pay interest (19%)	repay loan	tax interest saving (30%)	tax dep'n saving (18%)	effective annual cost	16% discount factor	net present cost (NPC) at 16% discount rate
1	−11,400		+3,420	+3,420	−4,740	× 0.8621	−4,086
2	−11,400		+3,420	+3,420	−4,740	× 0.7432	−3,523
3	−11,400		+3,420	+3,420	−4,740	× 0.6407	−3,037
4	−11,400	−60,000	+3,420	+3,420	−64,740	× 0.5523	−35,756
							−46,402

The annuity equivalent is $46,402 × 0.3574 = $16,584

Hire purchase

With the hire purchase option the farmer pays one-third as deposit ($20,000), and four annual payments, each of $10,000. There are tax savings on both interest and depreciation. Depreciation is 18% per year and interest is 17% simple. This case is shown in Table 9.9. The equivalent annual cost at 16% discount rate is $48,940 \times 0.3574 = $17,790$.

Table 9.9: Hire purchase of a $60,000 tractor at one-third deposit, 17% interest, 30% tax rate

year	deposit	pay	owe	interest (17%)	tax interest saving (30%)	18% per year dep'n	tax dep'n saving (30%)	effective cost per year	net present cost (NPC)
0	20,000	—	40,000	—	—	—	—	−20,000	−20,000
1	—	10,000	30,000	6,800	2,040	10,800	3,240	−11,520	−9,931
2	—	10,000	20,000	5,100	1,530	8,856	2,657	−10,913	−8,110
3	—	10,000	10,000	3,400	1,020	7,262	2,179	−10,210	−6,541
4	—	10,000	0	1,700	510	5,955	1,786	−9,404	−5,194
									−49,776

The annuity equivalent is $49,776 \times 0.3574 = $17,790$

The comparison is for an annual cost of $16,584 for the bank bill option, $17,790 for the hire purchase option, and $18,098 with the leasing option. There cannot be much difference in these different ways of financing a machinery deal, because of the way competitive financial markets work. In effect, all options are different ways of borrowing other people's money for a given time. A little more research into the possible 'add on' costs associated with each option could prove fruitful.

Interpreting farm management budgets

One of the major benefits from budgeting is the learning which is involved in the activity. The process of preparing budgets, of thinking about what goes where and why, improves the eventual decision by informing the decision makers better. The key to doing and to using farm management budgets well is making good judgements about the items and numbers which go into budgets. Reasons why the costs and returns might not turn out as expected need to be considered with care. To interpret the results of a budget, it is vital to specify what key things might affect the outcome such as the major environmental and economic hazards and risks, and the changes which could occur to important parts of a project during its life.

Budgets are about the future and so they have to be based on what might happen. For many reasons, many of the numbers that are used in farm budgets are 'soft'. People doing and using budgets do not always recognize this fact. The harder the data, the more clearly one can state how they were derived and the more accurately the figures used, reflect reality. It is well known that figures for future yields, prices, and costs are often soft. The reason is that some of the figures used are opinions. Such items can include:

- the amount which capital could be earning elsewhere;
- the worth of a piece of machinery;
- the annual depreciation cost;
- annual supplementary feed cost;
- the worth of the operator's labour and management;
- the likely yields and prices;
- future rates of inflation and interest rates.

Budgets are based on the expected yields, costs, prices, and inflation. These best estimates rarely ever happen. That is why it is useful to do budgets in terms of a range of prices and costs, as well as the 'most likely' outcomes.

When using budgets about the farm business to evaluate courses of action the numbers and the predicted outcomes must be interpreted with care. Focus only on the key numbers: those which have a major impact on the final outcome if they vary from the expected. The bottom line cannot be less variable than the variability of the key numbers which produce it. A tendency to read too much into 'the numbers' is folly particularly if you do not pay enough attention to the broader aspects of the proposal.

In farm management planning, the budgets should contain the best information available at the time the decisions are taken. As time passes, new conditions arise and apply. So new strategies have to be formed and old estimates modified or changed. As well, new decisions need to be made on the basis of all of the newly available data.

With some decisions the course could be clear-cut. For example, the outcomes from not buying the neighbouring block of land could be totally unacceptable (i.e., being forced out of business a few years later). Perhaps the aim of using capital in a specific way could stem from the aim of meeting a number of important non-economic objectives. This action may have the proviso that the economics of it are not 'bad'.

Good decision making depends on both good judgement and good arithmetic. The techniques of budgeting are straightforward but the relationships they embrace are complex. The process of doing budgets is one of the keys to making good decisions, believing in them, and acting on them. That is partly why the process of budgeting is important. In this process, the decision maker is forced to confront, and come to terms with, the key elements of cost, yields, prices, alternative choices, and the risks. It is this process, allied to analytical techniques, which is the basis of both making good decisions and making them work.

The first need in preparing reliable budgets is to know the relevant technical aspects of the farm's operations. Relevant, simple farm records can be a help to put numbers on such things as the present use of inputs of labour; machinery; fuel; seed; fertilizer and so on, in relation to the output of crops and livestock in the current farm plan.

Getting the technical basis of farm budgets right is often hard and always critical. To do so it is a 'must' to draw on the farmer's detailed knowledge and experience of production on the farm. Local farmers on comparable land who use similar technology, and local agricultural professionals and service people are also valuable sources. Experimental results coming from research plots and stations have to be adjusted to be relevant to the specific situation on each farm. Researchers claims about achievable yields ought to be examined critically. Scientists are usually concerned with advances in technical efficiency and increased yields. Gains in economic efficiency and increased profits are not their main concern. The differences between what is technically achievable under research conditions and what is economically feasible on the farm are often massive. Yields used in budgets have to be those which are possible using economic levels of inputs on the particular farm.

The major benefits in analysing and planning a farm business using farm budgets come from:

- finding out more about how the bits of a farm fit together to make income;
- identifying the strengths and weaknesses of the business;
- using this information to help in making decisions about using limited resources;
- comparing actual against budgeted cash flows, so letting the farmer take action to either exploit or remedy the situation;
- revealing information about the prospects and potential profitability of parts of the farm business. This is the information which the decision maker can draw on when forming his or her attitude to taking or avoiding the risk which may be involved.

If in an advisory role, analyses should be accompanied by recommendations. Often effective advice requires one or two actions to be taken quickly and soundly. Once proper analyses have been done with the decision maker(s), the course of action is usually reasonably clear-cut.

An adviser is usually a second opinion, a sounding board for the farmer. It makes sense to be equivocal before the analysis is done and before the facts of the matter are established as best they can be, but the adviser should be less equivocal after the analysis is done. If the analysis is any good, out of it will evolve soundly based views about appropriate actions. This is the information which farm decision makers require.

9

Questions for discussion

1   Identify the major factors involved in analysing and in planning a change.

2   The key to project analysis is the question 'compared with what?'
    What do we mean by this claim?

3   In farm management budgets many of the numbers are soft.
    What do we mean by this?

4   Explain what a partial budget is and how it is used.
    What are the difficult parts in doing a partial budget and interpreting the results?

5   When should you use:
    (a) real dollars;
    (b) nominal dollars, in evaluating a project with a life of more than three to four years?

6   What would be the real rate of return in a year's time of lending $100, if the inflation rate is 10% and 19% interest on the $100 is charged?

7   What does this statement mean:
    'Project A has an NPV of $100,000 using a nominal discount rate of 15%?

8   What assumptions underlie the use of discounted cash flow techniques?

9   Why is the IRR a less useful measure of profitability sometimes than the NPV?

10 NPV, IRR and B:C do not give the answer; they merely provide further information, the usefulness of which depends on the validity, as events unfold, of all the assumptions which have been made. Evaluate this statement.

11 In accounting for risk, fudge the numbers but leave alone the discount rate. Discuss.

12 Salvage value can be most important in appraising the economics of a farm development program. What is it? How do you estimate it?

13 If you have compared different ways of developing the same piece of land using real values for yields, costs and returns, you then have to do the budgets in nominal dollars. This involves making some guesses about future inflation rates. Why do we recommend using nominal dollars in the financial budget?

14 During a farm development program it is necessary to keep track of the expected assets and liabilities of:
    (a) the development project;
    (b) the whole farm.
    Why is this precaution needed?

15 If activity A has a gross margin of $35, and activity B has a gross margin of $25, you should always expand activity A and reduce activity B.
    This statement is not necessarily true. Why not?

16 Usually a change involves more than just changes in the variable costs of an activity. Other costs and returns are affected, and often so, too, are other activities. Thus more often than not activity gross margins analysis is not enough; partial or even whole farm budgets are required.
    Evaluate this claim.

9
Further reading

Barnard, C. S. and Nix, J. S., *Farm Planning and Control* (2nd edn), Cambridge University Press, Cambridge, 1986.

Barry, P. J., Hopkin, J .A., & Baker, C. B., *Financial Management in Agriculture* (3rd edn), The Interstate Printers and Publishers Inc., Illinois, 1988.

Boehlje, M. D. and Eidman, V. R., *Farm Management*, John Wiley & Sons, New York, 1983.

Calkins, P. H. and DiPietre, D. D., *Farm Business Management: Successful Decisions in a Changing Environment*, Macmillan Publishing Co. Inc., New York, 1983.

Castle, E. N., Becker, M. H., & Nelson, A. G., *Farm Business Management—The Decision Making Process*, Macmillan Publishing Company, New York, 1987.

Cocks, K. D., 'Creep Budgeting', *Review of Marketing and Agricultural Economics*, 32(3), 1964, pp. 137–148.

Dent, J. B. et al., *Farm Planning with Linear Programming*, Butterworths, London, 1986.

Pollard, V. J. and Obst, W. J., *Practical Farm Business Management* (2nd edn), Inkata Press, Melbourne, 1988.

Turner, J. and Taylor, M., *Applied Farm Management*, BSP Professional Books, Oxford, 1989.

10

They Use The Snaffle And The Curb Alright, But Where's The Bloody Horse?:
Farm Management History

This chapter is not for everyone. In it is given a 'birds eye' view of what has happened in the attempts to apply 'academic farm management' to 'real life farm management' since the early 1940s.

For those interested in how fashions change with the advent of new thoughts and techniques, insights are provided about past attempts to 'get it right'. We are a lot closer now than we were 50 years back. So we should be! But we believe that there are still people dealing with aspects of farm management who are unaware of some of the lessons from past experience, or who are misguidedly persisting in attempting to re-invent the wheel.

The emphases in academic work in farm management have ranged over a few broad fields. First, the emphasis was technical, with some book-keeping and arithmetic, describing 'what is' on the farm. Then came a theoretical framework built around production economics. This enabled emphasis on 'what ought to be'. The 'whole farm' approach and emphasis on management followed. Then came the computer. This opened the possibility of large-scale data recording and analysis, and the use of the quantitative techniques of decision analysis, such as linear programming, decision theory, utility analysis, and systems simulation.

All of these emphases came and went because they did not really hit the mark, although each contributed by focusing on important parts of farm

---

* Some of the material in this chapter derives from 'Fifty Years of Farm Management in Australia', by L. R. Malcolm, *RMAE*, April 1991.

management questions. The shortcomings of accounting and record-keeping; cost of production estimates; comparative analysis of gross margins and technical efficiency ratios; production economics; decision theory; linear programming; utility analysis and systems simulation are well documented in the farm management and agricultural economics literature of the past 50 years. This does not stop all of these approaches to decision making in farm management being re-discovered and re-emphasized regularly. What follows is a summary of what some workers in farm management have learnt about these emphases in those years.

In essence, we argue that the world is too complex for the complex but ultimately narrow-in-scope quantitative (operations research) type approaches to analysing farm decisions. Ironically, because of the complexity of the real world, the relatively simple farm management analytical techniques such as the traditional budgets are more useful because they better allow the full dimensions and complex inter-relationships of the problem at hand to be appreciated and to some extent to be taken into account in the decision-making process.

Good farm management decision analysis is all about having the appropriate breadth of scope and the appropriate depth of detailed analysis focused on the critical aspects of the problem. This is not easy, as it requires both breadth and depth of knowledge and sound judgement. For these reasons many people prefer to focus on part of the problem, and specialize in technical, economic or sociological aspects of a problem. Such emphases are necessary, but, alone, are insufficient to adequately answer questions about, and solve problems to do with, the operation of the whole farm in all its complicated glory.

Cost of production

Theoretical objections to research aimed at determining the unit production costs of specific agricultural products come from concern with the relationships and interdependence which exist between each farm activity, the items to include, and the value to use.

For individual activities there is the problem of identifying and allocating breakdown of shared costs, such as overheads, in the same way as they are actually incurred in one of several activities. This allocation has to be arbitrary, and a wide range of estimates can be defined as being 'true'.

The interdependence of activities means that simply comparing the so-called 'cost of production' of a crop or livestock enterprise with the price received is not enough to indicate how much to expand or contract an activity. Changes in farm organization have to be assessed not by their effect on the returns from a single activity, but have to be judged by their effect on the whole farm. For example a complementary activity could appear to have low profitability, but if it were removed, whole farm profitability could fall greatly. Or, an activity could have high costs and low profits, because it is on too small a scale, but it could be highly profitable if expanded. To reduce it or abandon it on the basis of cost accounting alone would be wrong.

Accounting and records and comparative analysis

A belief in the 1960s was that better farm record-keeping and analysis was needed for farm management. Further, standardized accounting procedures would drag the accounting profession into the farm management field (if not the paddock). Linked to this was a big push to develop comparative analysis as the corner-stone of farm management accounting. It was thought that farm accountants would prepare the financial statements and estimate efficiency ratios and technical standards. In that decade the agricultural economics and farm management profession had instigated a major attempt to develop a standardized farm accounting system, known as the Australian Chart and Code for Rural Accounting (ACCRA) system.

This was partly in response to the perceived potential for more elaborate record-keeping and analysis made possible by the developments in computers during the 1960s, allied to the belief that accounting, recording, and comparative analysis were highly useful to the management of farms.

Also, there was widespread recognition that the taxation accounts prepared for farm businesses by accountants were inadequate for farm management uses. Hopes had been high regarding the possibilities unleashed by accountants being able to standardize farm data and prepare farm management orientated net worth statements, profit budgets, cash budgets, and even partial budgets and investment analyses for farmer clients.

Eventually a few variations of the ACCRA coding system were adopted by a few accountants, but the hopes held for it during the 1960s and early 1970s did not materialize. Hoskins (1972) had noted that with rural accounting systems in other countries 'failure has been more common than success' and identified three major potential problems with the ACCRA system.

There was the lack of interest of farmers in record-keeping; and accountants' predilection for concentrating almost exclusively on tax accounting. Thirdly, there was the existence of alternative existing, competing accounting systems.

A flaw in the ACCRA system was that the usefulness of historical (original) records to farm management remained as limited as had always been the case. Further, when it came to forward-looking analyses for management and planning, technical matters were either omitted or inadequately included in the analysis. That is, accountants with little knowledge of farm technology could not carry out useful farm management analyses. This initial extremely limiting factor seemed to be largely overlooked in the excitement about the potential for computers to undertake large-scale data-recording and analysis.

A major fallacy was the belief that historical records, and comparative analysis of technical ratios and average activity gross margins, achieved on different farms were useful for farm management analysis. They are not very useful. Farm management is about dealing with what might happen. What happened in different, past circumstances is of limited relevance. The weaknesses of emphasis on accounting and recording is that generally it leaves out of the analyses the critical technical and human aspects and the management economics way of thinking, and has a past, not future, orientation.

While mastery of information is one of the keys to good management, it is information about adopting and applying new technology; about what is happening in the markets for both inputs and outputs; about expected future cash flows; and implications for gearing and growth, which is most valuable. Physical information about what happened in particular paddocks or to production by animals is needed and is useful. It is more useful in practice than out-of-date financial (often taxation) information about what happened sometime in different circumstances in the previous year, on your own and on other people's farms.

Comparative analysis

Technical ratios of output per animal or per ha tell nothing about profitability and can give opposite indications of what should be done, depending, for instance, on whether output per head or output per ha is the standard which is desired to maximize (Candler and Sargent 1962).

Gross margins for activities are the result of many interactions within an activity and between activities, and cannot be meaningfully compared between farms. Full analysis of all resources available and all output resulting in the whole farm system is necessary for each unique farm situation.

Comparisons of gross margins between farms, and 'league tables' of activity gross margins tell little about management of particular farms. A farm achieving relatively high gross margins could be doing so because of very good resources, and could be doing so despite a poor standard of farm management. Alternatively a farm with apparently poor gross margins could be achieving this despite poor resources and be doing so because of very high standards of farm management.

'League tables' of high and low gross margins and technical efficiency ratios imply a cause and effect which might not be true. The implication is that 'this' action is done in a particular activity, and the activity has a gross margin or efficiency ratio of 'that': therefore, the reasoning goes, 'this' caused 'that'. There is more to the story. Even if 'this' caused 'that' in the activity on this farm, whether the same can be expected on another farm depends on all the details of the farm, and many important aspects of farms are unique. Each farm is made up of different physical and financial resources, and different gearing, as well as farmers having different skills, goals, interests, labour forces, stage of life and so on.

Even if comparative analysis were sound in theory, which it is not, then it is still likely to be unreliable in practice as a guide to action. Measurement errors and differences as a result of subjective valuations involved about livestock valuations or machinery operating costs can easily be greater than the differences between estimated gross margins. If differences in gross margins are not large, comparison of gross margins is no guide to action. Conversely, when the differences in gross margins are large, the reasons are usually obvious to a competent observer.

Gross margins of one activity might include the effects of a complementary relationship with another activity, whilst not measuring this contribution as part of the gross margin of the contributing activity. For example, the complementary contribution of cattle production to sheep activities through their effect on pasture composition and output, on labour requirements, and animal health, shows up as a higher sheep gross margin.

Finally the average gross margin of an activity is not relevant to decisions at the margin. It is the marginal gross margin which counts. Despite comparative analysis of gross margins between farms being intellectually flawed, this remains one of the most widespread techniques of farm management analysis.

Mauldon and Schapper made such valuable contributions to the debate about farm records and comparative analysis in the early 1970s that they warrant repeating here in detail. They wrote 'Random Numbers for Farmers', an important article which had implications for the use of comparative analyses of farm performance ratios (Mauldon and Schapper 1970). They started with a forceful assertion:

The connection between the title and content of this paper is that the purposes served by those who want statistical comparisons of key or efficiency ratios and of historical gross margins between different farms and between activities within a farm, could be met costlessly and punctually by sets of (almost) random numbers. This is because such comparisons and margins are of slight use in planning, budgeting and diagnosing strengths and weaknesses in farm management, and are untimely, expensive, and inaccurate. This represents . . . a direct challenge to the proposed adoption by some State Departments of Agriculture of interfarm comparisons as a component of their extension programmes in farm management.

These authors noted that Candler and Sargent (1962) showed that farm efficiency ratios which were used as the basis of the inter-farm comparisons were capable of logically opposite conclusions. Furthermore, profit maximization required that marginal productivities per dollar spent of inputs were equal, if capital was limited, or, that marginal productivity of inputs equalled their price if capital was not limiting. Thus inter- and intra-farm comparisons of efficiency all based on calculations of average productivities are of little relevance.

Despite this, recommendations and demands for the use of comparative analysis and historical gross margins continued to be made in Australia. As Mauldon and Schapper argue, efficiency ratios are compounds of numerous factors and their use could lead to conflicting diagnoses and decisions. Technical ratios are not measures of economic efficiency in any case.

Frequently efficiency ratios are grouped according to whether they relate to farms with above average, below average or average net farm income. The implications of this are that (1) there is a causal relationship between the selected technical efficiency ratio and the net farm income; and (2) the average and below average farmer could reach the higher income group by achieving the same values for his or her efficiency ratios.

In fact, some below average farms might be at a maximum income and some above average farms might be below maximum income. Mauldon and Schapper (1970) continued:

Comparisons only seemingly allow the farm manager or consultant to by-pass the application of cost–price ratios and factor–product, factor–factor, and product–product relationships. Despite the claims made for comparisons in their use for increasing net farm income, planned increases that do occur through farm re-organisation (as distinct from increases to farm size) in fact and in theory come from planned changes both of and within these relationships.

Mauldon and Schapper argued that people doing comparisons of gross margins cannot derive marginal productivities, or infer marginal productivities from average data, or know which ratios are causally related to net farm income. Even if they could, each ratio is compounded of so many possible causal factors that the analyst would still be no better informed. Furthermore, the records on which the comparative calculations are made are not 'perfectly accurate' and have to be adjusted. The adjustment can exceed the size of the differences in the ratios between farms.

Mauldon and Schapper added that some comparisons were, however, of some use: first, comparisons of two or more years of results from the same farm, then comparison of actual results with planned results for the same farm during the one year; and comparisons of two or more sets of plans and budgets for the same farm for a future year. They concluded:

The sources and calculations of the best technical estimates for planning a particular farm are the farmer's experiences, properly designed and conducted experiments, and knowledge of the principles of plant and animal husbandry. The experience of other farmers is also a source of technical information. But to be of use it must be both relevant and operationally detailed. This is best achieved through well designed case study analysis.

These two authors also wrote about the sensitivity of inter-farm comparisons to inaccuracies of measurement and valuation (Mauldon and Schapper 1971). They said that inter-farm comparisons of ratios and margins were 'so untimely, so expensive, so inaccurate, so historical and so inherently ambiguous in their economic meaning as to be of slight usefulness for reliable planning, budgeting and diagnosis in farm management'.

For this article they focused on the tacit assumption which underlay comparative analysis, viz., that the source data are perfectly accurate or insignificantly innaccurate. Such correctness implies that (1) recorded sources and uses reconciled with actual sources and uses for both physical and financial flows; (2) valuations were known for certain; and objectively, and (3) farmers in the comparisons allocated items to activities in the same manner. When these above-mentioned conditions did not hold, the potential value of comparisons was considerably reduced, possibly to uselessness.

If errors of measurement were not randomly distributed but were biased by the methods of selection and valuation which were adopted, or if the errors could exceed the differences between farms, then the effects of errors were not neutral in inter-farm comparisons. As well, values of some items, such as land, plant, stock, inventories, were 'inevitably the expected values of subjective probability distributions'. These values were meaninglessly mixed up with objectively valued items such as cash balances. Mauldon and Schapper showed how various adjustments to figures for failure to reconcile or for differences in valuation altered the average level of performance within groups of farms, and the rankings of levels of performance.

A related issue to comparative analysis of farm performance standards is the issue of the setting-up of demonstration farms. The limitations of comparative analysis between farms apply with even more force to demonstration farms. This is particularly the case when demonstration farms are not operated as a fully commercial operation, as is inevitably the case. It is often thought that the term 'commercial operation' refers to a business simply operating without an obvious subsidy from government. However the concept of being commercial is more subtle than this. A common but sometimes not obvious factor in the operation of any farm is risk. For a demonstration farm to be comparable to a fully commercial private farm, the decisions about the operation of the demonstration farm have to be made under the same conditions of commercial risk (as well as everything else) as borne by operators of private farm businesses. Differences in the consequences of risk, and, of course, in individual farmers' attitudes to such risk, can go a long way towards explaining why farmers will or will not adopt a change which seems beneficial, in technological terms at least. Differences in goals, family situation, and stage of life also explain a lot.

Production economics

Farming is a dynamic, uncertain activity. Good technology is the key to success. The relevance of production economic reasoning, based on static situations, which assumes certainty and technical efficiency, is obviously limited.

T. W. Schultz in 1939 saw limitations to production economic theory and 'optimum combinations' approaches for farm management which stemmed 'from gaps in the theoretical apparatus of formal economics'.

Interestingly K. O. Campbell (1978) regarded this contribution by Schultz as being the start of the modern era of farm management. The essence of Schultz's view of relevant farm management research is captured in the following extract:

... If ... (a) ... pending change involves in addition an element of uncertainty, which is usually the case, the firm also assumes the additional function of uncertainty bearing ... In the real world the production processes of the firm are being altered continuously. Routine procedure will not suffice. Change born out of dynamic circumstances, is ever present. Adjustments are called for. It is the entrepreneur who decides what must be done. The decisions of the entrepreneur are carried out within the framework of the firm. Two interrelated decisions must be made, (a) the amount of adjustment that is necessary, (b) the method for making the adjustment; that is, what to do and how to do it. It is these adjustments of the firm that gives us the key to what we need to look for in our farm management research. To understand the basic nature of these adjustments is to know what is fundamental to the entrepreneurial problem in farming. Since the existence of the firm of necessity arises out of and is dependent upon dynamic conditions, it would appear that both the size of the firm and the success of the firm must be determined within a framework that allows for 'time' and 'change'.

A number of deficiencies of production economics stand out, as it relates to farm management. Economics, like farm management, is about decisions; but economics is about the outcomes of decisions, whereas farm management concerns both the process of decision making and the outcomes.

The neo-classical theory of the firm is an abstract model for predicting the overall results of the decisions of individual producers, and explaining and predicting changes in observed prices. Production economic theory is not intended as a working model of the decision-making process within firms, nor does it predict the actual responses of any particular farm firm to a change in relative prices.

While the history and financial position of a firm are properly excluded as irrelevant in production economic theory, these are important elements of the decision-making processes of individual firms. Static theory obviously does not fit the dynamic nature of agricultural production and management processes. In farming it is hard to identify and measure all inputs and outputs.

One of the major criticisms of the production economic model in terms of farm management is that it emphasizes the allocation of resources at an assumed level of technical efficiency, when farming is really about 'moving towards a continually improving and adjusting efficiency' (Harle 1974, p. 156; Longworth and Menz 1980).

Further, the partial and static emphasis of production economics and agricultural economic analysis means that it is of limited relevance to questions of management, which is essentially dynamic (Kaldor 1934; Hicks 1939; Schultz 1939; Williams 1959, 1968). Attempts to incorporate dynamic elements of the management function in analytical tools, such as dynamic programming, while successful in an agricultural economic sense (Kennedy 1981), are of limited usefulness for farm management.

The major relevance of production economic theory to Australian agriculture in practice seems to have been to provide a formalized way of thinking for making rational decisions. Dillon (1978) put the position plainly, saying that at the end of the 1970s it was the increasingly accepted view that 'training in farm management based on production economics has lost or must inevitably lose touch with farmers' needs and the practicality of farming because of its emphasis on logically attractive but largely inapplicable theory'.

Farm management is a dynamic and uncertain process, in which mastery of technology is the key, and the theoretical foundations of analyses into farm management had to fully allow for this fact. Production economic theory was essentially static in approach, and left out the technology and management, which limited the relevance of production economics to business management.

Linear programming

Linear programming (LP) is a technique which can be used to derive the most profitable combination of activities for a farm, for a well-defined set of resources available on the farm and the resources required by each activity. An optimum mix of activities is defined for the expected resources required and available and prices of inputs and outputs.

In practice a number of alternative near 'optimum' solutions exist which promise similar farm total gross margins. Then, decisions on combinations of activities are based only partly on the information contained in the results from standard static linear programming analysis, and partly on all the other factors not included, such as long-term aims and effects of activities over time, cash flow and gearing concerns, management skills and preferences, risk factors, and complementary effects and supplementary effects between activities—effects which are not all fully represented in the LP model. For example, with LP analysis of crop sequences, it is difficult to realistically capture many of the possible effects of the technical characteristics of different paddocks on activity yields and GMs at different stages of a crop sequence, allowing for the many combinations and permutations of seasons, yields, prices, weed status, in each year and in subsequent years.

Linear programming has rarely been used to solve questions about combinations of activities in Australian farming. This is because few choices are involved, and often when they are, simple gross margins selection are adequate. When there are a few major resources, and activities compete for resources in approximately the same proportions, such as cropping activities grown at the same time of the year, LP is not necessary to decide which crop to grow this year and simple budgeting is adequate.

Further, risk is such that longer term objectives of income stability influence, and can even override, considerations about short-term 'profit maximizing' combinations of activities. Costs and risks of changing from one situation to another also raise the importance of longer term planning and objectives, more so than is implied by the standard LP approaches. Climatic uncertainty further reduces the usefulness of precise planning techniques. There is also the question of technical proficiency. The way you do what you do is as important, or more important, than what you do on the farm.

LP received a lot of attention during the 1960s, in particular, refinements to the standard static, linear model. A major review of LP was done by Musgrave (1963). The use of non-linear segments and integer programming were refinements which had been developed for situations where the assumption of constant returns as activities expanded, and perfectly divisible resources such as machinery and paddocks, was not acceptable. Quadratic risk programming enabled variability to be considered in analyses.

The major part of an LP study is the specification of the problem. There are particular difficulties with LP, such as assuming that rigid joint relationships prevail over the whole range of possibilities, and on the other hand assuming a flexibility which was not feasible because of asset fixity.

Musgrave (1963) saw some scope for the use of representative 'benchmark' type studies to give guides to changes, from which extension workers could extrapolate, with appropriate budgeting, to individual farms. The use of LP as a research tool was seen by Musgrave as beyond dispute, and he saw potential for the establishment of a centralized farm management laboratory which provided LP as one means by which LP could come to have greater usefulness for farm management extension.

Cocks (1963, 1964) had also appraised the use of LP for farm management purposes. He said that farm management was an applied science which was never subject to definite tests of efficiency, and that 'even the most elaborately formulated model is only a partial description of the possible and actual cause–effect relationships on a particular farm'. Cocks considered that the development of a 'programming attitude' would be the useful spin-off from LP.

While LP could give a better solution than other applications of the programming attitude, there was still a need for farm planning methods which advisers 'could work through in a day with the farmer by his [or her] side making intuitive judgements'. Hence, Cocks concluded that a method was needed which could cope with incremental changes within enterprises; that is, some form of partial budgeting. Cocks advocated a method called 'creep budgeting'.

Static single-value linear programming might be sufficiently operational, and might provide enough information cheaply enough to take its place in some situations alongside the traditional farm management budgeting tools for farm management planning.

In most cases though, farming in Australia is so risky, or has such limited choices, or so involves choices between activities competing fairly strictly for the same resources at the same time, that the potential role of the formal programming techniques in practical farm management is limited.

Programming methods can be criticised for their focus on optimizing combinations of activities. There are always a range of farm plans which are similar in total gross margin but differ in technical requirements, or cash flow and gearing implications, so decisions on product combinations are then made on 'other' criteria.

The technical proficiency with which any of the often small number of options that are feasible are carried out is as important to improving net farm income as having an allocatively 'optimum' combination of activities.

Also, the implicit goal of maximizing total gross margin in any single year does not fit well with farmers' objectives, which usually involve many dimensions over a span of time longer than one year.

Making programming techniques more realistic and relevant by attempting to allow for real world dynamics, for uncertainty and variability, and for the multiplicity of decision-maker's objectives becomes such a complex procedure that such techniques are not operational or economical enough to be tools for farm management, useful as they are for research (Nuthall and Moffatt 1975).

With multi-period programming the information produced leads to better decisions about the first period of the plan (Anderson 1972; Trebeck and Hardaker 1972) but the marginal gain is unlikely to compare well with the marginal costs of producing that information.

Decision theory: expected utility analysis

The essence of the decision theory approaches to farm management is that it is an attempt to correct for the neglect of uncertainty and attitudes to risk, and the emphasis on maximizing money, returns, found in the alternative approaches to decision analysis.

An aim of these approaches is to incorporate into the analysis of a farm management decision explicit consideration of the reality that it is under conditions of uncertainty the decision has to be made.

Also, it attempts to cope with the reality that the decision maker(s) will have a particular attitude(s) to the degree of uncertainty, as well as having a number of objectives to try and to meet.

One contention of the proponents of decision theory was that risk was an important influence on farmers' decisions and that risk aversion or preference could be quantified using utility analysis. The criterion used was that of maximizing expected utility.

Officer and Anderson (1968) dealt more fully with utility and decision making under risk. They claim that whereas the criterion of maximization of expected profit fitted with economic theory, and held for conditions of certainty, it was found wanting when considerations of risk were introduced. The only alternative criterion to maximizing expected income which had been strongly proposed was the criterion of maximizing expected utility.

Dillon (1971) attempted to resolve the question 'Is Utility Futility?' Dillon was optimistic that the utility approach would prove to be productive because choices have to be made between probability distributions of outcomes. As well, uncertainty impinges on the choice and ranking of goals.

Though this may sound all too difficult, Dillon said, farm managers manage to make decisions in the face of incredible uncertainties and lack of information. A formal system of organizing as much relevant information about expected returns and riskiness as possible was a sensible approach.

Scrutiny of decision theory came after the publication of the book *Agricultural Decision Analysis* by Anderson, Dillon, & Hardaker (1977). Petit suggested that for decision making, less sophisticated analysis could still lead to similar conclusions; that the main problem in agricultural decision analysis 'is not so much to find the "best decision" but rather to understand how decisions are actually made, for what reasons, on the basis of which information and with which consequences' (Petit 1978). Sturgess (1978) noted that decision analysis is something that you believe (or do not).

McInerney's (1979) more substantive criticism of formal decision theory concerned the unworldliness of trying to 'deal with the unpredictability of future events by concentrating on the search for "better" pre-decision optimization procedures', and he concluded:

What they (decision theory exponents) really mean is that the reality of agricultural management is not easily handled analytically in their (or any one else's) formal decision-making framework. Quite obviously it is handled in practice, and often quite successfully, by people not well versed in decision analysis. Their secret seems to lie not just in making a considered choice based on a rational interpretation of the available information and consistent with their preferences and beliefs about the risks involved. Rather, having made a decision, whatever it is, they then make it work and keep things on an acceptable track. Their management is a matter of continually reacting to where they are, rather than periodically trying to pre-determine where they are going. Making a good fist of those initial planning decisions is important, sure, but let's also see some emphasis on management as a reactive, rather than a solely proactive, process.

A further consideration in the debate about utility analysis is the possibility that the way of achieving an objective, and the objective itself, are dependent (Cary and Holmes 1983) so that the utility derived from particular actions can come from reaching the desired objectives as well as from going through the process of reaching the desired objective.

Wright (1983) also casts doubt on the relevance of the decision theory approaches to management decisions, which had dominated the farm management literature of the late 1960s and early 1970s. He said that management scientists dissented from the view that decision theory was widely useful.

He questioned how well decision theory approaches were able to describe behaviour, and observed that there is a widespread tendency of people to breach the axioms which underlie decision theory. He was also concerned with the elicitation of subjective probability distributions and utility functions, and particularly criticized the use of the hypothetical gambling device to represent real decision choices.

Utility analysis has the assumption that all relevant beliefs an individual holds about an uncertain parameter can be summarized in a single profitability distribution. If this were not so, and there exists 'ambiguity' (probability of probability estimates) about probability estimates, then Wright maintains that this ambiguity should be taken into consideration in advising decision makers.

The point is that if all relevant beliefs were not captured in a single probability distribution, then the application of decision theory could lead to irrational action, simply because relevant information would be left out of the decision analysis. If so, then analysis based on maximizing expected utility would not lead to the appropriate action.

A prosaic test of the value of a technique for farm management decision making is whether it is applied. Utility analysis has rarely been used for research, and less, if ever, for farm management decisions.

With utility approaches to farm management decision making you are either 'of the faith'; accept the axioms; and believe that a monotonic utility index which reflects completely a person's preference among risky alternatives can be defined sensibly; or you do not. If the axioms are accepted, the theoretical and the practical controversies surrounding them are resolved to the believers' satisfaction; then expected utility approaches to decision problems can be seen as valid decision techniques.

However, where doubt, both theoretical and practical, seems proper, and the faith is missing, assessment of the usefulness of utility analysis is less generous (Shoemaker 1982; Stigum and Wenstop 1983).

Protagonists of utility could have taken an overly singular view of the role of decision making and risk in farm management. That is, the process of decision making is the beginning of a journey in a general direction. Much will happen along the way!

They could have overstated the case in their belief that utility functions can, both theoretically and practically, be sensibly elicited. They may have underestimated the importance of the interdependence between desired ends and means and the fluctuations of hope. There is also the issue of the decision-maker's future utility function, though this question is part of all decision analysis.

Perhaps most importantly, the utility theorists devised a technique whose use could only be worth considering for major decisions. It failed to focus attention on the critical practical considerations in major decisions, such as the technology; gearing; growth; time; cash flows; debt-servicing ability; and farmers' skills.

From observable evidence it is difficult to believe in a big future for utility analysis for farm management decision making. It could be that expected utility analysis is more sensibly about the theory of producer behaviour in the microeconomic sense, and is thus relevant to agricultural economics, if not farm management (Hardaker 1979).

The question is unresolved, though Simon (1983) concluded that 'subjective expected utility theory does not provide a good prediction—not even a good approximation—of actual behaviour'.

Maybe the importance given to risk will be the most important and enduring contribution of the decision theory approaches to decision analysis.

Though the necessary mathematics of probability analysis are well established, the essential information, and the large number of events required in a period, is usually missing.

An axiom of formal decision theory is that probability distribution can be derived about the uncertain factors which will help shape the outcome of a decision (Wright 1983). As with the axiom of utility analysis, the advocacy, and aceptance, of the use of probabilities in farm management decisions are matters of belief (Wright 1983). The belief has to be that the approach and the estimates pass tests of commonsense.

In practice, decision makers have to take a gamble and bear the consequences. Judgements about probabilities have to be made, either explicitly or implicitly (Officer and Anderson 1968). Decision makers are thus conscripts to the faith of probability approaches to decision making. Given this, some thinking about 'the odds' in decisions is useful in practice. It is worth noting that farmers take a multitude of actions to set themselves and their businesses up in a way which will assist them to cope with the risks of their game, while planning to stay in the game with a winning chance over the long haul.

Systems approaches

As people working in academic farm management came to realize that traditional production economics covered only part of the management story and was not appropriate for farm management, some started to cast around for an approach which might be more useful. Hence the appeal of systems approaches came into being.

Dillon (1978) recommended that training in farm management should be reorientated away from the traditional production economic, joint farm and national policy focus of the agricultural economists, to a farm systems approach orientated solely to farmers, retaining the essentially useful bits of the production economic way of thinking. Dillon noted that systems analysis is the appropriate conceptional way of thinking for farm management. He added although that farm management remains 'too complex' and 'too human' a process for much progress to be made in the 'systems' direction.

Inquiries into farm management require a particular interdisciplinary balance if they are to be truly about farm management. Having a good understanding of relevant elements of each discipline involved is the key to understanding the interactions between the technology; the economic and financial factors; and the human behaviour which comprise the process of farm management.

A discipline is a distinguishable set of analytics, theory and principles focusing on a particular bit of the world. Disciplines do not have clear boundaries though people working at solving problems are usually able, with a little faith, to distinguish between truly disciplinary and truly interdisciplinary pursuits. Broadly, each discipline is about searching out, understanding, and explaining that part of the world which is its focus, in order to derive general principles. The understandings and explanations are most usefully seen as being transitory, subject to swings in fashion and acceptance, and as being valid until they are replaced by more complete or new understandings and explanations. As well, there are always many competing explanations for the same phenomena. This is shown by rigorous and vigorous academic debates in every discipline.

Agricultural economics is primarily economic, and narrow enough in scope to be seen as disciplinary. Conversely, farming systems approaches to describe and to explain agricultural realities are not disciplinary but are interdisciplinary.

The process of analysing the choices and decisions facing the manager of a farm business is an interdisciplinary activity. Farm management, being interdisciplinary, comes within the realm of what Von Bertalanffy (1968) called 'general systems theory'. Boulding, the father of modern systems theory (1956) asserts that general systems theory is not:

a single self contained general theory of practically everything, to replace all the special theories of particular disciplines. Such a theory would be almost without content, for we always pay for generality by sacrificing content, and all we can say about practically everything is almost nothing.

Boulding says that somewhere between the specific that has no meaning (mathematical abstractions) and the general that has no content, there must be optimum degrees of generality, for particular purposes. And, 'it is the contention of the General Systems Theorists that this optimum degree of generality in theory is not always reached by the particular sciences'.

A further view about systems approaches, relatively commonly expressed, is that increasing specialization inhibits communication between disciplines, with a concomitant increase in the danger of specializing into irrelevancy.

The farm management worker has to be conversant with key aspects of many disciplines, and be able to communicate with various disciplinary specialists.

The question of 'optimum degree of generality' (or specificity) is the core of the debate on the allocation of limited research and educational resources between disciplinary and interdisciplinary study and research.

Students of agriculture need to do more than describe 'what is' on a farm. They need to be able to explain and analyse. To do so they need to be able to draw on disciplinary principles and knowledge of the inter-relationships between the many important aspects of a farm business.

In the article 'General Systems as a Point of View', Boulding (1974) pointed out the danger of superficiality inherent in (descriptive) systems approaches in an empirical world which is far beyond the capacity of any one mind to know. He put the case for disciplinary specialization, viz:

My wife has a standard formula, for which I endeavour to be grateful, for deflating me whenever my general systems visions soar too high. She says simply, 'If you are going to be the great integrator you ought to know something'.

He continued:

One obvious safeguard against the worst forms of superficiality is a firm foundation of knowledge in at least one empirical discipline. Before the general systems man takes off into the outer space of his ignorance, he ought at least to have a launching pad in some discipline where he can reasonably claim to be an expert. He must have the courage not merely to take refuge in a well-tended little plot of specialized knowledge but he should also feel that his most important and most secure contributions comes when he brings back and applies to his own specialized fields the insights which have come to him during his aerial surveys of the whole empirical universe. The ideal general systems man must be willing to talk nonsense outside his own field but must be equally unwilling to talk nonsense inside it.

Central to questions about systems approach is the emphasis placed on disciplinary versus interdisciplinary areas of study. 'Interdisciplinary means no discipline' is more than a tautology; it also reflects the view that mere knowledge of inter-relationships is not sufficient to enable one to understand and explain the operation of the whole, unless the interdisciplinary knowledge is backed by and built on a sound disciplinary basis.

Leeper (1959) defended disciplinary-based study in 'Holism, A Menace to Science', challenging the view that 'You cannot understand or make a sensible statement about a thing unless you know everything about it', with Bertrand Russell's riposte 'How then can knowledge ever begin?'

In farm management, the key to understanding the outcome of the interactions between technology, economics, and human behaviour, and to understanding the interactions themselves, is to have a good grasp of relevant elements of each discipline.

Of these disciplines, economics is a particularly important discipline for farm management. Economic considerations integrate the many diverse components that determine the output of a farm business. Most farmers are motivated to a large degree by the aim of making a profit.

The complexity of each farm business means that farm management analysis and planning has to be at once 'very general' and 'very specific'. The uncertainty about the precise relationships between all the inputs and all the outputs, and even what all the inputs and outputs are, for a particular farm and a particular time, means that farm management analyses and plans have to be built on broad approximations of points on response functions.

The complexity of farm business means that the 'optimal degree of generality' for farm management inquiries, as dictated by the ability of anyone to know more and more about more and more, is very general indeed. Furthermore farm management is about analysis for decisions in specific cases. It is difficult to derive general principles about farm management from the detailed analyses of diverse cases.

Systems modelling approaches to farm problems are limited because of flaws of holism. There is the flaw, from the view of scientific research, of being unable to say anything about anything until you know everything about it, the end of scientific discovery.

There is also the flaw, from the view of depth of knowledge, of limitations to knowing more and more and more and more, i.e., advancing knowledge in both depth and breadth. Thus in academic work in farming systems which goes into greater depth than the systems work of the farm management professionals, there are problems with the question of where the boundaries of the system are drawn.

The inadequacy of the farm systems modelling approaches for farm management purposes is compounded when the focus is essentially agricultural science–systems, with important economic, financial, behavioural, and institutional factors either unheard of, caricatured or considered as an afterthought.

Systems approach which attach 'some economics' at the end, and then become deductive, overlook the reality that economics is the discipline which is involved throughout the operation of the system; from first playing a major role in setting the agenda for the operation of the farm business to being involved in every input decision within the system.

Further, of course, there is the important question of including the time, dynamics and riskiness which affects the farm system. The opposite case, economic models which are inadequate on technical and behavioural aspects, are just as irrelevant for farm management decision-making purposes.

Anderson (1974) and Dalton (1974) recognized the possible, even probable, inappropriateness of decision analysis using systems simulation as a basis for individual farm management decision making. Anderson cautioned against the 'overselling' of the prospects for simulation in agricultural economics, reminding us that 'simulation can be an expensive tool for solving simple problems'.

Blackie and Dent (1974) asserted that, despite sophisticated simulation methodology being developed to assist analysis and planning of the farm business, the impact had been limited because the real information requirements of the farmer had not been met, i.e., the necessary requirements for feedback between performance and the established plan had usually been missing.

They hoped that skeleton models would become a useful method whereby simulation models could be constructed for use at low cost to the individual firm (Dent and Blackie 1974, 1979; Dent 1975). They saw simulation as, at least, providing a general planning facility for 'typical' farms which advisory personnel can use to 'develop a feel for management action' (Richie, Dent, & Blackie 1978).

Farming systems approaches need not fail. Farm systems approaches can be a practical solution to understanding and analysing farm management problems, as shown at the level at which good farm management professionals have always operated. It is a matter of having the right balance of disciplinary emphases to be able to analyse and to help solve farmers' problems.

But, for the above-mentioned reasons, farm management economists, who are concerned with the technical, economic, financial, institutional, and human aspects of farm businesses, assert that farm management could well be about 'farming systems' but 'farming systems', as the term is generally used, is not about farm management.

Farm management practitioners and farming systems researchers seem to differ in their view as to what is 'the optimal degree of generality'. The unappealing reality to technical systems researchers is that the 'optimal degree of generality' could be general indeed. The other unappealing reality to farming systems devotees is that each farm business 'system' is unique.

Arguably, a major reason for continued use of the traditional budgeting methods in farm management is that these allow a sufficiently comprehensive view of the problems, in enough interdisciplinary depth and breadth, to allow rational judgements to be confidently made about farm management actions. It is better to address the whole of the problem (system) and devise some solution than to elaborately model and 'solve' a part of the problem (system) extremely well.

Attempts to model 'representative' whole farm systems, as distinct from modelling discrete parts of a system, for farm management purposes, run into the problem that the operation of farm businesses is so complex, stochastic, and unique that even very elaborate models of the operation of representative whole farm business are still too general to be used to give sensible, individual farm management advice.

Once timing of inputs is recognized as, in some ways, an input itself, and variability of inputs considered, it is evident that there are innumerable different, and precise, farm systems. Systems approaches have made little progress at the farm level because attempts to model the particular on-farm complexities sufficiently realistically to be able to analyse decisions and give farm-by-farm management advice result in an intractable model (Dent 1975).

The best systems simulation can do in farm management is provide expert systems which can produce information about specific, usually technical aspects of a farm management decision. This information is then assimilated with all the other information needed in a farm management decision.

Farming might be, as Dillon (1978) put it, both too complex and too human an activity for much progress to be made in this direction. Hence practical farm management analyses will continue to have to be built on approximations of uncertain and shifting response functions which are based on broad groupings of inputs and outputs, allied to judgements and expectations about imperfectly known factors, giving full account to management's objectives, skills, and needs.

Traditional budgets and the quantitative methods

Techniques for analysing a decision on a farm can be categorized, arbitrarily, into two broad approaches. There are elaborate quantitative techniques, e.g. systems simulation, mathematical programming and expected utility methods. These have proved to be essentially non-operational tools of decision analysis for farm management, and often do not focus on the critical considerations.

The other approach, is cruder and simpler, and uses budgeting techniques, is less elaborate. This approach is used relatively widely and, even though it is relatively simple, it is more likely to focus on the important aspects in the analysis.

The quantitative methods aim at capturing, more fully, some of the relationships between the numerous parts which, in sum, go to make up a farm business. Users of these techniques try to account formally for the reality that decisions about what to do on the farm usually have a number of objectives which need to be satisfied, and that there is a large number of constraints on reaching those objectives. There are numerous discussions, examples and critiques of this type of decision technique in the literature.

Many of the limitations and inappropriateness of these approaches for individual farm management are acknowledged in the aforementioned literature. The 'curse of dimensionality' (Hardaker 1979) which restricts the capacity of any of the quantitative tools to account sufficiently for the full complexities of the operation of a farm business is acknowledged generally.

Interestingly, two researchers who, from the late 1960s through to the end of the 1970s, explored the possibilities of the quantitative decision techniques in immense depth and breadth, Anderson and Hardaker 1979, concluded towards the end of the 1970s that farm managers' intuition was paramount in decision analysis and decision making, and thus this significantly limited the scope for the elaborate quantitative techniques to contribute to comprehensive decision analysis (Anderson and Hardaker 1979).

The traditional farm management budgets continue in practice to be the core of farm management analyses. Nearly all of the quantitative techniques have never been used for decision analysis at the farm level, other than in the initial research and development phases of the techniques. There are many valid reasons for the lack of application of these techniques.

The quantitative techniques are prone to the failing of 'the technique defining the problem', when the critical art in farm management is identifying what is the problem. These methods often sacrifice breadth for depth. The high level of quantitative precision they require can be gained, in the current state of things, only by reducing the scope of what is analysed so much that some of the most important problems remain outside the analysis.

As well, focus on the quantitative analytics, which tended to be rigorous and logical, often took focus away from the farm family decision makers, who may exhibit neither of these features.

Though the simple budgeting techniques use broad measures of expected quantities of inputs and outputs, prices, risk and variability; and the focus is usually on a number of single measures, such as most likely extra profit; rate of growth in equity; likely cash flow and debt-service capability; and magnitude of possible losses; the total dimension of the situation is more readily included in the analysis.

The decision maker is then about to focus on the wide range of technical, economic, financial, institutional and human factors which are important in the decision and which will affect the outcomes. As well, the process of doing the simple budgets, whether the decision maker works alone or with an adviser, involves much weighing of relevant information.

A technological development has enhanced the usefulness of the traditional budgets for farm management. The computer spreadsheet has greatly improved the analytical power of the traditional farm management budgets in a number of ways.

Academic farm management work of the past has been characterized by an inappropriate balance between the various disciplinary fields involved in farm management. Whereas the agricultural economists have long eschewed the agricultural element, other than as a description of their area of applied economic interest, and appropriately so too, farm management workers cannot afford this luxury if they are to be relevant.

The development of the computer spreadsheet offers the best chance to date for incorporating all of the important elements in farm management analysis in an interdisciplinary balance which makes for relevant farm management analysis.

Despite the limitations of the relevance of formal production theory to farming practice, key ideas of production economics such as diminishing returns; substitution; equi-marginality and opportunity cost; fixed and variable costs; and the key concept of production surfaces; remain sufficiently valuable to farm management to be the subject of research efforts, and can, to some extent, be incorporated in the spreadsheet–budgeting approach. The computer spreadsheet enhances the potential analytical uses of farm activity budgets and could have a role in giving production economic principles greater relevance to real-farm management.

Budgeting, using the spreadsheet, makes possible explicit considerations of changes over time, risks, technical efficiency, and managerial objectives and preferences. For instance, the spreadsheet offers the budget analyst great scope to efficiently 'creep' around 'production surfaces' to technically feasible, increasingly profitable farm plans, under a range of changed circumstances.

Certainly the scope now is greater than Cocks (1964) could have envisaged when he advocated creep budgeting as a practical alternative to formal programming approaches, or by Schultz (1939) when he stressed the importance of adjustment to changed circumstances and the role of expectations in agricultural production.

The technology, the management–human element, and to a large degree dynamic–financial aspects such as gearing and growth were relatively neglected in farm management work up until the 1980s. The traditional budgets offer the best prospects of the available techniques for ensuring that all of the important dimensions of a decision are properly considered. The use of budgets on the spreadsheet enables the following to be incorporated into analyses to varying degrees of usefulness:

1 The technology as it applies to individual activities, through activity budgets.
2 The useful equi-marginal or substitution or opportunity cost ways of thinking.
3 The management–human element through the spreadsheet model being specific and unique to each situation, incorporating intimate knowledge of possibilities and constraints, and decision-makers' preferences and beliefs, in the activities analysed and the numbers put in the budgets.
4 The financial aspects by whole farm cash budgeting of different scenarios, through time, for different gearing ratios, rates of return and interest rates.
5 The uncertainty through the incorporation of the decision-makers' preferences and beliefs in, and about, the 'what-if' scenarios and sensitivity testings.

The scope for 'what-if' testing of parts of farm plans using the spreadsheet gives the decision maker some idea of the magnitude of various consequences, and a range of possible outcomes.

The likelihood of these events happening can then be weighed and judgements formed. While the problems of the lack of information about future happenings remain restrictive, the spreadsheet enables numerous calculations to be done easily, enabling a usefully comprehensive 'risk picture' to be built.

The problem then changes slightly from the difficulties stemming from having too little information to frame a good market, to the difficulties of having too much information from the 'what-if' pictures for the decision maker to assimilate and make a good decision. It is useful to work towards the end of saying 'If you take this gamble and these outcomes occur, these are the possible consequences, and the chances of these outcomes occurring might be. . . That's the best current information, make of it what you will.'

There is one other possible advantage stemming from the use of the computer spreadsheet and the traditional budgets. It is to do with the need to evaluate the research ideas and results of agricultural science in terms of the whole farm (Williams 1958).

The inevitable gap between research and application can be narrowed with simple budget approaches to analyses. It helps improved assessment of the possible ranges of values of changes to production systems at the whole farm level and, conversely, helps improved 'before the race' evaluation of research proposals.

This happens in two ways: despite the uncertainty about the ultimate net effects on whole farm performance of changes within the production system, ranges of possible whole farm outcomes can be explored using the spreadsheet; and judgements about the likelihood of various 'scenarios' then have to be made.

Second, if the costs of a possible but yet-to-be-researched change to the system are identified, then the levels of performance can be defined which would be required from the components of the production system under study, for the change to show a satisfactory return on capital. Assessment has to be on the basis of whole farm performance. If the economically required levels of performance have a sufficiently high probability of being achievable, then the research is worth doing.

Whole farm budgeting on a spreadsheet framework offers scope to capture all of the important effects of changes to agricultural production systems and establish a 'picture' of the 'worth' of a particular development, for a particular farm or for *ex ante* evaluation of research proposals.

Some (of many) incisive and useful comments made in the past about farm management

In this section are some comments we believe to be incisive and useful, made by a number of researchers in the past. These include Campbell's comments on research (1967), Williams on extension and the fallacy of the foolish farmer (1958), Musgrave on farm management (1976), Menz and Longworth (1976) and Buggie (1976) on allocative ability and on the limitations imposed on the role of sophisticated farm planning and record-keeping approaches in farm management by the limited ability of the potential users to use them, and the need for a range of methods and techniques in keeping with the range of abilities of people in farming.

Research: Campbell 1957

At the inaugural conference of the Australian Agricultural Economics Society Campbell (1957) contributed to a Symposium titled 'Contemporary Agricultural Economics in Australia'. He looked at agricultural economics research. His major criticism of agricultural economics research in Australia is worth quoting:

If I were asked to diagnose the major deficiency of agriculture economics research in Australia in the past decade, I would say that it lacked analytical orientation. I realise that this is a rather serious indictment, because to my mind, the essence of research is the attempt to confirm or deny hypotheses about the nature of reality. In the absence of clearly-formulated hypotheses or models, it is arguable whether what is done is research in the strict sense at all. Many field surveys have been undertaken in this country simply with the hazy idea of getting 'the facts about a specific region'. Too often when these studies have been completed, we have witnessed (to paraphrase Lionel Robbins) the disconcerting spectacle of research workers rediscovering the crashing truisms of agriculture and economics and leaping from the bath, so to speak, with Archimedean enthusiasm running naked through the city recommending them stridently to all and sundry.

Campbell avoided criticism of Australian agricultural economics which had been expressed by Sir Samuel Wadham, viz:

I have never known whether I deserve to be called an agricultural economist because my concept of an economist is one who is much more interested in the processes of investigating economic problems than I am, and further, one who is often so wrapped up in building up an academic facade around the problems that he becomes less interested in the problems themselves (cited in Campbell 1957).

Farm management was described by Campbell (1957) as an important field of study that had often been dominant in agricultural economics research, but which had not made much impact.

Campbell said that real progress in farm management depended upon farmers getting individual farm management advice by hiring farm management consultant services operated by private enterprise or possibly by universities and agricultural colleges. Public agencies could not afford to provide the highly specialized attention to individual farm businesses required for effective farm management.

Extension: Williams 1958

Williams (1958) criticized neglect of the social sciences by agricultural scientists which showed up when advisers attempted to use research results for extension purposes, and found the results inadequate for developing an extension program.

Allied to these criticisms was what Williams called the 'fallacy of the foolish farmer'. This fallacy 'leads the agriculturalist to act as if he knows better than the farmer what is good for him, and to believe that farmers who don't adopt his recommendations are foolish indeed'. He went on:

Failure to take account of the real motives behind decisions by farmers is based on the fallacy that they all have, or should have, identical motives when they set about their farm operations. Advice about mechanization, pasture improvement, fodder conservation, drought feeding or the need for structural improvements, is sometimes given in a way which suggests that the farmers are all motivated by the same desire to increase income. But significant differences exist between farmers as to problems of raising the necessary capital, bearing the risks involved, or achieving the higher level of management which the change requires. Quite often the position is set out in the form of the little sum, which may even take the form of a budget of costs and returns. If one believed the sum, the farmer would indeed be foolish not to plunge headlong into the proposal. But so often the sum does not portray the position as the farmer sees it; so often the scientist has to move beyond the firm basis of his scientific knowledge to shrewd guesses as to what motivates the particular farmer concerned. Instead of relying on shrewd guesses, we need to widen the frontier of scientific knowledge to cover the problems of human motivation. Then we can increase the range of circumstances in which it is feasible to take advantage of such major research findings as those relating to farm mechanization, pasture improvement and drought feeding.

Farm management: Musgrave 1976

Musgrave had this to say:

In the field of farm management many techniques have been called but most have been found wanting. Superficially the impression could be gained that, after the first ecstatic breakthrough with the application of budgeting procedures, there has been a sustained rummaging through a job lot of techniques, mainly of a programming nature, which, while producing many masters and Ph.D. theses and perhaps a few unthinking technicians, has not produced many useful farm management recommendations of either a general or a specific nature. It is not surprising that, outside the unilluminating category of 'research technique', most of the concentration on methodology was in the field of farm management.

However, Musgrave considered that all had not been wasted:

The conceptual apparatus which production economics provided for the guidance of resource and product combinations was very powerful indeed. The techniques of regression and linear programming, coupled with computers, enable the empirical testing of these concepts in an increasingly ambitious way. However, with the passage of time it became obvious that the concepts and techniques were not powerful enough in relation to the managerial problems which their use had enabled us to define. The restricted information content of the various deterministic models which had been developed did not warrant the expenditure of more than small sums of money on their use in practical farm management.

Following these discoveries there has been a search for ways of overcoming these problems posed by time and the refusal of decision makers to restrict their objectives to profit maximizing. This has led, increasingly to the study of the role of uncertainty in decision making. As a result the door has been opened on a vast and complex field well beyond the neoclassical starting points of the profession in Australia ... Maybe success when it arrives will be somewhat anti-climatic for it is possible, as Anderson and Hardaker suggest, that the scope for intuition will always be high in farm management and that our techniques will be restricted to the definition of efficient solution sets.

In conclusion Musgrave (1976) said:

In the field of farm management proper I have argued that the profession, while not being directly productive at the farm level, has not engaged in a sterile and repetitive use of irrelevant techniques. Rather it should be regarded as having been engaged on a long search for theories and models of the management process which will reinforce budgeting as the most important technique in the field. Rather than remaining trapped in a sterile positivistic trap it has been in the main conditionally normative and I would say that the main thrust in the field is now distinctly normative and that the political economists would applaud this development. However, it cannot be denied that a theoretician–practitioner gap remains. I detect a feeling among workers in farm management that the problem is too great and the potential rewards too few for a more analytical approach to replace or strengthen significantly the present inductive, intuitive approach. Even if this is true, the work must be continued because of the conceptual basis it provides for practical farm management workers. The problem is that material suport for such work may become attenuated because its shadow price is less immediately obvious to the allocators of research funds.

Allocative ability: Menz and Longworth (1976)

In one of the diminishing number of articles about farm management which appeared in the professional journal literature during the latter parts of the decade, Menz and Longworth (1976) wrote an important article about allocative ability, information processing, and farm management. They commented that the range of formal farm planning models which had been developed from the 1950s to the mid-1970s were rarely used by commercial farmers.

One 'overwhelming' reason for this they considered may have been 'that these mathematical models are not really capable of representing the actual decision problems of greatest interest to farm managers'. The essential feature which was missing from the planning models was the need by managers to constantly adjust operations as information feeds back from the dynamic system. The ability to adjust they termed 'allocative ability', which is the ability to acquire and use information efficiently. They continued:

Allocative ability is extremely important in modern agriculture. Overseas, technological change has received attention as a major factor constantly altering the conditions under which farmers operate. For example, Harle says: 'in practice, one is always moving towards a continually improving and adjusting technical efficiency, rather than allocating at a state of technical efficiency'. In the Australian context, the climatic, disease, price and even political uncertainties and instabilities faced by farm managers, guarantee the importance of allocative ability without the added challenge of new technology. In many Australian farming situations, timely short-term adjustments are likely to be more important in determining the long-run economic result than the general farming system employed.   (Menz and Longworth 1976)

As Menz and Longworth saw it, allocative ability is linked to information processing. Farm operators placed less emphasis on data than physical and labouring skills. The traditional approach to farm management information had emphasized the keeping of records, but often as an end in itself. The main reason farmers did not keep adequate records was that they lacked the data-handling skills to make use of recorded information. They concluded:

It is often claimed that 'you can't teach management'. Such statements imply that experience or intuition plays the dominant role in successful management. However, 'experience' and 'intuition' are merely terms used to describe various information processing systems. A preferable term is 'allocative ability' which highlights the constant need to adjust resources in the light of changing circumstances. Allocative ability can be enhanced by education related to the acquision and manipulation of data and by specific data processing techniques (allowing the speed and scope of manipulation to be increased). Perhaps more emphasis could be devoted to this aspect of farm management by the relevant training, extension and research institutions.   (Menz and Longworth 1976)

Buggie (1977) responded to Menz and Longworth. Buggie regarded 'allocative ability' as possibly being largely intelligence. If this is so he said then the possibilities for improvement in allocative ability through education and better farmer use of data-handling techniques could be overstated. Buggie concluded:

I agree with Menz and Longworth that there is need for farm planning models that are more relevant to farmers. However, this does not necessarily imply a need to develop farm planning/farm record-keeping models that are more sophisticated and more complex. As farmers have different levels of intellectual capacity, there is need for a range of models. Indeed, I suggest that there are many farmers whose intellectual capacity and other attributes are such that they are not going to significantly benefit from attempts to teach them decision making/record-keeping procedures that are different to those they now use.

Further, on this theme of adapting the content of extension and education to the learner, there should always be consideration of the possibility that more might be achieved (by a given teacher and a given learner) from concentrating on agricultural technology rather than on farm business management.

Concluding comments

Most of the main emphases in the past to farm management problems came and went without too many farmer decision makers even noticing them. For very good reasons, computerized record analysis, comparative gross margins, and commercial linear programming services have waxed and waned a little in popularity, ranging from negligible to negligible in the amount of their use by farmers. However, these emphases have all added positively in various ways to what we know now.

Farm management is a complex, interdisciplinary, uncertain and changing process. Most importantly, the balance of the many parts which constitute the process of farm management has to be 'right'; otherwise the best of bits of work on parts of the problem will be to no avail.

The literature of the Australian agricultural economic and farm management profession since the early 1940s contains evidence of numerous emphases which have prevailed at various times; emphases which reflect different weightings applied to the balance of the farm management mixture.

It was inevitable that new developments in any one of these areas could only come about from increasing specialization; and thus the new emphases that prevailed at different times and the new techniques that were developed, inevitably weighted the balance of the field of inquiry in the direction of the part of the process with which the new development was concerned.

The major reason for the limited relevance of a good deal of academic work in farm management to farm management is probably to be found in the methodology. The basic production economic model leaves out most of the really important things for farm management, viz., the technology, the human element, the risk, the dynamics, and time.

However, there are many other reasons why academic work in farm management ended up so many pathways which Candler (1962) described as 'blind alleys'. Some reasons are to do with the nature of the farming environment. Campbell (1957) was correct when he suggested that farm management as a 'science' had not made much headway in Australia because of insufficient whole farm emphasis, the inadequacy of the essentially static theory for Australia's highly uncertain agriculture, the extensive and diversified nature of farming activities, and the regular occurrence of significant technological improvements which at any time reduced the importance of making more efficient use of current technology.

The same can be said for the comments by Williams about the complexity and uniqueness of the farm management situation, and the importance of the human, social, and institutional factors, and the dynamic aspects, in determining the eventual outcome of the process called 'farm management'.

Farmers have little scope for control over outcomes, thus planning and decision analysis is relatively of less importance in a range of competing management needs and objectives (Wright 1983). Further, planning is a continuous process. It might be that the most important factor in management success is having technical skills, mastery of information, and plenty of equity. It might well be that institutional factors beyond the farmer's control are more significant determinants of the state of the farm business than is 'farm management'.

Approaches to farm management questions which have been judged to have not been highly relevant or directly useful as theoretical or practical contributions to farm management still have a part to play as part of rigorous and well-rounded courses in agricultural economics and agricultural science. Methodological pluralism is essential for progress to be made in any field.

Understanding of the whole farm, composed as it is of many complex bits, is a useful field of study for students of agricultural science and agricultural economics. An educational imperative is that interdisciplinary linkages be seen by students even if, being a field for specialist generalists, farm management itself does not lead to the deeper specialist knowledge engendered by higher research in the strictly disciplinary pursuits.

Further, intra-disciplinary linkages are important. Economists are all the better trained if they also have a feel for key factors which govern production possibilities and performance at the production–management level. The reverse of this is also true. It is becoming more important that people involved in farm management have a good understanding of the dynamics at work in the modern economy 'beyond the farm gate'.

In a theoretical sense, the most significant benefit from studying farm management is that a good appreciation of the complexities and the subtleties involved, deriving as it must from a sound knowledge of the relevant disciplines and their interactions, provides stark and salutary reminders about the limitations of the disciplines involved. Appreciating the limitations of ruling paradigms is not anti-intellectual but, to the contrary, is the essence of intellectual inquiry.

The importance placed on the timing of a change in farm plan or financial tactics by a farmer *vis-à-vis* the industry, and, equally important, the clear recognition of the role of industry-level arbitrage between all markets, are two of the most outstanding features which distinguish good farm management advisers.

Exposing agricultural scientists to serious economic ideas, particularly those who could later become systems devotees, could be the most suitable means for dispelling the tendency of agricultural scientists to embrace 'folk economics' (Boulding 1974) which derive largely by analogy from individual experience to the economic system as a whole, the conclusions from which are very often fallacious.

Academic work in farm management economics can make a large contribution to the production of better agricultural economists and scientists by highlighting the severe limitations of their models of reality. And, almost as a bonus, if we were to get it right, academic work in farm management should also make some contributions to the process of farm management.

Farmers and their advisers need to adapt constantly to change, though the nature of the questions, and the thinking processes which constitute farm analysis and planning have changed little over time. The focus of academic work in farm management has been through several major phases, as fashions come and go, and as technology changes. In future the nature of the questions facing farmers will be little different from those questions farmers have faced, have answered, and have acted on throughout history.

Obviously the importance of devising good answers to the right questions becomes greater as pressures on farm financial circumstances continue to intensify. The use of traditional budgets and the spreadsheet to explore and to help solve problems about the management of farms in a dynamic environment might contribute to narrowing the gap which always exists between the findings of research into aspects of farm management and the application of these findings to the management of particular farms.

Because of the difficulties involved, and because future developments along the lines discussed will not require major new methodological tricks, progress in farm management will probably continue to occur at the relatively sedate rate of the past. Progress will also be slow because in future, as in the past, the challenges and the rewards for most will be greater in agricultural economics research, rather than in work in farm management. For those so inclined, there is plenty to be going on with.

10

References

Anderson, J. R. (1972), 'An overview of modelling in agricultural management', *Review of Marketing and Agricultural Economics*, 40 (3), 111–123.

————(1974), 'Simulation: methodology and application in agricultural economics', *Review of Marketing and Agricultural Economics*, 42 (1), 3–55.

Anderson, J. R., Dillon, J. L., & Hardaker, J. B. (1977), *Agricultural Decision Analysis*, Iowa State University Press, Ames.

Anderson, J. R. and Hardaker J. B. (1979), 'Economic Analysis in Design of New Technologies for Small Farmers, in Valdes A., Scobie G., & Dillon, J. L. (eds), *Economics and the Design of Small-Farmer Technology*, Iowa State University Press, Ames, pp.11–26.

Boulding, K. E. (1956), 'General systems theory: The skeleton of science', *Management Science*, 2 (3), 197–208.

————(1974), 'General Systems as a Point of View' in Singell, L. D. (ed.), *Collected Papers Vol.4. Toward a General Social Science*, Colorado Associated University Press, Boulder Colorado, pp.209–222.

Buggie, G. (1977), 'Allocative ability and farm management: A comment', *Review of Marketing and Agricultural Economics*, 45 (1–2), 51–55.

Campbell, K. O. (1957), 'Contemporary agricultural economics in Australia', *Review of Marketing and Agricultural Economics*, 25 (1–2), 24–33.

————(1978), 'Review of *Survey of Agricultural Economics Literature. Volume 1*. edited by Martin, L. R.', *Australian Journal of Agricultural Economics*, 22 (1), 76–77.

Candler, W. and Sargent, D. (1962), 'Farm standards and the theory of production', *Journal of Agricultural Economics*, 15 (2), 282–290.

Cary, J. W. and Holmes, W. E. (1982), 'Relationships among farmers' goals and farm adjustment strategies: Some empirics of a multidimensional approach', *Australian Journal of Agricultural Economics*, 26 (2), 114–130.

Cocks, K. D. (1963), 'Review of Farm *Business Management: The Decision Making Process*' (by Castle, E. N., Becker, M. M., Macmillan, New York), *Australian Journal of Agricultural Economics*, 7 (1), 80–81.

————(1964), 'Creep budgeting', *Review of Marketing and Agricultural Economics*, 32 (3), 137–148.

Dalton, G. E. (ed.) (1974), *Study of Agricultural Systems*, Applied Science Publishers Ltd, London.

Dent, J. B. (1975), 'The application of systems theory in agriculture', Chapter 3 in Dalton, G. E. (ed.), *Study of Agricultural Systems*, Applied Science Publishers Ltd, London.

Dent, J. B. and Blackie, M. J. (1979), *Systems Simulation in Agriculture*, Applied Science Publishers Ltd, London.

Dillon, J. L. (1971a), 'An expository review of Bernoullian decision theory in agriculture', *Review of Marketing and Agricultural Economics*, 39 (1), 3–80.

————(1978), An Evaluation of the State of Affairs in Farm Management, Paper to Annual Conference of the Agricultural Economics Society of South Africa, Stellenbosch.

Hardaker, J. B. (1979), 'A Review of Some Farm Management Research Methods for Small-Farm Development in LDCs', *Journal of Agricultural Economics*, 30, 315–324.

Harle, J. T. (1974), 'Further towards a more dynamic approach to farm planning —a technically based model of the farm firm', *Journal of Agricultural Economics*, 25 (1), 153–164.

Hicks, J. R. (1939), *Value and Capital*, Oxford University Press, London.

Hoskins, W. R. (1972), The ACCRA System—Progress and Promise, Paper to the 16th Annual Conference of the Australian Agricultural Economics Society, Sydney.

Kaldor, N. (1934), 'The equilibrium of the firm', *The Economic Journal*, 44, 60–67.

Kennedy, J. O. S. (1981), 'Applications of dynamic programming to agriculture, forestry and fisheries: Review and prognosis', *Review of Marketing and Agricultural Economics*, 49 (3), 141–173.

Leeper, G. W. (1959), 'Holism, a Menace to Science', *Agros*, School of Agriculture, University of Melbourne, 9–12.

Longworth, J. and Menz, K. (1980), 'Activity analysis: Bridging the gap between production economic theory and practical farm management procedures', *Review of Marketing and Agricultural Economics*, 48 (1), 7–20.

Mauldon, R. (1958), 'An introduction to the application of linear programming to farming problems', *Journal of the Australian Institute of Agricultural Science*, 24 (3), 191–198.

Mauldon, R. and Schapper, H. (1970), 'Random numbers for farmers', *Journal of the Australian Institute of Agricultural Science*, 36 (4), 279–284.

—— (1971), 'The sensitivity of interfarm comparisons to inaccuracies of measurement and valuation', *Review of Marketing and Agricultural Economics*, 39 (2), 107–118.

McInerney, J. P. (1979), 'Review of *Agricultural Decision Analysis*' (by Anderson, J. R., Dillon, J. C., Hardaker, J. B., Iowa State University Press, Iowa 1977), *Journal of Agricultural Economics*, 30, 80–82.

Menz, K. and Longworth, J. (1976), 'Allocative ability, information processing and farm management', *Review of Marketing and Agricultural Economics*, 44 (4), 203–205.

Musgrave, W. F. (1963), 'Linear programming: An evaluation', *Australian Journal of Agricultural Economics*, 7 (1), 35–41.

——'Problems of change in Australian agricultural economics', *Australian Journal of Agricultural Economics*, 20 (3), 133–143.

Nuttall, P. and Moffatt, J. R. (1968), 'On the Use of Deterministic Linear Programming for Planning in a Non-Certain Environment', *Review of Marketing and Agricultural Economics*, 43 (4), 185–195.

Officer, R. R. and Anderson, J. R. (1968), 'Risk, uncertainty and management decisions', *Review of Marketing and Agricultural Economics*, 36 (1), 3–19.

Petit, M. (1978), 'Review of *Agricultural Decision Analysis* by Anderson, J. R. *et al.*' *Australian Journal of Agricultural Economics*, 22 (2), 140–141.

Richie, I. J., Dent, J. B., & Blackie, M. J. (1978), 'Irrigation management: An information approach', *Agricultural Systems*, 3, 67–74.

Schultz, T. W. (1939), 'Theory of the firm and farm management research', *American Journal of Agricultural Economics*, 21, 570–586.

Shoemaker, Paul (1982), 'The expected utility model: Its variants, purposes, evidence and limitations', *Journal of Economic Literature*, 20, 529–563.

Simon, H. A. (1983), 'Rational decision making in business organizations', Chapter 15 in Marr, W. L. and Baldey, R. (eds) *How Economists Explain*, University of America Press, New York, pp.281–315.

Stigum, B. P. and Werstop, F. (1983), *Foundations of Utility and Risk: Theory with Applications*, D. Reidel Publishing Co., (Holland).

Sturgess, N. H. (1978), 'Review of *Agricultural Decision Analysis* by Anderson, J. R. *et al.*', *Review of Marketing and Agricultural Economics*, 46 (2), 157–159.

Trebeck, D. B. and Hardaker, J. (1972), 'The integrated use of simulation and stochastic programming for whole farm planning under risk', *Australian Journal of Agricultural Economics*, 16 (2), 115–126.

Williams, D. B. (1958), 'Facts, Fancies and Fallacies, for Unscientific Scientists', *Journal of the Australian Institute of Agricultural Science*, 24 (2), 124–131.

——(1959), 'Extension economics in Australian extension services', *Australian Journal of Agricultural Economics*, 3, 24–34.

Wright, V. (1983), 'Some Bounds to the Relevance of Decision Theory', *Australian Journal of Agricultural Economics*, 27 (2), 221–230.

10

Questions for discussion

1   Comparisons of gross activity margins between different farms are of little use for farm management analysis. Discuss.

2   The average gross margin of an activity is irrelevant to a decision about a change in the size of an activity. Is this correct?

3   It is better to solve the whole of the problem roughly than solve part of the problem precisely. Is it?

4   The strength of the traditional farm management budgets is that they readily allow the full dimensions of the case at hand to be considered and thus enable all the important aspects to be appropriately weighted. What does this statement mean?

5   The key to farm management analysis is correct identification of the problem, once all the relevant information is gathered, the solution is usually obvious. Is this correct?

6   Good farm management analysis requires an appropriate balance to be given to the human, technical, financial, economic risk, and beyond-the-farm factors. Discuss.

Appendix

Table A: Growth at compound interest

Terminal value of a unit of original principal for a term of n periods at a compound rate of interest i per period $(1 + i)^n$

period	interest rate i						
n	.01(1%)	.02(2%)	.03(3%)	.035(3½%)	.04(4%)	.045(4½%)	.05(5%)
1	1.0100	1.0200	1.0300	1.0350	1.0400	1.0450	1.0500
2	1.0201	1.0404	1.0609	1.0712	1.0816	1.0920	1.1025
3	1.0303	1.0612	1.0927	1.1087	1.1249	1.1417	1.1576
4	1.0406	1.0824	1.1255	1.1475	1.1699	1.1925	1.2155
5	1.0510	1.1041	1.1593	1.1877	1.2167	1.2462	1.2763
6	1.0615	1.1262	1.1941	1.2293	1.2653	1.3023	1.3401
7	1.0721	1.1487	1.2299	1.2723	1.3159	1.3609	1.4071
8	1.0829	1.1717	1.2668	1.3168	1.3686	1.4221	1.4775
9	1.0937	1.1951	1.3048	1.3629	1.4233	1.4861	1.5513
10	1.1046	1.2190	1.3439	1.4106	1.4802	1.5530	1.6289
11	1.1157	1.2434	1.3842	1.4600	1.5395	1.6229	1.7103
12	1.1268	1.2682	1.4258	1.5111	1.6010	1.6959	1.7959
13	1.1381	1.2936	1.4685	1.5640	1.6651	1.7722	1.8856
14	1.1495	1.3195	1.5126	1.6187	1.7317	1.8519	1.9799
15	1.1610	1.3459	1.5580	1.6753	1.8009	1.9353	2.0798
16	1.1726	1.3728	1.6047	1.7340	1.8730	2.0224	2.1829
17	1.1843	1.4002	1.6528	1.7949	1.9479	2.1134	2.2920
18	1.1961	1.4282	1.7024	1.8575	2.0258	2.2085	2.4066
19	1.2801	1.4568	1.7535	1.9225	2.1068	2.3079	2.5270
20	1.2202	1.4859	1.8061	1.9898	2.1911	2.4117	2.6533

period	interest rate i						
n	.055(5½%)	.06(6%)	.065(6½%)	.07(7%)	.075(7½%)	.08(8%)	.09(9%)
1	1.0550	1.0600	1.0650	1.0700	1.0750	1.0800	1.0900
2	1.1130	1.1236	1.1342	1.1449	1.1556	1.1664	1.1881
3	1.1742	1.1910	1.2079	1.2250	1.2423	1.2597	1.2950
4	1.2388	1.2625	1.2865	1.3108	1.3355	1.3605	1.4116
5	1.3070	1.3382	1.3701	1.4026	1.4356	1.4693	1.5386
6	1.3788	1.4185	1.4591	1.5007	1.5433	1.5869	1.6771
7	1.4547	1.5036	1.5540	1.6058	1.6590	1.7138	1.8280
8	1.5347	1.5938	1.6550	1.7182	1.7835	1.8509	1.9926
9	1.6191	1.6895	1.7626	1.8385	1.9172	1.9990	2.1719
10	1.7081	1.7908	1.8771	1.9672	2.0610	2.1589	2.3674
11	1.8021	1.8983	1.9991	2.1049	2.2156	2.3316	2.5804
12	1.9012	2.0122	2.1291	2.2522	2.3818	2.5182	2.8127
13	2.0058	2.1329	2.2675	2.4098	2.5604	2.7196	3.0658
14	2.1161	2.2609	2.4149	2.5785	2.7524	2.9372	3.3417
15	2.2325	2.3966	2.5718	2.7590	2.9589	3.1722	3.6425
16	2.3553	2.5404	2.7390	2.9522	3.1808	3.4259	3.9703
17	2.4848	2.6928	2.9170	3.1588	3.4194	3.7000	4.3276
18	2.6215	2.8543	3.1067	3.3799	3.6758	3.9960	4.7171
19	2.7656	3.0256	3.3086	3.6165	3.9515	4.3157	5.1417
20	2.9178	3.2071	3.5236	3.8697	4.2479	4.6601	5.6044

continued

period	interest rate i					
n	.10(10%)	.11(11%)	.12(12%)	.13(13%)	.14(14%)	.15(15%)
1	1.1000	1.1100	1.1200	1.1300	1.1400	1.1500
2	1.2100	1.2321	1.2544	1.2769	1.2996	1.3225
3	1.3310	1.3676	1.4049	1.4429	1.4815	1.5209
4	1.4641	1.5181	1.5735	1.6305	1.6890	1.7490
5	1.6105	1.6851	1.7623	1.8424	1.9254	2.0114
6	1.7716	1.8704	1.9738	2.0819	2.1950	2.3131
7	1.9487	2.0762	2.2107	2.3526	2.5023	2.6600
8	2.1436	2.3045	2.4760	2.6584	2.8526	3.0590
9	2.3579	2.5580	2.7731	3.0040	3.2519	3.5179
10	2.5937	2.8394	3.1058	3.3946	3.7072	4.0456
11	2.8531	3.1518	3.4785	3.8359	4.2262	4.6524
12	3.1384	3.4984	3.8960	4.3345	4.8179	5.3502
13	3.4523	3.8833	4.3635	4.8980	5.4924	6.1528
14	3.7975	4.3104	4.8871	5.5347	6.2613	7.0757
15	4.1772	4.7846	5.4736	6.2543	7.1379	8.1371
16	4.5950	5.3109	6.1304	7.0673	8.1372	9.3576
17	5.0545	5.8951	6.8660	7.9861	9.2765	10.7613
18	5.5599	6.5435	7.6900	9.0243	10.5752	12.3754
19	6.1159	7.2633	8.6128	10.1974	12.0557	14.2318
20	6.7275	8.0623	9.6463	11.5231	13.7435	16.3665

period	interest rate i					
n	.16(16%)	.17(17%)	.18(18%)	.19(19%)	.20(20%)	.21(21%)
1	1.1600	1.1700	1.1800	1.1900	1.2000	1,2100
2	1.3456	1.3689	1.3924	1.4161	1.4400	1.4641
3	1.5609	1.6016	1.6430	1.6852	1.7280	1.7716
4	1.8106	1.8739	1.9388	2.0053	2.0736	2.1436
5	2.1003	2.1924	2.2878	2.3863	2.4883	2.5937
6	2.4364	2.5652	2.6995	2.8398	2.9860	3.1384
7	2.8262	3.0012	3.1855	3.3793	3.5832	3.7975
8	3.2784	3.5114	3.7589	4.0214	4.2998	4.5950
9	3.8030	4.1084	4.4354	4.7854	5.1598	5.5599
10	4.4114	4.8068	5.2338	5.6947	6.1917	6.7275
11	5.1173	5.6240	6.1759	6.7767	7.4301	8.1403
12	5.9360	6.5801	7.2876	8.0642	8.9161	9.8497
13	6.8858	7.6987	7.5994	9.5964	10.6993	11.9182
14	7.9875	9.0074	10.1472	11.4198	12.8392	14.4210
15	9.2655	10.5387	11.9737	13.5895	15.4070	17.4494
16	10.7480	12.3303	14.1290	16.1715	18.4884	21.1138
17	12.4677	14.4264	16.6722	19.2441	22.1861	25.5477
18	14.4625	16.8789	19.6732	22.9005	26.6233	30.9127
19	16.7765	19.7484	23.2144	27.2516	31.9480	37.4043
20	19.4608	23.1056	27.3930	32.4294	38.3376	45.2592

Table B: Present value of a future lump sum

Present value of a unit amount due in n periods at a discount rate of i per period

period	interest rate i						
n	.01(1%)	.02(2%)	.03(3%)	.035(3½%)	.04(4%)	.045(4½%)	.05(5%)
1	0.9901	0.9804	0.9709	0.9662	0.9615	0.9569	0.9524
2	0.9803	0.9615	0.9426	0.9335	0.9246	0.9157	0.9070
3	0.9706	0.9423	0.9151	0.9019	0.8890	0.8763	0.8638
4	0.9610	0.9238	0.8885	0.8714	0.8548	0.8386	0.8227
5	0.9515	0.9057	0.8626	0.8420	0.8219	0.8205	0.7835
6	0.9420	0.8880	0.8375	0.8135	0.7903	0.7679	0.7462
7	0.9327	0.8706	0.8131	0.7860	0.7599	0.7348	0.7107
8	0.9235	0.8535	0.7894	0.7594	0.7307	0.7032	0.6768
9	0.9143	0.8368	0.7664	0.7337	0.7026	0.6729	0.6446
10	0.9053	0.8203	0.7441	0.7089	0.6756	0.6439	0.6139
11	0.8963	0.8043	0.7224	0.6849	0.6496	0.6162	0.5847
12	0.8874	0.7885	0.7014	0.6618	0.6246	0.5897	0.5568
13	0.8787	0.7730	0.6810	0.6394	0.6006	0.5643	0.5303
14	0.8700	0.7579	0.6611	0.6178	0.5775	0.5400	0.5051
15	0.8613	0.7430	0.6419	0.5969	0.5553	0.5167	0.4810
16	0.8528	0.7284	0.6232	0.5767	0.5339	0.4945	0.4581
17	0.8444	0.7142	0.6050	0.5572	0.5134	0.4732	0.4363
18	0.8360	0.7002	0.5874	0.5384	0.4936	0.4528	0.4155
19	0.8277	0.6864	0.5703	0.5202	0.4746	0.4333	0.3957
20	0.8195	0.6730	0.5537	0.5026	0.4564	0.4146	0.3769

period	interest rate i						
n	.055(5½%)	.06(6%)	.065(6½%)	.07(7%)	.075(7½%)	.08(8%)	.09(9%)
1	0.9479	0.9434	0.9390	0.9346	0.9302	0.9259	0.9174
2	0.8985	0.8900	0.8817	0.8734	0.8653	0.8573	0.8417
3	0.8516	0.8396	0.8278	0.8163	0.8050	0.7938	0.7722
4	0.8072	0.7921	0.7773	0.7629	0.7488	0.7350	0.7084
5	0.7651	0.7473	0.7299	0.7130	0.6966	0.6806	0.6499
6	0.7252	0.7050	0.6853	0.6663	0.6470	0.6302	0.5963
7	0.6874	0.6651	0.6435	0.6227	0.6028	0.5835	0.5470
8	0.6516	0.6274	0.6042	0.5820	0.5607	0.5403	0.5019
9	0.6176	0.5919	0.5674	0.5439	0.5218	0.5002	0.4604
10	0.5854	0.5584	0.5327	0.5083	0.4852	0.4632	0.4224
11	0.5549	0.5268	0.5002	0.4751	0.4813	0.4285	0.3875
12	0.5260	0.4970	0.4699	0.4440	0.4199	0.3971	0.3555
13	0.4986	0.4688	0.4410	0.4150	0.3906	0.3677	0.3262
14	0.4726	0.4423	0.4141	0.3878	0.3633	0.3405	0.2992
15	0.4479	0.4173	0.3888	0.3624	0.3380	0.3192	0.2745
16	0.4246	0.3936	0.3651	0.3387	0.3144	0.2919	0.2519
17	0.4024	0.3714	0.3428	0.3166	0.2925	0.2703	0.2311
18	0.3815	0.3503	0.3219	0.2959	0.2720	0.2502	0.2120
19	0.3616	0.3305	0.3022	0.2765	0.2531	0.2317	0.1945
20	0.3427	0.3118	0.2838	0.2584	0.2354	0.2145	0.1784

continued

period	interest rate i						
n	.10(10%)	.11(11%)	.12(12%)	.13(13%)	.14(14%)	.15(15%)	.16(16%)
1	0.9091	0.9009	0.8929	0.8849	0.8772	0.8696	0.8621
2	0.8264	0.8116	0.7972	0.7831	0.7695	0.7561	0.7432
3	0.7513	0.7312	0.7118	0.6930	0.6750	0.6575	0.6407
4	0.6830	0.6587	0.6355	0.6133	0.5921	0.5717	0.5523
5	0.6209	0.5934	0.5674	0.5428	0.5194	0.4972	0.4761
6	0.5645	0.5346	0.5066	0.4803	0.4556	0.4323	0.4104
7	0.5132	0.4817	0.4523	0.4251	0.3996	0.3759	0.3538
8	0.4665	0.4339	0.4039	0.3762	0.3506	0.3269	0.3050
9	0.4241	0.3909	0.3606	0.3329	0.3075	0.2843	0.2629
10	0.3855	0.3522	0.3220	0.2946	0.2697	0.2472	0.2267
11	0.3505	0.3173	0.2875	0.2607	0.2366	0.2149	0.1954
12	0.3186	0.2858	0.2567	0.2307	0.2076	0.1869	0.1685
13	0.2897	0.2575	0.2292	0.2042	0.1821	0.1625	0.1452
14	0.2633	0.2320	0.2046	0.1807	0.1597	0.1413	0.1252
15	0.2394	0.2090	0.1827	0.1599	0.1401	0.1229	0.1079
16	0.2176	0.1883	0.1631	0.1415	0.1229	0.1069	0.0930
17	0.1978	0.1696	0.1456	0.1252	0.1078	0.0929	0.0802
18	0.1799	0.1528	0.1300	0.1108	0.0946	0.0808	0.0691
19	0.1635	0.1377	0.1161	0.0981	0.0829	0.0703	0.0596
20	0.1486	0.1240	0.1037	0.0868	0.0728	0.0611	0.0514

period	interest rate i						
n	.17(17%)	.18(18%)	.19(19%)	.20(20%)	.21(21%)	.22(22%)	.23(23%)
1	0.8547	0.8475	0.8403	0.8333	0.8264	0.8197	0.8130
2	0.7305	0.7182	0.7062	0.6944	0.6830	0.6719	0.6610
3	0.6244	0.6086	0.5934	0.5787	0.5645	0.5507	0.5374
4	0.5336	0.5158	0.4987	0.4822	0.4665	0.4514	0.4369
5	0.4561	0.4371	0.4190	0.4019	0.3855	0.3700	0.3552
6	0.3898	0.3704	0.3521	0.3349	0.3186	0.3033	0.2888
7	0.3332	0.3139	0.2959	0.2791	0.2633	0.2486	0.2348
8	0.2848	0.2660	0.2487	0.2326	0.2176	0.2038	0.1909
9	0.2434	0.2255	0.2090	0.1938	0.1799	0.1670	0.1552
10	0.2080	0.1911	0.1758	0.1615	0.1486	0.1369	0.1262
11	0.1778	0.1619	0.1476	0.1346	0.1228	0.1122	0.1026
12	0.1520	0.1372	0.1240	0.1122	0.1015	0.0920	0.0834
13	0.1299	0.1163	0.1042	0.0935	0.0839	0.0754	0.0678
14	0.1110	0.0985	0.0876	0.0779	0.0693	0.0618	0.0551
15	0.0949	0.0835	0.0736	0.0649	0.0573	0.0506	0.0448
16	0.0811	0.0708	0.0618	0.0541	0.0474	0.0415	0.0364
17	0.0693	0.0600	0.0520	0.0451	0.0391	0.0340	0.0296
18	0.0592	0.0508	0.0437	0.0376	0.0323	0.0279	0.0241
19	0.0506	0.0431	0.0367	0.0313	0.0267	0.0229	0.0196
20	0.0433	0.0365	0.0308	0.0261	0.0221	0.0187	0.0159

Table C: Present value of an annuity

Present value P of an annuity of particular value per period for a term of n periods at a compound interest rate i per period $\left[\dfrac{(1+i)^n - 1}{i(1+i)^n}\right]$

period				interest rate i			
n	.01(1%)	.02(2%)	.03(3%)	.035(3½%)	.04(4%)	.045(4½%)	.05(5%)
1	0.9901	0.9804	0.9709	0.9662	0.9615	0.9569	0.9524
2	1.9704	1.9416	1.9135	1.8997	1.8861	1.8727	1.8594
3	2.9410	2.8839	2.8286	2.8016	2.7751	2.7490	2.7232
4	3.9020	3.8077	3.7171	3.6731	3.6299	3.5875	3.5459
5	4.8534	4.7135	4.5797	4.5150	4.4518	4.3900	4.3295
6	5.7955	5.6014	5.4172	5.3285	5.2421	5.1579	5.0757
7	6.7282	6.4720	6.2303	6.1145	6.0020	5.8927	5.7864
8	7.6517	7.3255	7.0197	6.8739	6.7327	6.5959	6.4632
9	8.5660	8.1622	7.7861	7.6077	7.4353	7.2688	7.1078
10	9.4713	8.9826	8.5302	8.3166	8.1109	7.9127	7.7217
11	10.3676	9.7868	9.2526	9.0015	8.7605	8.5289	8.3064
12	11.2551	10.5753	9.9540	9.6633	9.3851	9.1186	8.8632
13	12.1337	11.3484	10.6349	10.3027	9.9856	9.6829	9.3936
14	13.0037	12.1062	11.2961	10.9205	10.5631	10.2228	9.8986
15	13.8650	12.8493	11.9379	11.5174	11.1184	10.7395	10.3797
16	14.7179	13.5777	12.5611	12.0941	11.6523	11.2340	10.8378
17	15.5622	14.2919	13.1661	12.6513	12.1657	11.7072	11.2741
18	16.3983	14.9920	13.7535	13.1897	12.6593	12.1600	11.6896
19	17.2260	15.5785	14.3238	13.7098	13.1339	12.5933	12.0853
20	18.0455	16.3514	14.8775	14.2124	13.5903	13.0079	12.4622

period				interest rate i			
n	.055(5½%)	.06(6%)	.065(6½%)	.07(7%)	.075(7½%)	.08(8%)	.09(9%)
1	0.9479	0.9434	0.9390	0.9346	0.9302	0.9259	0.9174
2	1.8463	1.8334	1.8206	1.8080	1.7956	1.7833	1.7591
3	2.6979	2.6730	2.6485	2.6243	2.6005	2.5771	2.5313
4	3.5051	3.4651	3.4258	3.3872	3.3493	3.3121	3.2397
5	4.2703	4.2124	4.1557	4.1002	4.0459	3.9927	3.8897
6	4.9955	4.9173	4.8410	4.7665	4.6938	4.6229	4.4859
7	5.6830	5.5824	5.4845	5.3893	5.2966	5.2064	5.0329
8	6.3346	6.2098	6.0887	5.9713	5.8573	5.7466	5.5348
9	6.9522	6.8017	6.6561	6.5152	6.3789	6.2469	5.9952
10	7.5376	7.3601	7.1888	7.0236	6.8641	6.7101	6.4177
11	8.0925	7.8869	7.6890	7.4987	7.3154	7.1390	6.8052
12	8.6185	8.3838	8.1587	7.9427	7.7353	7.5361	7.1607
13	9.1171	8.8527	8.5997	8.3576	8.1258	7.9038	7.4869
14	9.5896	9.2950	9.0138	8.7455	8.4892	8.2442	7.7862
15	10.0376	9.7122	9.4027	9.1079	8.8271	8.5595	8.0607
16	10.4622	10.1059	9.7678	9.4466	9.1415	8.8514	8.3126
17	10.8646	10.4773	10.1106	9.7632	9.4340	9.1216	8.5436
18	11.2461	10.8276	10.4325	10.0591	9.7060	9.3719	8.7556
19	11.6077	11.1581	10.7347	10.3356	9.9591	9.6036	8.9501
20	11.9504	11.4699	11.0185	10.5940	10.1945	9.8181	9.1285

continued

period	interest rate i					
n	.10(10%)	.11(11%)	.12(12%)	.13(13%)	.14(14%)	.15(15%)
1	0.9091	0.9009	0.8929	0.8849	0.8772	0.8696
2	1.7355	1.7125	1.6900	1.6681	1.6467	1.6257
3	2.4868	2.4437	2.4018	2.3611	2.3216	2.2832
4	3.1699	3.1024	3.0373	2.9745	2.9137	2.8550
5	3.7908	3.6959	3.6048	3.5172	3.4331	3.3522
6	4.3553	4.2305	4.1114	3.9975	3.8887	3.7845
7	4.8684	4.7122	4.5638	4.4226	4.2883	4.1604
8	5.3349	5.1461	4.9676	4.7988	4.6389	4.4873
9	5.7590	5.5370	5.3282	5.1317	4.9464	4.7716
10	6.1446	5.8892	5.6502	5.4262	5.2161	5.0188
11	6.4951	6.2065	5.9377	5.6869	5.4527	5.2337
12	6.8137	6.4924	6.1944	5.9176	5.6603	5.4206
13	7.1034	6.7499	6.4325	6.1218	5.8424	5.5831
14	7.3667	6.9819	6.6282	6.3025	6.0021	5.7245
15	7.6061	7.1909	6.8109	6.4624	6.1422	5.8474
16	7.8237	7.3792	6.9740	6.6039	6.2651	5.9542
17	8.0215	7.5488	7.1196	6.7291	6.3729	6.0472
18	8.2014	7.7016	7.2497	6.8399	6.4674	6.1280
19	8.3649	7.8393	7.3658	6.9380	6.5504	6.1982
20	8.5136	7.9633	7.4694	7.0247	6.6231	6.2593

period	interest rate i				
n	.16(16%)	.17(17%)	.18(18%)	.19(19%)	.20(20%)
1	0.8621	0.8547	0.8475	0.8403	0.8333
2	1.6052	1.5852	1.5656	1.5465	1.5278
3	2.2459	2.2096	2.1743	2.1399	2.1065
4	2.7982	2.7432	2.6901	2.6386	2.5887
5	3.2743	3.1993	3.1272	3.0576	2.9906
6	3.6847	3.5892	3.4976	3.4098	3.3255
7	4.0386	3.9224	3.8115	3.7057	3.6046
8	4.3436	4.2072	4.0776	3.9544	3.8372
9	4.6065	4.4506	4.3030	4.1633	4.0310
10	4.8332	4.6586	4.4941	4.3389	4.1925
11	5.0286	4.8364	4.6560	4.4865	4.3271
12	5.1971	4.9884	4.7932	4.6105	4.4392
13	5.3423	5.1183	4.9095	4.7147	4.5327
14	5.4675	5.2293	5.0081	4.8023	4.6106
15	5.5755	5.3242	5.0916	4.8759	4.6755
16	5.6685	5.4053	5.1623	4.9377	4.7296
17	5.7487	5.4746	5.2223	4.9897	4.7746
18	5.8178	5.5338	5.2732	5.0333	4.8122
19	5.8774	5.5845	5.3162	5.0700	4.8435
20	5.9288	5.6278	5.3527	5.1009	4.8696

Table D: Annuity whose present value is one

Annuity A whose present value is one for a term of n periods at a compound rate of interest i per period $\left[\dfrac{i(1+i)^n}{(1+i)^n-1}\right]$

period				interest rate i			
n	.01(1%)	.02(2%)	.03(3%)	.035(3½%)	.04(4%)	.045(4½%)	.05(5%)
1	1.0100	1.0200	1.0300	1.0350	1.0400	1.0450	1.0500
2	0.5075	0.5150	0.5226	0.5264	0.5302	0.5340	0.5378
3	0.3400	0.3468	0.3535	0.3569	0.3603	0.3638	0.3672
4	0.2563	0.2626	0.2690	0.2723	0.2755	0.2787	0.2820
5	0.2060	0.2122	0.2184	0.2215	0.2246	0.2278	0.2310
6	0.1725	0.1785	0.1846	0.1877	0.1908	0.1939	0.1970
7	0.1486	0.1545	0.1605	0.1635	0.1666	0.1697	0.1728
8	0.1307	0.1365	0.1425	0.1455	0.1485	0.1516	0.1547
9	0.1167	0.1225	0.1284	0.1314	0.1345	0.1376	0.1407
10	0.1056	0.1113	0.1172	0.1202	0.1233	0.1264	0.1295
11	0.0965	0.1022	0.1081	0.1111	0.1141	0.1172	0.1204
12	0.0888	0.0946	0.1005	0.1035	0.1066	0.1097	0.1128
13	0.0824	0.0881	0.0940	0.0971	0.1001	0.1033	0.1065
14	0.0769	0.0826	0.0885	0.0916	0.0947	0.0978	0.1010
15	0.0721	0.0778	0.0838	0.0868	0.0899	0.0931	0.0963
16	0.0679	0.0737	0.0796	0.0827	0.0858	0.0890	0.0923
17	0.0643	0.0700	0.0760	0.0790	0.0822	0.0854	0.0887
18	0.0610	0.0667	0.0727	0.0758	0.0790	0.0822	0.0855
19	0.0581	0.0638	0.0698	0.0729	0.0761	0.0794	0.0827
20	0.0554	0.0612	0.0672	0.0704	0.0736	0.0769	0.0802

period				interest rate i			
n	.055(5½%)	.06(6%)	.065(6½%)	.07(7%)	.075(7½%)	.08(8%)	.09(9%)
1	1.0550	1.0600	1.0650	1.0700	1.0750	1.0800	1.0900
2	0.5416	0.5454	0.5493	0.5531	0.5569	0.5608	0.5685
3	0.3707	0.3741	0.3776	0.3811	0.3845	0.3880	0.3950
4	0.2853	0.2886	0.2919	0.2952	0.2986	0.3019	0.3087
5	0.2342	0.2374	0.2406	0.2439	0.2472	0.2505	0.2571
6	0.2002	0.2034	0.2066	0.2098	0.2130	0.2163	0.2229
7	0.1760	0.1791	0.1823	0.1856	0.1888	0.1921	0.1987
8	0.1579	0.1610	0.1642	0.1675	0.1707	0.1740	0.1807
9	0.1438	0.1470	0.1502	0.1535	0.1568	0.1601	0.1668
10	0.1327	0.1359	0.1391	0.1424	0.1457	0.1490	0.1558
11	0.1236	0.1268	0.1301	0.1334	0.1367	0.1401	0.1469
12	0.1160	0.1193	0.1226	0.1259	0.1293	0.1327	0.1396
13	0.1097	0.1130	0.1163	0.1197	0.1231	0.1265	0.1336
14	0.1043	0.1076	0.1109	0.1143	0.1178	0.1213	0.1284
15	0.0996	0.1030	0.1064	0.1098	0.1133	0.1168	0.1240
16	0.0956	0.0990	0.1024	0.1059	0.1094	0.1130	0.1203
17	0.0920	0.0954	0.0989	0.1024	0.1060	0.1096	0.1170
18	0.0889	0.0924	0.0959	0.0994	0.1030	0.1067	0.1142
19	0.0862	0.0896	0.0932	0.0968	0.1004	0.1041	0.1117
20	0.0837	0.0872	0.0908	0.0944	0.0981	0.1018	0.1095

continued

period	interest rate i					
n	.10(10%)	.11(11%)	.12(12%)	.13(13%)	.14(14%)	.15(15%)
1	1.1000	1.1100	1.1200	1.1300	0.1400	1.1500
2	0.5762	0.5839	0.5917	0.5995	0.6073	0.6151
3	0.4021	0.4092	0.4163	0.4235	0.4307	0.4380
4	0.3155	0.3223	0.3292	0.3362	0.3432	0.3503
5	0.2638	0.2706	0.2774	0.2843	0.2913	0.2983
6	0.2296	0.2364	0.2432	0.2501	0.2572	0.2642
7	0.2054	0.2122	0.2191	0.2261	0.2332	0.2404
8	0.1874	0.1943	0.2013	0.2084	0.2156	0.2228
9	0.1736	0.1806	0.1877	0.1949	0.2022	0.2096
10	0.1627	0.1698	0.1770	0.1843	0.1917	0.1992
11	0.1540	0.1611	0.1684	0.1758	0.1834	0.1911
12	0.1468	0.1540	0.1614	0.1690	0.1767	0.1845
13	0.1408	0.1481	0.1557	0.1633	0.1712	0.1791
14	0.1357	0.1432	0.1509	0.1587	0.1666	0.1747
15	0.1315	0.1391	0.1468	0.1547	0.1628	0.1710
16	0.1278	0.1355	0.1434	0.1514	0.1596	0.1679
17	0.1247	0.1325	0.1405	0.1486	0.1569	0.1654
18	0.1219	0.1298	0.1379	0.1462	0.1546	0.1632
19	0.1195	0.1276	0.1358	0.1441	0.1527	0.1613
20	0.1175	0.1256	0.1339	0.1423	0.1510	0.1598

period	interest rate i				
n	.16(16%)	.17(17%)	.18(18%)	.19(19%)	.20(20%)
1	1.1600	1.1700	1.1800	1.1900	1.2000
2	0.6230	0.6308	0.6387	0.6466	0.6545
3	0.4453	0.4526	0.4599	0.4673	0.4747
4	0.3574	0.3645	0.3717	0.3790	0.3863
5	0.3054	0.3126	0.3198	0.3270	0.3344
6	0.2714	0.2786	0.2859	0.2933	0.3007
7	0.2476	0.2549	0.2624	0.2698	0.2774
8	0.2302	0.2377	0.2452	0.2529	0.2606
9	0.2171	0.2247	0.2324	0.2402	0.2481
10	0.2069	0.2147	0.2225	0.2305	0.2385
11	0.1989	0.2068	0.2148	0.2229	0.2311
12	0.1924	0.2005	0.2086	0.2169	0.2253
13	0.1872	0.1954	0.2037	0.2121	0.2206
14	0.1829	0.1912	0.1997	0.2082	0.2169
15	0.1794	0.1878	0.1964	0.2051	0.2139
16	0.1764	0.1850	0.1937	0.2025	0.2114
17	0.1739	0.1827	0.1915	0.2004	0.2094
18	0.1719	0.1807	0.1896	0.1987	0.2078
19	0.1701	0.1791	0.1881	0.1972	0.2065
20	0.1687	0.1777	0.1868	0.1960	0.2054

Table E: Terminal value of a unit annuity where $\dfrac{(1 + i)^n - 1}{i}$

(Terminal value of an annuity of unit per value per period for a term of n periods at a compound rate of interest i per period)

period				interest rate i			
n	.01(1%)	.02(2%)	.03(3%)	.035(3½%)	.04(4%)	.045(4½%)	.05(5%)
1	1.0000	1.0000	1.0000	1.0000	1.0000	1.0000	1.0000
2	2.0100	2.0200	2.0300	2.0350	2.0400	2.0450	2.0500
3	3.0301	3.0604	3.0909	3.1062	3.1216	3.1370	3.1525
4	4.0604	4.1216	4.1836	4.2149	4.2465	4.2782	4.3101
5	5.1010	5.2040	5.3091	5.3625	5.4163	5.4707	5.5256
6	6.1520	6.3081	6.4684	6.5502	6.6330	6.7169	6.8019
7	7.2135	7.4343	7.6625	7.7794	7.8983	8.0192	8.1420
8	8.2857	8.5830	8.8923	9.0517	9.2142	9.3800	9.5491
9	9.3685	9.7546	10.1591	10.3685	10.5828	10.8021	11.0266
10	10.4622	10.9497	11.4639	11.7314	12.0061	12.2882	12.5779
11	11.5668	12.1687	12.8078	13.1420	13.4864	13.8412	14.2068
12	12.6825	13.4121	14.1920	14.6020	15.0258	15.4640	15.9171
13	13.8093	14.6803	15.6170	16.1130	16.6268	17.1599	17.7130
14	14.9474	15.9739	17.0863	17.6770	18.2919	18.9321	19.5986
15	16.0969	17.2934	18.5989	19.2957	20.0236	20.7841	21.5786
16	17.2579	18.6393	20.1569	20.9710	21.8245	22.7193	23.6575
17	18.4304	20.0121	21.7616	22.7050	23.6975	24.7417	25.8404
18	19.6147	21.4123	23.4144	24.4997	25.6454	26.8551	28.1324
19	20.8109	22.8406	25.1169	26.3572	27.6712	29.0636	30.5390
20	22.0190	24.2974	26.8704	28.2797	29.7781	31.3714	33.0660

period				interest rate i			
n	.055(5½%)	.06(6%)	.065(6½%)	.07(7%)	.075(7½%)	.08(8%)	.09(9%)
1	1.0000	1.0000	1.0000	1.0000	1.0000	1.0000	1.0000
2	2.0550	2.0600	2.0650	2.0700	2.0750	2.0800	2.0900
3	3.1680	3.1836	3.1992	3.2149	3.2306	3.2464	3.2781
4	4.3423	4.3746	4.4072	4.4399	4.4729	4.5061	4.5731
5	5.5811	5.6371	5.6936	5.7507	5.8084	5.8666	5.9847
6	6.8881	6.9753	7.0637	7.1533	7.2440	7.3359	7.5233
7	8.2669	8.3898	8.5229	8.6540	8.7873	8.9228	9.2004
8	9.7216	9.8975	10.0769	10.2598	10.4464	10.6366	11.0285
9	11.2563	11.4913	11.7319	11.9780	12.2298	12.4876	13.0210
10	12.8754	13.1808	13.4944	13.8164	14.1471	14.4866	15.1929
11	14.5835	14.9716	15.3716	15.7836	16.2081	16.6455	17.5603
12	16.3856	16.8699	17.3707	17.8885	18.4237	18.9771	20.1407
13	18.2868	18.8821	19.4998	20.1406	20.8055	21.4953	22.9534
14	20.2926	21.0151	21.7673	22.5505	23.3659	24.2149	26.0192
15	22.4087	23.2760	24.1822	25.1290	26.1184	27.1521	29.3609
16	24.6411	25.6725	26.7540	27.8881	29.0072	30.3243	33.0034
17	26.9964	28.2129	29.4930	30.8402	32.2580	33.7502	36.9737
18	29.4812	30.9057	32.4101	33.9990	35.6774	37.4502	41.3013
19	32.1027	33.7600	35.5167	37.3790	39.3532	41.4463	46.0185
20	34.8683	36.7856	38.8253	40.9955	43.3047	45.7620	51.1601

continued

period			interest rate i			
n	.10(10%)	.11(11%)	.12(12%)	.13(13%)	.14(14%)	.15(15%)
1	1.0000	1.0000	1.0000	1.0000	1.0000	1.0000
2	2.1000	2.1100	2.1200	2.1300	2.1400	2.1500
3	3.3100	3.3421	3.3744	3.4069	3.4396	3.4725
4	4.6410	4.7097	4.7793	4.8498	4.9211	4.9934
5	6.1051	6.2278	6.3528	6.4803	6.6101	6.7424
6	7.7156	7.9129	8.1152	8.3227	8.5355	8.7537
7	9.4872	9.7833	10.0890	10.4047	10.7305	11.0668
8	11.4359	11.8594	12.2997	12.7573	13.2328	13.7268
9	13.5795	14.1640	14.7756	15.4157	16.0853	16.7858
10	15.9374	16.7220	17.5487	18.4197	19.3373	20.3037
11	18.5312	19.5614	20.6546	21.8143	23.0445	24.3493
12	21.3843	22.7132	24.1331	25.6502	27.2707	29.0017
13	24.5227	26.2116	28.0291	29.9847	32.0886	34.3519
14	27.9750	30.0949	32.3926	34.8827	37.5811	40.5047
15	31.7725	34.4054	37.2797	40.4175	43.8424	47.5804
16	35.9497	39.1899	42.7533	46.6717	50.9803	55.7715
17	40.5447	44.5008	48.8837	53.7391	59.1176	65.0751
18	45.5992	50.3959	55.7497	61.7251	68.3941	75.8363
19	51.1591	56.9395	63.4397	70.7494	78.9692	88.2118
20	57.2750	64.2028	72.0524	80.9468	91.0249	102.4436

period			interest rate i			
n	.16(16%)	.17(17%)	.18(18%)	.19(19%)	.20(20%)
1	1.1000	1.0000	1.0000	1.0000	1.0000
2	2.1600	2.1700	2.1800	2.1900	2.2000
3	3.5056	3.5389	3.5724	3.6061	3.6400
4	5.0665	5.1405	5.2154	5.2913	5.3680
5	6.8771	7.0144	7.1542	7.2966	7.4416
6	8.9775	9.2068	9.4420	9.6829	9.9299
7	11.4139	11.7720	12.1415	12.5227	12.9159
8	14.2401	14.7732	15.3270	15.9020	16.4991
9	17.5185	18.2847	19.0858	19.9234	20.7989
10	21.3215	22.3931	23.5213	24.7089	25.9587
11	25.7329	27.1999	28.7551	30.4035	32.1504
12	30.8502	32.8239	34.9311	37.1802	39.5805
13	36.7862	39.4040	42.2187	45.2445	48.4966
14	43.6720	47.1027	50.8180	54.8409	59.1959
15	51.6595	56.1101	60.9653	66.2607	72.0351
16	60.9250	66.6488	72.9390	79.8502	87.4421
17	71.6730	78.9791	87.0680	96.0217	105.9305
18	84.1407	93.4056	103.7403	115.2659	128.1167
19	98.6032	110.2845	123.4135	138.1664	154.7400
20	115.3797	130.0329	146.6280	165.4180	186.6880

Table F: Annuity whose terminal value is one

Amount A which would need to be set aside each year to yield a particular terminal value at a compound interest rate i per period $\left[\dfrac{i}{(1+i)^n - 1}\right]$

period				interest rate i			
n	.01(1%)	.02(2%)	.03(3%)	.035(3½%)	.04(4%)	.045(4½%)	.05(5%)
1	1.0000	1.0000	1.0000	1.0000	1.0000	1.0000	1.0000
2	0.4975	0.4950	0.4926	0.4914	0.4902	0.4890	0.4878
3	0.3300	0.3267	0.3235	0.3219	0.3203	0.3188	0.3172
4	0.2463	0.2426	0.2390	0.2372	0.2355	0.2337	0.2320
5	0.1960	0.1921	0.1883	0.1865	0.1846	0.1828	0.1810
6	0.1625	0.1585	0.1546	0.1527	0.1508	0.1489	0.1470
7	0.1386	0.1345	0.1305	0.1285	0.1266	0.1247	0.1227
8	0.1201	0.1165	0.1124	0.1105	0.1085	0.1066	0.1047
9	0.1067	0.1025	0.0984	0.0964	0.0945	0.0926	0.0907
10	0.0956	0.0913	0.0872	0.0852	0.0839	0.0776	0.0795
11	0.0864	0.0822	0.0781	0.0761	0.0741	0.0722	0.0704
12	0.0788	0.0745	0.0705	0.0685	0.0665	0.0647	0.0628
13	0.0724	0.0681	0.0640	0.0621	0.0601	0.0583	0.0564
14	0.0669	0.0626	0.0585	0.0566	0.0547	0.0528	0.0510
15	0.0621	0.0578	0.0538	0.0518	0.0499	0.0481	0.0463
16	0.0579	0.0536	0.0496	0.0477	0.0458	0.0440	0.0427
17	0.0543	0.0500	0.0459	0.0440	0.0422	0.0404	0.0387
18	0.0510	0.0467	0.0427	0.0408	0.0389	0.0372	0.0355
19	0.0480	0.0438	0.0398	0.0379	0.0361	0.0344	0.0327
20	0.0454	0.0411	0.0372	0.0354	0.0336	0.0319	0.0302

period				interest rate i			
n	.055(5½%)	.06(6%)	.065(6½%)	.07(7%)	.075(7½%)	.08(8%)	.09(9%)
1	1.0000	1.0000	1.0000	1.0000	1.0000	1.0000	1.0000
2	0.4866	0.4854	0.4842	0.4831	0.4819	0.4808	0.4785
3	0.3157	0.3141	0.3126	0.3110	0.3095	0.3080	0.3050
4	0.2303	0.2285	0.2269	0.2252	0.2235	0.2219	0.2187
5	0.1792	0.1774	0.1756	0.1739	0.1722	0.1705	0.1671
6	0.1451	0.1434	0.1415	0.1398	0.1380	0.1363	0.1329
7	0.1210	0.1191	0.1174	0.1155	0.1138	0.1121	0.1087
8	0.1029	0.1010	0.1000	0.0980	0.0961	0.0940	0.0907
9	0.0893	0.0877	0.0855	0.0840	0.0820	0.0801	0.0768
10	0.0781	0.0763	0.0746	0.0725	0.0709	0.0690	0.0658
11	0.0686	0.0668	0.0650	0.0634	0.0617	0.0601	0.0569
12	0.0610	0.0593	0.0576	0.0559	0.0543	0.0527	0.0496
13	0.0547	0.0530	0.0513	0.0496	0.0481	0.0465	0.0436
14	0.0493	0.0476	0.0459	0.0443	0.0428	0.0413	0.0384
15	0.0446	0.0430	0.0414	0.0398	0.0383	0.0368	0.0340
16	0.0406	0.0390	0.0374	0.0358	0.0344	0.0330	0.0303
17	0.0370	0.0354	0.0349	0.0324	0.0310	0.0296	0.0270
18	0.0341	0.0324	0.0308	0.0294	0.0280	0.0267	0.0242
19	0.0311	0.0296	0.0281	0.0267	0.0254	0.0241	0.0217
20	0.0287	0.0272	0.0258	0.0244	0.0231	0.0218	0.0195

period	interest rate i					
n	.10(10%)	.11(11%)	.12(12%)	.13(13%)	.14(14%)	.15(15%)
1	1.0000	1.0000	1.0000	1.0000	1.0000	1.0000
2	0.4762	0.4739	0.4717	0.4695	0.4673	0.4651
3	0.3021	0.2992	0.2963	0.2935	0.2907	0.2880
4	0.2155	0.2123	0.2092	0.2062	0.2032	0.2003
5	0.1638	0.1606	0.1574	0.1543	0.1513	0.1483
6	0.1296	0.1264	0.1232	0.1201	0.1172	0.1142
7	0.1054	0.1022	0.0991	0.0961	0.0932	0.0904
8	0.0874	0.0843	0.0813	0.0784	0.0756	0.0728
9	0.0736	0.0706	0.0677	0.0649	0.0622	0.0596
10	0.0627	0.0598	0.0570	0.0543	0.0517	0.0492
11	0.0540	0.0511	0.0484	0.0458	0.0434	0.0411
12	0.0468	0.0440	0.0414	0.0390	0.0367	0.0345
13	0.0408	0.0381	0.0357	0.0333	0.0312	0.0291
14	0.0357	0.0332	0.0309	0.0287	0.0266	0.0247
15	0.0315	0.0291	0.0268	0.0247	0.0228	0.0210
16	0.0278	0.0255	0.0234	0.0214	0.0196	0.0179
17	0.0247	0.0225	0.0205	0.0186	0.0169	0.0154
18	0.0219	0.0198	0.0179	0.0162	0.0146	0.0132
19	0.0195	0.0176	0.0158	0.0141	0.0127	0.0113
20	0.0175	0.0156	0.0139	0.0123	0.0110	0.0098

period	interest rate i				
n	.16(16%)	.17(17%)	.18(18%)	.19(19%)	.20(20%)
1	1.0000	1.0000	1.0000	1.0000	1.0000
2	0.4630	0.4608	0.4587	0.4566	0.4545
3	0.2853	0.2826	0.2799	0.2773	0.2747
4	0.1974	0.1945	0.1917	0.1890	0.1863
5	0.1454	0.1426	0.1398	0.1370	0.1344
6	0.1114	0.1086	0.1059	0.1033	0.1007
7	0.0876	0.0849	0.0824	0.0798	0.0774
8	0.0702	0.0677	0.0652	0.0629	0.0606
9	0.0571	0.0547	0.0524	0.0502	0.0481
10	0.0469	0.0447	0.0425	0.0405	0.0385
11	0.0389	0.0368	0.0348	0.0329	0.0311
12	0.0324	0.0305	0.0286	0.0269	0.0253
13	0.0272	0.0254	0.0237	0.0221	0.0206
14	0.0229	0.0212	0.0197	0.0182	0.0169
15	0.0194	0.0178	0.0164	0.0151	0.0139
16	0.0164	0.0150	0.0137	0.0125	0.0114
17	0.0139	0.0127	0.0115	0.0104	0.0094
18	0.0119	0.0107	0.0096	0.0087	0.0078
19	0.0101	0.0091	0.0081	0.0072	0.0065
20	0.0087	0.0077	0.0068	0.0060	0.0054

Glossary

Here are some of the commoner, fairly general terms in farm management economics.

activity a particular method of producing a commodity; a more specific term than 'enterprise', e.g. spring wheat, winter-fattened steers

activity gross income the total value of the output of a farm activity, whether the output was sold or not

activity gross margin activity gross income less the variable costs of that activity

amortization loan loan with equal annual repayments made up of varying amounts of interest and principal

annuity an equal annual sum spent or received

bank bill a financial instrument which can be bought. A form of interest-only loan, for specified short periods with full principal repayment at the end of the period. Can be 'rolled-over' into a new bank bill loan.

budget a detailed statement of expected costs and returns

budget control the process of comparing the actual performance of an aspect of farm production with the performance which was expected when the budget was drawn up

capital items which have not been used up including land, equipment, livestock and money (See also 'fixed' and 'working)

capital gains increase in the value of capital items owing to a rise in their market price, less any money spent on improvements to these capital items

capital investment money spent on equipment, stock or on improvement that has a life of more than one year and which should add to the productive capacity of the farm

cash flow the movement of cash in and cash out of an enterprise or whole farm

cash flow budget a budget of the expected cash in (receipts) and cash out (payments) associated with a particular farm plan or investment

cast for age (cfa) a reject animal that is past its economic life for particular conditions

certainty equivalent the sure happening that a decision maker regards as being equal to some particular risky happening. Can be used in assessing risky decisions

collateral security for a loan

comparative analysis comparison of the performance of aspects of a particular farm with some 'standard' level of performance. Usually the 'standard' is the average performance of the same aspect in a group of broadly similar farms

compounding adding interest to a sum of money, including interest on the interest and capital accumulated each year, i.e., calculation of the future value of a present sum

compound interest rate the rate of interest used in compounding

constant dollar dollars expressed in the same values as apply in some particular period, e.g. dollars in present dollar values projected into the future

contingency allowance allowance included in a budget to cover unexpected events, e.g. a drought resulting in severe losses of cattle or crops

debt-serving capacity ability of a business to pay interest and prinicipal repayments. Annual farm net cash flow before deducting interest and loan repayments

decision analysis a procedure for ensuring that a decision maker makes decisions that are consistent with personal beliefs about the risks faced and personal preferences for possible consequences from the decision

decision tree a diagrammatic representation of a risky decision problem

demand the amounts of a product or service that will be bought at various prices

depreciation the loss in value of capital equipment

depreciation allowance the sum of money which is deducted from income each year so that funds are available to replace equipment when it is worn out

development budget a budget used when planning major changes in a farm which will take some time to reach full capacity

diminishing returns the phenomenon that increases in variable inputs to a production process results in smaller and smaller increases in total output. The principle of diminishing returns indicates that extra variable input will add to the profit from the production process so long as the extra return exceeds the extra cost

discounting calculation of the present value of a future sum

discounting factor the value by which a future cash flow must be multiplied to calculate its present value

dry sheep equivalent (dse) amount of feed required to maintain a 48 kg wether for a period, usually one year

elasticity of demand the responsiveness of quantity demanded to a change in price or a change in income

enterprise the production of a particular commodity or groups of related commodities; a more general term than 'activity', e.g. wheat

equity total assets less total liabilities; net worth

equity capital the value of the owner's capital stake in the business (total assets less total liabilities). The amount the owner would end up with after all assets were sold and debts paid

equity per cent equity capital as percentage of total farm capital, i.e.,
$$\frac{\text{assets minus liabilities}}{\text{assets}} \times \frac{100}{1}$$

finance budget a budget showing nominal cash flows

fixed capital land, buildings, other improvements

fixed costs costs that must be met and are not affected by the size and output of the activities in the farm operations; also called 'overhead costs'

futures quantities of a commodity of defined quality for delivery at an agreed future date, as specified in a contract tradeable in a futures market

gearing the ratio of debt to equity; also called 'leverage'

gross margin gross income less variable costs

gross margins planning a procedure whereby activities are selected on the basis of the gross margin from a unit of input, such as land, feed, labour, capital

hedging protection against a loss on holding stocks of a commodity owing to a price change during the period of ownership, achieved by taking an opposite position on a futures market

income elasticity the responsiveness of quantity demanded of a good to changes in income

inflation an increase in the supply of money in relation to the goods and services available and, in consequence, a decline in the value of money

intermediate activity the production of a commodity which is not sold directly but becomes an input for other activities of the farm, e.g. stubble for grazing

internal rate of return the discount rate at which the present value of income from a project equals the present value of total expenditure (capital and annual costs) on the project; the break-even discount rate

investment appraisal an evaluation of the profitability of an investment

linear programming a mathematical, computer-based, farm planning technique that can be used to determine the combination of activities which maximizes total gross margin, or minimizes costs

livestock feed budget a budget comparing feed requirements of livestock with the feed available

livestock gross income the value of livestock production in the form of animals and produce, adjusted for inventory changes

livestock month amount of energy required by a 48 kg wether for one month, grazing medium-quality pasture with a 35% exercise allowance

marginal economists' word for 'extra' or 'added'. Principle of marginality emphasizes the importance of evaluating changes for extra effects, not the average level of performance

marginal cost the extra cost incurred in growing or selling an additional unit of product

marginal product the change in output arising from using an extra unit of an input

marginal revenue the extra net income obtained from growing or selling one additional unit of product

marginal value product the value of an extra unit of output; the marginal physical product of a unit of output times the price per unit of the product

marketing margin the difference between the farm-level purchase price and price of a product at further stages of the marketing chain

monopoly there is only one seller of a certain product or service

mortgage a claim on assets put up as collateral for a loan

net cash flow the difference between the money received and the money spent in any period

net farm income   operating profit less interest; return to equity

net present value   (NPV) the sum of the discounted values of the future income and costs associated with a farm project or plan

net worth   the value of total assets less the value of total liabilities

nominal dollar   the value of one dollar with any inflation effects included; the actual dollar sum involved at any time

nominal interest rate   interest rate including a component for expected inflation. The market rate of interest (m); usually comprising a component of real gain (r) plus an inflation component (f), i.e., $m = r + f + rf$

oligopoly   there are only a few sellers of a certain product or service so that each will be affected substantially by a change in policy on the part of another

operating profit   gross income less variable and overhead costs

opportunity cost   the opportunity cost of a farm management decision is the amount of money which is given up by choosing one alternative rather than another

overhead costs   costs which do not vary greatly as the level of production or mixture of activities change; also called 'fixed costs'

parametric budget   a planning technique which takes varying prices and yields into account

partial budget   a budget drawn up to estimate the effect on whole farm operating profit of a proposed change affecting only part of the farm

principle of comparative advantage   an economic principle recognizing that various crops and livestock will be produced in areas where they can be produced relatively more cheaply or more profitably there than alternative crops or livestock

production function   the relationship between the level of inputs and the level of output for some production process

provisional tax   a form of pay-as-you-earn (PAYE) tax. It is a means by which the Treasury is able to obtain tax during the year in which income is earned from businessses with periodic income

quantity demanded   the amount of a good someone will buy at a particular price

quantity supplied   the amount of a good someone will produce at a particular price

real dollar   the value of one dollar at a certain time with the effects of inflation removed; refers to the purchasing power of the dollar

real interest   interest rate with the effects of inflation removed

return to total capital   the annual operating profit expressed as a percentage of total capital. Measures the efficiency of resource use

risk premium   an amount which a person requires before being willing to accept a particular risk

risk   the threat posed by an uncertain outcome

scenario   a sketch of a possible outcome(s)

sensitivity testing   checking the effect on a planned outcome of a change in one of the factors contributing to that outcome

spot price   the price for a product for immediate delivery; cash price

stock equivalents　units used in livestock feed budgeting whereby the energy needs of different categories of livestock are expressed in terms of one type of livestock, e.g. dry sheep equivalents (dse), cow days (cds)

subjective probability　an individual's belief about the likelihood of a particular event occurring

substitution　the giving of one input or activity for another input or activity

supply　the amounts of a product or service that will be offered for sale at various prices

term loan　loan with interest paid on the outstanding sum and principal repaid in equal annual parts

variable costs (also direct costs)　costs which change according to the size of the activity, e.g. fuel, seed

whole farm budget　budget showing the operating profit from the whole farm plan

whole farm planning　planning for the mix of activities on the entire farm, as distinct from partial budget planning

working capital　capital needed for the day-to-day operation of a farm

Index